Towards a Critical Edition of the *Celestina*

The University of Wisconsin Press

# Towards a Critical Edition of the

# Celestina

*A filiation of early editions*

J. HOMER HERRIOTT

Madison and Milwaukee, 1964

*Published by*
THE UNIVERSITY OF WISCONSIN PRESS
Madison and Milwaukee

Mailing address: P.O. Box 1379,
Madison, Wisconsin 53701
Editorial offices: 430 Sterling Court
Madison



Printed in the United States of America
by the George Banta Company, Inc., Menasha, Wisconsin

Library of Congress Catalog Card Number 64-25079

## *Foreword*

One of the needs to which scholars should devote more attention, if ever the Hispanic field is to gain the esteem and prestige which its culture and literature merit, is critical editions. Neither foreign scholars nor Spaniards themselves can afford to rely on texts that are not trustworthy. A work cannot be evaluated judiciously and fully if the writer's choice of words, his style, is in doubt. Deletion of words or phrases, additions, substitutions, and changes made by later copyists or editors cannot be accepted. It is partly owing to the lack of reliable editions that two of the greatest masterpieces of Spanish literature, the *Libro de Buen Amor* and the *Celestina,* are scarcely known throughout the world, even by name, except by Hispanists.

The *Celestina,* a sixteen-act play to be read, not presented on the stage, was written in the last decade of the fifteenth century. The only copy of the earliest extant edition, Burgos 1499, is in the Library of the Hispanic Society of America. The author, who states that he "found" the first act, was Fernando de Rojas, a student at the University of Salamanca. When the book was published, some critics were of the opinion that the love affair it recounted moved forward too rapidly; they also felt that the work was a tragedy rather than a comedy. Thereupon Rojas inserted five more acts in the drama, making a total of twenty-one; made numerous insertions and changes, varying from a word or two to whole paragraphs; and changed the title from *Comedia de Calisto y Melibea* to *Tragicomedia de Calisto y Melibea.* This revision was first published, we believe, in Salamanca in 1500, and immediately achieved a success.

Fernando de Rojas was a genius who was more than a century ahead of his time in the art of dialogue and character portrayal. His leading character, Celestina, is probably the greatest creation of the go-between in the world's literature. The play became known as *La Celestina* early in the sixteenth century.

Leon Amarita, who prepared an edition of the play that appeared in Madrid in 1822, states in his Prologue that thirty editions may have been published in Spain in the sixteenth century. So far the list in a bibliography that we are preparing contains 187 editions dated before 1600. However we have not been able to locate a considerable number of these, and others represent bibliographical errors. Adaptations for the stage were also made: in Spain by P. M. Ximénez de Urrea, with the title *Egloga de la Tragicomedia de Calisto y Melibea* (1513); in England by John Rastell, with the title *Interlude of Calisto and Melibea* (1530?).

A revival of interest in the *Celestina* has been taking place during the last twenty-five years. In France since 1942 Paul Achard's adaptation has been presented in Paris more than eight hundred times, and Jean Anouilh also has written a stage version. Three years earlier, Camus playing the role of Calisto, directed the staging of an adaptation in the Théâtre de l'équipe in Algiers. In Italy Sarah Ferrati, who played the role of Celestina in Carlo Terron's adaptation, won the San Genesio Award for the best interpretation of the year 1962. An opera *La Celestina* was presented in 1963 in Florence. In January 1964 plans were announced for the first production of a film in Rome. Within the past nine years three new English translations of the *Celestina* have been published.

With the aim of determining the wording of the original, or princeps, edition of the Tragicomedia, this book presents what we believe to be the filiation of early editions—all but one Spanish. An integral part of the study is a series of graphs on which appear some of the most significant of about ten thousand variants found in these editions. Comments on the interrelationships shown in the graphs among the editions and among the four stemmas, or families of editions, accompany the graphs. The commentary is limited to words in the text of the *Celestina* without reference to contemporary usage.

It is hoped that the findings presented in this volume may enable scholars, teachers, and students to see the relationship of any early edition to the others examined here and to select with greater assurance the words that Fernando de Rojas wrote in the Tragicomedia.

Some of the material in this book was presented at the meetings of the Modern Language Association in Chicago in December 1959 and in Philadelphia in December 1961.

We are deeply grateful to the University of Wisconsin Research Committee which has sponsored the project through the years and to the many students who have ably assisted in our investigations.

Among those who have shown interest in the research and have contributed generously with counsel and encouragement may be cited the late María Rosa Lida de Malkiel, Otis H. Green, Rafael Lapesa, Clara L. Penney, Lolita S. de Vilanova, Kathleen A. Nelson, Mary A. Boudreau, James O. Crosby, Erna R. Berndt, Cándido Ayllón, and Diego Catalán Menéndez Pidal. Any errors in fact or judgment however are our own.

J. H. H.

*Madison, Wisconsin*
*May, 1964*

## *Contents*

Towards a Critical Edition of the *Celestina*

# CHAPTER 1

# Catalog of Editions Used in This Study

The catalog of early editions of the *Celestina* presented in this chapter is arranged according to date of publication whenever possible, even though the date of some may be uncertain. It is our opinion that the variants of the early editions of the *Celestina* fall into four stemmas or families, of which the prototype of each has been lost. We have constructed a graph illustrating the interrelationship among early editions which will be described in Chapter 2. We find it necessary to refer in the catalog in this chapter to these four lost editions which are indicated by an asterisk *A, *E, *F and *G. *A represents the princeps edition of the Comedia, in sixteen acts; *E the princeps edition of theTragicomedia, in twenty-one acts; *F and *G represent later versions of the Tragicomedia. *A is the prototype of Stemma I, *E the prototype of Stemma II, while *F and *G those of Stemmas III and IV respectively. Whenever an asterisk appears elsewhere before an edition, it also indicates that no extant copy is known.

R. Foulché-Delbosc drew up a filiation of early editions which was published posthumously under the title "Observations sur la *Célestine,* III" in the *Revue Hispanique,* No. 174 (April 1930), pp. 544–99. His filiation corresponds only at times to ours. His classification, identified by the initials F–D, is placed in parentheses immediately following ours in the catalog. Our classification is new, although four of the editions—*A, B, D, and M—bear the same letter that Foulché-Delbosc utilized. We shall first merely list the nineteen editions, giving the location of at least one copy, if known, and information concerning modern editions, as well as references to Clara L. Penney, *The Book Called "Celestina,"* The Hispanic Society, New York, 1954. Miss Penney offers more detailed data on each edition. Later we shall present some of our reasons for selecting or positing the nineteen editions in our classification.

### *Comedia*

*Act I. Before 1499? Rojas states that he "found" Act I.

*A (F–D: *A, Toledo?). Before 1499? Princeps edition?

B (F–D: B). 1499? Burgos? Fadrique de Basilea? *[Comedia de Calisto y Melibea.]* Hispanic Society of America, New York. Reproduced in facsimile edition, New York, De Vinne Press, 1909, by Archer M. Huntington. Reprinted by R. Foulché-Delbosc in Bibliotheca hispanica, Barcelona, Madrid, 1902. See Penney, pp. 28–33 and 94.

C (F–D: C, 1500? Salamanca?). 1500, Toledo [Pedro Hagenbach?]. *Comedia de Calisto ⁊ Melibea.* Bibliotheca Bodmeriana, Cologny-Genève, Switzerland. Reproduced in facsimile edition by the Bibliotheca Bodmeriana, 1961, with a Foreword by Daniel Poyán Díaz.

D (F–D: D). 1501? Sevilla? Stanislao Polono? ———. Bibliothèque Nationale, Paris, Yg. 63. Reprinted by Foulchì-Delbosc in Bibliotheca hispanica, Barcelona, Madrid, 1900. See Penney, pp. 95–96.

### *Tragicomedia*

*E 1500? Salamanca? *[Tragicomedia de Calisto y Melibea.]* Princeps edition?

*F 1501? [———.] The prototype of Stemma III in our classification. See Chapter 2 for a discussion of the four stemmas.

*G 1501? [———.] The prototype of Stemma IV in our filiation. See Chapter 2 for a discussion of the four stemmas.

*Note:* Scholars have questioned the date and place of publication of some of the next six editions. We place question marks in the catalog after all six, leaving the decisions in each case to specialists in the history of typography and printing. The question marks do not appear on the graphs.

H (F–D: G). 1502? Toledo? [Pedro Hagenbach?] *Tragicomedia de Calisto y Melibea.* British Museum, C. 20. b. 9. There are many lacunae. See Penney, p. 99.

I (F–D: E). 1502? Sevilla? [Stanislao Polono?] ———. British Museum, C. 20. c. 17. See Penney, p. 96.

J (F–D: N). 1502? Sevilla? [Stanislao Polono?] ———. See Penney, p. 98, where the locations of six extant copies are listed.

K [1502? Sevilla? No colophon.] ———. University of Michigan Library, Ann Arbor. Eight folios are missing. See Penney, p. 97.

L (F–D: F). 1502? Sevilla? [Stanislao Polono?] *Libro de Calisto y Melibea y de la puta vieja Celestina.* Facsimile edition, A. Antonio Pérez y Gómez, Valencia, 1958. Edited by M. Criado de Val and G. D. Trotter, Madrid, C.S.I.C., 1958, under the title *Tragicomedia de Calixto y Melibea. Libro también llamado "La Celestina."* Biblioteca Nacional, Madrid, R 26575. See Penney, p. 97.

M (F–D: M). 1502? Salamanca? [Juan de Porras?] *Tragicomedia de Calisto y Melibea.* Hispanic Society of America; British Museum, G. 10224. See Penney, pp. 33–40 and 96.

N (F–D: H). 1506, January 29. Rome, per Magistrum Eucharium Silber alias Franck. *Tragicocomedia di Calisto e Melibea.* Italian translation by Alfonso de Ordóñez. See Penney, p. 119.

O (F–D: J). [1507, Zaragoza, Jorge Coci.] Tomás Gorchs used the Zaragoza 1507 edition, now lost, as one of the basic sources for his 1841 edition of *La Celestina,* which we refer to as O. O was reprinted in Barcelona, 1842. See Penney, p. 99.

P (F–D: K). 1514, February 21. Valencia, Juan Joffre. *Tragicomedia de Calisto y Melibea.* Biblioteca Nacional, Madrid, R 4870. See Penney, p. 99.

U (F–D: L). 1518, Valencia, Juan Joffre. ———. British Museum, C. 64. d. 4. See Penney, p. 100.

V 1529, Valencia, Juan Viñao. *Tragicomedia de Calisto ⁊ Melibea.*

Amarita. 1822, Madrid, Don León Amarita. *La Celestina o Tragicomedia de Calisto y Melibea, Nueva edición.* 2nd. ed., Madrid, 1835.

The first section of the bibliography of the *Celestina* that we are compiling lists at present more than sixty editions printed or supposed to have been printed before 1530. However, many of these are phantom editions, errors, or lost editions. In addition to the editions listed in the catalog above, there are to our knowledge fifteen other editions in existence today from the period before 1529, including seven Italian translations, two issues of a French translation, one German translation, and one Hebrew partial translation or imitation in a manuscript of uncertain date. Only four of the fifteen are Spanish editions. Like the Zaragoza 1507 edition, a fifth Spanish edition, Barcelona, Carlos Amoros, 1525, has disappeared rather recently.

### *Early Extant Editions Not Used in This Study*

1514, June 23. Milan, Zanota da Castione. *Tragicocomedia di Calisto e Melibea.* Italian translation. British Museum; University of Bologna. See Penney, p. 119.

1515, January. Milan, In officina libraria Minutiana, Nicolai de Gorgonzola. ———. British Museum, 117. 15. aa. 9; Biblioteca Nacional, Madrid, R 1473. See Penney, p. 120.

1515, April 12. Venice, Pincius? ———. University of Bologna; British Museum. See Penney, p. 120.

1519, March 16. Milan, Ioanne Angelo Scinzenzeler. ———. Biblioteca Agusta, Palazzo del Comune, Perugia, I–O–69 (1). See Penney, p. 120.

1519, December 10. Venice, Cesaro Arriuabeno. *Celestina. Tragicomedia di Calisto e Melibea.* Italian translation. Biblioteca Nacional, Madrid, R 1434. See Penney, p. 120.

1520, December 20. Augsburg, Sigismund Grymm Vnnd Marx Wirsung. *Ain hipsche tragedia.* German translation by Christoph Wirsung. Facsimile edition, Augsburg, 1923. J. Peeters-Fontainas Library, Louvain. See Penney, pp. 118–19.

1520? Hebrew translation by Joseph Sarfatti (Giuseppe Gallo). We have been unable as yet to locate and obtain a reproduction of this MS. See J. D. Cassuto, "A Poem of Joseph Samuel ben Zarfati on the First Hebrew Comedy," in *Jewish Studies in Memory of George A. Kohut.* New York (1935), 121–28.

Q (F–D: O). 1523. Sevilla (Venice?), Juan Batista Pedrezano? *Tragicomedia de Calisto y Melibea.* Hispanic Society of America; British Museum, C. 63. e. 8. See Penney, p. 100.

[(F–D: P). 1525. Barcelona, Carlos Amoros. ———.] Not included in list of extant editions since the copy has disappeared. See Penney, p. 100.

R (F–D: Q). 1525, November. Sevilla, Jacobo Cromberger y Juan Cromberger. ———. British Museum, G 10223. See Penney, p. 101.

1525, November. Venice, Gregorio de Gregorii. *Celestina. Tragicomedia di Calisto e Melibea.* Italian translation. Biblioteca Nacional, Madrid, R 8746. See Penney, p. 120.

1525, November. Venice, Francesco Caron. ———. University of Pennsylvania. See Penney, p. 120.

S (F–D does not classify). 1526, June 23. Toledo, Casa de Remon de Petras. *Tragicomedia de Calisto y Melibea.* British Museum, C. 63. c. 24. See Penney, p. 101.

1527, August 1. Paris, Nicolas Cousteau [for] Galliot du Pre. *La Célestine.* French translation. Issue A. Bibliothèque Nationale, Paris, Rés. Yg. 307. See Gerard J. Brault: *Célestine. A Critical Edition of the First French Translation.* Detroit, Wayne University Press (1963), p. 213.

1527. ———. Issue B. See Brault, p. 213.

T (F–D does not classify). 1528, March. [Sevilla,] Jacobo Cromberger Aleman y Juan Cromberger. *Tragicomedia de Calisto y Melibea* (without *El auto de Trasso*). Hispanic Society of America; Biblioteca Nacional, Madrid, R 30.275.

Early in our investigations the four Spanish editions represented by the letters Q, R, S, and T according to the date of publication were included among the editions collated. In the final form of the graph, Q, the Seville 1523 edition, was deleted because the editor follows Stemma III closely; so were R, S, and T (Seville 1525, Toledo 1526, and Seville 1528), all of which follow Stemma IV. None of these four editions would help the reader at the present time to understand the early development of the text; their presence would merely clutter up the graphs. Perhaps at a later date a more extensive graph will be designed which will include not only all early Spanish editions but also translations.

CHAPTER 2

# Filiation of the Early Editions

This chapter presents additional data on the editions used in this study, the interrelationship of editions and stemmas, and the procedure used throughout the book to help the reader interpret and evaluate the variants. The graph is explained and exemplified on pages 17–19.

Collation of the twelve selected early Spanish editions of the *Celestina* which are extant revealed some ten thousand variants, when not only textual changes but all orthographic variations were included. More than 85 percent of the words in the text of these editions proved to have no variants. Perhaps this fact will bring encouragement to the reader if keeping the characteristics of so many editions in mind should prove difficult. As further aid, points are intentionally repeated throughout this book in our commentary on the words on the graphs.

Even before the collation was completed it was evident that certain variants were peculiar to only two or three editions, others to many more. There was little or no doubt that J consistently followed the errors of I. Efforts to discover any further direct relationships were unsuccessful, although we posited from one to as many as ten lost editions before 1502. At this stage of our research we were going on the premise that an editor used only one basic text.

Then we began to test the variants on the premise that an editor utilized two basic texts instead of one. At this point a filiation began slowly to take form. It appeared that three editors, whose editions are of great importance in our efforts to reconstruct the lost princeps edition *E, used two basic editions from different stemmas: Gorchs in preparing O had Amarita and the Zaragoza 1507 editions before him and used now one, now the other; the editor of H normally preferred the variant of *F but at times selected a word from *E; and the editor of P used *E primarily but occasionally turned to I.

Another example of an editor who used two texts from different stemmas proved to be in K, which generally follows *G but from time to time prefers the variant of *F. K is much less significant than O, H, or P as an aid in reconstructing the lost princeps edition *E, but it is included in our catalog in order to give a more complete view of the filiation of early texts.

As will be indicated by this study, not only most of the textual changes but the great majority of the orthographic variants follow the pattern of falling into one or more of the stemmas. The exceptions found are most frequently instances where the editor based his text on two editions in different stemmas and chose the variant now of one, now of the other.

### *Comments on the Editions*

Additional comments on the editions in the catalog may help the reader to fix some of the characteristics of each in memory.

### *Comedia*

*A (Before 1499?) has normally been accepted as the designation for the lost princeps edition of the Comedia. We accept the hypothesis that such an edition existed. It is our opinion that the Comedia was not written before 1496.

B (Burgos? 1499?). Some scholars have questioned both date and place of publication. We accept B at present as the oldest extant edition of the Comedia, although we put a question mark after date and place.

C (Toledo, 1500). Until the discovery of this edition it was necessary to rely chiefly on the Seville 1501 edition (D) in attempting to reconstruct the princeps edition of the Comedia. C represents the earliest appearance of much of the preliminary and all of the final materials, and thus throws light on many problems that have been plaguing scholars in the twentieth century. These materials of course appear in the facsimile edition of C, but they are included here for the reader's convenience.

*Preliminary Materials*

1. Title: Comedia de Calisto ꝛ Melibea
2. Subtitle: "la qual contiene demas de su agradable ꝛ dulce estilo ———"
3. Heading: "El autor a vn su amigo"
4. "Carta a vn su amigo"

5. Heading for eleven acrostic octaves: "El autor escusandose de su yerro."
6. Eleven acrostic octaves
7. Statement: "siguese la comedia de Calisto ʒ Melibea compuesta en reprehension de los locos enamorados . . . ."
8. Argumento [General]: "Calisto fue de noble linaje . . . ."
9. Text of the sixteen acts, each with its Argumento

*Final Materials*

10. Heading: "Alonso de Proaza: corrector de la impression al lector"
11. Three octaves
12. Heading: "Dize el modo que se ha de tener leyendo esta comedia"
13. One octave
14. Heading: "Declara vn secreto que el autor encubrio en los metros que puso al principio del libro"
15. One octave
16. Heading: "Descriue el tiempo en que la obra se imprimio"
17. Final octave

D (Sevilla? 1501?). This edition, like C, is complete and contains all the preliminary and final materials listed above for C. In addition, between the title and subtitle appears this statement: "Con sus argumentos nueuamente añadidos."

***Tragicomedia***

*E [Salamanca? 1500?]. The principal object of our investigations is to reconstruct the text of this lost edition, which in our opinion was the princeps edition of the Tragicomedia. Some scholars since 1900 have been willing to posit a lost Salamancan edition of 1500; many others have rejected this premise. Among reasons for accepting this edition as more than a probability the following may be considered:

This edition is the one cited in the colophon of the Valencia 1514 edition (P) as follows:

> El carro Phebeo después de auer dado
> Mill ʒ quinientas bueltas en rueda,
> Ambos entonçes los hijos de Leda
> A Phebo en su casa teníen possentado,
> Quando este muy dulce y breue tratado
> Después de reuisto ʒ bien corregido,

Con gran vigilancia puntado y leydo,
Fué en Salamanca impresso acabado.

Menéndez Pelayo and Krapf were convinced, partly because of the colophon, that the Valencian edition followed this lost Salamancan edition and that the latter was probably the princeps edition. Therefore Krapf based his new edition on the Valencian text, as the title indicates: Eugenio Krapf, *La Celestina . . . conforme a la edición de Valencia de 1514, reproducción de la Salamanca de 1500, con una introducción del doctor d. M. Menéndez y Pelayo.* 2 vols. Vigo, Librería de Eugenio Krapf, 1900.

Krapf accepted almost all the text of P for *E, supporting his decisions often on N or O. Many of his decisions were valid, others were not. U and V are included along with P in our filiation because, while they often follow P blindly, U sometimes corrects P's numerous errors and V sometimes selects a variant from another edition.

Dr. Emma Scoles in a recent study entitled "Note sulla prima traduzione italiana della *Celestina*," *Studi Romanzi*, Vol. 33 (1961), presents additional data indicating that the words of N and P often appeared also in the Comedia and were different from those of the six editions of the Tragicomedia tentatively dated 1502 in our catalog.

Our hypothesis, developed in Chapter 4, is that when Fernando de Rojas prepared the Tragicomedia he used a printed copy of the Comedia, making small changes on the margin, turning to sheets of paper for long additions. For this reason we should normally expect the wording of *A and *E to be the same apart from his or his editor's changes and any typographical errors.

As will be seen later in this study, our investigations have led us to conclude that usually the Comedia (*ABCD or Stemma I) and *EPUV (or Stemma II in the Tragicomedia), often supported by H or N or O or any combination of these three editions, present the same word, whereas the other 1502 editions may have a variant. The six 1502 editions fall into two families: the group HIJ with its lost prototype *F in Stemma III, and the group KLM with its lost prototype *G in Stemma IV.

*F (1501?). The lost prototype, in our classification, of Stemma III, which includes also HIJ. Although the editor of *F used the princeps edition *E, apparently the only one available, as his basic text, for some reason he made a considerable number of changes from its text. The variants of *F and Stemma III reflect a later development in the text of the Tragicomedia than do those of Stemma II.

*G (1501?). The lost prototype, in our filiation, of Stemma IV, which includes also KLM. *G normally uses *F as a basic text and in turn is usually followed by KLM and Amarita. The text of *G must be reconstructed from the words in L and M, and also K when the latter does not use *F as a basic text.

H (Toledo? 1502?). This edition is occasionally very helpful in efforts to reconstruct *E, since the editor from time to time chose a word from *E although he generally followed *F. The lacunae in the unique copy are much to be regretted.

I (Sevilla? 1502?). Foulché-Delbosc believed that this edition, E in his classification, was the princeps edition of the Tragicomedia.

J (Sevilla? 1502?). When we first endeavored to establish a filiation among the early editions there was, as we have said, only one relationship about which we had little or no doubt: J followed I. Many errors were made in I and copied by J. I could not have used J as a basic text, for J has a great many additional errors which are not reflected in I. The graphs and summaries show that often the group IJ has a unique variant which is an error.

K (Sevilla? 1502?). Some scholars have believed K to be another edition of or closely related to I. However our data indicate that I normally belongs to the family *FHIJ (Stemma III) whereas K usually belongs to the family *GKLM (Stemma IV). The rather frequent use of different words in I and K may be observed on the graphs. The editor of K had two basic texts before him, *F and *G. When he preferred a word from *F, the text of K differs from that of L and M.

L (Sevilla? 1502?). This edition belongs to the group *GKLM (Stemma IV). Although the text of L often coincides with that of K and M, it does not derive from either. All three texts are based on the same lost text, *G.

M (Salamanca? 1502?). This edition also belongs to the group *GKLM. Although it has many errors and omissions, it is based on *G.

N (Rome, 1506). This is the earliest Italian translation. The translator, Alfonso de Ordóñez, a Spaniard, dates his preface 1505, but the first edition was probably published in 1506. N is very important in the process of reconstruction since like P it uses *E as a basic text. Sometimes N, even though it is a translation, uses the exact word of the Spanish text. At other times the word in the Italian translation indicates that its source is *E. Thus N represents the early stage of the development of the text, as opposed to the variants in Stemmas III or IV or both, which represent a later development. Occasionally the Italian word corresponds to that in one or another edition other than *E. The translator may have had any of the editions earlier than 1506 at hand; our data so far do not indicate which. We look for further enlightment on this problem to Dr. Emma Scoles. When the word or words in N do not reflect the word or meaning of any Spanish words on the graph, we do not include the Italian text on the graph. On the other hand, whenever the Italian words faithfully reflect *E, we capitalize them.

O (Barcelona, 1841; 1842). Tomás Gorchs published a "critical" edition of the *Celestina* in Barcelona in 1841. It was reprinted in 1842. The editor used two basic texts: Amarita's, published in 1822, and the Zaragoza 1507 edition. The reader will observe on the graphs that when Gorchs does not follow Amarita his word almost always coincides with *E, although he generally modernizes the spelling. Unfortunately since Gorchs published his edition the Zaragoza edition has disappeared. However Gorchs' edition O has scores of examples of how the Zaragoza edition read. In order not to clutter up the graph we indicate that O came directly from *E; it should be kept in mind that the lost Zaragoza edition was the intermediary.

P (Valencia, 1514). Cited under notes on *E. Believing that P followed *E, Krapf accepted the reading of P in his 1900 edition unless it was an obvious error. However, as the data on our graphs indicate, the editor of P makes a considerable number of errors which can be detected only by examining the variants of the early editions. At times he utilizes the text of I as well. In spite of this, P is more helpful than any other edition in our endeavor to reconstruct *E.

In this study we call P and the two following editions, U and V, the Valencian tradition.

U (Valencia, 1518) is used in preference to translations which are earlier, because at times it corrects the error of P. Otherwise U normally follows P.

V (Valencia, 1529), the latest of the early editions in the catalog, was produced eleven years after U, and the editor had available more texts from which to select variants. He normally follows U but at times selects a variant from another edition, as may be seen on the graphs.

The group PUV reflects the lost princeps edition *E more closely than do either Stemmas III or IV.

Amarita (Madrid, 1822, 1835). For various reasons, of which the Inquisition apparently was the primary one, no edition of the *Celestina* that we know of was published in Spain after that of Pamplona 1633 (together with a French translation) until the appearance of Amarita's in 1822. Amarita is included in this study because Gorchs in editing his Barcelona edition of 1841 (O) often followed Amarita, although frequently he preferred *E, as reflected in the Zaragoza 1507 edition. We are not interested here in the sources of Amarita, but the reader may observe that it normally follows Stemma IV.

As the preceding notes indicate, we are accepting certain hypotheses and premises at the present time; for example, that B is the oldest extant edition of the Comedia. The reasons for accepting some premises and rejecting others will be brought out later as each edition and its relationship with other editions are discussed.

### *Procedure Followed in Presenting Variants*

The usual procedure throughout most of this book is (1) to quote a brief passage from the text of the *Celestina* so that the reader may see a selected word in its context; (2) to present on the accompanying graph the selected word and its variants in each edition; (3) to summarize in the text the matter shown on the graph and comment briefly on the pattern of variants illustrated. The graphs are the core of the study, and at times little or no comment is necessary.

With few exceptions we have refrained from citing in commentaries and summaries editions later than those in catalog and graphs. References to an edition shown on the graph are by its letter; the work of its editor, corrector, or printer is not distinguished unless that seems necessary. In editions *A and *E the work of the author, similarly, is not distinguished from that of corrector or printer; all is covered in our references to what "the author created."

Quotations from the text of the *Celestina* are always taken from the edition of Julio Cejador y Frauca, Madrid, 1913 (referred to as Cej.). Cejador's 1943 edition is cited in brackets. C-T represents the edition of M. Criado de Val and G. D. Trotter, *Tragicomedia de Calixto y Melibea,* Madrid, C.S.I.C., 1958.

Cejador's editions are not only more available than other editions but in our opinion closer to the lost princeps edition *E. The text however, as is well known, shows carelessness in the use of accents and punctuation. In order to help the reader we at times delete or add accents and change punctuation; we never alter the spelling unless there is an obvious error.

The textual summaries of the graph list each variant, followed by the editions in which each appears. The word or words that we believe the author created in Comedia, Tragicomedia, or both are placed first, and in capitals; they are distinguished thus by position from other variants. In addition other words are placed in capitals, whenever in our opinion they derive directly or indirectly from one or both of the two princeps editions, *A and *E. For example in the cases of Amarita and O, the two modern editions, we usually capitalize the witness even though the spelling has been modernized. However, at times, especially in a complicated set of variants, these two editions are classified apart.

### *Definitions and Symbols*

Some of the terms and symbols used in commentaries, graphs, and summaries need explanation.

1. *A blank* appears on the graph a few times where the word or variant would ordinarily be. This occurs only in N, the Italian translation, when the variant is unique and is either an error or offers no aid to the reader in interpreting the graph.

2. *Blank line:* ———. A blank line normally is limited to Stemma I and indicates that an addition made in the Tragicomedia never existed in Stemma I. However the blank line is also used when the word under discussion never existed in any of the editions except for one or a group of two or three where the first editor has made an addition.

3. *Omissions in editions: (———).* Used when an edition omits a word.

4. *(Falta).* There is only one known copy of several of the editions represented on the graph. Unfortunately some of these editions, especially H and K, have considerable lacunae, where the text was originally complete but someone has torn out one or more folios. In such cases, when the text is wanting, we use (falta), always in parentheses.

5. *Words in capital letters.* Capital letters for word or phrase on graph or in summary and commentary indicate our belief that the word was in *A or *E or both, or that in meaning the word reflects the one in *E, as in the Italian translation. On Graph 23, for example, VALER appears in Stemma II (*EPUV) and also in O. Stemmas III and IV and Amarita present the variant *ver.* N's use of the Italian

AIUTAR, which like VALER means "to help," leaves no doubt that the translator of N used a Spanish text with VALER, not *ver*.

6. *Words which appear in lower case letters*. Lower case letters for a word or phrase in graph, summary, and commentary indicate our belief that the variant does not reflect the word in *A or *E or both, but instead represents a corrupt text. Normally when only one word of a group is corrupt, all the words in the group are lower case. However in a complicated group of variants, as on Graphs 209 and 213, where first one word and then another presents a variant, only the varying word is considered. This procedure may enable the reader to comprehend and evaluate the graph more quickly. If there is any doubt in our mind about a word or variant in an edition, especially in the Italian translation, we leave the word lower case or place a question mark after it.

7. *Witness*. A "witness" as used in this book is normally a printed word that appears in one of the early extant editions or in a later edition which we know followed one or more of the earlier editions. The texts of the editions which have been lost, *A, *E, *F, and *G, have to be reconstructed from the support of the witnesses in other editions and therefore cannot provide witnesses themselves. However, since 85 percent of the words in the fifteen extant editions of the *Celestina* studied have no variants, we extend the use of the term witness to include all of these nonvariant words in the lost editions *A, *E, *F, and *G. The only possible exceptions would be a few errors of *A stemming from the printer or the carelessness of the corrector. Likewise when we are convinced from all the data that a reconstructed word in any one of the lost editions is the only word that can be ascribed to that edition, we again extend the use of the term "witness." If we did not do this the stemmas in the summaries would be perpetually broken up and it would be difficult for the reader to grasp their significance.

On the other hand, whenever there is any doubt about the hypothetical reconstruction of a word in a lost edition, a question mark is placed in graph and summary after the letter or word of the edition concerned. In short, the reconstruction of the text of lost editions is determined by the support of printed witnesses provided the latter are trustworthy and convincing. The question marks appearing in the catalog for date and place of publication of B, the six 1502 editions and others are never represented on the graphs.

8. *Unique*. "Unique" may refer to one edition or one stema. Since there are several groups of editions such as BC, BCD, IJ, PUV, etc., which we wish to emphasize in order that the reader may better grasp

their significance on a graph and in the complete filiation of texts, the use of the word "unique" is extended to refer to a group.

9. *Addition.* The word "addition" has a special meaning when it appears in commentary introducing a quotation from the *Celestina;* here it refers to the additions that the author made to the Comedia when he transformed it into the Tragicomedia. At times editors made additions on their own; this different sense of the word is clear from the text.

### *The Graph*

#### *Graph 1. Placing of Editions on the Graph—by Date*

The date of publication of most of the editions on the graph is indicated by their level with respect to the dates at left. The asterisk indicates lost editions.

*Left-hand column:* The Comedia, or earliest form of the *Celestina* (16 acts). Four editions: *A, B, C, and D. *A, the posited lost princeps edition, may have appeared before 1499. B, C, and D we believe were published respectively in 1499, 1500, and 1501.

*Under the arrows:* The Tragicomedia (21 acts). Fifteen editions: *E through V and Amarita.

*E, the posited lost princeps edition of the Tragicomedia, may have been published in 1500. It is placed on that date level, like C.

*F and *G, also posited lost editions, must have been published later than *E but before 1502. They are placed on the 1501 date level, like D.

The six editions H, I, J, K, L, and M are tentatively dated 1502, although one or more of them may have been published some years later. Even if all of these except I should prove to have appeared several years later, the validity of the graph and the filiation it shows would be affected very little or not at all. I could not have been published after 1514.

N, the first Italian translation of the Tragicomedia, was published at Rome in 1506.

P, U, and V were published in Valencia in 1514, 1518, and 1529 respectively.

Only O (Gorchs' 1841 edition) and Amar. (Amarita, 1822) are not at their proper chronological level, because of need to keep the graph condensed spatially.

#### *Graph 2. Stages of the Text and Relationship of Editions*

Stemma I represents the Comedia and consists of four editions: *A, B, C, and D.

Stemma II, the earliest stage of the Tragicomedia, consists of four editions: *E, P, U, and V. The first Italian translation, N, is placed near Stemma II since the translator used *E as a basic text.

Stemma III, a later stage in the development of the Tragicomedia, consists of four editions: *F, H, I, and J.

Stemma IV, the last stage in development of the Tragicomedia, consists of four editions: *G, K, L, and M. Amarita normally follows this stemma.

The dotted lines indicate relationships of editions. The editors of H, N, and P, for example, all drew on *E. Four editions (H, K, P, and O) were based on two sources; for example, P on both *E and I. The editor of O used both Amarita and the Zaragoza 1507 edition (since lost), which reflected *E. To simplify the graph the line bypasses the Zaragoza edition, running directly from *E to O.

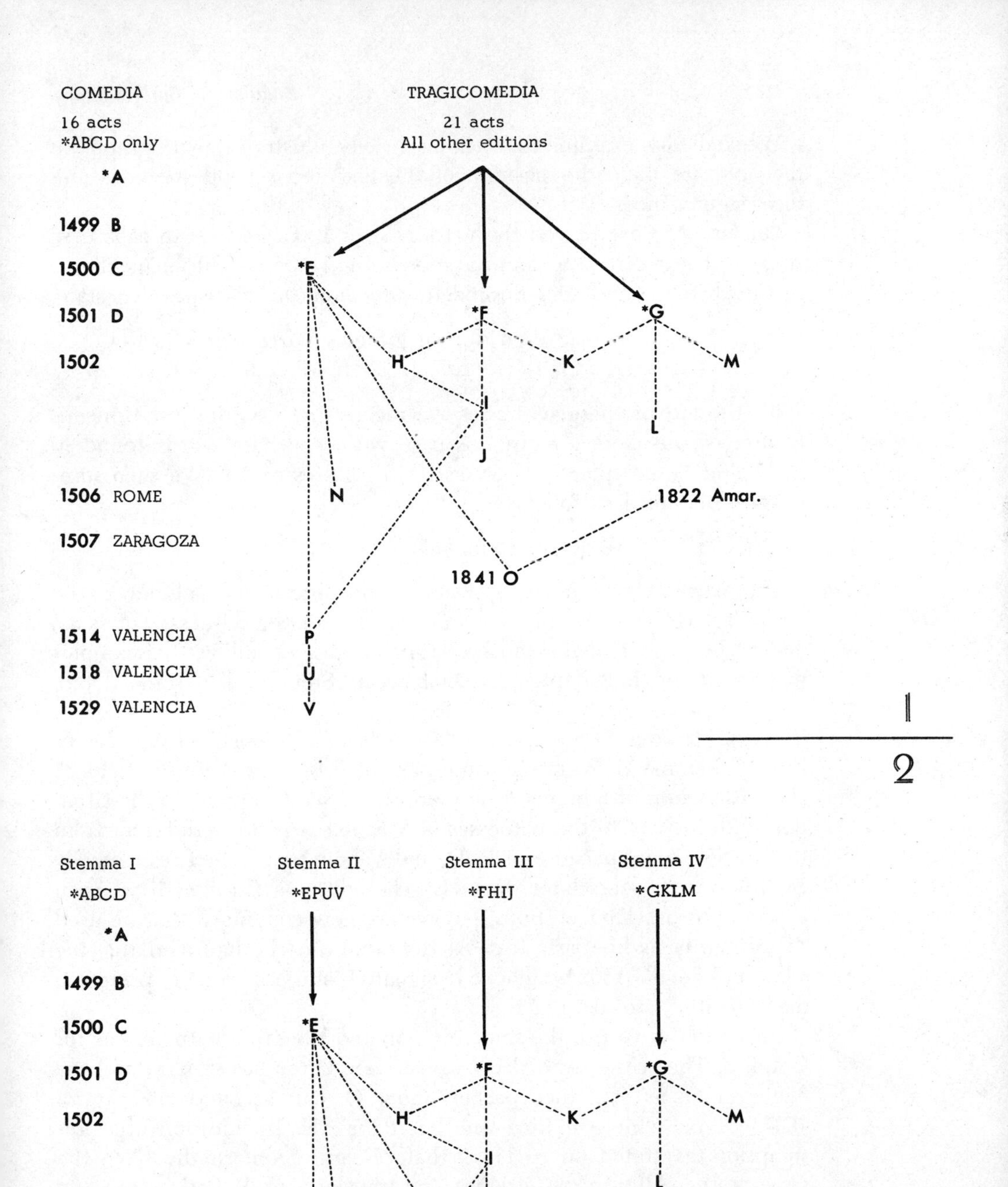
COMEDIA
16 acts
*ABCD only
TRAGICOMEDIA
21 acts
All other editions
*A
1499 B
1500 C
1501 D
1502
1506 ROME
1507 ZARAGOZA
1514 VALENCIA
1518 VALENCIA
1529 VALENCIA
*E
*F
*G
H
K
M
I
L
J
N
1822 Amar.
1841 O
P
U
V
1
2
Stemma I
*ABCD
Stemma II
*EPUV
Stemma III
*FHIJ
Stemma IV
*GKLM
*A
1499 B
1500 C
1501 D
1502
1506 R.
1507 Z.
1514 V.
1518 V.
1529 V.
*E
*F
*G
H
K
M
I
L
J
N
1822 Amar.
1841 O
P
U
V

We shall now examine the stemmas briefly, illustrating with graphs on the opposite page the position of the first and second stemmas and their significance.

On Graph 3 are placed the witnesses for B, C, and D: in each case SE DAN. The words appear in a speech by Tristán as he hears shouts in the distance and sees Sosia returning home in a disheveled state.

> . . . No sé qué me diga de tan grandes vozes como SE DAN.
> *(Cej. II, XIII, 115, l. 17 [107, l. 12]; C–T, 229, l. 20)*

With the aid of these witnesses we reconstruct *A, the lost princeps edition of the Comedia. In this case we accept the words found in B, C, and D and place SE DAN as the witnesses of *A. We then summarize Stemma I as follows:

SE DAN  *ABCD (or Stemma I)

The word "error" never appears on the graph and seldom in the summary. However at times we cannot accept the witnesses of B, C, and D because B makes an error and C and D follow B. Examples may be found in Chapter 5, which treats Stemma I in some detail.

From Stemma I, represented by the four editions *ABCD, let us turn to Stemma II, which is also represented by four editions, *EPUV. (For discussion of Stemma II in more detail see Chapter 6.) The situation with respect to the witnesses of Stemma II is quite different from that in Stemma I because of P, U, and V being published respectively 14, 18, and 29 years later than *E. The editor of P might have been expected to use later editions, but we are now convinced that he used *E primarily as his basic text. At the same time he had available the edition of Seville 1502 which we designate I, and occasionally preferred the variant of I to that of *E.

On Graph 4 we use the same citation and the same witnesses as for Graph 3. The witnesses of PUV are SE DAN. O too has SE DAN; and the editor of O, as explained earlier under O, had at hand a Zaragoza 1507 edition which in turn was based on *E. In addition our presumption, as stated on p. 11, is that *E and *A normally have the same words. Alfonso de Ordóñez, the translator of N, had before him a copy of *E, which he usually followed, but here he chose a variant. Using these witnesses, we reconstruct *E. We accept the words that appear in PUV and O, that is SE DAN.

We then summarize the witnesses of Stemmas I and II as follows:

SE DAN  *ABCD*EPUV + O (or Stemmas I and II + O)
sento  N

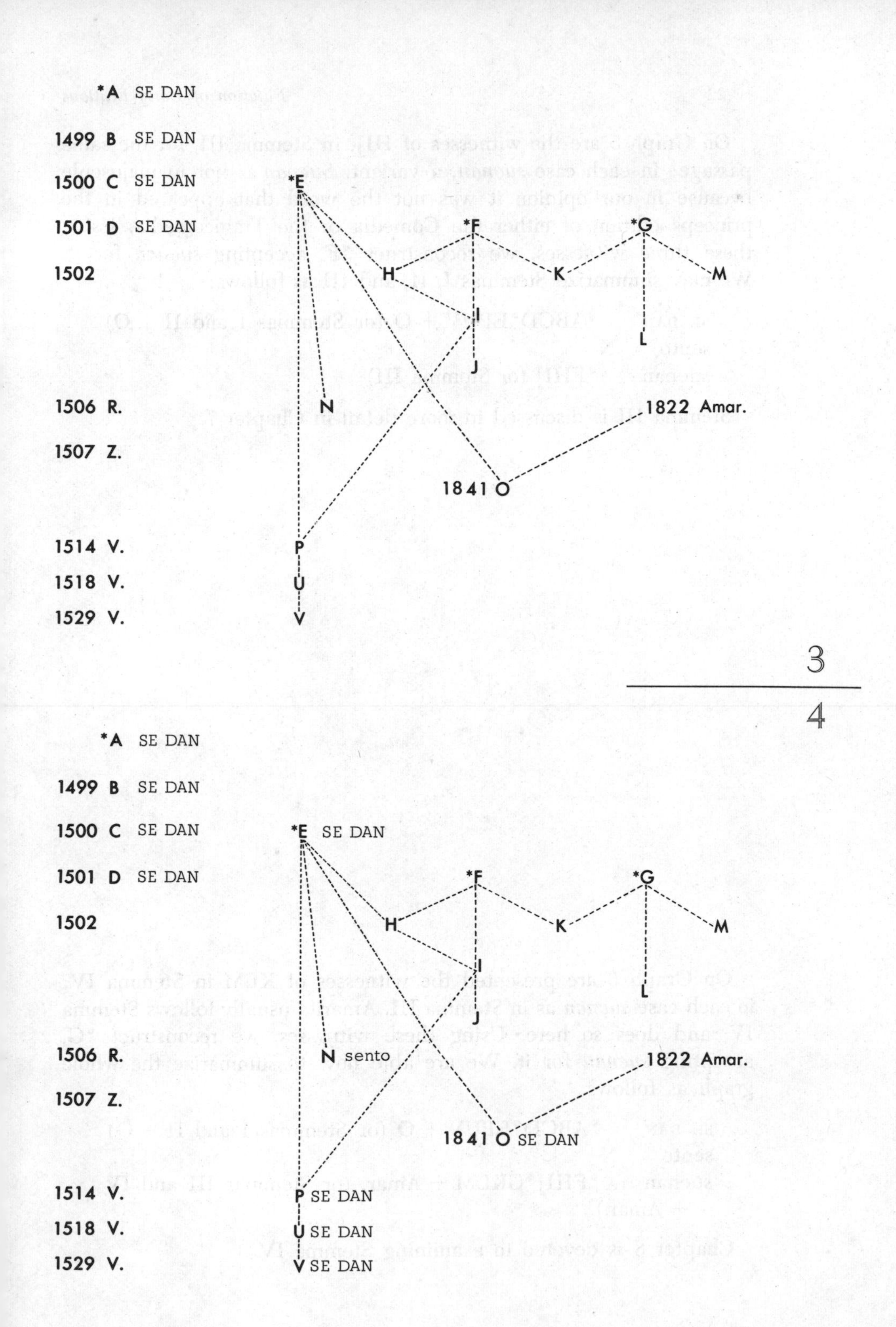
*A SE DAN
1499 B SE DAN
1500 C SE DAN
1501 D SE DAN
1502
1506 R.
1507 Z.
1514 V.
1518 V.
1529 V.
*E
*F
*G
H
K
M
J
L
J
N
1822 Amar.
1841 O
P
U
V
3
4
*A SE DAN
1499 B SE DAN
1500 C SE DAN
1501 D SE DAN
1502
1506 R.
1507 Z.
1514 V.
1518 V.
1529 V.
*E SE DAN
*F
*G
H
K
M
I
L
J
N sento
1822 Amar.
1841 O SE DAN
P SE DAN
U SE DAN
V SE DAN

On Graph 5 are the witnesses of HIJ, in Stemma III, for the same passage: in each case *suenan,* a variant. *Suenan* is not in majuscule because in our opinion it was not the word that appeared in the princeps edition of either the Comedia or the Tragicomedia. Using these three witnesses, we reconstruct *F, accepting *suenan* for it. We may summarize Stemmas I, II, and III as follows:

SE DAN *ABCD*EPUV + O (or Stemmas I and II + O)
sento N
suenan *FHIJ (or Stemma III)

Stemma III is discussed in more detail in Chapter 7.

On Graph 6 are presented the witnesses of KLM in Stemma IV: in each case *suenan* as in Stemma III. Amarita usually follows Stemma IV, and does so here. Using these witnesses, we reconstruct *G, accepting *suenan* for it. We are able now to summarize the whole graph as follows:

SE DAN *ABCD*EPUV + O (or Stemmas I and II + O)
sento N
suenan *FHIJ*GKLM + Amar. (or Stemmas III and IV + Amar.)

Chapter 8 is devoted to examining Stemma IV.

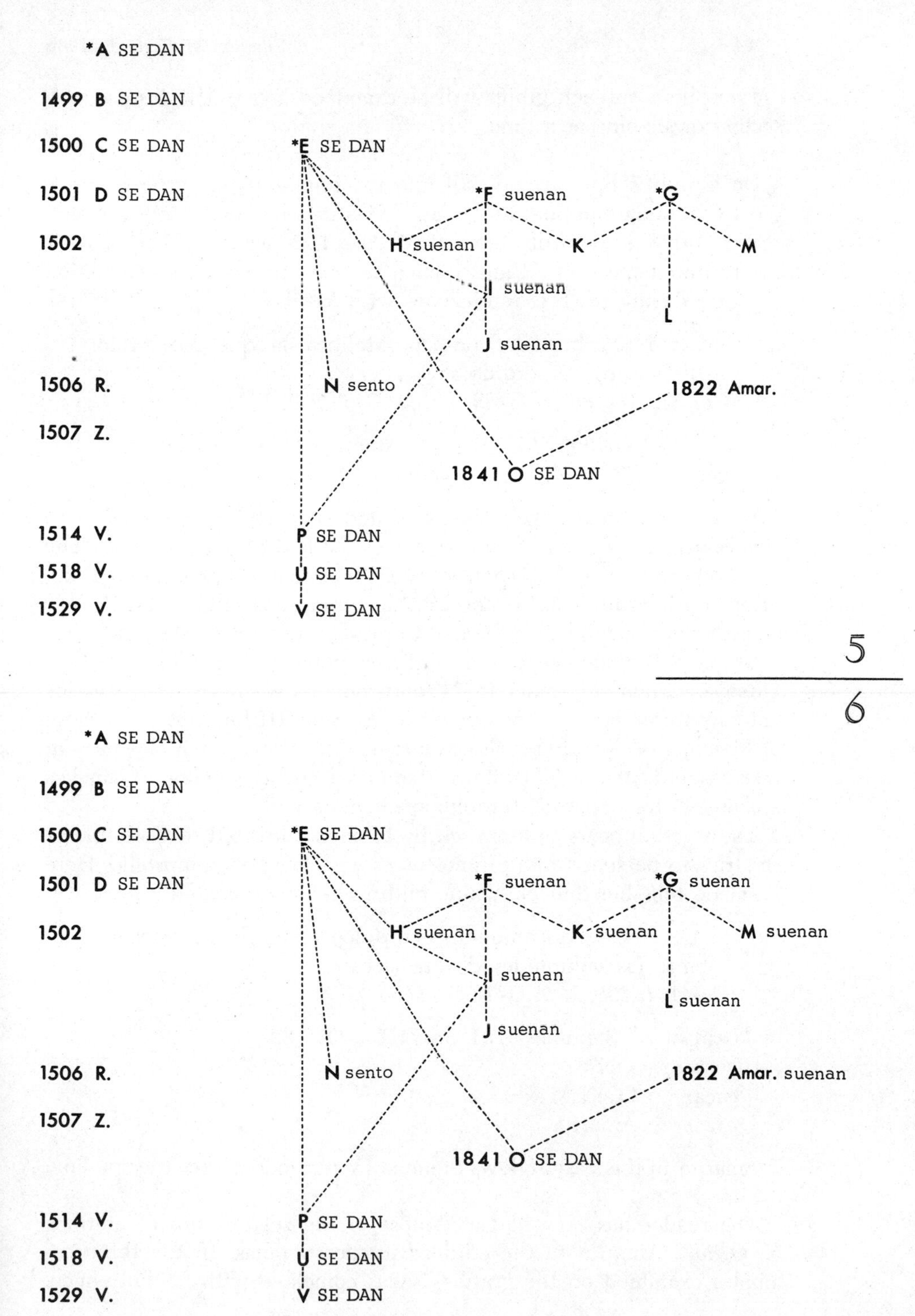

*A SE DAN
1499 B SE DAN
1500 C SE DAN
*E SE DAN
1501 D SE DAN
*F suenan
*G
1502
H suenan
K
M
I suenan
L
J suenan
1506 R.
N sento
1822 Amar.
1507 Z.
1841 O SE DAN
1514 V.
P SE DAN
1518 V.
U SE DAN
1529 V.
V SE DAN
5
6
*A SE DAN
1499 B SE DAN
1500 C SE DAN
*E SE DAN
1501 D SE DAN
*F suenan
*G suenan
1502
H suenan
K suenan
M suenan
I suenan
L suenan
J suenan
1506 R.
N sento
1822 Amar. suenan
1507 Z.
1841 O SE DAN
1514 V.
P SE DAN
1518 V.
U SE DAN
1529 V.
V SE DAN

From here on each graph will be examined as a whole instead of a section or stemma at a time.

On Graph 7 the variants fall into the four-stemma pattern, but N gives additional support to *E and Amarita chooses to follow Stemmas I and II instead of Stemma IV. Also H is wanting. The word is taken from a speech by Calisto when he hears Lucrecia's voice behind the gate during his first rendezvous with Melibea.

> —Cierto soy burlado: no ERA Melibea la que me habló. ¡Bullicio oygo, perdido soy!
> (*Cej. II, XII, 88, 1. 7 [82, 1. 18]; C–T, 209, 1. 1*)

ERA *ABCD*EPUV + N + Amar. + O
será *FIJ*GKLM (H falta)

Both the examples we have presented suggest that there are two significant stages in the development of the text of the *Celestina.* The first and oldest state is represented by Stemmas I and II, a later development by Stemmas III and IV. This premise is so important in our opinion that Chapter 3 is devoted to presenting additional data.

Graph 8 provides an example of a stemma with a unique variant. Often a variant originates in *F and then, as we have seen, spreads not only throughout all the editions of Stemma III but also to all those of Stemma IV, including the prototype *G. However in the present case *F and Stemma III follow Stemmas I and II whereas *G makes a change which spreads throughout Stemma IV.

The word appears in a speech by Pármeno directed to Celestina as she tries to persuade him to join forces with her and Sempronio. Here Pármeno tells her that he has no faith in her sugar-coated pills.

> . . . hizieron sectas embueltas en dulce veneno para CAPTAR é tomar las voluntades de los flacos . . . .
> (*Cej. I, I, 108, 1. 9; C–T, 57, 11. 5–6*)

CAPTAR Stemmas I, II, and III + O
gustare N
caçar *GKLM
cazar Amarita

Amarita in this case follows Stemma IV but modernizes the spelling.

The reader has now had a glimpse of the relationship of editions N, O, and Amarita to the editions in the stemmas. In the three examples examined on the graphs, N has coincided with *E only once,

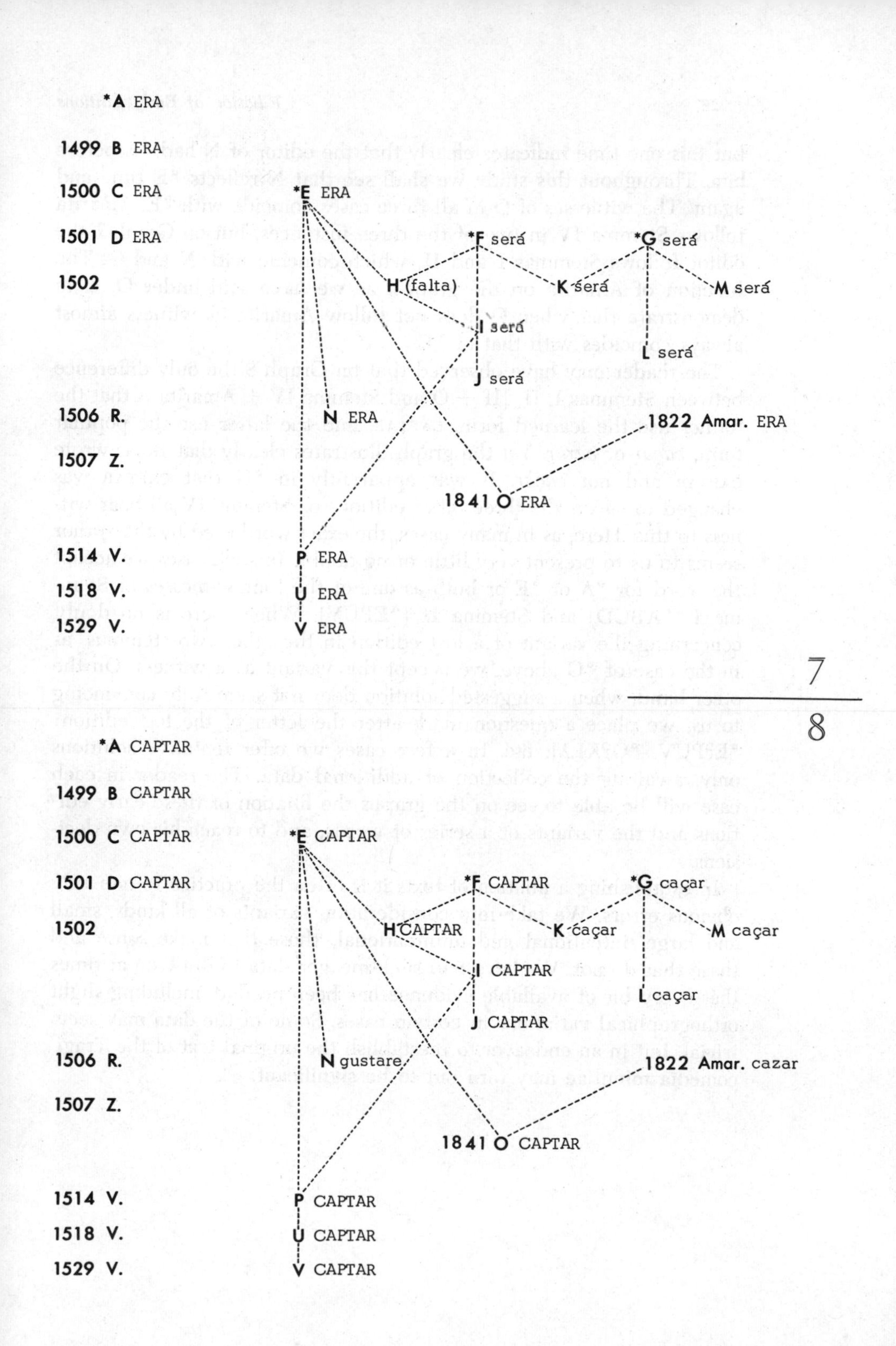

*A ERA
1499 B ERA
1500 C ERA
*E ERA
1501 D ERA
*F será
*G será
1502
H (falta)
K será
M será
I será
L será
J será
1506 R.
N ERA
1822 Amar. ERA
1507 Z.
1841 O ERA
1514 V.
P ERA
1518 V.
U ERA
1529 V.
V ERA
*A CAPTAR
1499 B CAPTAR
1500 C CAPTAR
*E CAPTAR
1501 D CAPTAR
*F CAPTAR
*G caçar
1502
H CAPTAR
K caçar
M caçar
I CAPTAR
L caçar
J CAPTAR
1506 R.
N gustare
1822 Amar. cazar
1507 Z.
1841 O CAPTAR
1514 V.
P CAPTAR
1518 V.
U CAPTAR
1529 V.
V CAPTAR

but this one time indicates clearly that the editor of N had *E before him. Throughout this study we shall see that N reflects *E time and again. The witnesses of O in all three cases coincide with *E. Amarita follows Stemma IV in two of the three instances, but on Graph 7 the editor follows Stemmas I and II, which coincide with N and O. The function of Amarita on the graphs, as we have said under O, is to demonstrate that when O does not follow Amarita its witness almost always coincides with that of *E.

The reader may have observed that on Graph 8 the only difference between Stemmas I, II, III + O and Stemma IV + Amarita is that the former use the learned form, CAPTAR, and the latter use the popular form, *caçar* or *cazar.* Yet the graph illustrates clearly that Rojas wrote CAPTAR and not *caçar.* It was apparently in *G that CAPTAR was changed to *caçar;* the three other editions of Stemma IV all bear witness to this. Here, as in many cases, the exact word used by the author seems to us to present very little or no doubt. In such cases we accept the word for *A or *E or both as one of the four witnesses of Stemma I (*ABCD) and Stemma II (*EPUV). When there is no doubt concerning the variant of a lost edition in the other two stemmas, as in the case of *G above, we accept this variant as a witness. On the other hand, when a suggested solution does not seem fully convincing to us, we place a question mark after the letter of the lost edition: *E?PUV, *G?KLM, etc. In a few cases we offer tentative solutions only, awaiting the collection of additional data. The reader in each case will be able to see on the graphs the filiation of these early editions and the variants of a series of words, and to reach his own decisions.

In establishing a filiation of texts it is often the practice to cite only obvious errors. We take into consideration variants of all kinds, small and large, intentional and unintentional, those that make sense and those that do not. We have had such meager data to draw on at times that every bit of available evidence has been needed, including slight orthographical variations in certain cases. Some of the data may seem trivial, but in an endeavor to reestablish the original text of the Tragicomedia minutiae may turn out to be significant.

CHAPTER 3

## Stemmas I and II versus III and IV

We have examined three variants in the preceding chapter and have seen that the witness of each edition falls into one of four stemmas. In two of the examples cited, Stemmas I and II provide one witness and Stemmas III and IV a different one. In the third example the witnesses of Stemma IV are unique and present an error. Stemmas with a unique witness are infrequent in the *Celestina* except in the additions, where Stemma I of course is missing. Then Stemma II is frequently unique.

This chapter furnishes additional data illustrating with graphs the sharp division between the witnesses of Stemmas I and II on the one hand and III and IV on the other. If the witnesses appear in an addition, the contrast will be limited to Stemma II versus Stemmas III and IV. The reader, we believe, will gradually become convinced that Stemmas I and II, or Stemma II in the case of an addition, reflect the words of the author insofar as we are able to determine them today. As we have stated, Stemma I represents the Comedia or oldest state of the text; Stemma II the revision of the text by Fernando de Rojas, or the Tragicomedia; while *F and *G represent a later stage in the development of the text.

Graph 9 presents each witness of the four stemmas, without reconstructing the prototypes *A, *E, *F, *G. Graph 10 reconstructs with the reader each prototype.

The word appears in a speech by Celestina as she cajoles Areúsa in her room.

> — No lo sé. A las obras creo; que las palabras, de balde, las venden dondequiera. PERO el amor nunca se paga sino con puro amor é á las obras con obras.
> *(Cej. I, VII, 253, 1. 11; C–T, 143, 1. 12)*

It is evident from the witnesses in Stemma I that the word in *A was PERO and from the witnesses of Stemma II that PERO was the word in *E. On the other hand the witnesses of Stemma III indicate that the word in *F was *porque* just as those of Stemma IV indicate that this was the word in *G. Therefore the summary of the graph runs as follows:

PERO *ABCD*EPUV + O
che N
porque Stemmas III and IV + Amar.

In scores of cases Stemmas I and II are supported, as here, by the witness of O. In these cases Gorchs has preferred the variant of the Zaragoza 1507 edition to that of Amarita.

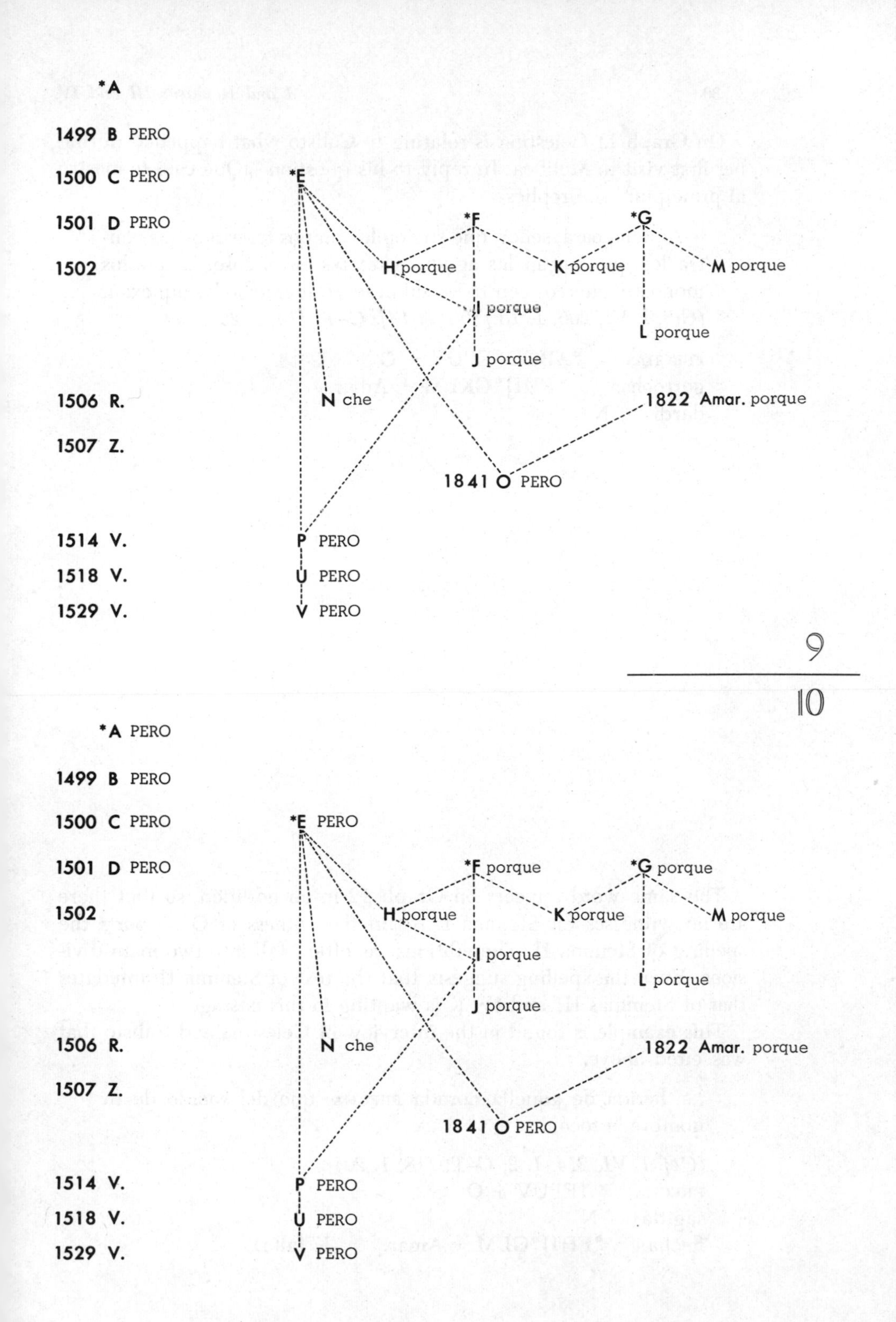
*A
1499 B PERO
1500 C PERO
1501 D PERO
1502
1506 R.
1507 Z.
1514 V.
1518 V.
1529 V.
*E
*F
*G
H porque
K porque
M porque
I porque
J porque
L porque
N che
1822 Amar. porque
1841 O PERO
P PERO
U PERO
V PERO
9
10
*A PERO
1499 B PERO
1500 C PERO
1501 D PERO
1502
1506 R.
1507 Z.
1514 V.
1518 V.
1529 V.
*E PERO
*F porque
*G porque
H porque
K porque
M porque
I porque
J porque
L porque
N che
1822 Amar. porque
1841 O PERO
P PERO
U PERO
V PERO

On Graph 11 Celestina is relating to Calisto what happened during her first visit to Melibea. In reply to his question "¿Qué cara te mostró al principio?" she replies:

—Aquella cara, señor, que suelen los brauos toros mostrar contra los que lançan las agudas FRECHAS en el coso, la que los monteses puercos contra los sabuesos, que mucho los aquexan. *(Cej. I, VI, 206, l. 13 [206, l. 13]; C–T, 113, l. 25)*

FRECHAS *ABCD*EPUV + O
garrochas *FHIJ*GKLM + Amar.
dardi N

The same word appears on Graph 12 in an addition, so that there are no witnesses for Stemma I. Again the witness of O supports the spelling of Stemma II. The editions (as often) fall into two main divisions. Even the spelling suggests that the text of Stemma II antedates that of Stemmas III and IV. K is wanting in this passage.

This example is found in the interview of Celestina and Calisto that was cited above.

. . . herida de aquella dorada FRECHA, que del sonido de tu nombre le tocó, . . . .

*(Cej. I, VI, 214, l. 2; C–T, 118, l. 20)*
FRECHA *EPUV + O
sagitta N
flecha *FHIJ*GLM + Amar. (K falta)

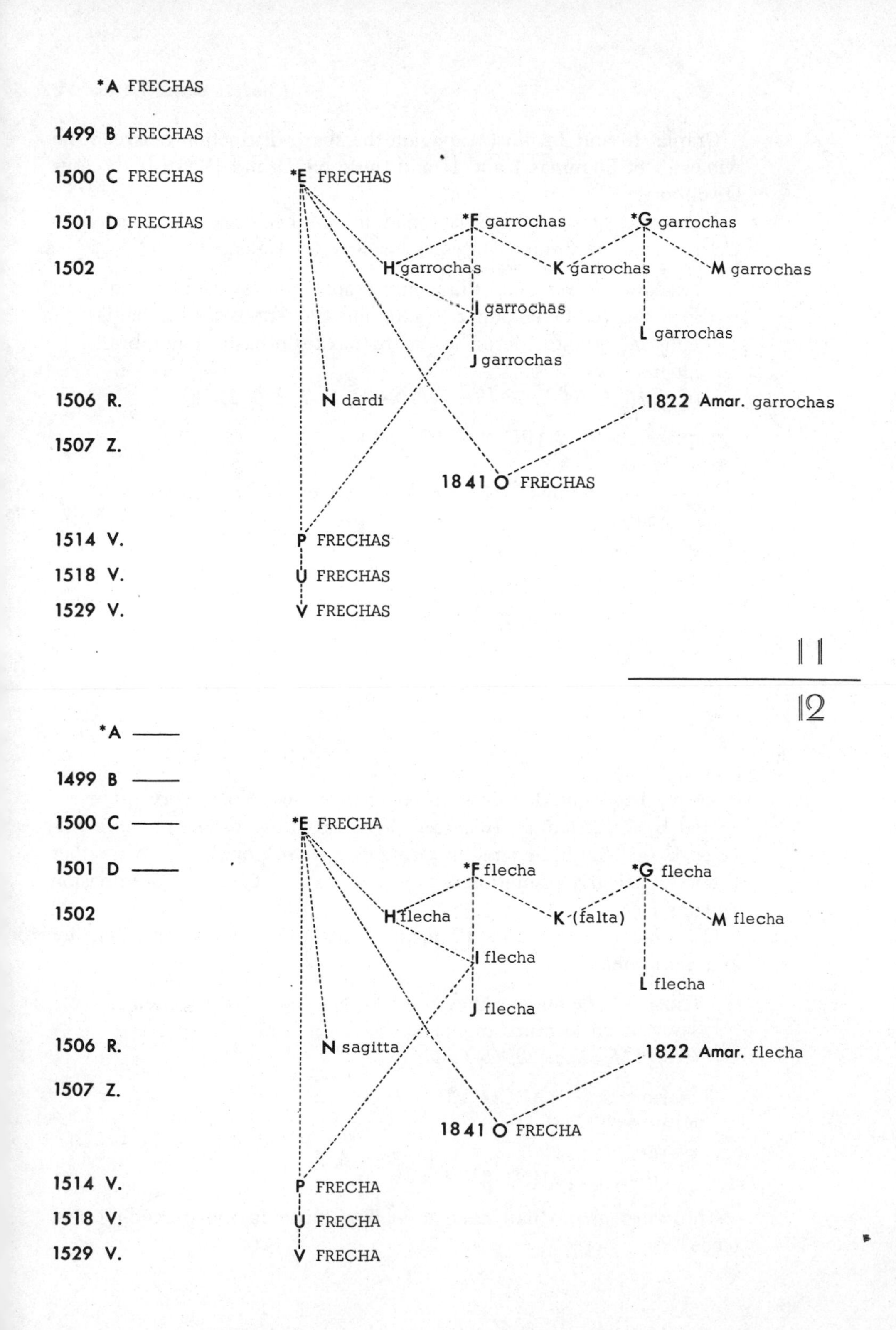

*A FRECHAS
1499 B FRECHAS
1500 C FRECHAS
*E FRECHAS
1501 D FRECHAS
*F garrochas
*G garrochas
1502
H garrochas
K garrochas
M garrochas
I garrochas
L garrochas
J garrochas
1506 R.
N dardi
1822 Amar. garrochas
1507 Z.
1841 O FRECHAS
1514 V.
P FRECHAS
1518 V.
U FRECHAS
1529 V.
V FRECHAS
11
12
*A ——
1499 B ——
1500 C ——
*E FRECHA
1501 D ——
*F flecha
*G flecha
1502
H flecha
K (falta)
M flecha
I flecha
L flecha
J flecha
1506 R.
N sagitta
1822 Amar. flecha
1507 Z.
1841 O FRECHA
1514 V.
P FRECHA
1518 V.
U FRECHA
1529 V.
V FRECHA

Graphs 13 and 14 illustrate again the sharp distinction between the witnesses of Stemmas I and II and those of III and IV. In both cases O supports *E.

The word on Graph 13 is found in Melibea's speech directed to Celestina as the former confesses her love for Calisto.

> . . . Muchos é muchos días son passados que esse noble caualllero me habló en amor. Tanto me fué ENTONCES su habla enojosa, quanto, después que tú me le tornaste a nombrar, alegre.
> *(Cej. II, X, 64, l. 23 [61, ll. 19–20]; C–T, 190, l. 18)*

ENTONCES *ABCD*EPUV + O
AL HORA N
(———) Stemmas III and IV + Amar., where the word is omitted.

As we have noted, the editorial changes in *F are very often accepted by *G. At times there are slight variations in one or more editions. U on Graph 14 possibly presents a more popular form (neither U nor V is clearly printed in the original text), but the twofold division remains clear-cut.

Celestina is persuading Pármeno to abandon Calisto and join her and Sempronio.

> CEL. . . . Quando somos tentados per moços é no bien INSTRUTOS en lo mundano, . . . .
> *(Cej. I, I, 93, l. 20; C–T, 48, l. 19)*

INSTRUTOS *ABCD*EPV? + O
ISTRUTOS? U
INSTRUCTI N
astutos *FHIJ*GKLM + Amar.

The word *astuto* had been used by Calisto in the preceding sentence.

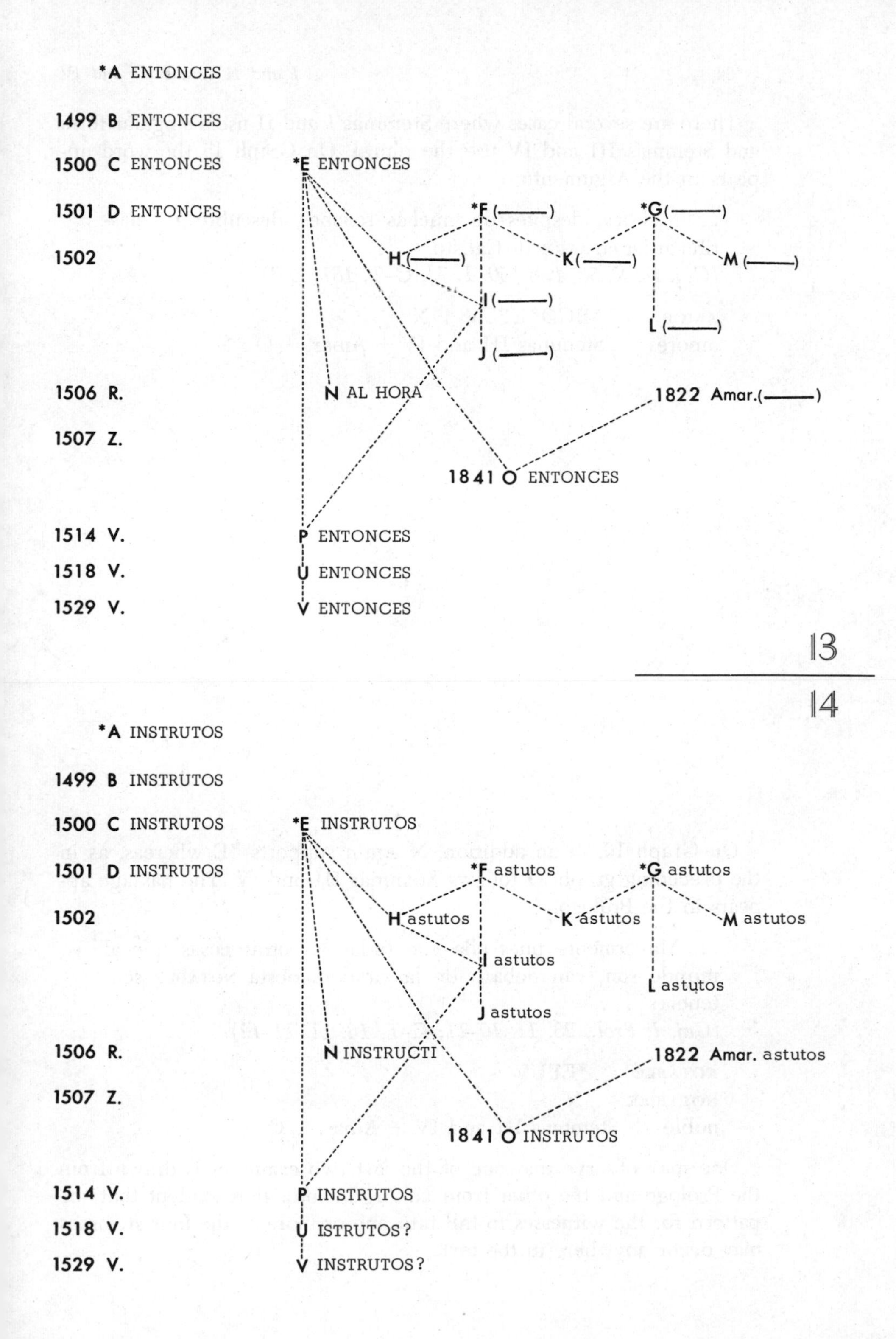

*A ENTONCES
1499 B ENTONCES
1500 C ENTONCES
*E ENTONCES
1501 D ENTONCES
*F (———)
*G (———)
1502
H (———)
K (———)
M (———)
I (———)
L (———)
J (———)
1506 R.
N AL HORA
1822 Amar. (———)
1507 Z.
1841 O ENTONCES
1514 V.
P ENTONCES
1518 V.
U ENTONCES
1529 V.
V ENTONCES
13
14
*A INSTRUTOS
1499 B INSTRUTOS
1500 C INSTRUTOS
*E INSTRUTOS
1501 D INSTRUTOS
*F astutos
*G astutos
1502
H astutos
K astutos
M astutos
I astutos
L astutos
J astutos
1506 R.
N INSTRUCTI
1822 Amar. astutos
1507 Z.
1841 O INSTRUTOS
1514 V.
P INSTRUTOS
1518 V.
U ISTRUTOS?
1529 V.
V INSTRUTOS?

There are several cases where Stemmas I and II use a singular form and Stemmas III and IV use the plural. On Graph 15 the word appears in the Argumento of Act X.

> . . . Melibea, después de muchas razones, descubre á Celestina arder en AMOR de Calisto.
> *(Cej. II, X, 53, 1. 8 [50, 1. 7]; C–T, 181, 1. 6)*

AMOR *ABCD*EPUV + N
amores Stemmas III and IV + Amar. + O

On Graph 16, in an addition, N again supports *E whereas, as in the preceding graph, O follows Stemmas III and IV. The passage appears in the Prólogo.

> . . . Mayormente pues ella con todas las otras cosas que al mundo son, van debaxo de la vandera desta NOTABLE sentencia: . . . .
> *(Cej. I, Pról., 23, 11. 10–11; C–T, 16, 11. 11–12)*

NOTABLE *EPUV
NOTABILE N
noble Stemmas III and IV + Amar. + O

One may observe that one of the last two examples is drawn from the Prólogo and the other from an Argumento. It is evident that the pattern for the witnesses to fall into one or more of the four stemmas may occur anywhere in the text.

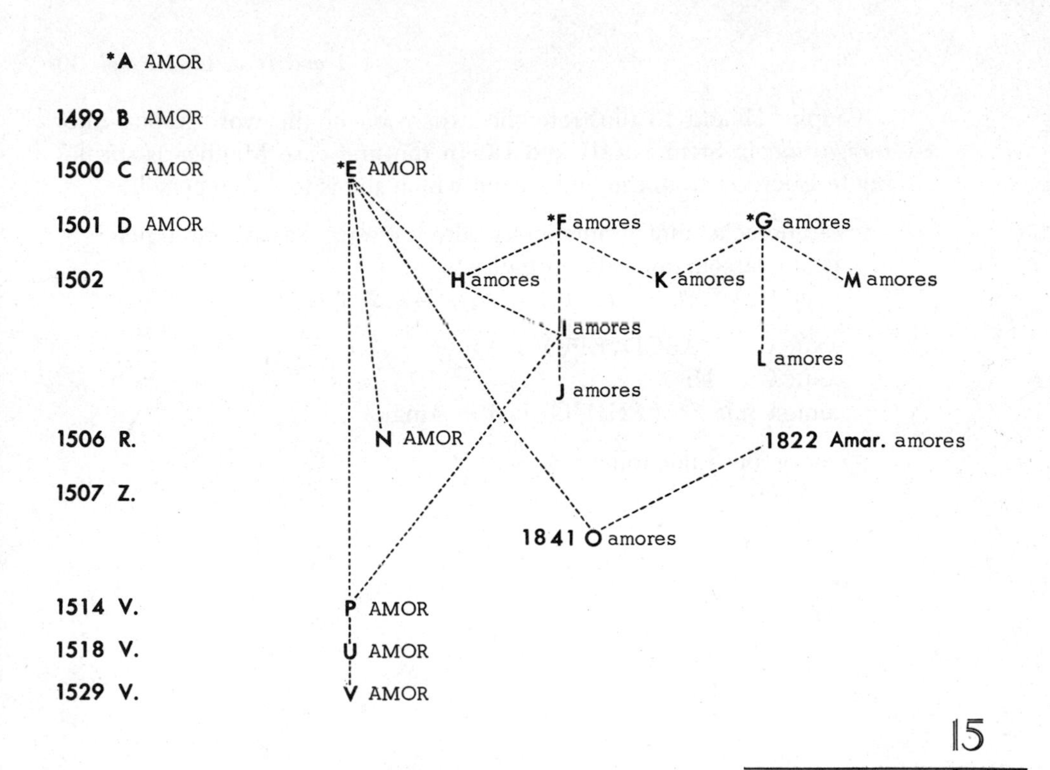
*A AMOR
1499 B AMOR
1500 C AMOR
*E AMOR
1501 D AMOR
*F amores
*G amores
1502
H amores
K amores
M amores
I amores
L amores
J amores
1506 R.
N AMOR
1822 Amar. amores
1507 Z.
1841 O amores
1514 V.
P AMOR
1518 V.
U AMOR
1529 V.
V AMOR





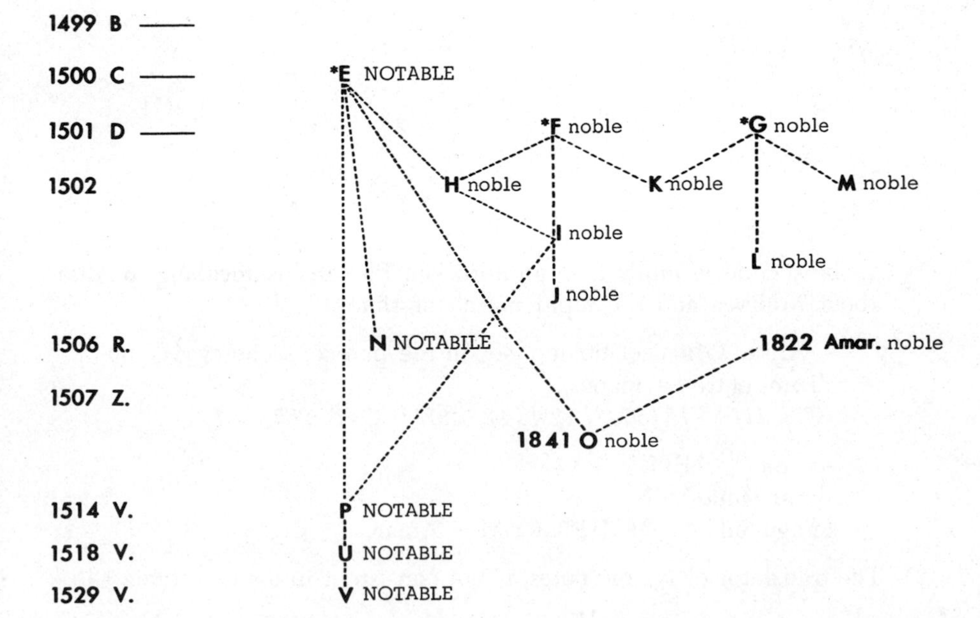
*A ——
1499 B ——
1500 C ——
*E NOTABLE
1501 D ——
*F noble
*G noble
1502
H noble
K noble
M noble
I noble
L noble
J noble
1506 R.
N NOTABILE
1822 Amar. noble
1507 Z.
1841 O noble
1514 V.
P NOTABLE
1518 V.
U NOTABLE
1529 V.
V NOTABLE

Graphs 17 and 18 illustrate the expansion of the word AMIGA into *amiga mía* in Stemmas III and IV. In the first case Melibea is speaking to Lucrecia from the tower from which she is to throw herself.

—Lucrecia, amiga mía, muy alto es esto. Ya me pesa por dexar la compañía de mi padre.
*(Cej. II, XX, 206, l. 13 [191, l. 13]; C–T, 288, l. 3)*

AMIGA *ABCD*EPUV + O
AMICA N
amiga mía *FHIJ*GKLM + Amar.

Cejador does not follow B.

The second example is in an addition. Pleberio is speaking to Alisa about Melibea and the rapid march of time.

—Alisa, AMIGA, el tiempo, según me parece, se nos va, como dizen, entre las manos.
*(Cej. II, XVI, 155, l. 12 [144, l. 11]; C–T, 265, l. 1)*

AMIGA *EPUV + O
donna mia N
amiga mía *FHIJ*GKLM + Amar.

The translator of N, one notes, is not consistent in his rendition.

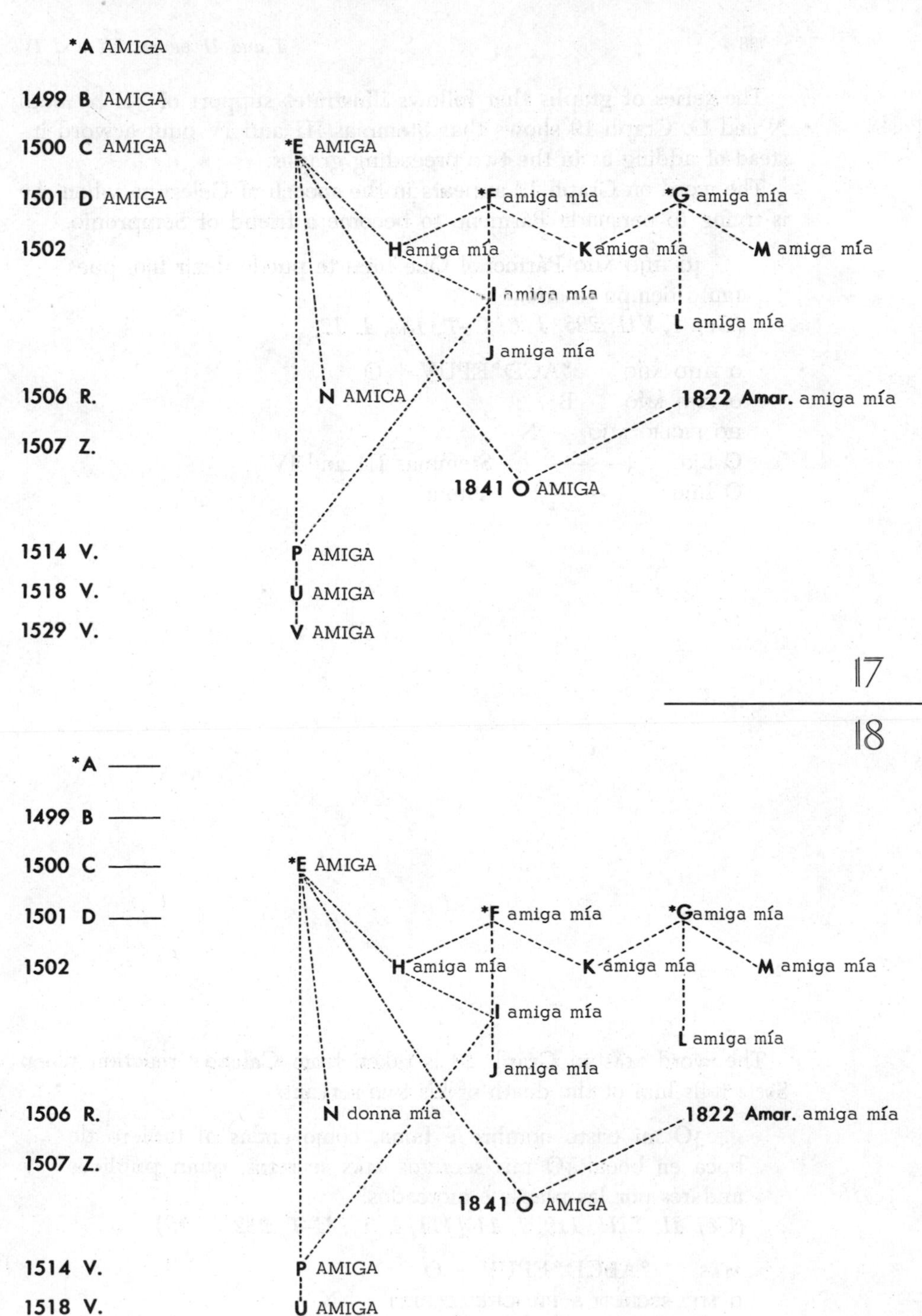
*A AMIGA
1499 B AMIGA
1500 C AMIGA
*E AMIGA
1501 D AMIGA
*F amiga mía
*G amiga mía
1502
H amiga mía
K amiga mía
M amiga mía
I amiga mía
L amiga mía
J amiga mía
1506 R.
N AMICA
1822 Amar. amiga mía
1507 Z.
1841 O AMIGA
1514 V.
P AMIGA
1518 V.
U AMIGA
1529 V.
V AMIGA
17
18
*A
1499 B
1500 C
*E AMIGA
1501 D
*F amiga mía
*G amiga mía
1502
H amiga mía
K amiga mía
M amiga mía
I amiga mía
L amiga mía
J amiga mía
1506 R.
N donna mía
1822 Amar. amiga mía
1507 Z.
1841 O AMIGA
1514 V.
P AMIGA
1518 V.
U AMIGA
1529 V.
V AMIGA

The series of graphs that follows illustrates support of *E by both N and O. Graph 19 shows that Stemmas III and IV omit a word instead of adding as in the two preceding graphs.

The word on Graph 19 appears in the speech of Celestina when she is trying to persuade Pármeno to become a friend of Sempronio.

> . . . ¡O HIJO MÍO Pármeno! Que bien te puedo dezir fijo, pues tanto tiempo te crié.
> *(Cej. I, VII, 236, 1. 6; C–T, 133, 1. 12)*

O HIJO MÍO *ACD*EPUV + O
O FIJO MÍO B
HO FIGLIO MIO N
O fijo (———) Stemmas III and IV
O hijo (———) Amar.

The word MÁS in Graph 20 is taken from Calisto's reaction when Sosia tells him of the death of his two servants.

> . . . ¡O mi triste nombre é fama, cómo andas al tablero de boca en boca! ¡O mis secretos MÁS secretos, quán públicos andarés por las plaças é mercados!
> *(Cej. II, XIII, 119, 1. 11 [111, 1. 1]; C–T, 232, 1. 10)*

MÁS *ABCD*EPUV + O
O MEI SECRETI & PIU CHE SECRETI N
mis *FHIJ*GKLM + Amar.

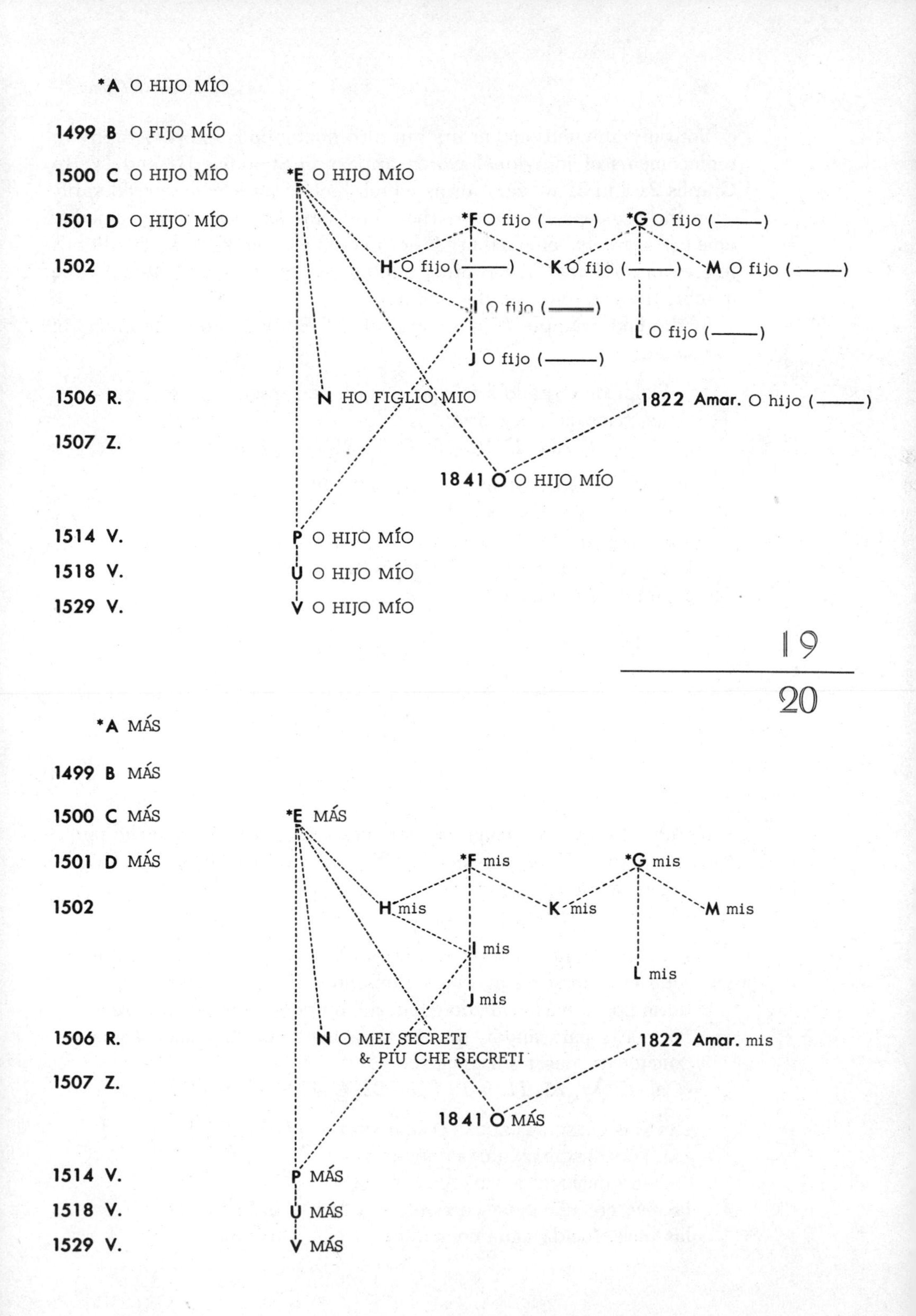
*A O HIJO MÍO
1499 B O FIJO MÍO
1500 C O HIJO MÍO
*E O HIJO MÍO
1501 D O HIJO MÍO
*F O fijo (——)
*G O fijo (——)
1502
H O fijo (——)
K O fijo (——)
M O fijo (——)
I O fijo (——)
L O fijo (——)
J O fijo (——)
1506 R.
N HO FIGLIO MIO
1822 Amar. O hijo (——)
1507 Z.
1841 O O HIJO MÍO
1514 V.
P O HIJO MÍO
1518 V.
U O HIJO MÍO
1529 V.
V O HIJO MÍO
19
20
*A MÁS
1499 B MÁS
1500 C MÁS
*E MÁS
1501 D MÁS
*F mis
*G mis
1502
H mis
K mis
M mis
I mis
L mis
J mis
1506 R.
N O MEI SECRETI & PIU CHE SECRETI
1822 Amar. mis
1507 Z.
1841 O MÁS
1514 V.
P MÁS
1518 V.
U MÁS
1529 V.
V MÁS

Not only unintentional errors but also fluctuations in orthography or replacements of individual words appear in Stemmas III and IV. In Graphs 21 and 22 we find forms which have drawn away considerably from the princeps edition of either the Comedia or the Tragicomedia. One can scarcely believe that *F or *G or any other of the eight editions in Stemmas III and IV was proofread against the original edition by the author, the corrector, or the editor.

In the first example Alisa is informing Celestina about the illness of her sister.

> —Dolor de costado é tal que, SEGÚN DEL MOÇO SUPE que quedaua, temo no sea mortal.
> *(Cej. I, IV, 163, 11. 18–19; C–T, 85, 11. 15–16)*

| | |
|---|---|
| SEGÚN DEL MOÇO SUPE | *ABCD*EPUV |
| SEGÚN DEL MOZO SUPE | O |
| SECONDO CHE IO SEPPE DAL FAMIGLIO | N |
| según dize el moço | *FHIJ*GKLM |
| según dice el mozo | Amar. |

Graph 22 shows a change of five consecutive words from the plural to the singular. H is lacking but otherwise the editions fall into the same classification as in the preceding graph.

Celestina is boasting to Calisto of her ability and power.

> . . . Mira, mira que está Celestina de tu parte é que, avnque todo te faltasse lo que en vn enamorado se requiere, te vendería por el más acabado galán del mundo, que te haría llanas las peñas para andar, que te faría LAS MÁS CRESCIDAS AGUAS CORRIENTES pasar sin mojarte.
> *(Cej. II, XI, 75, 11. 9–10 [71–72]; C–T, 200, 11. 1–2)*

| | |
|---|---|
| LAS MÁS CRESCIDAS AGUAS CORRIENTES | *ABD*EPUV |
| LAS MÁS CRECIDAS AGUAS CORRIENTES | C + O |
| LE PIU CURRENTE & CRESCENTE AQQUE | N |
| la más crecida agua corriente | *FI*GKLM + Amar. |
| las más crecida agua corriente | J (H falta) |

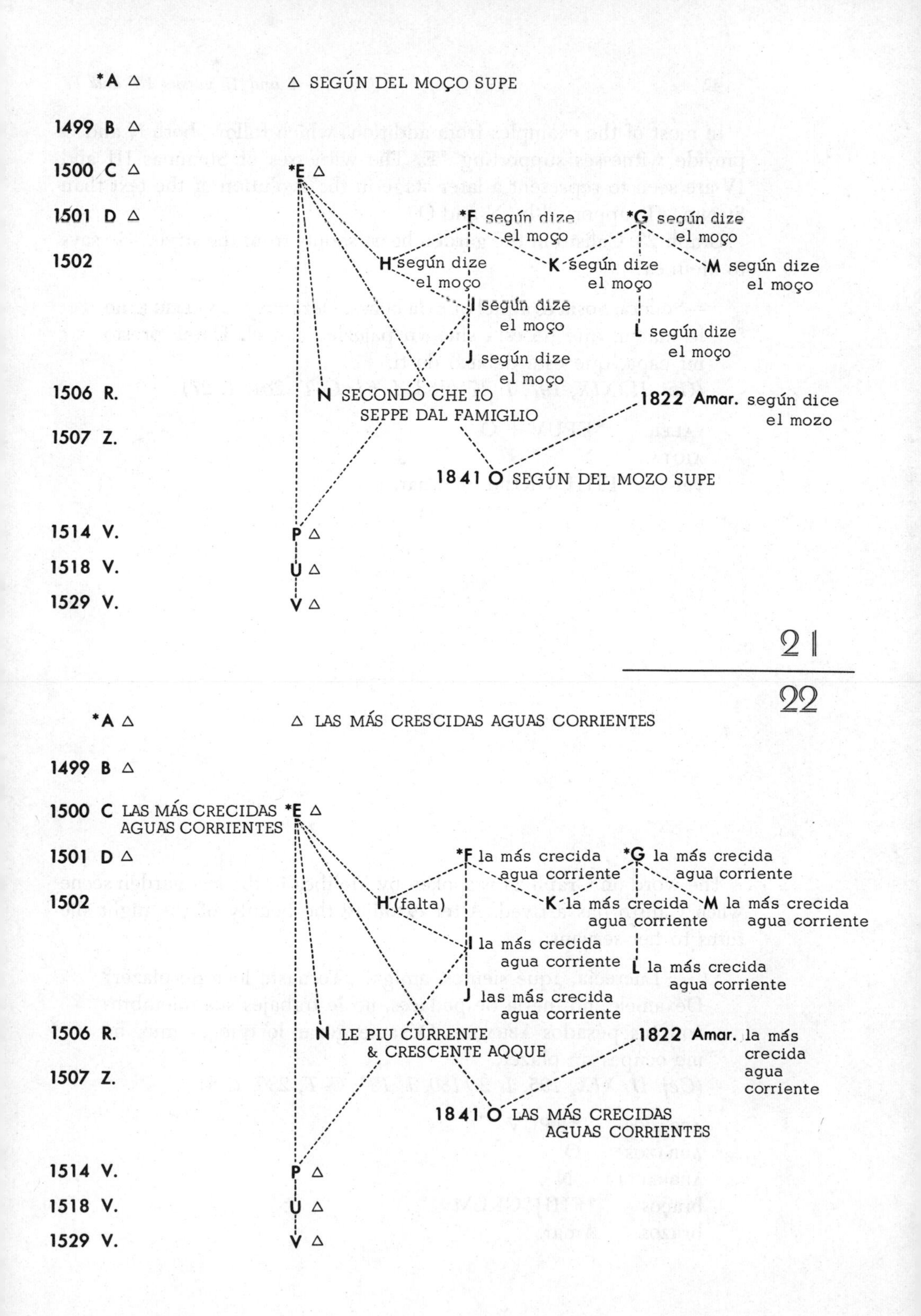
*A △
△ SEGÚN DEL MOÇO SUPE
1499 B △
1500 C △
*E △
1501 D △
*F según dize el moço
*G según dize el moço
1502
H según dize el moço
K según dize el moço
M según dize el moço
I según dize el moço
L según dize el moço
J según dize el moço
1506 R.
N SECONDO CHE IO SEPPE DAL FAMIGLIO
1822 Amar. según dice el mozo
1507 Z.
1841 O SEGÚN DEL MOZO SUPE
1514 V.
P △
1518 V.
U △
1529 V.
V △
21
22
*A △
△ LAS MÁS CRESCIDAS AGUAS CORRIENTES
1499 B △
1500 C LAS MÁS CRECIDAS AGUAS CORRIENTES
*E △
1501 D △
*F la más crecida agua corriente
*G la más crecida agua corriente
1502
H (falta)
K la más crecida agua corriente
M la más crecida agua corriente
I la más crecida agua corriente
L la más crecida agua corriente
J las más crecida agua corriente
1506 R.
N LE PIU CURRENTE & CRESCENTE AQQUE
1822 Amar. la más crecida agua corriente
1507 Z.
1841 O LAS MÁS CRECIDAS AGUAS CORRIENTES
1514 V.
P △
1518 V.
U △
1529 V.
V △

In most of the examples from additions which follow, both N and O provide witnesses supporting *E. The witnesses of Stemmas III and IV are seen to represent a later stage in the evolution of the text than Stemma II supported by N and O.

Graph 23. Calisto in the garden hears shouts from the street. He says to Melibea:

> —Señora, Sosia es aquel que da bozes. Déxame yr á VALERLE, no le maten, que no está sino vn pajezico con él. Dame presto mi capa, que está debaxo de tí.
> *(Cej. II, XIX, 197, 1. 17 [183, 1. 6]; C–T, 281, 1. 27)*

VALER *EPUV + O
AIUTAR N
ver *FHIJ*GKLM + Amar.

The word on Graph 24 is spoken by Melibea in the last garden scene when Calisto has arrived. After extolling the beauty of the night she turns to her servant:

> . . . Lucrecia, ¿qué sientes, amiga? ¿Tornaste loca de plazer? Déxamele, no me la despedaces, no le trabajes sus miembros con tus pesados ABRAÇOS. Déxame gozar lo que es mío, no me ocupes mi plazer.
> *(Cej. II, XIX, 195, 1. 2 [180, 1. 19]; C–T, 280, 1. 8)*

ABRAÇOS *EPUV
ABRAZOS O
ABBRACCI N
braços *FHIJ*GKLM
brazos Amar.

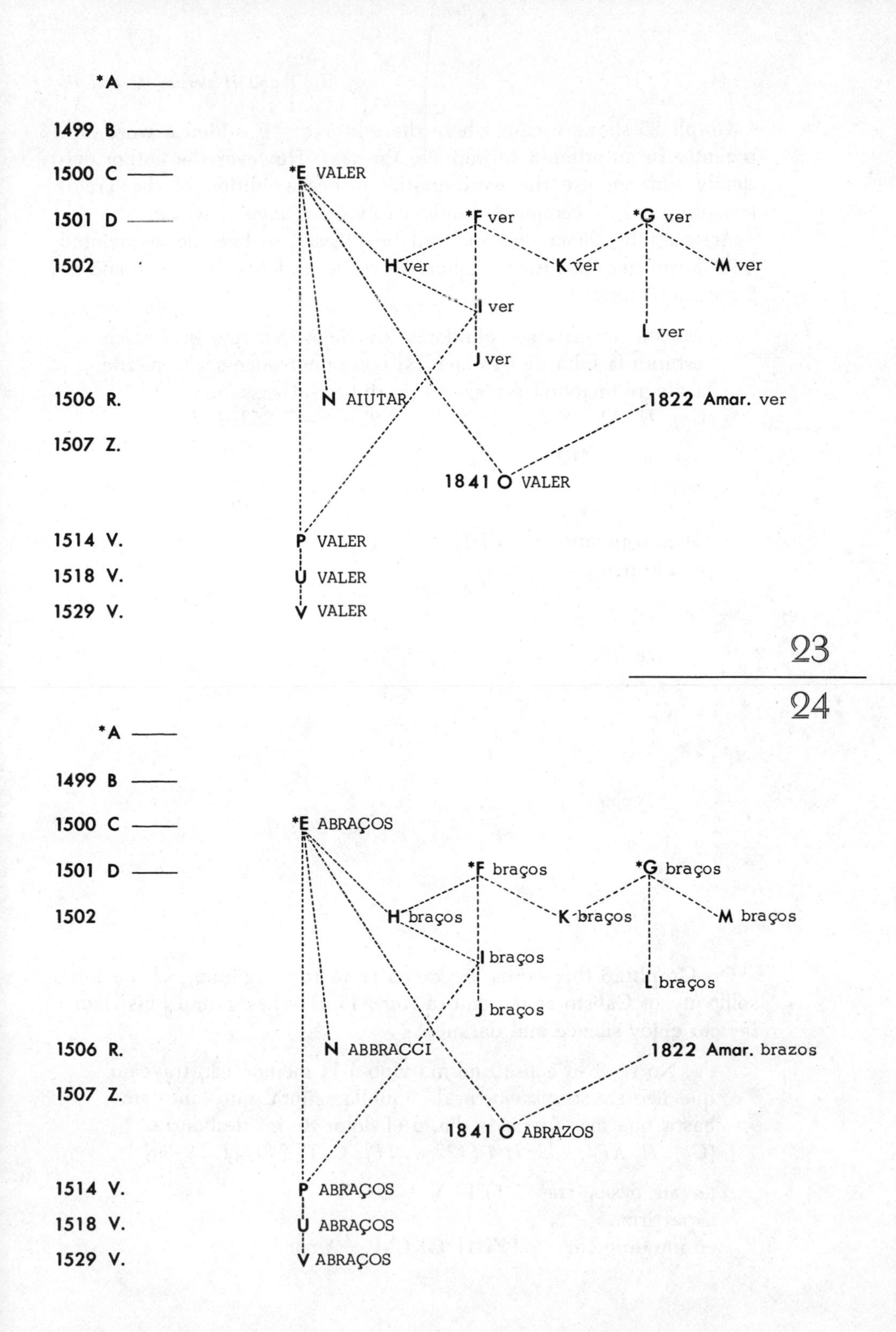

*A
1499 B
1500 C
1501 D
1502
1506 R.
1507 Z.
1514 V.
1518 V.
1529 V.
*E VALER
*F ver
*G ver
H ver
K ver
M ver
I ver
L ver
J ver
N AIUTAR
1822 Amar. ver
1841 O VALER
P VALER
U VALER
V VALER
23
24
*A
1499 B
1500 C
1501 D
1502
1506 R.
1507 Z.
1514 V.
1518 V.
1529 V.
*E ABRAÇOS
*F braços
*G braços
H braços
K braços
M braços
I braços
L braços
J braços
N ABBRACCI
1822 Amar. brazos
1841 O ABRAZOS
P ABRAÇOS
U ABRAÇOS
V ABRAÇOS

Graph 25 shows a case where the editor of *F added a word, apparently in an attempt to improve the text. However the author evidently did not use the word in the princeps edition of the Tragicomedia, and it becomes redundant following *nueuo sucessor.*

Areúsa tells Elicia that she will be pleased to become acquainted with Sosia and she invites Elicia to come and live with her and to forget her former lover.

> . . . Con nueuo amor oluidarás los viejos. Vn hijo que nasce restaura la falta de tres finados: con nueuo sucessor se pierde la alegre memoria é plazeres perdidos del PASSADO.
> *(Cej. II, XV, 152, 1. 11 [141, 1. 22]; C–T, 253, 1. 17)*

PASSADO *EPUV
PASSATO N
PASADO O
passado tiempo *FHIJ*GKLM
pasado tiempo Amar.

On Graph 26 the words are taken from the beginning of the long soliloquy of Calisto at the end of Act XIV. He has gone to his chambers to enjoy silence and darkness.

> . . . No sé si lo causa que me vino á la memoria la trayción, que fize EN ME DESPARTIR de aquella señora, que tanto amo, hasta que más fuera de día, ó el dolor de mi deshonrra.
> *(Cej. II, XIV, 132, 1. 4 [122, 1. 11]; C–T, 240, 11. 29–30)*

EN ME DESPARTIR *EPUV + O
a partirme N
en me despedir *FHIJ*GKLM + Amar.

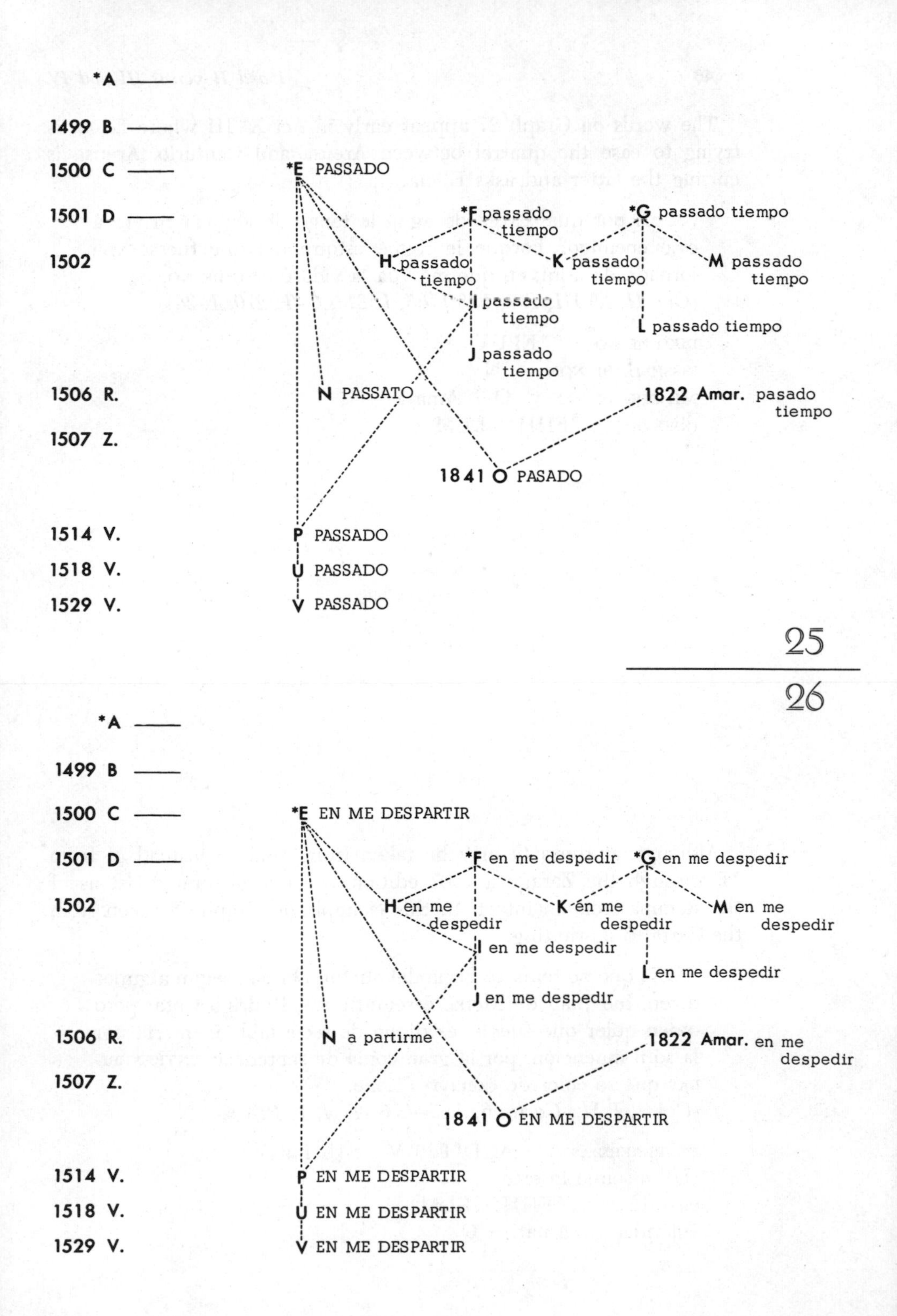
*A
1499 B
1500 C
1501 D
1502
1506 R.
1507 Z.
1514 V.
1518 V.
1529 V.
*E PASSADO
*F passado tiempo
*G passado tiempo
H passado tiempo
K passado tiempo
M passado tiempo
I passado tiempo
L passado tiempo
J passado tiempo
N PASSATO
1822 Amar. pasado tiempo
1841 O PASADO
P PASSADO
U PASSADO
V PASSADO
25
26
*A
1499 B
1500 C
1501 D
1502
1506 R.
1507 Z.
1514 V.
1518 V.
1529 V.
*E EN ME DESPARTIR
*F en me despedir
*G en me despedir
H en me despedir
K en me despedir
M en me despedir
I en me despedir
L en me despedir
J en me despedir
N a partirme
1822 Amar. en me despedir
1841 O EN ME DESPARTIR
P EN ME DESPARTIR
U EN ME DESPARTIR
V EN ME DESPARTIR

The words on Graph 27 appear early in Act XVIII where Elicia is trying to ease the quarrel between Areúsa and Centurio. Areúsa is cursing the latter and asks Elicia:

> . . . ¿E por quál carga de agua le tengo de abraçar ni ver á esse enemigo? Porque le rogué estotro día que fuesse vna jornada de aquí, en que me yua la vida é DIXO DE NO.
> *(Cej. II, XVIII, 179, 1. 3 [165, 1. 21]; C–T, 270, 1. 28)*

DIXO DE NO *EPUV
DISSEME DI NON N
ME DIJO DE NO O + Amar.
dixo no *FHIJ*GKLM

Although at times O may be taken from Amarita instead of from *E through the Zaragoza 1507 edition, the two general divisions of the stemmas remain intact. In this example on Graph 28 taken from the Carta, B is wanting.

> . . . Ví que no tenía su firma del auctor, el qual, según algunos dizen, fué Juan de Mena, é según otros, Rodrigo Cota; pero quien quier que fuesse, es digno de recordable memoria por la sotil inuención, por la gran copia de sentencias ENTREXERIDAS que so color de donayres tiene.
> *(Cej. I, P.M., Carta, 6, 1. 3–4; C–T, 4, 1. 12)*

ENTREXERIDAS *ACD*EPUV (B falta)
che ui sonno inserte N
enxeridas *FHIJ*GKLM
enjeridas Amar. + O

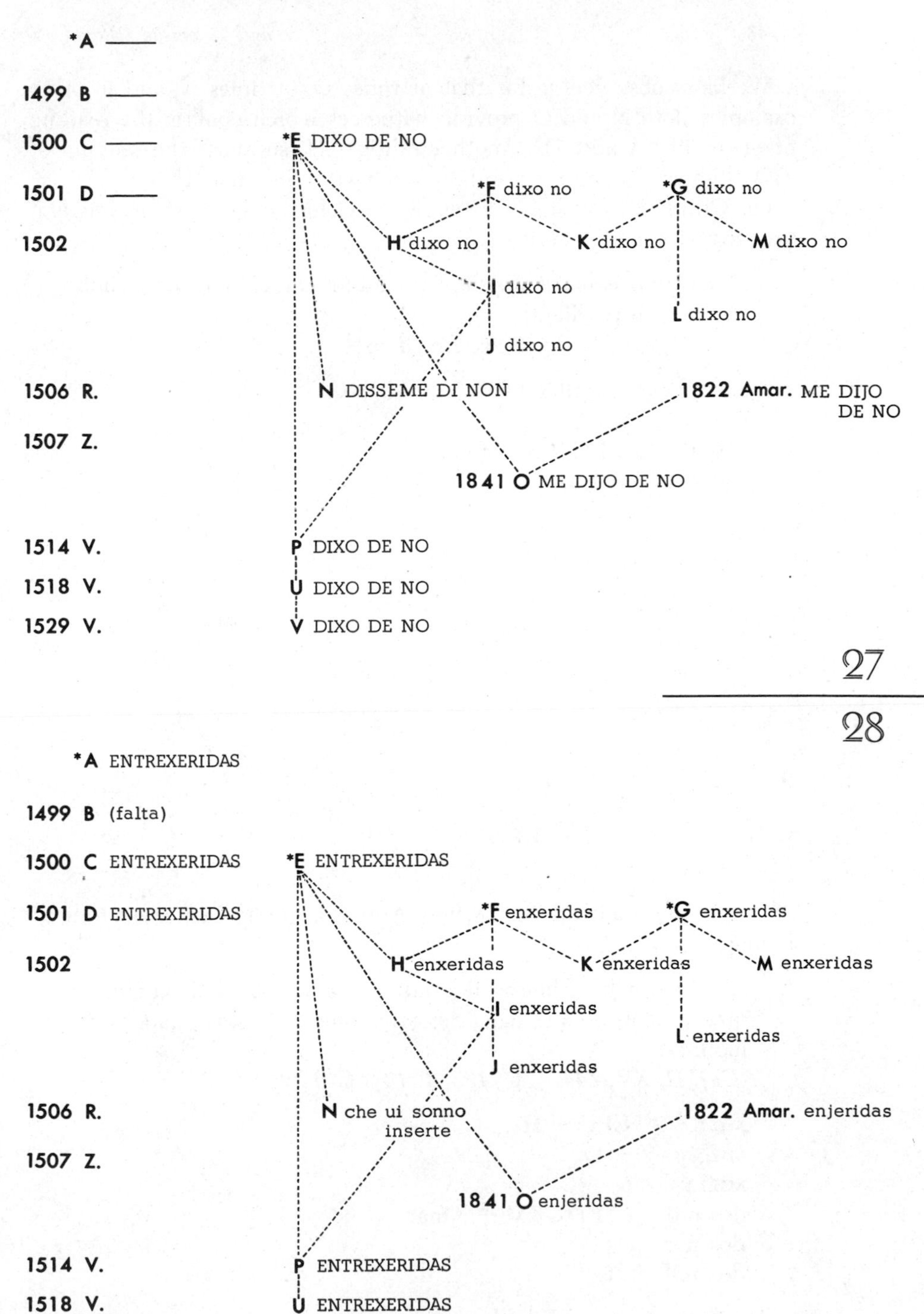

*A ——
1499 B ——
1500 C ——
1501 D ——
1502
1506 R.
1507 Z.
1514 V.
1518 V.
1529 V.
*E DIXO DE NO
*F dixo no
*G dixo no
H dixo no
K dixo no
M dixo no
I dixo no
L dixo no
J dixo no
N DISSEME DI NON
1822 Amar. ME DIJO DE NO
1841 O ME DIJO DE NO
P DIXO DE NO
U DIXO DE NO
V DIXO DE NO
27
28
*A ENTREXERIDAS
1499 B (falta)
1500 C ENTREXERIDAS
1501 D ENTREXERIDAS
1502
1506 R.
1507 Z.
1514 V.
1518 V.
1529 V.
*E ENTREXERIDAS
*F enxeridas
*G enxeridas
H enxeridas
K enxeridas
M enxeridas
I enxeridas
L enxeridas
J enxeridas
N che ui sonno inserte
1822 Amar. enjeridas
1841 O enjeridas
P ENTREXERIDAS
U ENTREXERIDAS
V ENTREXERIDAS

We have observed so far that at times O, at times N, and in other examples both N and O provide witnesses which confirm the reading of *E or of *A and *E. Another edition, H, supports the reading of *E at times, although it normally belongs in Stemma III.

On Graph 29 Calisto is listening to Celestina's report on her first visit to the home of Melibea.

> . . . ¿Qué más hazía aquella Tusca ADELETA, cuya fama, siendo tú viua, se perdiera?
> *(Cej. I, VI, 214–15; C–T, 119, 1. 8)*

ADELETA *ABCD*EPUV + H + O
Eletra N
Athleta *FIJ*GKLM
Adelecta Amar.

Graph 30 is in an addition where Areúsa is giving Centurio a tongue-lashing.

> . . . si no, por los huesos del padre que me hizo é de la madre que me parió, yo te haga dar MILL palos en essas espaldas de molinero.
> *(Cej. II, XV, 144, 1. 6 [133, 1. 14]; C–T, 249, 1. 3)*

MILL *EPU + H
MIL V + O
MILLE N
dos mil *FI*GKM + Amar.
dos mis J
dos mll L

The forms in J and L both represent errors by the typesetter.

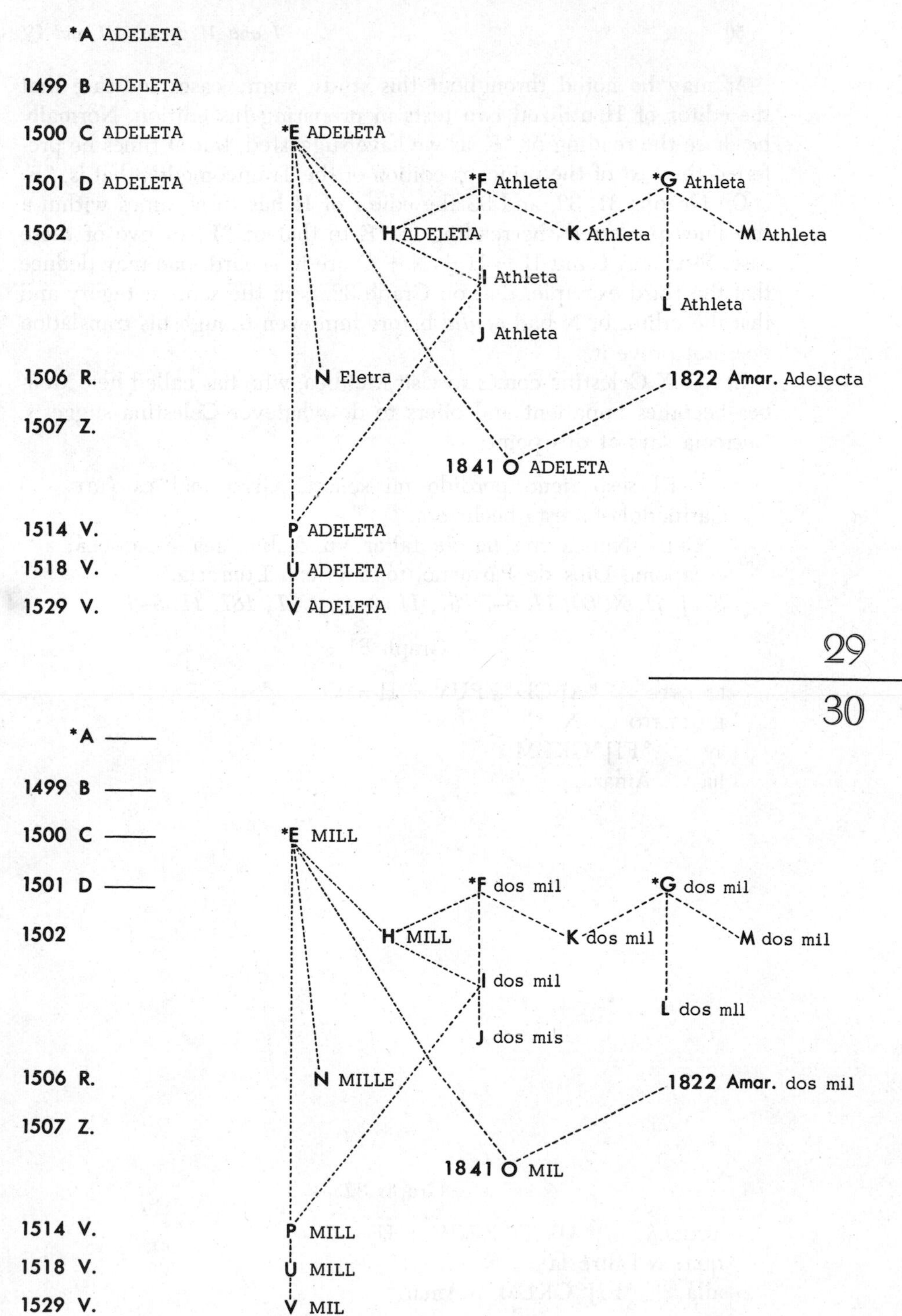

*A ADELETA
1499 B ADELETA
1500 C ADELETA
*E ADELETA
1501 D ADELETA
*F Athleta
*G Athleta
1502
H ADELETA
K Athleta
M Athleta
I Athleta
L Athleta
J Athleta
1506 R.
N Eletra
1822 Amar. Adelecta
1507 Z.
1841 O ADELETA
1514 V.
P ADELETA
1518 V.
U ADELETA
1529 V.
V ADELETA
29
30
*A ——
1499 B ——
1500 C ——
*E MILL
1501 D ——
*F dos mil
*G dos mil
1502
H MILL
K dos mil
M dos mil
I dos mil
L dos mll
J dos mis
1506 R.
N MILLE
1822 Amar. dos mil
1507 Z.
1841 O MIL
1514 V.
P MILL
1518 V.
U MILL
1529 V.
V MIL

As may be noted throughout this study, many cases indicate that the editor of H utilized two texts in preparing his edition. Normally he chose the reading of *F, as we have suggested, but at times he preferred the text of the princeps edition of the Tragicomedia, that is, *E.

On Graphs 31, 32, and 33 the editor of H has three times within a few lines preferred the reading of *E to that of *F. In two of these cases Stemmas I and II + H + N + O are in accord; one may deduce that the third example, that on Graph 32, is in the same category and that the editor of N had *acullá* before him even though his translation does not prove it.

In Act X Celestina comes to visit Melibea, who has called her. Melibea becomes impatient and offers to do whatever Celestina suggests. Lucrecia says at this point:

> —El seso tiene perdido mi señora. Gran mal ES ÉSTE. Catiuádola ha esta hechizera.
>
> CEL.—Nunca me ha de faltar vn diablo acá é ACULLÁ; escapóme Dios de Pármeno, tópome con Lucrecia.
>
> *(Cej. II, X, 60, 11. 5–7 [57, 11. 2–4]; C–T, 187, 11. 5–6)*

Graph 31

ES ÉSTE *ABCD*EPUV + H + O
E QUESTO N
ay *FIJ*GKLM
ha Amar.

Graph 32

ACULLÁ *ABCD*EPUV + H + O
qua: & l'altro la N
allá *FIJ*GKLM + Amar.

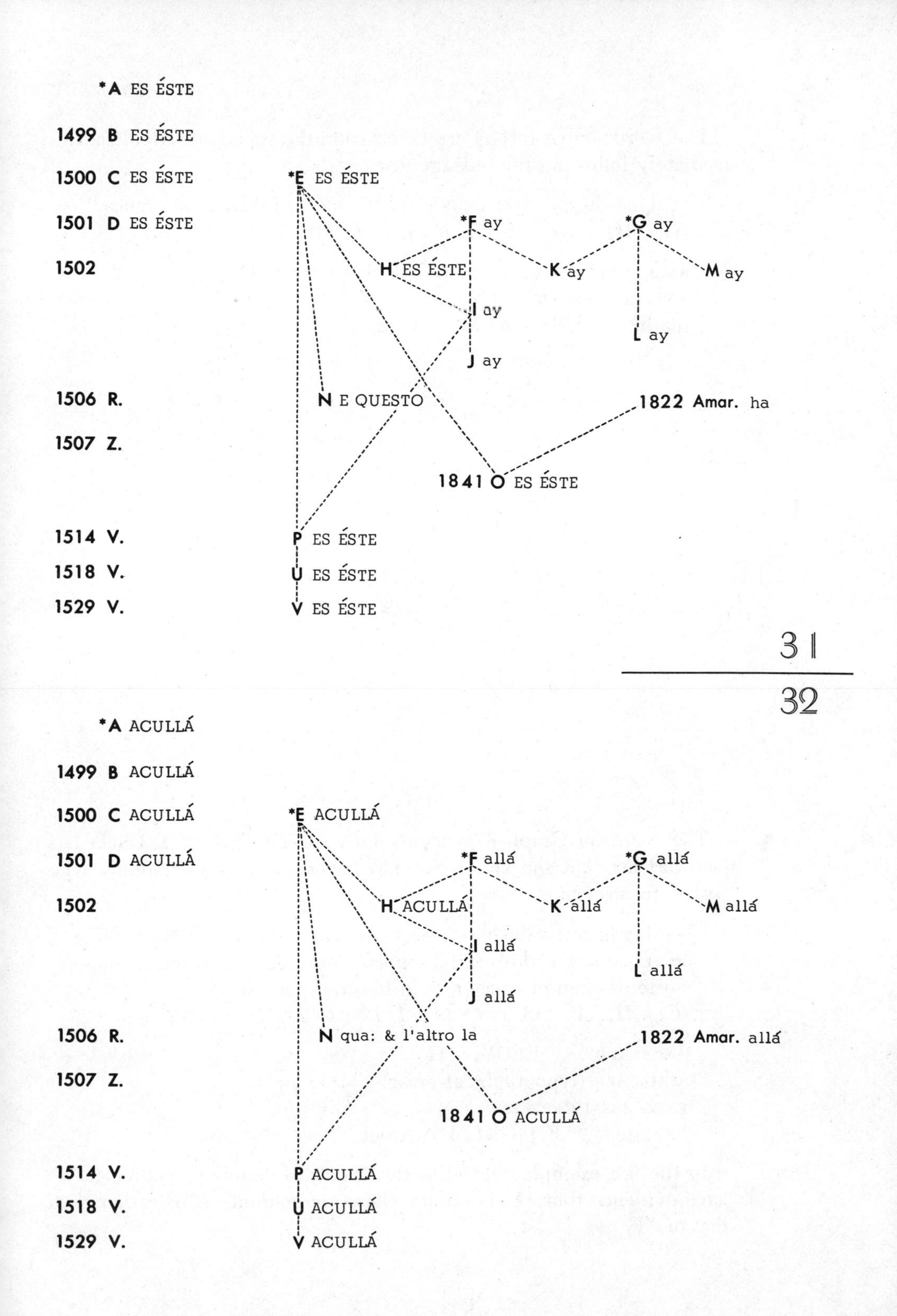
*A ES ÉSTE
1499 B ES ÉSTE
1500 C ES ÉSTE
1501 D ES ÉSTE
1502
*E ES ÉSTE
*F ay
*G ay
H ES ÉSTE
K ay
M ay
I ay
L ay
J ay
1506 R.
N E QUESTO
1822 Amar. ha
1507 Z.
1841 O ES ÉSTE
1514 V.
P ES ÉSTE
1518 V.
U ES ÉSTE
1529 V.
V ES ÉSTE
31
32
*A ACULLÁ
1499 B ACULLÁ
1500 C ACULLÁ
1501 D ACULLÁ
1502
*E ACULLÁ
*F allá
*G allá
H ACULLÁ
K allá
M allá
I allá
L allá
J allá
1506 R.
N qua: & l'altro la
1822 Amar. allá
1507 Z.
1841 O ACULLÁ
1514 V.
P ACULLÁ
1518 V.
U ACULLÁ
1529 V.
V ACULLÁ

The words on Graph 33 are taken from the speech by Melibea, immediately following the passage just cited.

—¿Qué dizes, AMADA MAESTRA? ¿Qué te fablaua essa moça?
*(Cej. II, X, 60, 1. 9 [57, 1. 6]; C–T, 187, 1. 8)*

AMADA MAESTRA *ABCD*EPUV + H + O
AMATA MAESTRA N
madre *FIJ*GKLM + Amar.

The word on Graph 34 appears in a speech of Areúsa. Elicia has just told her that she knows Sosia, a friend of Pármeno. Areúsa, who wishes to meet him, says:

—Mas hazme este plazer, que me embíes acá esse Sosia. Yo le HALAGARÉ é diré mill lisonjas é offrescimientos hasta que no le dexe en el cuerpo de lo hecho é por hazer.
*(Cej. II, XV, 152, 1. 1 [141, 1. 12]; C–T, 253, 1. 8)*

HALAGARÉ *EPUV + H
ALHAGARÉ (typographical error) O
FARO ASSAI CAREZZE N
hablaré *FIJ*GKLM + Amar.

In the last example as well as the five immediately preceding it, we have evidence that H sometimes chose the variant of *E rather than that of *F.

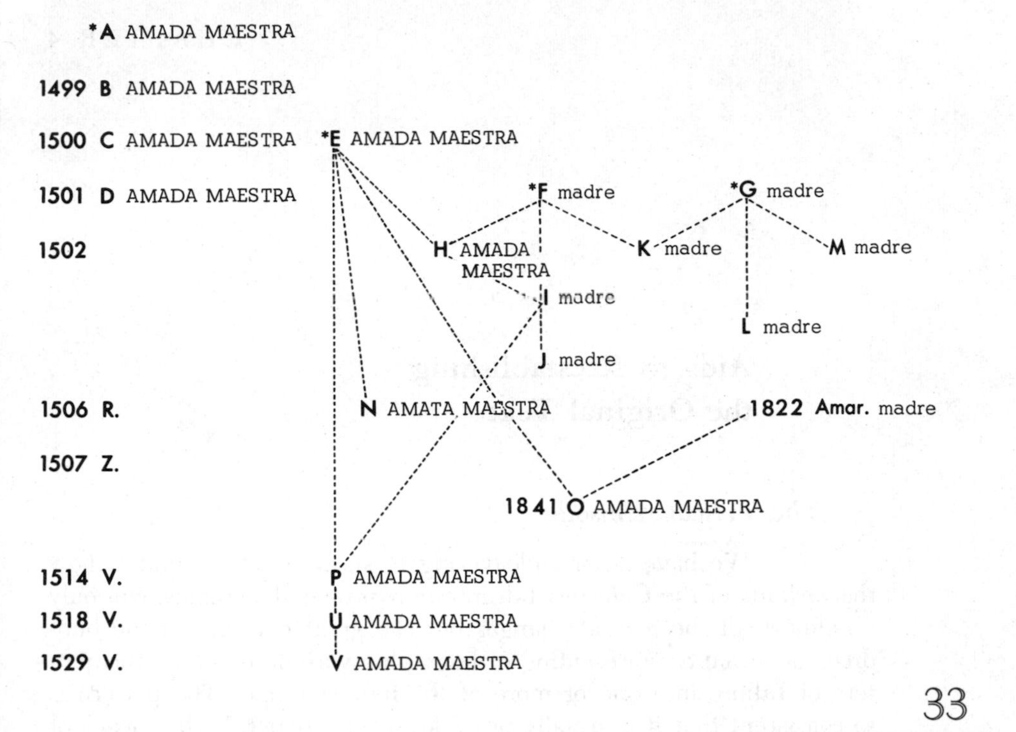

*A AMADA MAESTRA
1499 B AMADA MAESTRA
1500 C AMADA MAESTRA
*E AMADA MAESTRA
1501 D AMADA MAESTRA
*F madre
*G madre
1502
H AMADA MAESTRA
K madre
M madre
I madre
L madre
J madre
1506 R.
N AMATA MAESTRA
1822 Amar. madre
1507 Z.
1841 O AMADA MAESTRA
1514 V.
P AMADA MAESTRA
1518 V.
U AMADA MAESTRA
1529 V.
V AMADA MAESTRA






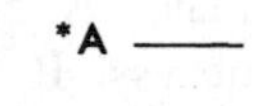

*A ——


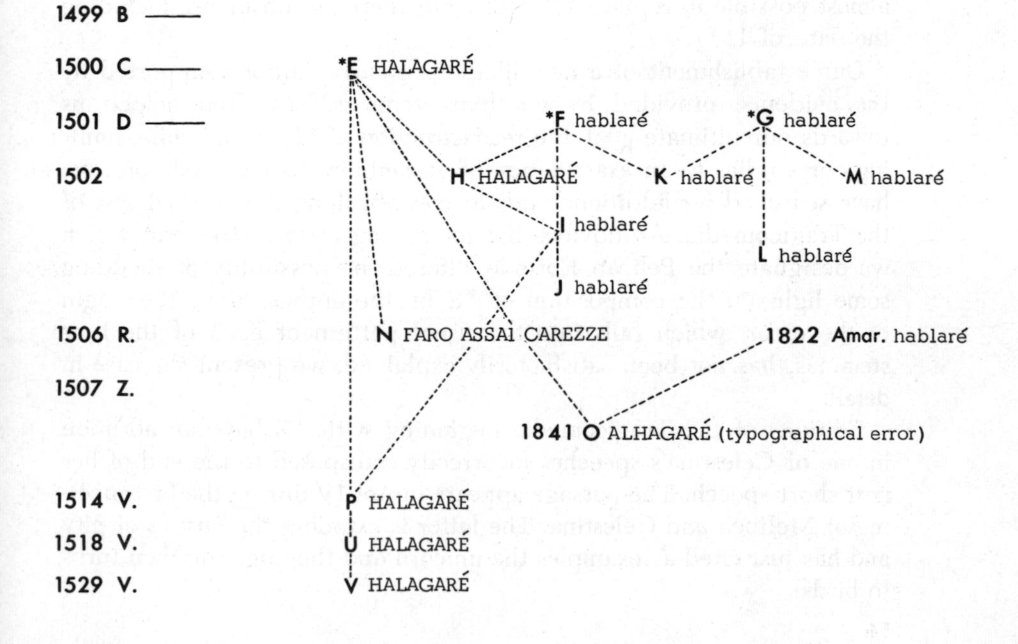

1499 B ——
1500 C ——
*E HALAGARÉ
1501 D ——
*F hablaré
*G hablaré
1502
H HALAGARÉ
K hablaré
M hablaré
I hablaré
L hablaré
J hablaré
1506 R.
N FARO ASSAI CAREZZE
1822 Amar. hablaré
1507 Z.
1841 O ALHAGARÉ (typographical error)
1514 V.
P HALAGARÉ
1518 V.
U HALAGARÉ
1529 V.
V HALAGARÉ

# CHAPTER 4

# Aids to Reestablishing the Original Text

## *The Pelican Episode*

We have been endeavoring to show in our examples how the variants of the *Celestina* fall into four principal stemmas. Not only do almost all the textual changes but the great majority of the hundreds of variants representing orthographic variations follow this pattern of falling into one or more of the four stemmas. The pattern is so consistent that it is usually possible to reconstruct *F by means of the witnesses H, I, J; and *G by means of the witnesses K, L, M. Originally we tried to reconstruct the prototypes of the stemmas, *E, *F and *G, with only one of the witnesses but without success. It is almost possible to replace *F with I but there are obstacles, including the date of I.

Our establishment of a new filiation of early editions supported by the evidence provided by the four stemmas has often helped us towards our ultimate goal, the reconstruction of *E. Meanwhile, limiting our studies to an examination of variants in the early editions, we have searched for additional aids to reestablishing the original text of the Tragicomedia. An obvious but interesting error in the text, which we designate the Pelican Episode, offered the possibility of shedding some light on the composition of *E by the author. Since the origin of the error, which falls into the usual pattern of each of the four stemmas, has not been satisfactorily explained, we present the case in detail.

Editions of the Tragicomedia beginning with *E have an addition in one of Celestina's speeches incorrectly transposed to the end of her next short speech. The passage appears in Act IV during the first meeting of Melibea and Celestina. The latter is extolling the virtues of pity and has just cited as examples the unicorn and the dog. She then turns to birds.

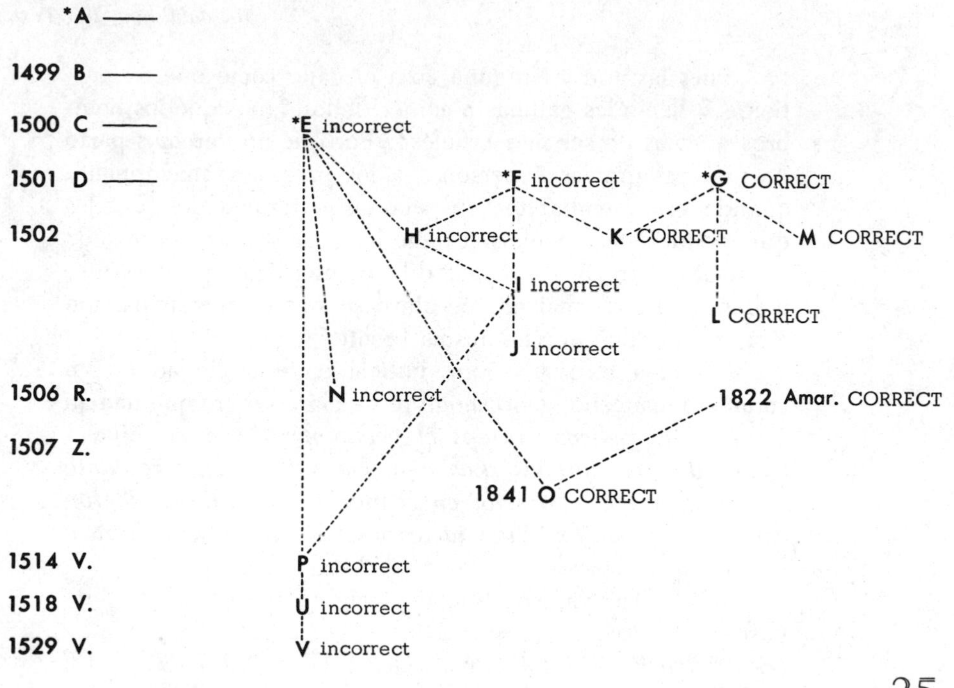
*A
1499 B
1500 C
1501 D
1502
1506 R.
1507 Z.
1514 V.
1518 V.
1529 V.
*E incorrect
*F incorrect
*G CORRECT
H incorrect
K CORRECT
M CORRECT
I incorrect
L CORRECT
J incorrect
N incorrect
1822 Amar. CORRECT
1841 O CORRECT
P incorrect
U incorrect
V incorrect

. . . ¿Pues las aues? Ninguna cosa el gallo come que no participe ꝛ llame las gallinas a comer dello: *¿por qué los hombres auemos de ser más crueles? ¿Por qué no daremos parte de nuestras gracias ꝛ personas a los próximos, mayormente quando están embueltos en secretas enfermedades, ꝛ tales que, donde está la melezina, salió la causa de la enfermedad?

MELIB.—Por Dios, sin más dilatar, me digas quién es esse doliente, que de mal tan perplexo se siente, que su passion ꝛ remedio salen de vna misma fuente.

CEL.—Bien ternás, señora, noticia en esta cibdad de vn cauallero mancebo, gentil hombre de clara sangre que llaman Calisto. **El pelicano rompe el pecho por dar a sus hijos a comer de sus entrañas. Las cigueñas mantienen otro tanto tiempo a sus padres viejos en el nido quanto ellos le dieron ceuo siendo pollitos. Pues tal conoscimiento dió la natura a los animales ꝛ aues.*

MELIB.—¡Ya, ya, ya! Buena vieja, no me digas más, no pases adelante. . .

*(Ed. Valencia 1514, fol. C v a. [Cej. I, IV, 176, 1. 7–177, 1. 18; C–T, 91, 1. 23–92, 1. 3.]*

We cite the text of P (Valencia, 1514) since Menéndez Pelayo and Krapf as well as Cejador restore the passage to its proper place. The transposed speech, indicated by asterisk and italics, should have been inserted at the first asterisk. Graph 35 shows that the error continues throughout Stemmas II and III and in N. It is passed on from N to many of the early Italian editions and it appears in the Spanish editions that are based on Stemma III. Therefore, we have the following division:

Passage transposed *EPUV*FHIJ + N
Passage in proper position *GKLM + Amar. + O

One might surmise that an edition of the Tragicomedia existed before *E and that *E made the error, that later *G used the archetype and restored the passage to its proper place. This possibility merely introduces new inexplicable problems. Our studies so far lead us to believe that the editor of *G utilized *F, and perhaps *E. He may have been a student or visitor in Salamanca and heard, possibly from Rojas himself, that the passage had been transposed. This might have encouraged him to bring out another, better edition.

A possible explanation of the error in *E may be found in a theory already mentioned: that the author of the Tragicomedia probably used the printed edition *A of the Comedia as he revised the text. When he made small changes of a word or two, he may have written them on the margins of the printed page, and inserted the longer additions on separate sheets of paper between the pages. In some way the typesetter, although he placed the addition in a speech of Celestina, as directed, placed it in the wrong speech. Perhaps the fact that the words preceding *el pelicano* in the two places end in *-to* and *-llo* had something to do with the error. This premise that Rojas used the printed text of the Comedia in composing the Tragicomedia has aided us at times in the reconstruction of *E, as may be seen later in this chapter. Moreover, this error and others apparently cropping out in *F and *G as well as *E make it seem unlikely that either Rojas or Proaza, the corrector of the Comedia, read the proof of any of them.

### *Orthographic Variants: Initial* H- *versus Initial* f-

When one reads the *Celestina,* he encounters not only problems of interpretation of difficult passages but also a hodgepodge of orthographic variants. He is likely to wonder if the author himself spelled a word in various ways or whether editor, corrector, or others were responsible—or rather irresponsible—in their haste. We have accumulated data on the characteristics of the various editors—their preferences, aversions, idiosyncrasies. We have also compiled a list of nonvariant words. Both are helpful in determining Rojas' probable spelling.

In the attempt to reconstruct the lost princeps edition of the Tragicomedia, one of the most troublesome problems is the chaotic use of initial H- and f-. We shall point out typical changes in spelling in which an editor switches from initial H- to f- almost at random. These occur frequently in one or more editions of the Comedia, but there are fewer examples of isolated changes in the other stemmas.

Graph 36 shows changes in all the stemmas except Stemma II. In Stemma I, B uses *fazer;* in Stemma III, I and J do so; and in Stemma IV, L does. We shall demonstrate later that *F sometimes uses H- and sometimes *f-*. In the present case both H and K provide witnesses for H- and only I for f-. J normally follows I.

The word on Graph 36 appears in Act IV where Celestina is speaking to Lucrecia.

> ... E avn darte he vnos poluos para quitarte esse olor de la boca, que te huele vn poco, que en el reyno no lo sabe *fazer* otra sino yo é no ay cosa que peor en la muger parezca. *(Cej. I, IV, 190, 1. 18; C–T, 100, 1. 8)*

HAZER *ACD*EPUV*FH*GKM
HACER Amar. + O

fazer B + IJ + L
fare N

On Graph 37 *fecho* is preferred to HECHO by L as well as by BCD. The word is in a speech by Calisto to Sempronio in Act I.

> —¡Maldito seas!, que *fecho* me has reyr, lo que no pensé ogaño.
> *(Cej. I, I, 45, 1. 1; C–T, 29, 1. 27)*
>
> HECHO *A + Stemmas II and III + *GKM + Amar. + O
> fecho BCDL
> facto N

The editor of L appears to favor f- and at times is the only one to use it:

> fagas——Cej. II, XX, 205, 1. 10 (190, 1. 9); C–T, 287, 1. 12
> fizo——Cej. II, XIII, 121, 1. 20 (113, 1. 8); C–T, 233, 1. 22
> fazer——Cej. II, XVI, 171, 1. 8 (159, 1. 1); C–T, 265, 1. 1

The nonvariant word list of the *Celestina* that we have compiled—omitting definite and indefinite articles, short prepositions, possessive adjectives, etc.—has three sections: nonvariant words in the sixteen-act editions, those in the additions, and finally those in the complete work. The section on the complete work shows that H- was used in all the forms of HABLAR 83 times and f- only once (*fablasse,* Cej. I, VI, 204, 1. 16; C–T, 112, 1. 22). We have not yet replaced *fablasse* with HABLASSE as the word we believe the author used, but it would not be surprising if someone, say a typesetter, used f- for H- in the princeps edition of the Comedia. The nonvariant forms of the verb HALLAR appear 28 times, with none for *fallar.* While nonvariant forms of HAZER occur almost 200 times, *fazer* appears only three times. HERMOSO appears four times, always with H-, and so does HERMOSURA. HIJO, HIJOS, HIJA, HIJAS show up 71 times as nonvariants, always spelled with H-. HUYR appears in various forms 28 times, always spelled with H-. There are no nonvariants with *f-* for HOLGAR.

These data lead us to believe that Rojas preferred initial H- to f-. The series of graphs that follows illustrates the peculiarities of the editors of some of the editions, and at the same time gives a glimpse of certain patterns which will be examined in more detail when the individual stemmas are discussed. On these graphs only one verb, HAZER, will be used, in its various forms.

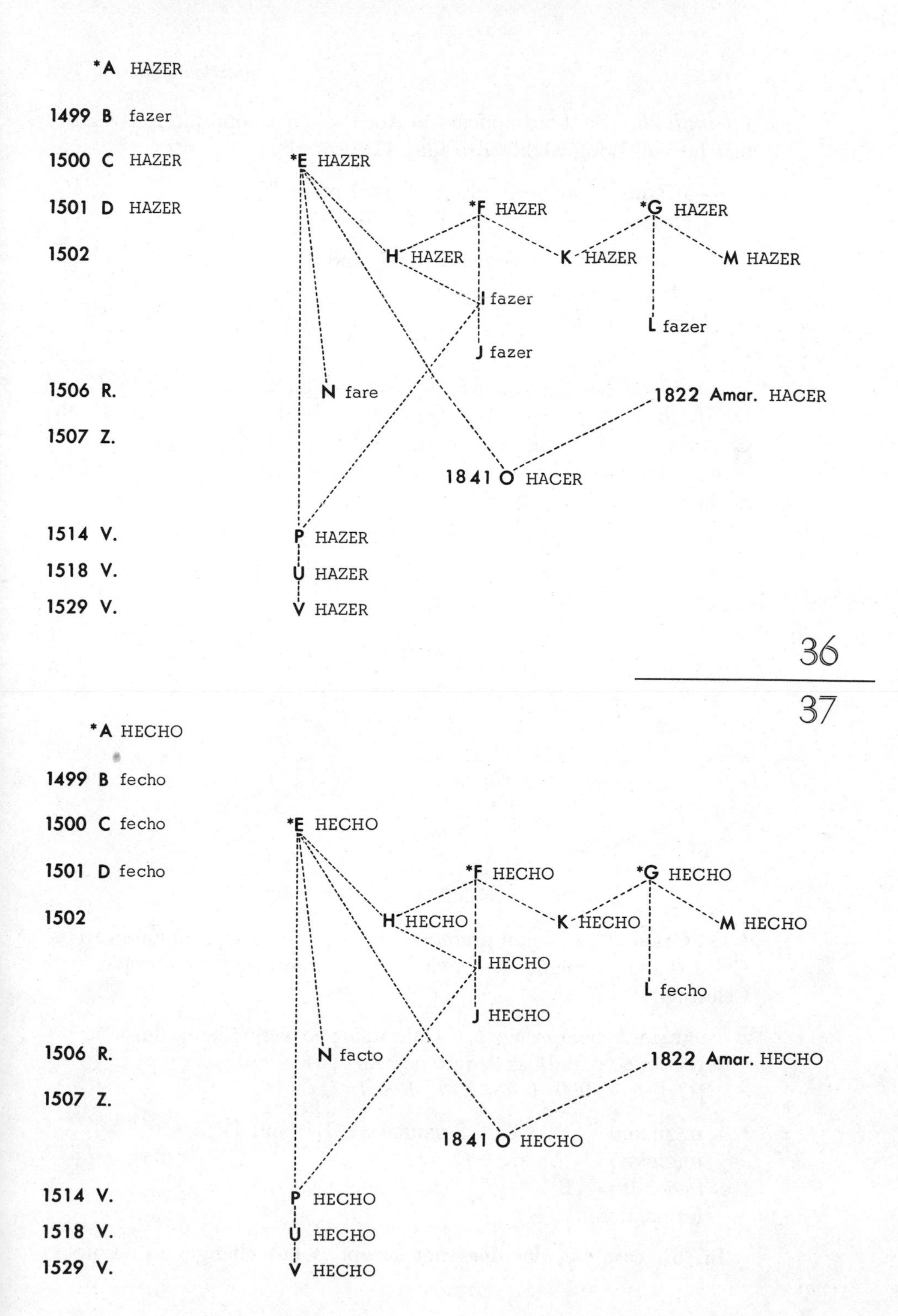
*A HAZER
1499 B fazer
1500 C HAZER
1501 D HAZER
1502
1506 R.
1507 Z.
1514 V.
1518 V.
1529 V.
*E HAZER
*F HAZER
*G HAZER
H HAZER
K HAZER
M HAZER
I fazer
J fazer
L fazer
N fare
1822 Amar. HACER
1841 O HACER
P HAZER
U HAZER
V HAZER
36
37
*A HECHO
1499 B fecho
1500 C fecho
1501 D fecho
1502
1506 R.
1507 Z.
1514 V.
1518 V.
1529 V.
*E HECHO
*F HECHO
*G HECHO
H HECHO
K HECHO
M HECHO
I HECHO
J HECHO
L fecho
N facto
1822 Amar. HECHO
1841 O HECHO
P HECHO
U HECHO
V HECHO

*Graph 38.* The word appears in Act I when Sempronio tells Calisto that he will bring Melibea to him. Calisto asks:

> —¿Cómo has pensado de *fazer* esta piedad?
> *Cej. I, I, 58, 1. 15; C–T, 35, 1. 25)*

HAZER *A + Stemmas II, III, and IV
HACER Amar. + O
fazer BCD
far N

It is evident that B has made an error, which was followed by C and D. If, as we believe, Rojas worked with the printed text of the Comedia in composing the Tragicomedia, it is highly unlikely that he or his editor would change one letter H- to f- in a text where almost all the nonvarying words had initial H- in preference to f-.

On Graph 39, B, again preferring f- to H-, presents a unique variant. Calisto and Pármeno are awaiting the return of Sempronio with Celestina.

> PÁRM.—A Sempronio é á Celestina veo venir cerca de casa, HAZIENDO paradillas de rato en rato . . . .
> *(Cej. I, V, 200, 1. 13; C–T, 108, 1. 11)*

HAZIENDO *ACD + Stemmas II, III, and IV
HACIENDO Amar. + O
faziendo B
fermandose N

In this case Cejador does not accept B but changes to HAZIENDO.

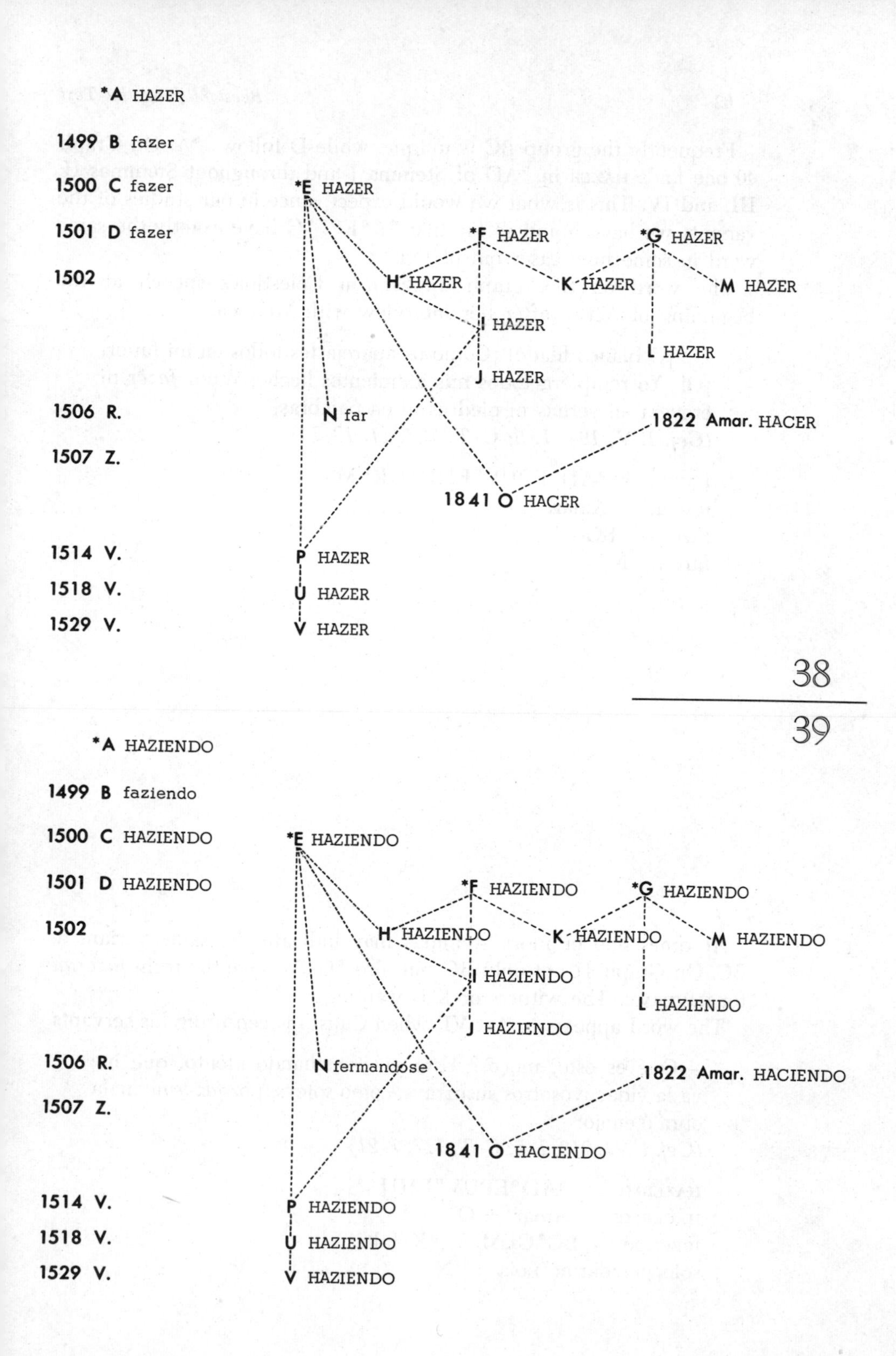
*A HAZER
1499 B fazer
1500 C fazer
1501 D fazer
1502
1506 R.
1507 Z.
1514 V.
1518 V.
1529 V.
*E HAZER
*F HAZER
*G HAZER
H HAZER
K HAZER
M HAZER
I HAZER
L HAZER
J HAZER
N far
1822 Amar. HACER
1841 O HACER
P HAZER
U HAZER
V HAZER
38
39
*A HAZIENDO
1499 B faziendo
1500 C HAZIENDO
1501 D HAZIENDO
1502
1506 R.
1507 Z.
1514 V.
1518 V.
1529 V.
*E HAZIENDO
*F HAZIENDO
*G HAZIENDO
H HAZIENDO
K HAZIENDO
M HAZIENDO
I HAZIENDO
L HAZIENDO
J HAZIENDO
N fermandose
1822 Amar. HACIENDO
1841 O HACIENDO
P HAZIENDO
U HAZIENDO
V HAZIENDO

Frequently the group BC is unique, while D follows *A. On Graph 40 one finds HAZER in *AD of Stemma I and throughout Stemmas II, III, and IV. This is what we would expect, since in our studies of the variants we have found so far that *A*E*F*G have exactly the same word in some nine cases out of ten.

The word on this graph appears in Celestina's speech at the beginning of Act V after her interview with Melibea.

> . . . ¡O blanco filado! ¡Cómo os aparejastes todos en mi fauor! ¡O! ¡Yo rompiera todos mis atamientos hechos é por *fazer* ni creyera en yeruas ni piedras ni en palabras!
> *(Cej. I, V, 194, 1. 5; C–T, 104, 11. 13–14)*

HAZER *AD*EPUV*FHIJ*GKLM
HACER Amar. + O
fazer BC
fare N

At times one or more stemmas may indicate the same variant as BC. On Graph 41 not only BC but also *GLM have the form *fazerme* for HAZERME. The witness of K is wanting.

The word appears in Act VI, when Calisto is censuring his servants.

> —¿Qué es esto, moços? Estó yo escuchando atento, que me va la vida; ¿vosotros susurrays, como soleys, por *fazerme* mala obra é enojo?
> *(Cej. I, VI, 212, 1. 5; C–T, 117, 1. 21)*

HAZERME *AD*EPUV*FHIJ
HACERME Amar. + O
fazerme BC*GLM (K falta)
solo per darme noia N

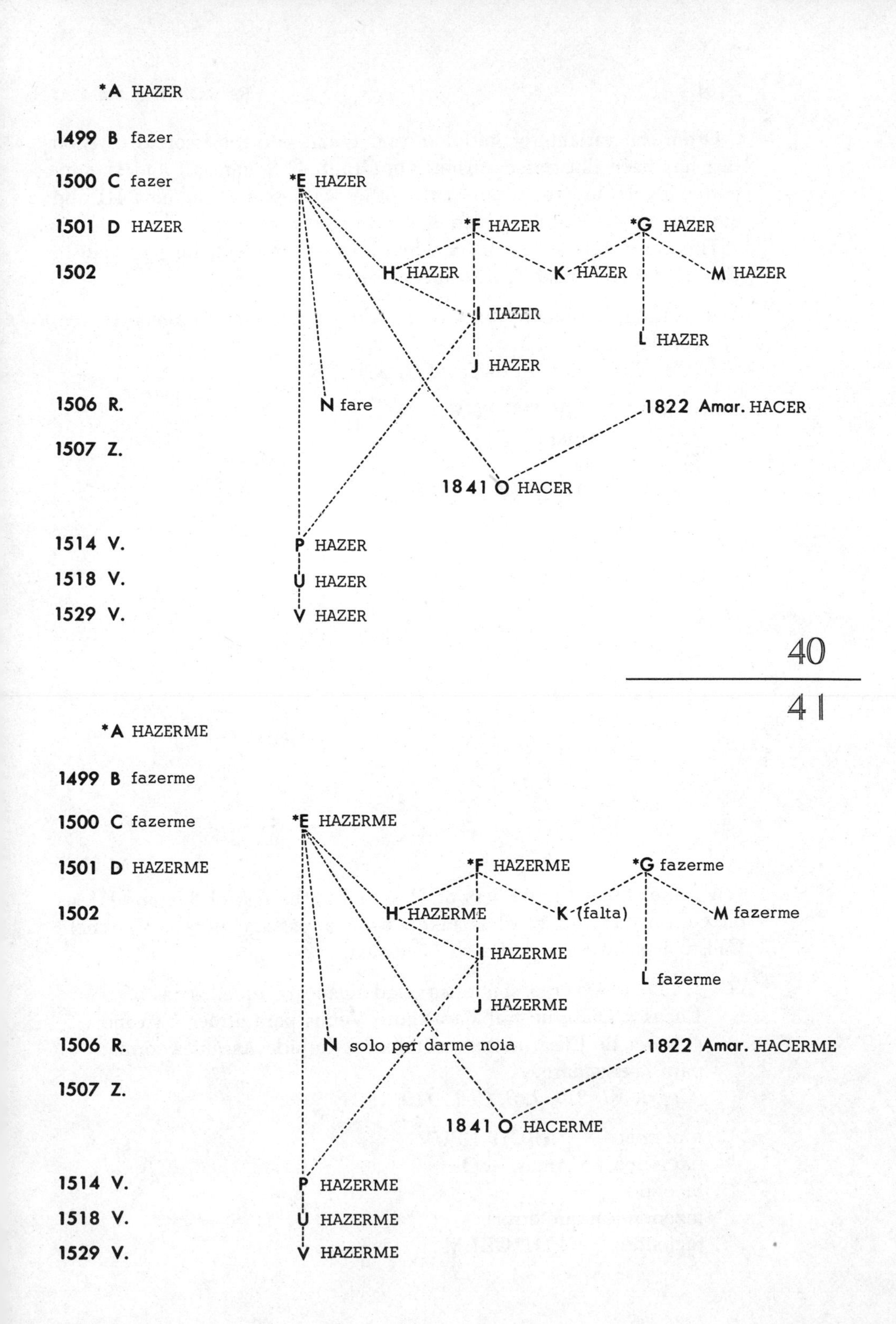
*A HAZER
1499 B fazer
1500 C fazer
*E HAZER
1501 D HAZER
*F HAZER
*G HAZER
1502
H HAZER
K HAZER
M HAZER
I HAZER
L HAZER
J HAZER
1506 R.
N fare
1822 Amar. HACER
1507 Z.
1841 O HACER
1514 V.
P HAZER
1518 V.
U HAZER
1529 V.
V HAZER
40
41
*A HAZERME
1499 B fazerme
1500 C fazerme
*E HAZERME
1501 D HAZERME
*F HAZERME
*G fazerme
1502
H HAZERME
K (falta)
M fazerme
I HAZERME
L fazerme
J HAZERME
1506 R.
N solo per darme noia
1822 Amar. HACERME
1507 Z.
1841 O HACERME
1514 V.
P HAZERME
1518 V.
U HAZERME
1529 V.
V HAZERME

Often the variants of initial H- and f- fall into the twofold division that has been illustrated earlier. On Graph 42 Stemmas I and II, supported by H, use H-, whereas the other witnesses of Stemma III and Stemma IV—except K, which is wanting—use f-.

The word appears in Act I when Pármeno is describing to Calisto Celestina and her stock in trade of drugs.

> . . . HAZÍA solimán, afeyte cozido, argentadas, bujelladas, cerillas, llanillas, . . .
> *(Cej. I, I, 74, 1. 2; C–T, 42, 1. 28)*

HAZÍA *ABCD*EPUV + H
HACÍA Amar. + O
faceua N
fazía *FIJ*GLM (K falta)

At other times the witness of H supports the rest of Stemma III, as on Graph 43. The word is taken from a passage in Act VI where Calisto is showering praise on Celestina.

> . . . De cierto creo, si nuestra edad alcançara aquellos passados Eneas é Dido, no trabajara tanto Venus para atraer á su fijo el amor de Elisa, HAZIENDO tomar á Cupido Ascánica forma, para la engañar; . . .
> *(Cej. I, VI, 216, 1. 3; C–T, 119, 1. 23)*

HAZIENDO *ABCD*EPUV
HACIENDO Amar. + O
facendo N
fazendo (unique error) J
faziendo *FHI*GKLM

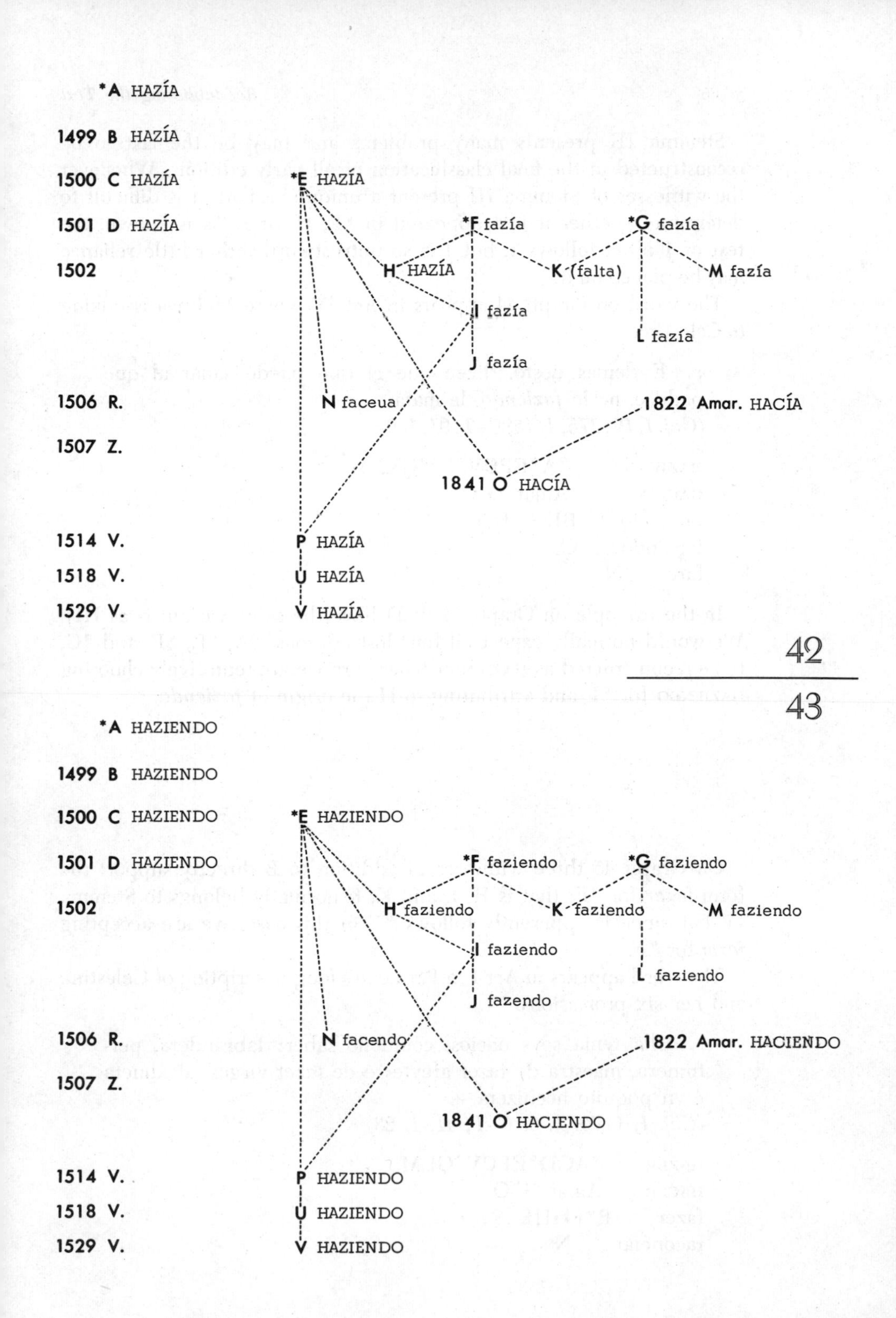
*A HAZÍA
1499 B HAZÍA
1500 C HAZÍA
*E HAZÍA
1501 D HAZÍA
*F fazía
*G fazía
1502
H HAZÍA
K (falta)
M fazía
I fazía
L fazía
J fazía
1506 R.
N faceua
1822 Amar. HACÍA
1507 Z.
1841 O HACÍA
1514 V.
P HAZÍA
1518 V.
U HAZÍA
1529 V.
V HAZÍA
42
43
*A HAZIENDO
1499 B HAZIENDO
1500 C HAZIENDO
*E HAZIENDO
1501 D HAZIENDO
*F faziendo
*G faziendo
1502
H faziendo
K faziendo
M faziendo
I faziendo
L faziendo
J fazendo
1506 R.
N facendo
1822 Amar. HACIENDO
1507 Z.
1841 O HACIENDO
1514 V.
P HAZIENDO
1518 V.
U HAZIENDO
1529 V.
V HAZIENDO

Stemma III presents many problems and may be the last to be reconstructed in the final classification of all early editions. Whenever the witnesses of Stemma III present a unique variant, it is difficult to determine whether it first appeared in *F, H, or I. As is known, the text of J often follows I, but J is so untrustworthy that little reliance may be placed on it.

The word on Graph 44 appears in Act IV where Melibea is talking to Celestina.

> . . . E demas desto, dizen que el que puede sanar al que padece, no lo *faziendo,* le mata.
> *(Cej. I, IV, 175, l. 15; C–T, 91, l. 9)*

HAZIENDO *A*EPUV*F?*GKLM
HACIENDO Amar. + O
faziendo BD + HIJ
façiendo C
fare N

In the example on Graph 44 BCD have the same variant f- as HIJ. We would normally expect all four lost editions, *A, *E, *F, and *G, to be reconstructed as HAZIENDO. Therefore we are tentatively choosing HAZIENDO for *F and attributing to H the origin of *faziendo.*

On Graph 45 three witnesses in addition to B directly support the form *fazer* for *F; that is H, I, and K. K normally belongs to Stemma IV but since it apparently follows *F in this case, we are accepting *fazer* for *F.

The word appears in Act I in Pármeno's long description of Celestina and her six professions.

> . . . Ella tenía seys oficios, conuiene saber: labrandera, perfumera, maestra de fazer afeytes é de *fazer* virgos, alcahueta é vn poquito hechizera.
> *(Cej. I, I, 70, l. 8; C–T, 41, l. 23)*

HAZER *ACD*EPUV*GLM
HACER Amar. + O
fazer B*FHIJK
raconciar N

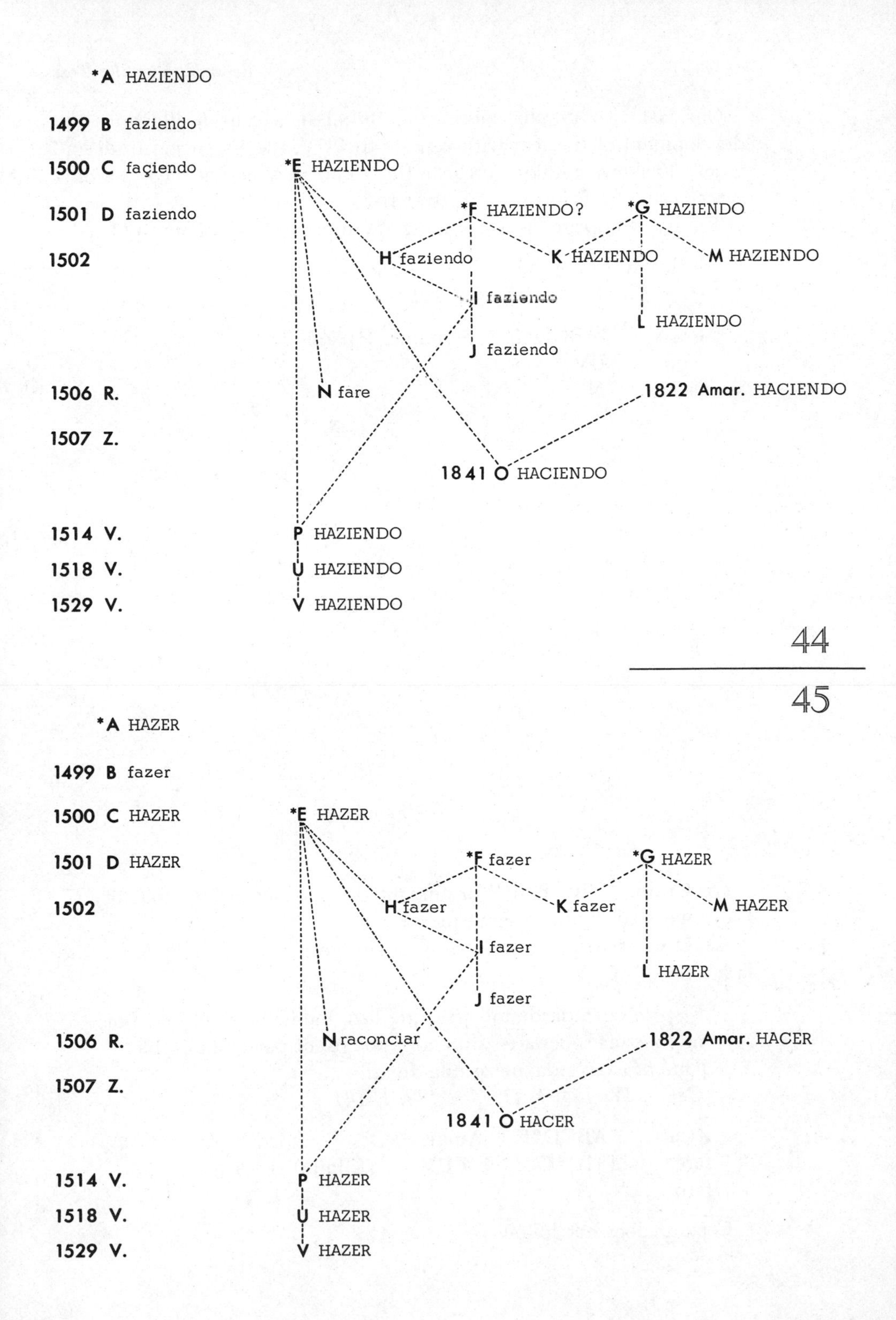

*A HAZIENDO
1499 B faziendo
1500 C façiendo
1501 D faziendo
1502
1506 R.
1507 Z.
1514 V.
1518 V.
1529 V.
*E HAZIENDO
*F HAZIENDO?
*G HAZIENDO
H faziendo
K HAZIENDO
M HAZIENDO
I faziendo
L HAZIENDO
J faziendo
N fare
1822 Amar. HACIENDO
1841 O HACIENDO
P HAZIENDO
U HAZIENDO
V HAZIENDO
44
45
*A HAZER
1499 B fazer
1500 C HAZER
1501 D HAZER
1502
1506 R.
1507 Z.
1514 V.
1518 V.
1529 V.
*E HAZER
*F fazer
*G HAZER
H fazer
K fazer
M HAZER
I fazer
L HAZER
J fazer
N raconciar
1822 Amar. HACER
1841 O HACER
P HAZER
U HAZER
V HAZER

Our last two graphs concerning initial H- versus f- illustrate the development of the text with respect to PUV, the Valencian tradition. Graph 46 shows a unique error in the group PUV and at the same time a preference of P for initial f- over H-.

The word appears in Act I where Sempronio is speaking to Calisto.

> —Haz tú lo que bien digo, é no lo que mal HAGO.
> *(Cej. I, I, 43, l. 23; C–T, 29, l. 9)*

HAGO *ABCD*E + Stemmas III and IV + Amar. + O
fago PUV
faccio N

On Graph 47 we find P preferring the reading of I to that of *E. Later we shall find the same preference.

Celestina is speaking to herself as she goes to visit Melibea for the first time.

> . . . ¡Ay, cuytada de mí! ¡En qué lazo me he metido! Que por me mostrar solícita é esforçada, pongo mi persona al tablero! ¿Qué *faré* cuytada, mezquina de mí, . . .
> *(Cej. I, IV, 154, l. 11; C–T, 80, l. 14)*

HARÉ *ABCD*E + Amar. + O
faré *FHIJ*GLM + PUV (K falta)
faro N

Cejador does not follow B.

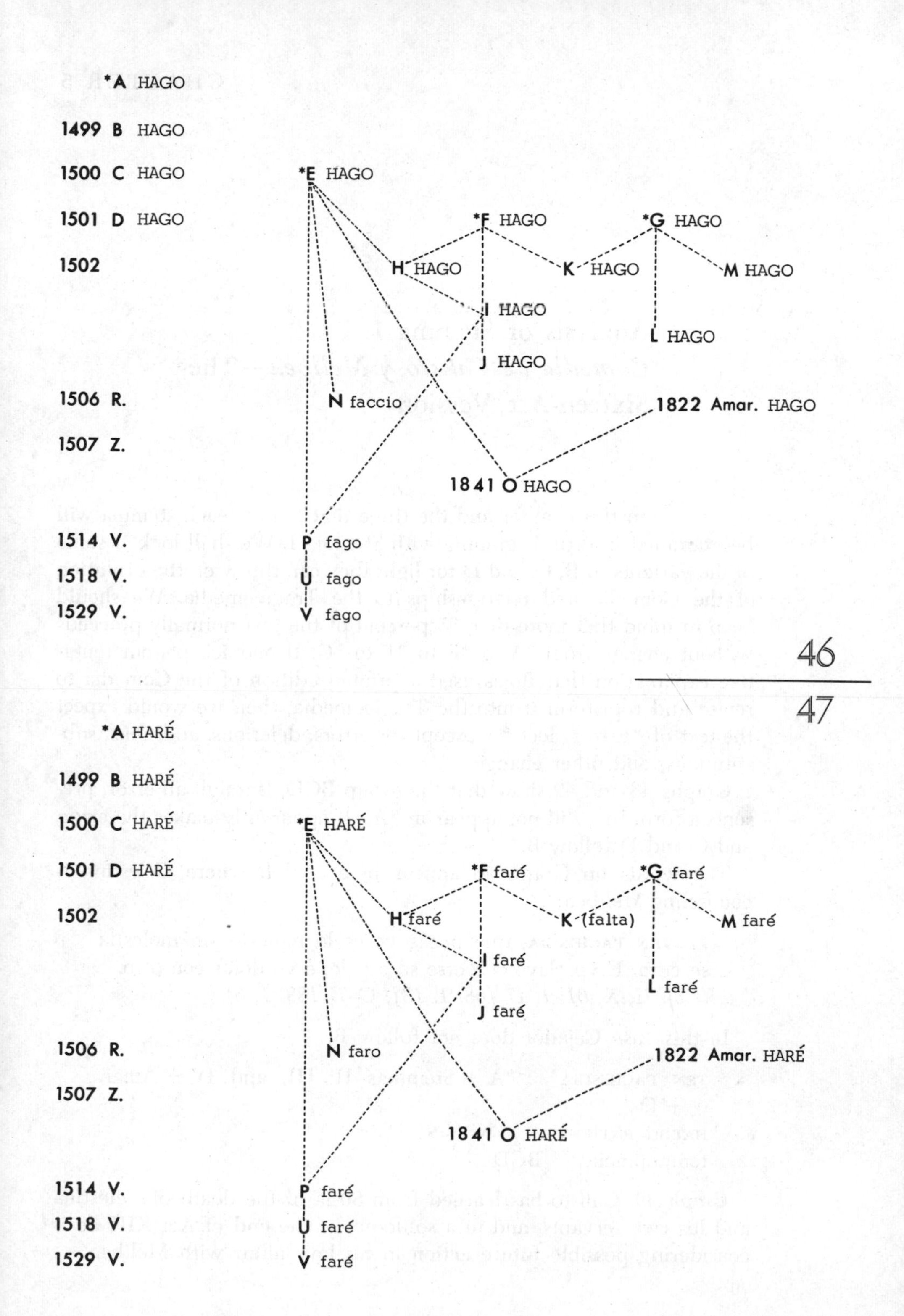
*A HAGO
1499 B HAGO
1500 C HAGO
*E HAGO
1501 D HAGO
*F HAGO
*G HAGO
1502
H HAGO
K HAGO
M HAGO
I HAGO
L HAGO
J HAGO
1506 R.
N faccio
1822 Amar. HAGO
1507 Z.
1841 O HAGO
1514 V.
P fago
1518 V.
U fago
1529 V.
V fago
46
47
*A HARÉ
1499 B HARÉ
1500 C HARÉ
*E HARÉ
1501 D HARÉ
*F faré
*G faré
1502
H faré
K (falta)
M faré
I faré
L faré
J faré
1506 R.
N faro
1822 Amar. HARÉ
1507 Z.
1841 O HARÉ
1514 V.
P faré
1518 V.
U faré
1529 V.
V faré

CHAPTER 5

# Analysis of Stemma I: *Comedia de Calisto y Melibea*—The Sixteen-Act Version

In this chapter and the three that follow, each stemma will be examined in turn, beginning with Stemma I. We shall look at some of the variants in B, C, and D for light they can throw on the evolution of the Comedia and relationships to the Tragicomedia. We should keep in mind that more than 85 percent of the text normally proceeds without change from *A to *E to *F to *G. If one accepts our tentative explanation that Rojas used a printed edition of the Comedia to revise and transform it into the Tragicomedia, then we would expect the text of *E to reflect *A except for errors, deletions, additions, substitutions, and other changes.

Graphs 48 and 49 show that the group BCD, through an error, presents a form that did not appear in *A. B apparently makes the error, and C and D follow B.

The words on Graph 48 appear in a speech where Celestina is counseling Melibea:

> . . . TEN PACIENCIA, que pocas vezes lo molesto sin molestia se cura. E vn clavo con otro se espele, é vn dolor con otro. *(Cej. II, X, 61, 1. 17 [58, 1. 13]; C–T, 188, 1. 6)*

In this case Cejador does not follow B.

TEN PACIENCIA  *A + Stemmas II, III, and IV + Amar. + O
HABBII PATIENTIA  N
temperancia  BCD

*Graph 49.* Calisto has learned from Sosia of the death of Celestina and his two servants, and in a soliloquy at the end of Act XIII he is considering possible future action in his love affair with Melibea.

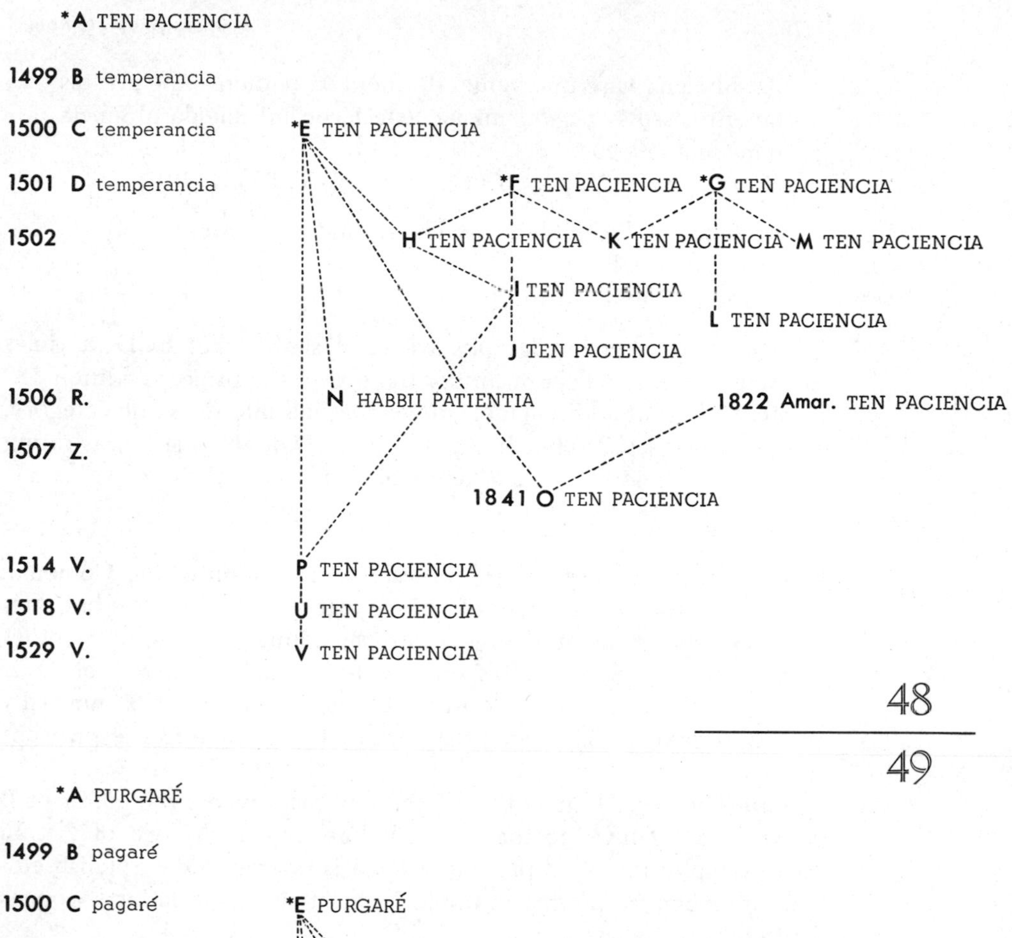


48
49

*A PURGARÉ

1499 B pagaré

1500 C pagaré

1501 D pagaré

1502

1506 R.

1507 Z.

1514 V.

1518 V.

1529 V.

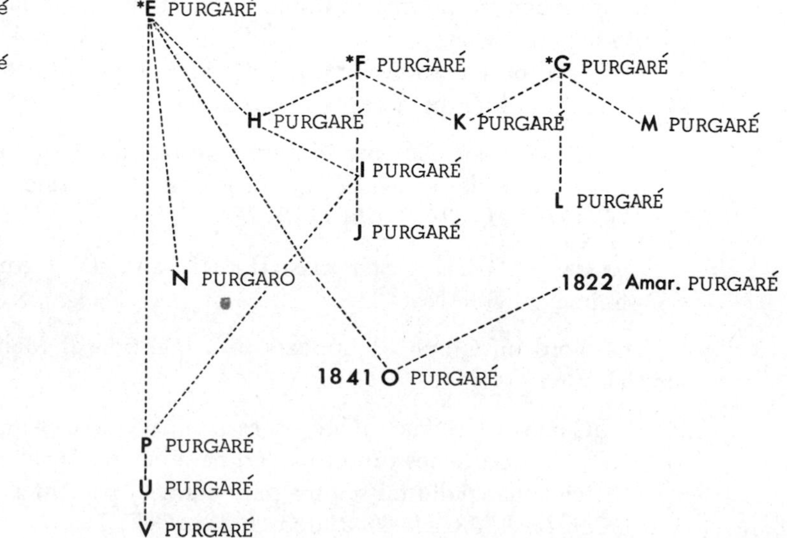

> . . . Mañana haré que vengo de fuera, si pudiere vengar estas muertes; si nó, *pagaré* mi inocencia con mi fingida absencia o me fingiré loco, . . .
> *(Cej. II, XIII, 121, 1. 18 [113, 1. 6]; C–T, 233, 1. 19)*

| | |
|---|---|
| PURGARÉ | *A + Stemmas II, III, and IV + Amar. + O |
| PURGARO | N |
| pagaré | BCD |

In the two preceding graphs we have shown that BCD at times apparently do not reflect faithfully the text of the princeps edition *A. Before we look at additional examples that fall into the same category, let us examine separately editions B, C, and D of Stemma I, illustrating with graphs some of the characteristics and peculiarities of each.

### *Edition B*

B is generally accepted as the oldest extant edition of the Comedia. It has a considerable number of unique orthographic variants but does not often replace the original text with substitute words or make other textual changes. At times B's error is followed by either C or D or both, as we have already observed. The witnesses of B normally command great respect since they are closest in time to the princeps edition.

Graphs 50 and 51 show two of the few cases where the editor of B preferred a synonym to the words before him in the text of *A. In both examples the word presented by B is unique to the Spanish editions, although in the first example N, the Italian translation, happens to use the same word.

The word on Graph 50 appears in a speech of Pármeno directed to Celestina in which he accepts her counsel.

> . . . E rogaré á Dios por el *ánima* de mi padre, que tal tutriz me dexó, é de mi madre, que á tal muger me encomendó.
> *(Cej. I, VII, 237, 1. 18; C–T, 134, 1. 17)*

| | |
|---|---|
| ALMA | *ACD + Stemmas II, III, and IV + Amar. + O |
| ánima | B + N |

The word on Graph 51 appears in a question of Melibea directed to Celestina:

> –¿Cómo, Celestina? ¿Qué es esse nueuo salario que pides? ¿De licencia tienes tú necessidad para me dar la salud? ¿Quál *físico* jamás pidió tal seguro para curar al paciente?
> *(Cej. II, X, 58, 11. 20–21 [55, 1. 18]; C–T, 186, 1. 2)*

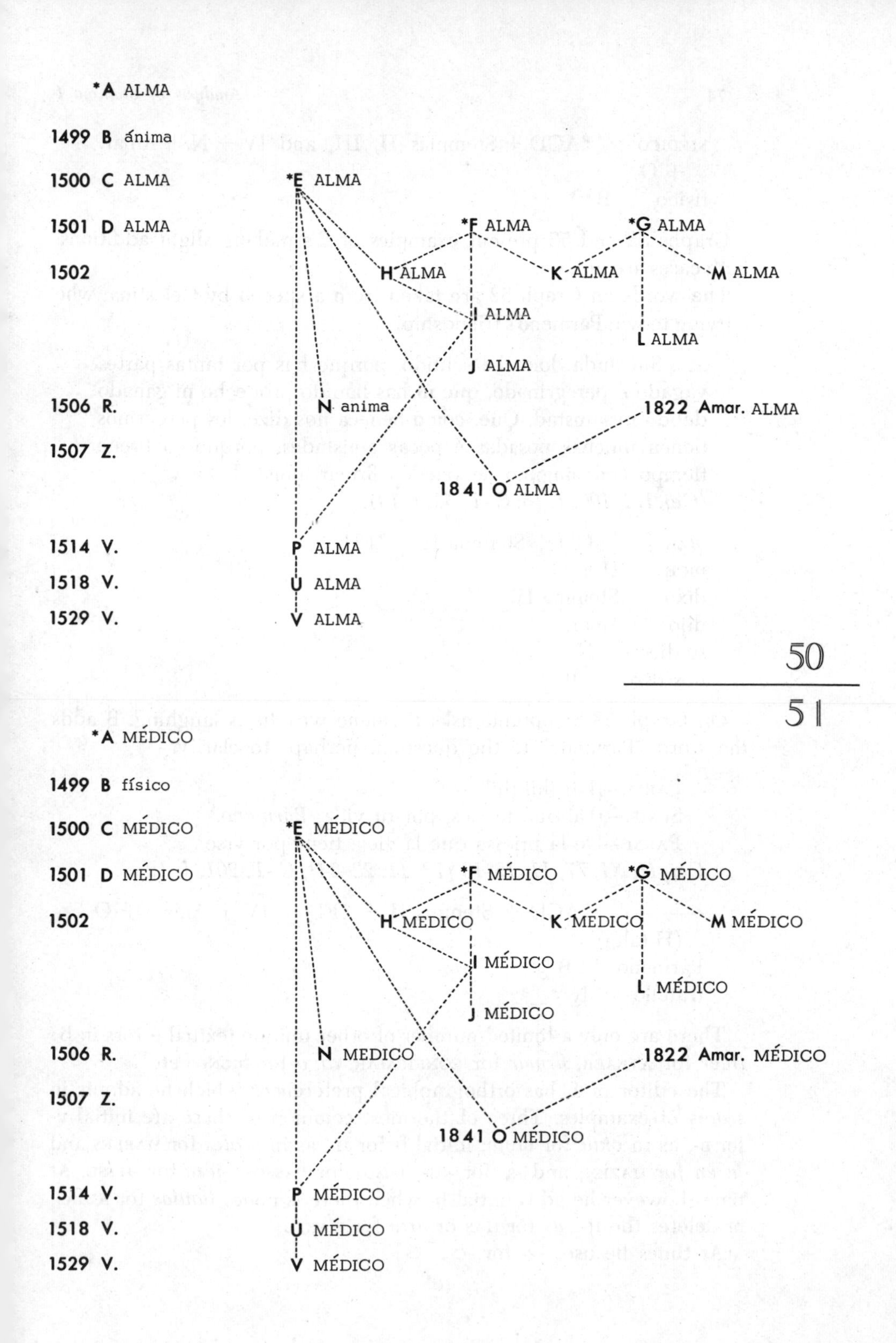
*A ALMA
1499 B ánima
1500 C ALMA
*E ALMA
1501 D ALMA
*F ALMA
*G ALMA
1502
H ALMA
K ALMA
M ALMA
I ALMA
L ALMA
J ALMA
1506 R.
N anima
1822 Amar. ALMA
1507 Z.
1841 O ALMA
1514 V.
P ALMA
1518 V.
U ALMA
1529 V.
V ALMA
*A MÉDICO
1499 B físico
1500 C MÉDICO
*E MÉDICO
1501 D MÉDICO
*F MÉDICO
*G MÉDICO
1502
H MÉDICO
K MÉDICO
M MÉDICO
I MÉDICO
L MÉDICO
J MÉDICO
1506 R.
N MEDICO
1822 Amar. MÉDICO
1507 Z.
1841 O MÉDICO
1514 V.
P MÉDICO
1518 V.
U MÉDICO
1529 V.
V MÉDICO

50

51

MÉDICO *ACD + Stemmas II, III, and IV + N + Amar. + O
físico B

Graphs 52 and 53 present examples of B's making slight additions. Both cases are unique.

The words on Graph 52 are taken from a speech by Celestina, who is trying to win Pármeno's friendship.

> . . . Sin duda dolor he sentido, porque has por tantas partes vagado é peregrinado, que ni has hauido prouecho ni ganado debdo ni amistad. Que, como Séneca *nos* dize, los peregrinos tienen muchas posadas é pocas amistades, porque en breue tiempo con ninguno no pueden firmar amistad.
> *(Cej. I, I, 100, l. 16; C–T, 52, l. 19)*

DIZE *ACD + Stemma II + *FIJ
DICE H + O
dixo Stemma IV
dijo Amar.
se dice N
nos dize B

On Graph 53 Sempronio asks Pármeno why he is laughing. B adds the word "Pármeno" to the question, perhaps to clarify.

> PÁRM.—¡Hi! ¡hi! ¡hi!
> SEMP.—¿De qué te ríes, por tu vida, *Pármeno*?
> PÁRM.—De la priessa que la vieja tiene por yrse.
> *Cej. II, XI, 77, ll. 12–13 [73, ll. 23–24]; C–T, 201, l. 12)*

——— *ACD + Stemma II + *FIJ + IV + Amar. + O (H falta)
Pármeno B
fratello N

There are only a limited number of other unique textual errors in B: *traer* for ATRAER, *firmar* for CONFIRMAR, *digo* for DIGNO, etc.

The editor of B has orthographical preferences which he adopts in scores of examples. Three of the most common of these are initial v- for B-, as in *viuir* for BIUIR; initial f- for H-, as in *fables* for HABLES and *fazen for* HAZEN; and -s- for -SS-, *pasos* for PASSOS, *-iese* for -IESSE. At times however he adds initial h- when there is none: *hauías* for AUÍAS; or deletes the H-: *as* for HAS or *arto* for HARTO.

At times he uses -z- for -C-:

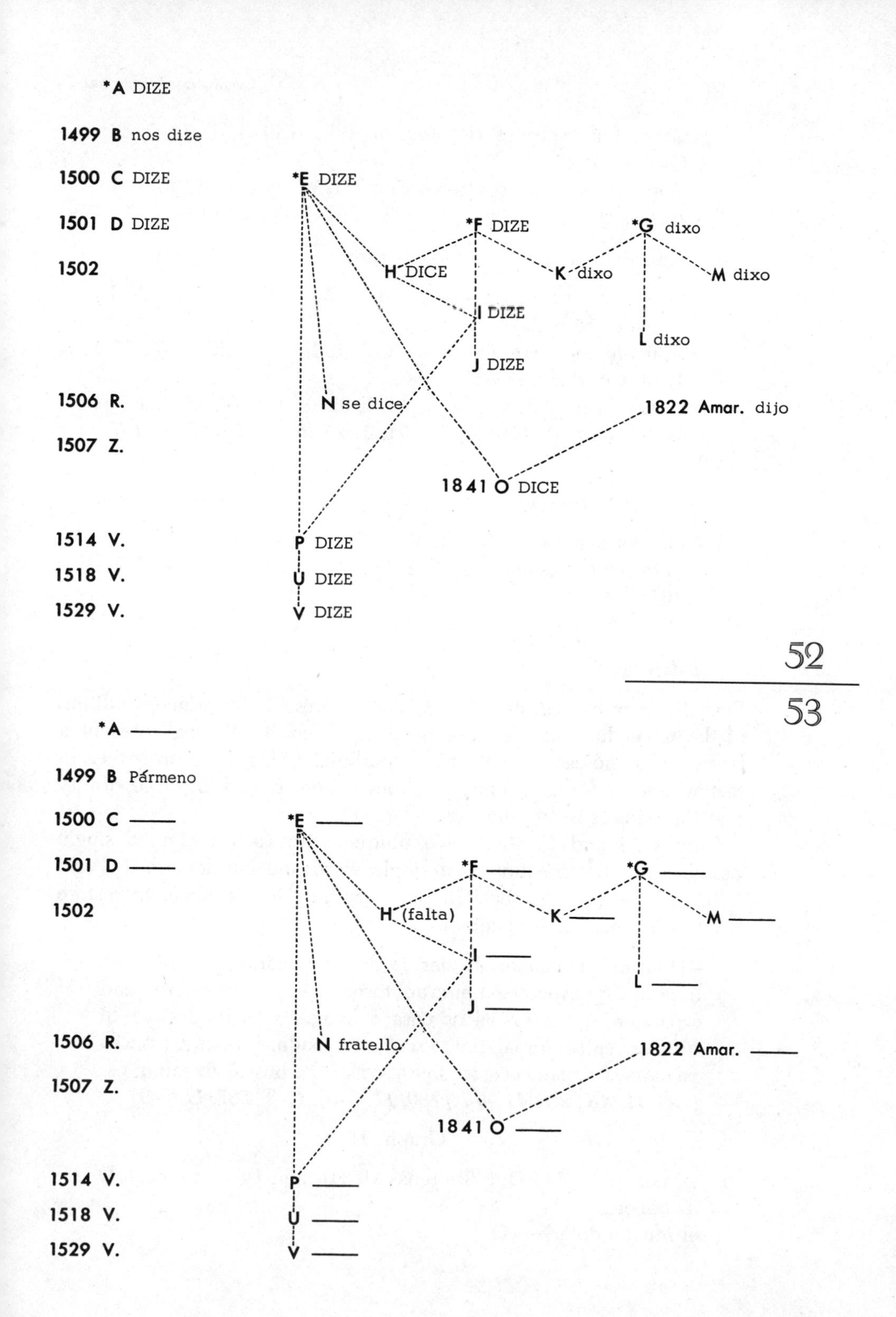

*A DIZE
1499 B nos dize
1500 C DIZE
1501 D DIZE
1502
1506 R.
1507 Z.
1514 V.
1518 V.
1529 V.
*E DIZE
*F DIZE
*G dixo
H DICE
K dixo
M dixo
I DIZE
L dixo
J DIZE
N se dice
1822 Amar. dijo
1841 O DICE
P DIZE
U DIZE
V DIZE
52
53
*A
1499 B Pármeno
1500 C
1501 D
1502
1506 R.
1507 Z.
1514 V.
1518 V.
1529 V.
*E
*F
*G
H (falta)
K
M
I
L
J
N fratello
1822 Amar.
1841 O
P
U
V

*faziones* for FACIONES (L: *fayciones*)——Cej. I, I, 74, l. 2; C–T, 42, l. 27
*luzentores* for LUCENTORES——Cej. I, I, 75, l. 2; C–T, 43, l. 1
*cozes* for COCES——Cej. I, II, 118, l. 3; C–T, 64, l. 19

He confuses -A- and -E- from time to time:

*auantaja for* AUENTAJA——Cej. I, I, 53, l. 7; C–T, 33, l. 1 (Cejador corrects)
*entreñable* for ENTRAÑABLE——Cej. I, I, 61, l. 22; C–T, 37, l. 14 (Cejador corrects)
*fragaron* for FREGARON——Cej. I, I, 92, l. 8; C–T, 48, l. 1
*seya* for SAYA——Cej. II, XI, 71, l. 25 (68, l. 21); C–T, 197, l. 27

From time to time he uses the singular of nouns for the plural:

*sueño* for SUEÑOS——Cej. I, V, 201, l. 2; C–T, 108, l. 21
*lagaña* for LAGAÑAS——Cej. II, IX, 32, l. 14 (31, l. 11); C–T, 167, l. 32

### *Edition C*

Recently it was suggested that C may represent the princeps edition of the Comedia and therefore have preceded B. We shall present a few graphs indicating that this hypothesis is highly improbable. In fact whenever C has a unique witness, there is very little possibility that the witness is not an error.

Graphs 54 and 55 show two unique witnesses of C in a single passage, one the addition of a single word and one longer. Pleberio is telling Melibea that he will do everything in his power to restore her health and peace of mind.

> –Hija, mi bienamada é querida del viejo padre, por Dios, no te ponga desesperación el cruel tormento desta tu enfermedad é passión, que á los flacos coraçones EL DOLOR los arguye. Si tú me cuentas tu mal, luego será remediado. Que NI FALTARÁN MEDICINAS NI MÉDICOS, NI SIRUIENTES para buscar tu salud, . . . *(Cej. II, XX, 205, ll. 4–7 [190, ll. 3–6]; C–T, 287, ll. 7–9)*

Graph 54

EL DOLOR  *ABD + Stemmas II, III, and IV + Amar. + O
IL DOLORE  N
el mucho dolor  C

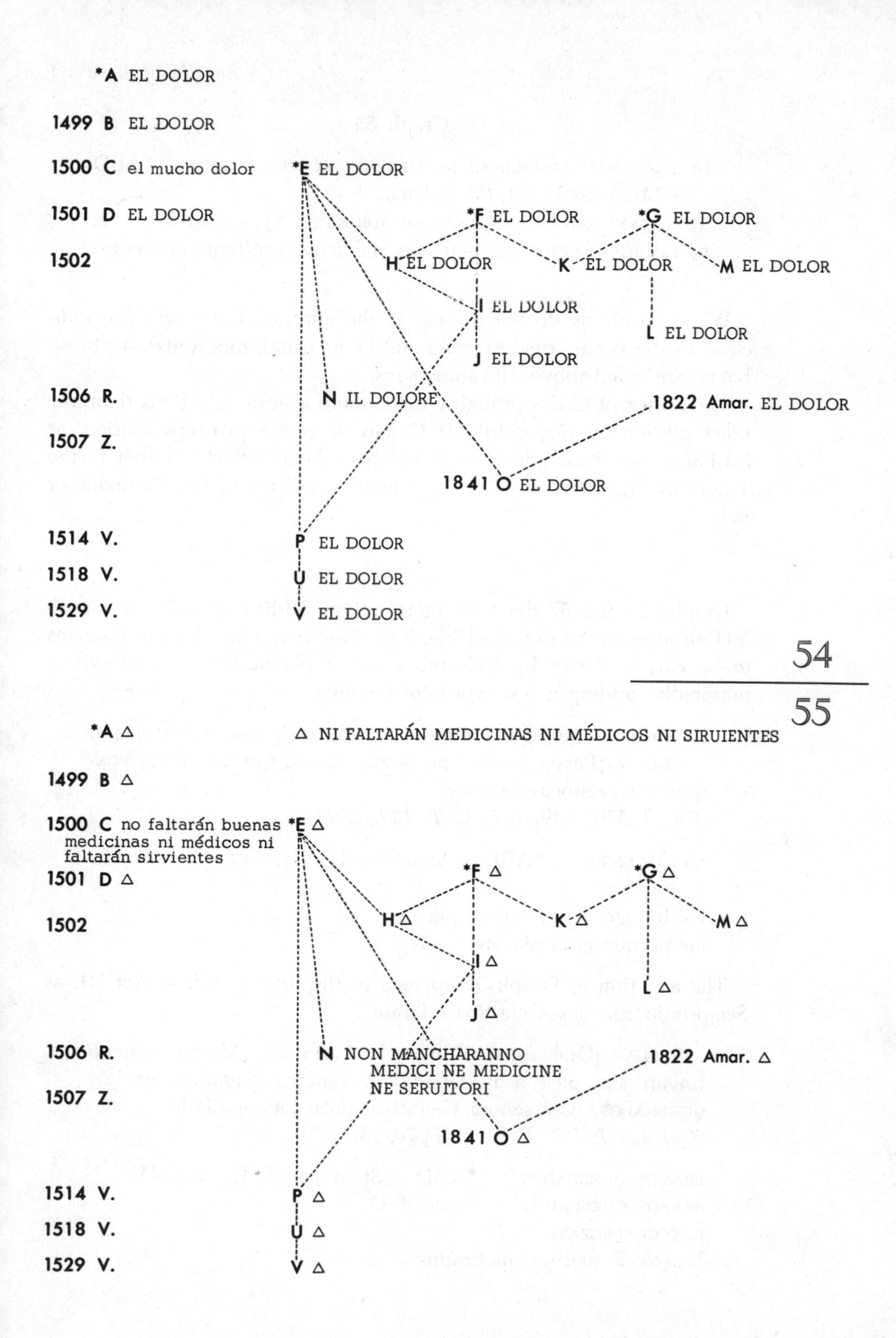

*A EL DOLOR
1499 B EL DOLOR
1500 C el mucho dolor
*E EL DOLOR
1501 D EL DOLOR
*F EL DOLOR
*G EL DOLOR
1502
H EL DOLOR
K EL DOLOR
M EL DOLOR
I EL DOLOR
L EL DOLOR
J EL DOLOR
1506 R.
N IL DOLORE
1822 Amar. EL DOLOR
1507 Z.
1841 O EL DOLOR
1514 V.
P EL DOLOR
1518 V.
U EL DOLOR
1529 V.
V EL DOLOR
54
55
*A △
△ NI FALTARÁN MEDICINAS NI MÉDICOS NI SIRUIENTES
1499 B △
1500 C no faltarán buenas medicinas ni médicos ni faltarán sirvientes
*E △
1501 D △
*F △
*G △
1502
H △
K △
M △
I △
L △
J △
1506 R.
N NON MANCHARANNO MEDICI NE MEDICINE NE SERUITORI
1822 Amar. △
1507 Z.
1841 O △
1514 V.
P △
1518 V.
U △
1529 V.
V △

### Graph 55

NI FALTARÁN MEDICINAS NI MÉDICOS NI SIRUIENTES *ABD + Stemmas II, III, IV + Amar. + O

NON MANCHARANNO MEDICI NE MEDICINE, NE SERUITORI N

*no* faltarán *buenas* medicinas ni médicos ni *faltarán* siruientes C

When additions do not appear in the citation, the words are italicized in the summaries. Amarita and O, as usual, modernize -U- to -V- but are included above with SIRUIENTES.

The editor of C has probably made more unique additions than any other edition on our graph. If C had been the princeps edition, at least some of these additions would have been reflected either in the Tragicomedia, especially *E, or in another edition of the Comedia, or in both.

Graphs 56 and 57 illustrate more unique additions of C. On Graph 56 Celestina, at Areúsa's bedside, is praising her. The editor of C seems to be carried away by Celestina's art of persuasion and intervenes personally, adding a few words of his own.

> . . . Déxame mirarte toda, á mi voluntad, que ME HUELGO.
> AREU.—¡Passo, madre, no llegues á mí, que me fazes coxquillas é prouocasme á reyr.
> *(Cej. I, VII, 249, l. 5; C–T, 140, l. 20)*

ME HUELGO *ABD + Stemmas II, III, and IV + Amar. + O

me huelgo ꝛ tomo gran plazer C

me prendo gran piacere N

The addition in Graph 57 appears in the first speech of Act III, as Sempronio reaches Celestina's house.

> SEMP.—¡Qué espacio lleua la barvuda! ¡Menos sosiego trayan sus pies á la venida! A dineros pagados, BRAÇOS QUEBRADOS. ¡Ce! señora Celestina, poco has aguijado.
> *(Cej. I, III, 127, l. 12; C–T, 70, ll. 2–3)*

BRAÇOS QUEBRADOS *ABD + Stemmas II, III, and IV

BRAZOS QUEBRADOS Amar. + O

BRACCI SPECZATI N

braços ꝛ piernos quebrados C

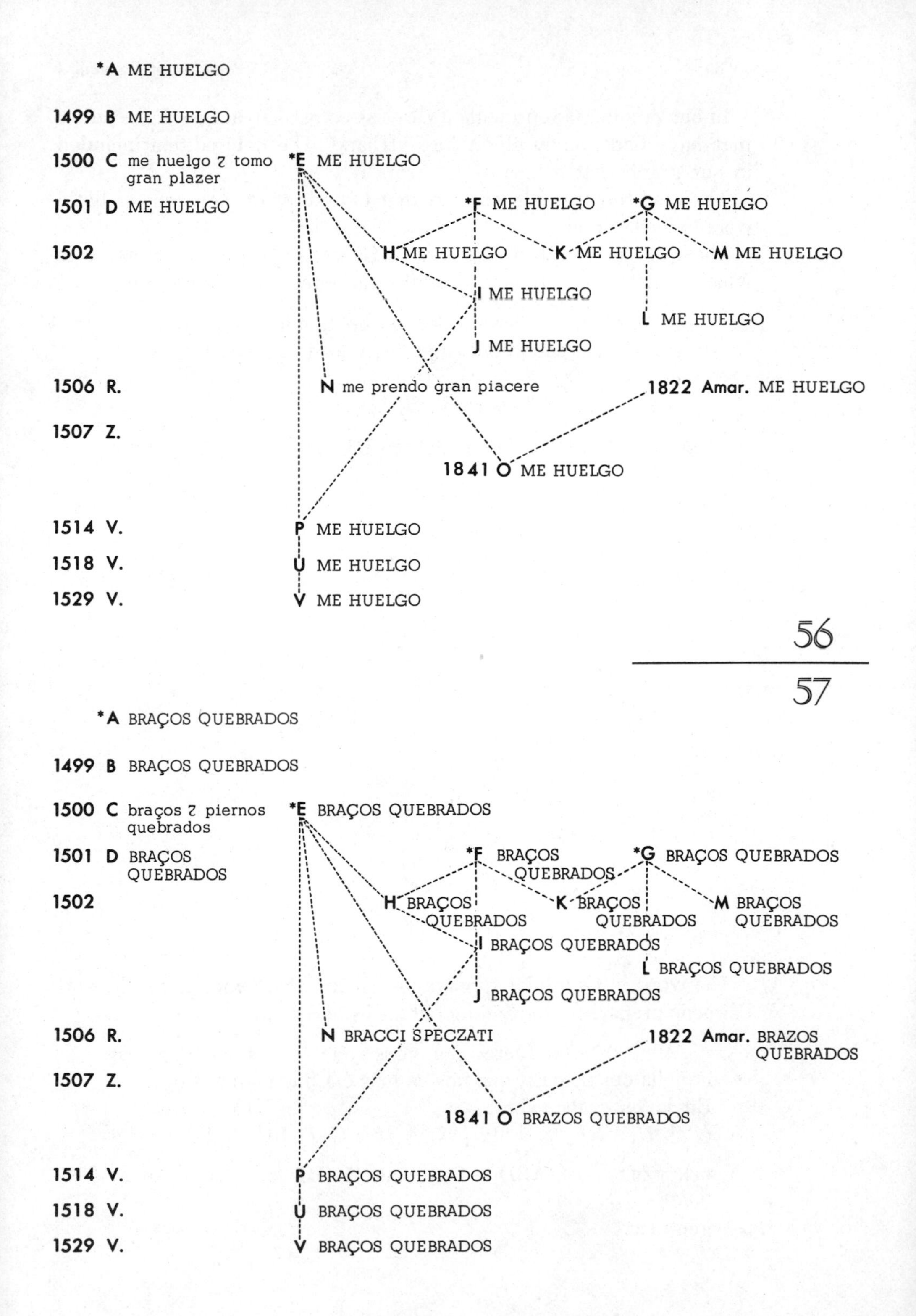
*A ME HUELGO
1499 B ME HUELGO
1500 C me huelgo ⁊ tomo gran plazer
*E ME HUELGO
1501 D ME HUELGO
*F ME HUELGO
*G ME HUELGO
1502
H ME HUELGO
K ME HUELGO
M ME HUELGO
I ME HUELGO
L ME HUELGO
J ME HUELGO
1506 R.
N me prendo gran piacere
1822 Amar. ME HUELGO
1507 Z.
1841 O ME HUELGO
1514 V.
P ME HUELGO
1518 V.
U ME HUELGO
1529 V.
V ME HUELGO
56
57
*A BRAÇOS QUEBRADOS
1499 B BRAÇOS QUEBRADOS
1500 C braços ⁊ piernos quebrados
*E BRAÇOS QUEBRADOS
1501 D BRAÇOS QUEBRADOS
*F BRAÇOS QUEBRADOS
*G BRAÇOS QUEBRADOS
1502
H BRAÇOS QUEBRADOS
K BRAÇOS QUEBRADOS
M BRAÇOS QUEBRADOS
I BRAÇOS QUEBRADOS
L BRAÇOS QUEBRADOS
J BRAÇOS QUEBRADOS
1506 R.
N BRACCI SPECZATI
1822 Amar. BRAZOS QUEBRADOS
1507 Z.
1841 O BRAZOS QUEBRADOS
1514 V.
P BRAÇOS QUEBRADOS
1518 V.
U BRAÇOS QUEBRADOS
1529 V.
V BRAÇOS QUEBRADOS

In our opinion C represents a careless copy of B, although the editor may have had a copy of *A also at hand. The only edition included in our graph that makes more errors is J.

The next three graphs suggest that C's editor or corrector, or both, were indeed careless.

The word in Graph 58 appears in Calisto's speech to Sempronio in which he is endeavoring to describe the effect of love on him.

> . . . ¿Quien tiene dentro del pecho aguijones, paz, guerra, tregua, amor, enemistad, injurias, pecados, sospechas, todo a vna CAUSA?
> *(Cej. I, I, 40, l. 4; C–T, 26, l. 29)*

CAUSA *ABD + Stemmas II, III, and IV + N + Amar. + O
casa C

The word in Graph 59 appears in a speech by Sempronio as he and Pármeno prepare for the banquet at Celestina's home.

> . . . Acuérdate, si fueres por conserua, apañes vn bote para aquella GENTEZILLA, que nos va más é á buen entendedor . . . . En la bragueta cabrá.
> *(Cej. II, VIII, 22, l. 19 [22, l. 16]; C–T, 161, l. 28)*

GENTEZILLA *ABD + Stemmas II, III, and IV + Amar. + O
gente N
gentileza C

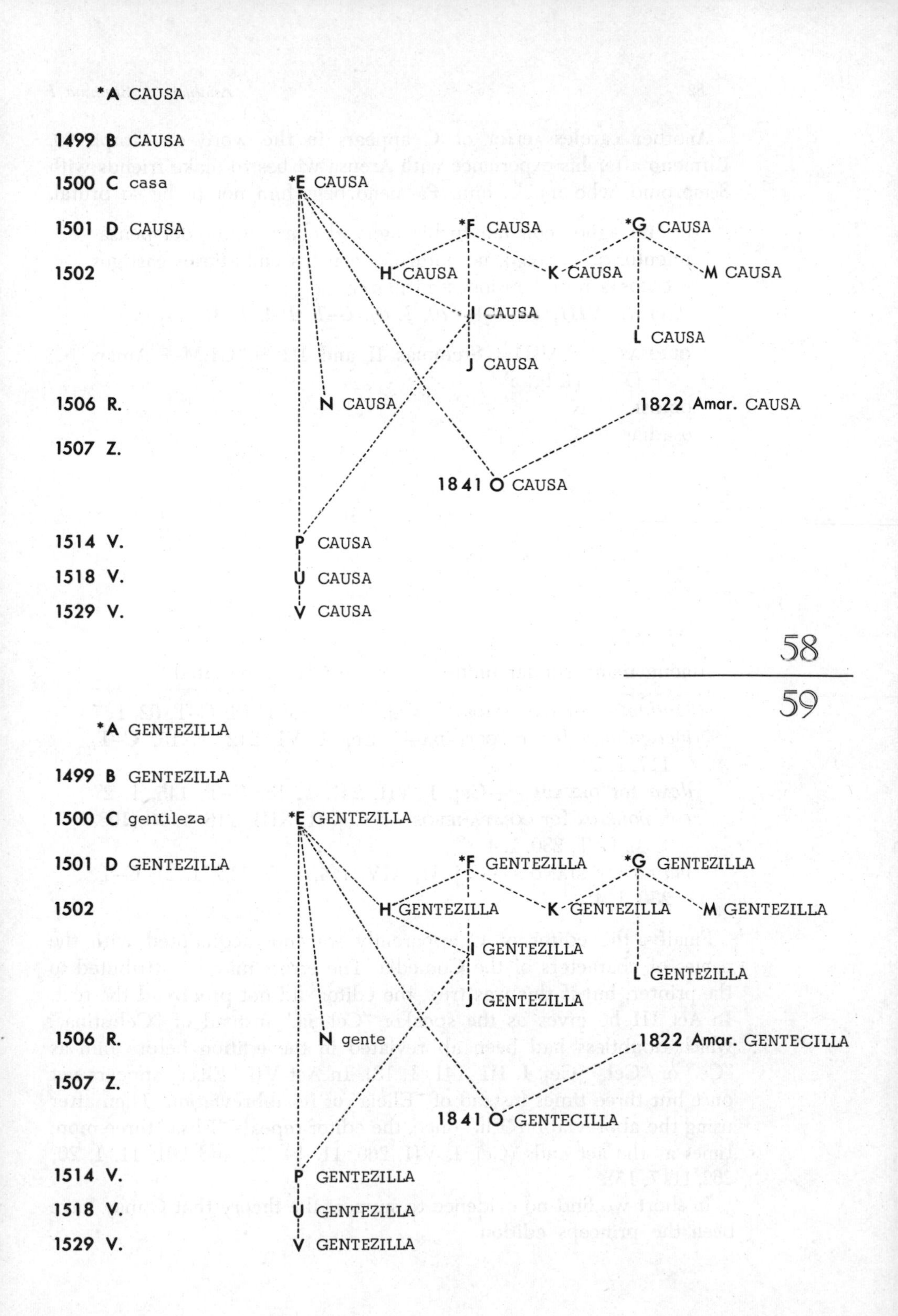

*A CAUSA
1499 B CAUSA
1500 C casa
*E CAUSA
1501 D CAUSA
*F CAUSA
*G CAUSA
1502
H CAUSA
K CAUSA
M CAUSA
I CAUSA
L CAUSA
J CAUSA
1506 R.
N CAUSA
1822 Amar. CAUSA
1507 Z.
1841 O CAUSA
1514 V.
P CAUSA
1518 V.
U CAUSA
1529 V.
V CAUSA
58
59
*A GENTEZILLA
1499 B GENTEZILLA
1500 C gentileza
*E GENTEZILLA
1501 D GENTEZILLA
*F GENTEZILLA
*G GENTEZILLA
1502
H GENTEZILLA
K GENTEZILLA
M GENTEZILLA
I GENTEZILLA
L GENTEZILLA
J GENTEZILLA
1506 R.
N gente
1822 Amar. GENTECILLA
1507 Z.
1841 O GENTECILLA
1514 V.
P GENTEZILLA
1518 V.
U GENTEZILLA
1529 V.
V GENTEZILLA

Another careless error of C appears in the word on Graph 60. Pármeno after his experience with Areúsa wishes to make friends with Sempronio, who mocks him. Pármeno begs him not to be so brutal.

> . . . no agües con tan turbia agua el claro liquor del pensamiento, que traygo, no enturuies con tus embidiosos castigos é ODIOSAS reprehensiones mi plazer.
> *(Cej. II, VIII, 10, 1. 9 [10, 1. 6]; C–T, 154, 1. 4)*

| | |
|---|---|
| ODIOSAS | *ABD + Stemmas II and III + *GLM + Amar. |
| + O | (K falta) |
| ODIOSE | N |
| osadías | C |

Among many similar unique errors in C may be cited:

*laudamos* for LA DAMOS——Cej. I, II, 113, 1. 18; C–T, 62, 1. 7
*incognitada* for INCOGITADA——Cej. I, VI, 212, 1. 15; C–T, 117, 1. 29
*dexa* for DEXADA——Cej. I, VII, 257, 1. 15; C–T, 145, 1. 27
*compoñeros* for COMPAÑEROS——Cej. II, XIII, 116, 1. 10 (108, 1. 3); C–T, 230, 1. 4
*mamo* for MANO——Cej. II, XIV, 124, 1. 2 (115, 1. 2); C–T, 236, 1. 4

Finally, the editor of C apparently was not acquainted with the names of characters of the Comedia. The errors may be attributed to the printer; but if this was true, the editor did not proofread the text. In Act III he gives as the speaker "Celicia," instead of "Celestina," which doubtless had been abbreviated in the edition before him as "Ce." or "Cel." (Cej. I, III, 141, 1. 13). In Act VII "Elisa" appears not once but three times instead of "Elicia" or its abbreviation. Then after using the abbreviation 'Eli." once, the editor repeats "Elisa" three more times as the act ends (Cej. I, VII, 260, 11. 19, 22, and 261, 11. 1, 20; 262, 11. 7, 15).

In short we find no evidence to support the theory that C may have been the princeps edition.

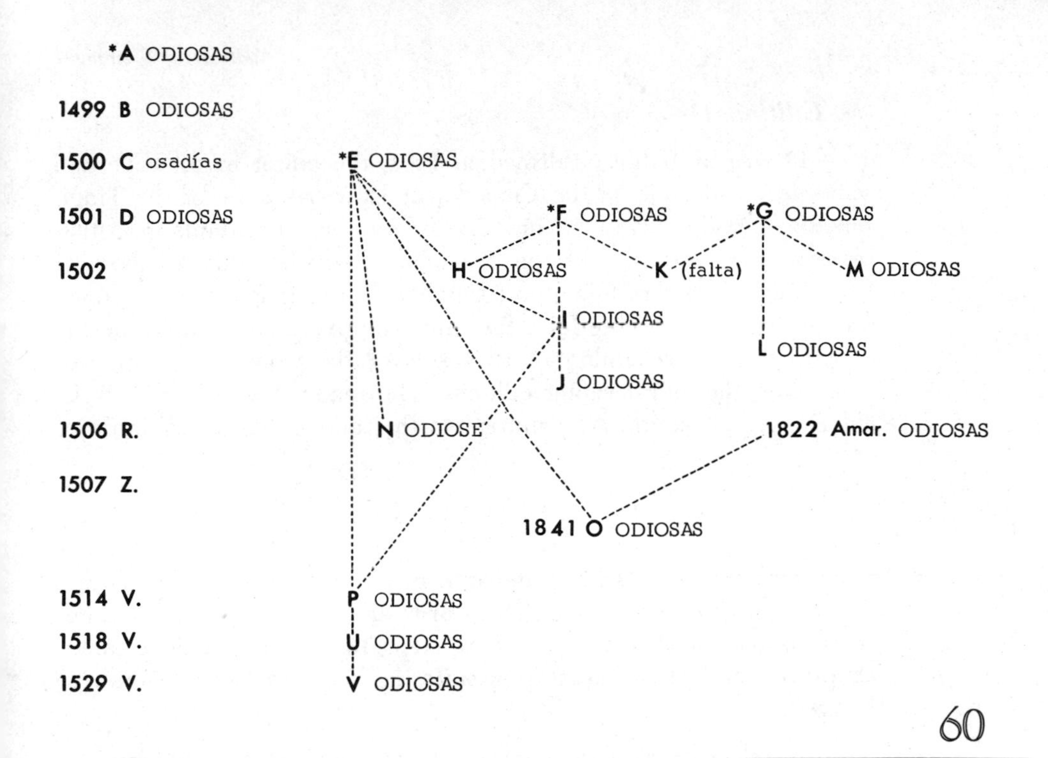
*A ODIOSAS
1499 B ODIOSAS
1500 C osadías
*E ODIOSAS
1501 D ODIOSAS
*F ODIOSAS
*G ODIOSAS
1502
H ODIOSAS
K (falta)
M ODIOSAS
I ODIOSAS
L ODIOSAS
J ODIOSAS
1506 R.
N ODIOSE
1822 Amar. ODIOSAS
1507 Z.
1841 O ODIOSAS
1514 V.
P ODIOSAS
1518 V.
U ODIOSAS
1529 V.
V ODIOSAS

## *Edition D*

Since D was probably published in 1501, the editor might have had available in addition to the Comedia at least one copy of the Tragicomedia, perhaps *E or *F or *G. The number of variants in D that correspond to witnesses of the Tragicomedia rather than to those of the Comedia appears to support this possibility. It is a mistake, however—to which we clung for some time—to give great credence to the authenticity and reliability of witnesses of the Comedia, in spite of their being the oldest extant editions. The reader has seen that B, C, and D may all at times be untrustworthy, and C has a multitude of errors.

The next two graphs illustrate some of the peculiarities of D. Graph 61 shows a unique omission. The words are spoken by Sempronio to Celestina as the two plan the next steps to take in the love affair. Sempronio states that hardship or suffering becomes more bearable as time passes.

> . . . Todo es assí, todo passa desta manera, TODO SE OLUIDA, todo queda atrás.
> *(Cej. I, III, 132, 11. 1–2; C–T, 71, 1. 23)*

TODO SE OLUIDA    *ABC + Stemma II + *FHI + Stemma IV + Amar. + O
ogni cosa se smentica    N
todo se aluida    J
(———)    D

The words on Graph 62 are those of Melibea as she awaits Calisto in the garden. The editor of D has reworded the text without changing the meaning.

> —Los ángeles sean en su guarda, su persona ESTÉ SIN PELIGRO, que su tardanza no me es pena.
> *(Cej. II, XIV, 124, 1. 4 [115, 1. 4]; C–T, 236, 11. 5–6)*

ESTÉ SIN PELIGRO    *ABC + Stemmas II, III, and IV + Amar. + O
STIA . . . SENZA PERICULO    N
no esté en peligro    D

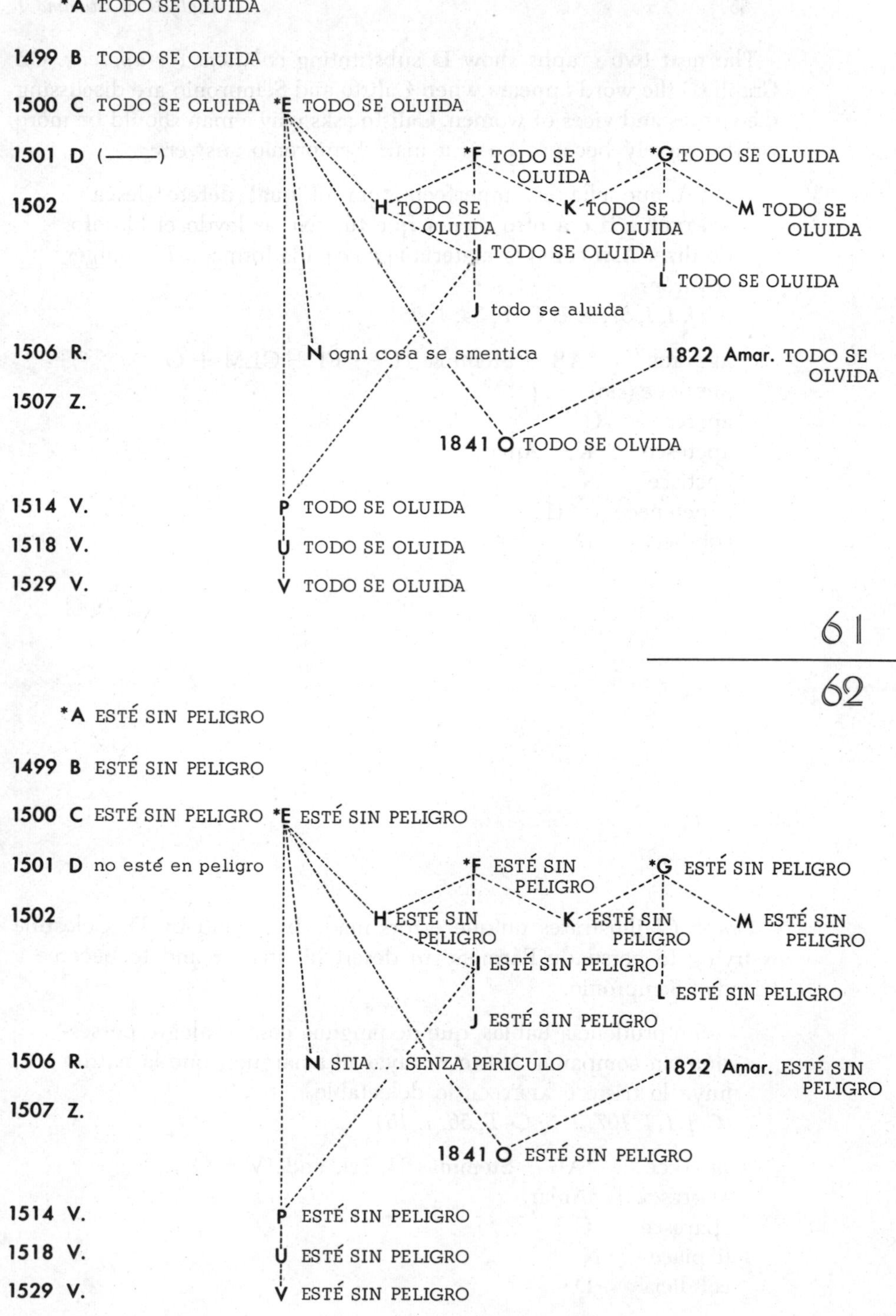
*A TODO SE OLUIDA
1499 B TODO SE OLUIDA
1500 C TODO SE OLUIDA
*E TODO SE OLUIDA
1501 D (——)
*F TODO SE OLUIDA
*G TODO SE OLUIDA
1502
H TODO SE OLUIDA
K TODO SE OLUIDA
M TODO SE OLUIDA
I TODO SE OLUIDA
L TODO SE OLUIDA
J todo se aluida
1506 R.
N ogni cosa se smentica
1822 Amar. TODO SE OLVIDA
1507 Z.
1841 O TODO SE OLVIDA
1514 V.
P TODO SE OLUIDA
1518 V.
U TODO SE OLUIDA
1529 V.
V TODO SE OLUIDA
61
62
*A ESTÉ SIN PELIGRO
1499 B ESTÉ SIN PELIGRO
1500 C ESTÉ SIN PELIGRO
*E ESTÉ SIN PELIGRO
1501 D no esté en peligro
*F ESTÉ SIN PELIGRO
*G ESTÉ SIN PELIGRO
1502
H ESTÉ SIN PELIGRO
K ESTÉ SIN PELIGRO
M ESTÉ SIN PELIGRO
I ESTÉ SIN PELIGRO
L ESTÉ SIN PELIGRO
J ESTÉ SIN PELIGRO
1506 R.
N STIA . . . SENZA PERICULO
1822 Amar. ESTÉ SIN PELIGRO
1507 Z.
1841 O ESTÉ SIN PELIGRO
1514 V.
P ESTÉ SIN PELIGRO
1518 V.
U ESTÉ SIN PELIGRO
1529 V.
V ESTÉ SIN PELIGRO

The next two graphs show D substituting *cobdicia* for *apetece*. On Graph 63 the word appears when Calisto and Sempronio are discussing the virtues and vices of women. Calisto asks why a man should be more worthy merely because he is a man. Sempronio answers:

> —En que ella es imperfecta, por el qual defeto desea é APETECE á tí é á otro menor que tú. ¿No as leydo el filósofo, do dize: Assí como la materia apetece á la forma, así la muger al varón?
> *(Cej. I, I, 57, 1. 1; C–T, 34, 1. 25)*

APETECE *AB + Stemma II + *FI + GLM + O
APETE CE (sic) J
aparece C
apetesce K + Amar.
apetisce N
a petenece H
cobdicia D

Graph 64 illustrates unique errors made by C and by D. Celestina is trying to persuade Pármeno to desert his master and to become a friend of Sempronio.

> —Sin prudencia hablas, que de ninguna cosa es alegre possesión sin compañía. No te retrayas ni amargues, que la natura huye lo triste é APETECE lo delectable.
> *(Cej. I, I, 107, 1. 6; C–T, 56, 1. 16)*

APETECE *AB + Stemmas II, III, and IV + O
APETESCE Amar.
aparesce C
li piace N
cobdicia D

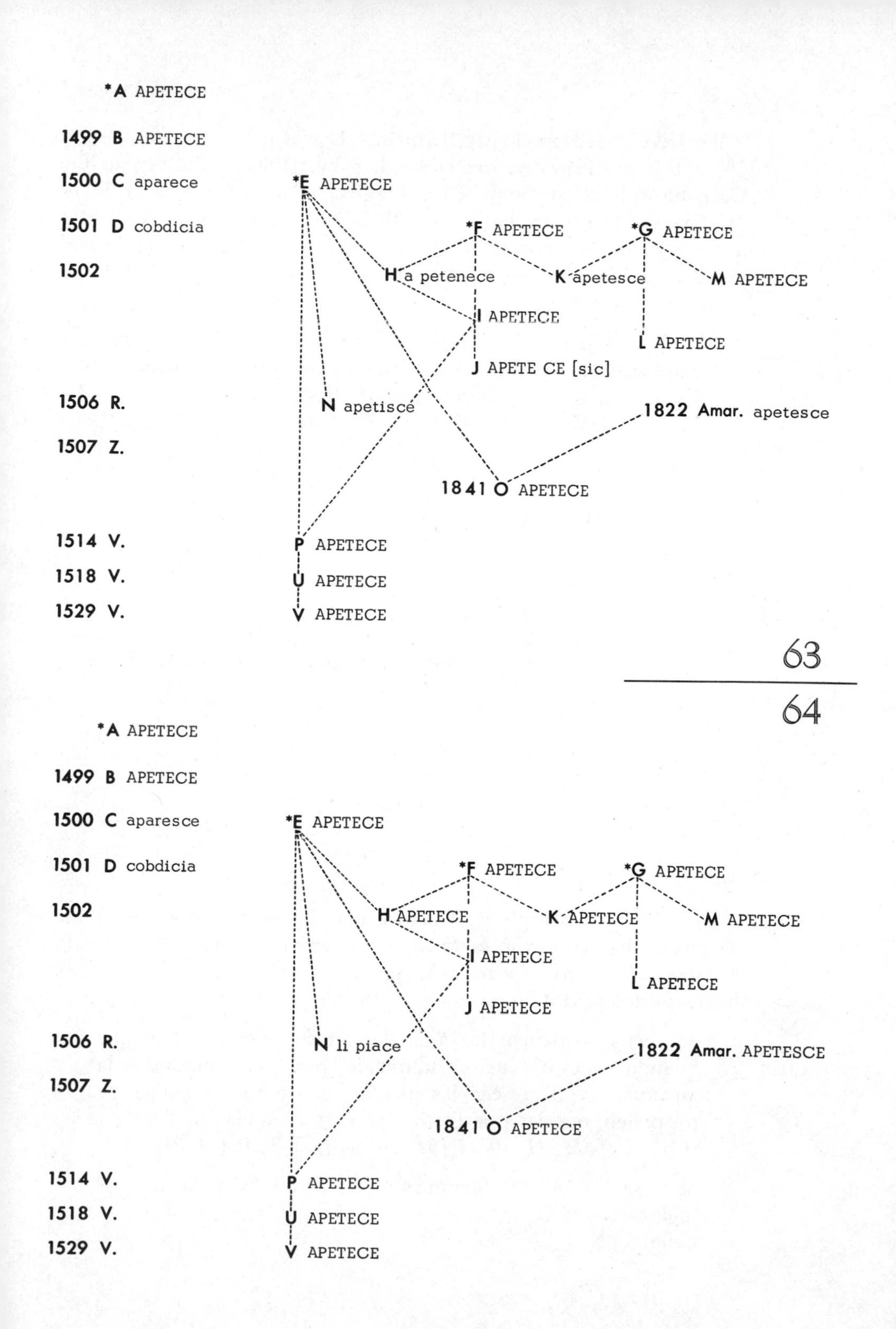
*A APETECE
1499 B APETECE
1500 C aparece
1501 D cobdicia
1502
1506 R.
1507 Z.
1514 V.
1518 V.
1529 V.
*E APETECE
*F APETECE
*G APETECE
H a petenece
K apetesce
M APETECE
I APETECE
L APETECE
J APETE CE [sic]
N apetisce
1822 Amar. apetesce
1841 O APETECE
P APETECE
U APETECE
V APETECE
63
64
*A APETECE
1499 B APETECE
1500 C aparesce
1501 D cobdicia
1502
1506 R.
1507 Z.
1514 V.
1518 V.
1529 V.
*E APETECE
*F APETECE
*G APETECE
H APETECE
K APETECE
M APETECE
I APETECE
L APETECE
J APETECE
N li piace
1822 Amar. APETESCE
1841 O APETECE
P APETECE
U APETECE
V APETECE

We have stated previously that, since D was probably published in 1501, it is possible that the editor had available in addition to the Comedia at least one copy of the Tragicomedia, perhaps *E or *F or *G. Graph 65 suggests that he had *F or *G rather than *E. The word may be found in a speech by Tristán directed to Sosia as they stand guard outside the garden. Both servants are attacking the selfishness and cruelty of Calisto.

> . . . Viuiendo con el Conde, que no matase al hombre, me daua mi MADRE por consejo. Veslos á ellos alegres é abraçados é sus seruidores con harta mengua degollados.
> *(Cej. II, XIV, 128, 11. 10–11 [119, 11. 1–2]; C–T, 238, 1. 30)*

MADRE *ABC + Stemma II + O
MATRE N
padre D + Stemmas III and IV + Amar.

To judge from Graph 66, D again may have utilized a text of the Tragicomedia. However tentatively we are reconstructing *A with MELENA. The word appears in a speech by Celestina, whom Melibea has requested to visit her.

> . . . mejor se doman los animales en su primera edad, que quando ya es su cuero endurecido, para venir mansos á la MELENA; mejor crescen las plantas, que tiernas é nueuas se trasponen, que las que frutificando ya se mudan; . . .
> *(Cej. II, X, 57, 11. 10–11 [54, 11. 8–9]; C–T, 184, 1. 31)*

MELENA *A?D + Stemmas II, III, and IV + Amar. + O
melezina BC
pelle N

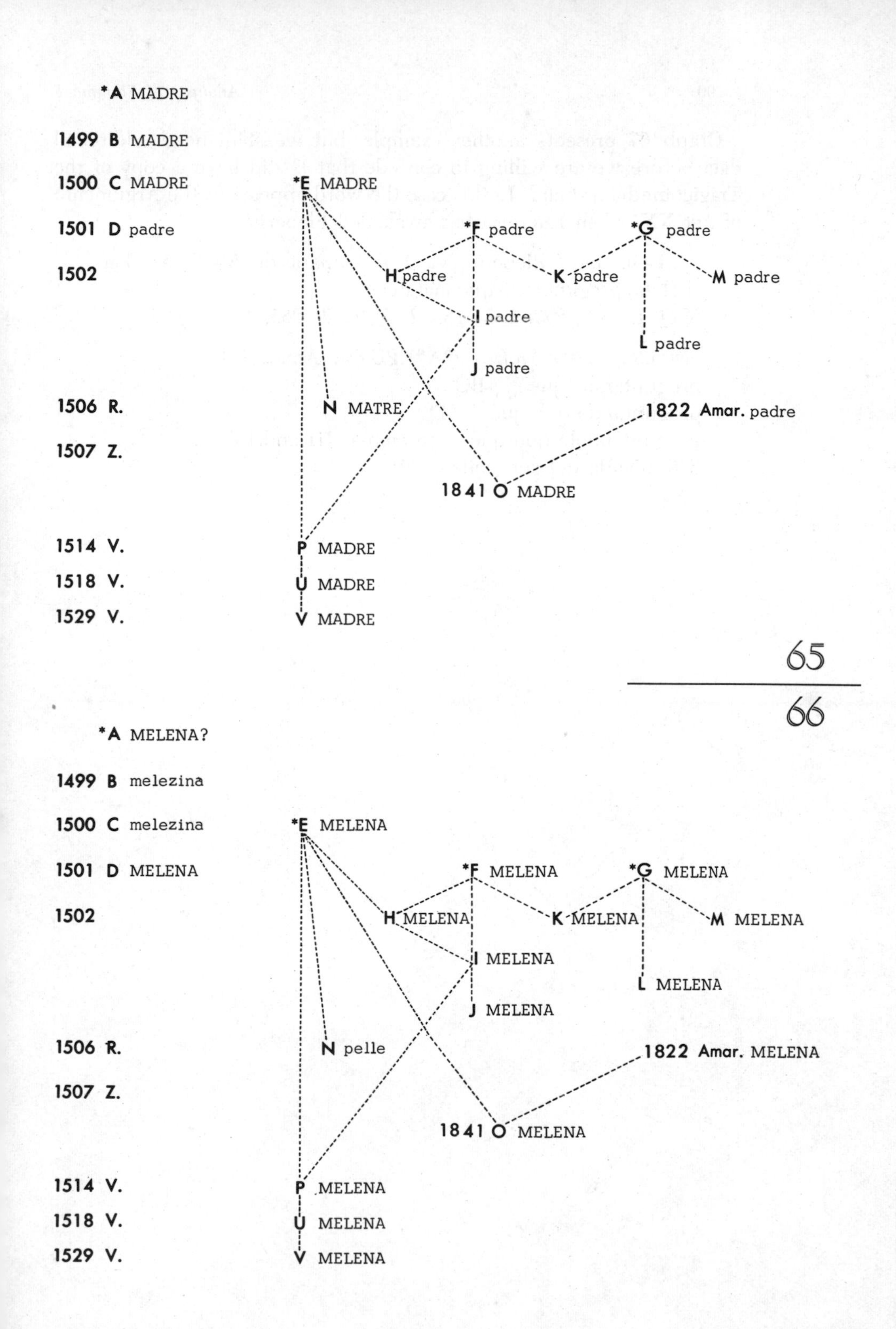
*A MADRE
1499 B MADRE
1500 C MADRE
*E MADRE
1501 D padre
*F padre
*G padre
1502
H padre
K padre
M padre
I padre
L padre
J padre
1506 R.
N MATRE
1822 Amar. padre
1507 Z.
1841 O MADRE
1514 V.
P MADRE
1518 V.
U MADRE
1529 V.
V MADRE
65
66
*A MELENA?
1499 B melezina
1500 C melezina
*E MELENA
1501 D MELENA
*F MELENA
*G MELENA
1502
H MELENA
K MELENA
M MELENA
I MELENA
L MELENA
J MELENA
1506 R.
N pelle
1822 Amar. MELENA
1507 Z.
1841 O MELENA
1514 V.
P MELENA
1518 V.
U MELENA
1529 V.
V MELENA

Graph 67 presents another example, but we shall need additional data before we are willing to concede that D did have a copy of the Tragicomedia at hand. In this case the word appears in the Argumento of Act XX, when Lucrecia has awakened Pleberio.

> . . . Leuantado Pleberio, va á la cámara de Melibea. Consuélala, *preguntando qué* mal tiene.
> *(Cej. II, XX, 203, 1. 7 [188, 1. 7]; C–T, 285, 11. 5–6)*

PREGUNTÁNDOLE QUÉ    *A*EPUV + Amar. + O
preguntando qué    BC
preguntando que qué    D
preguntándole que qué    Stemmas III and IV
li domanda del suo male    N

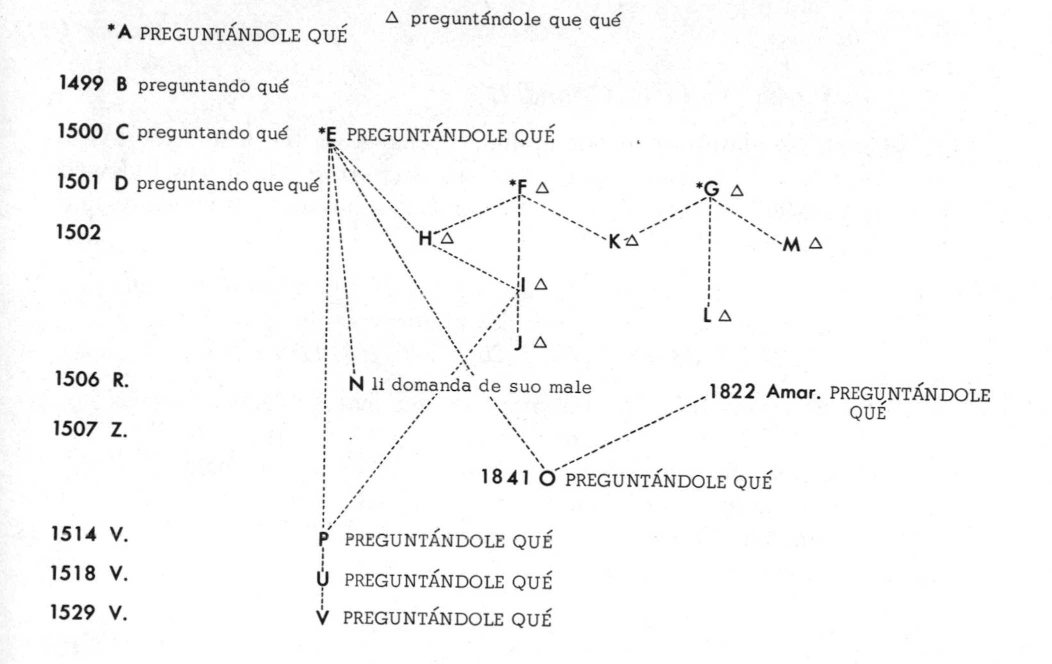
△ preguntándole que qué
*A PREGUNTÁNDOLE QUÉ
1499 B preguntando qué
1500 C preguntando qué
*E PREGUNTÁNDOLE QUÉ
1501 D preguntando que qué
*F △
*G △
1502
H △
K △
M △
I △
L △
J △
1506 R.
N li domanda de suo male
1822 Amar. PREGUNTÁNDOLE QUÉ
1507 Z.
1841 O PREGUNTÁNDOLE QUÉ
1514 V.
P PREGUNTÁNDOLE QUÉ
1518 V.
U PREGUNTÁNDOLE QUÉ
1529 V.
V PREGUNTÁNDOLE QUÉ

### *Variations in B, C, and D*

Graph 68 illustrates in our opinion a change in the text made by B. Then C tried to clarify and made another error, which was followed by D. Melibea has sent Lucrecia for Celestina and is now expressing her pleasure at the visit.

> . . . Pues, por amor de Dios, te despojes para *muy* diligente entender en mi mal é me dés algún remedio.
> *(Cej. II, X, 56, 1. 22 [53, 1. 20]; C–T, 184, 11. 19–20)*
>
> para MÁS diligente entender en mi mal  *A + Stemmas II, III, and IV + Amar. + O
> cio che PIU diligentemente possi intendere nel mio male  N
> para *muy* diligente entender en mi mal  B
> para *mí* diligente entender en mi mal  C
> para *mí* diligente *a* entender en mi mal  D

Graph 69 shows not only the witnesses of an error in B and C but also a variant initiated by *F and extending through Stemmas III and IV. K is wanting.

Pármeno tells Sempronio that he has spent the night with Areúsa. Sempronio expresses surprise and doubt.

> —Espantado me tienes. Mucho puede el contínuo trabajo: vna contínua gotera *horaca* vna piedra?
> *(Cej. II, VIII, 14, 11. 22–23 [14, 11. 14–15]; C–T, 156, 1. 24)*
>
> HORADA  *AD*EPUV + O
> horadará  *FHIJ*GLM + Amar.  (K falta)
> horaca  BC
> fu ora  N

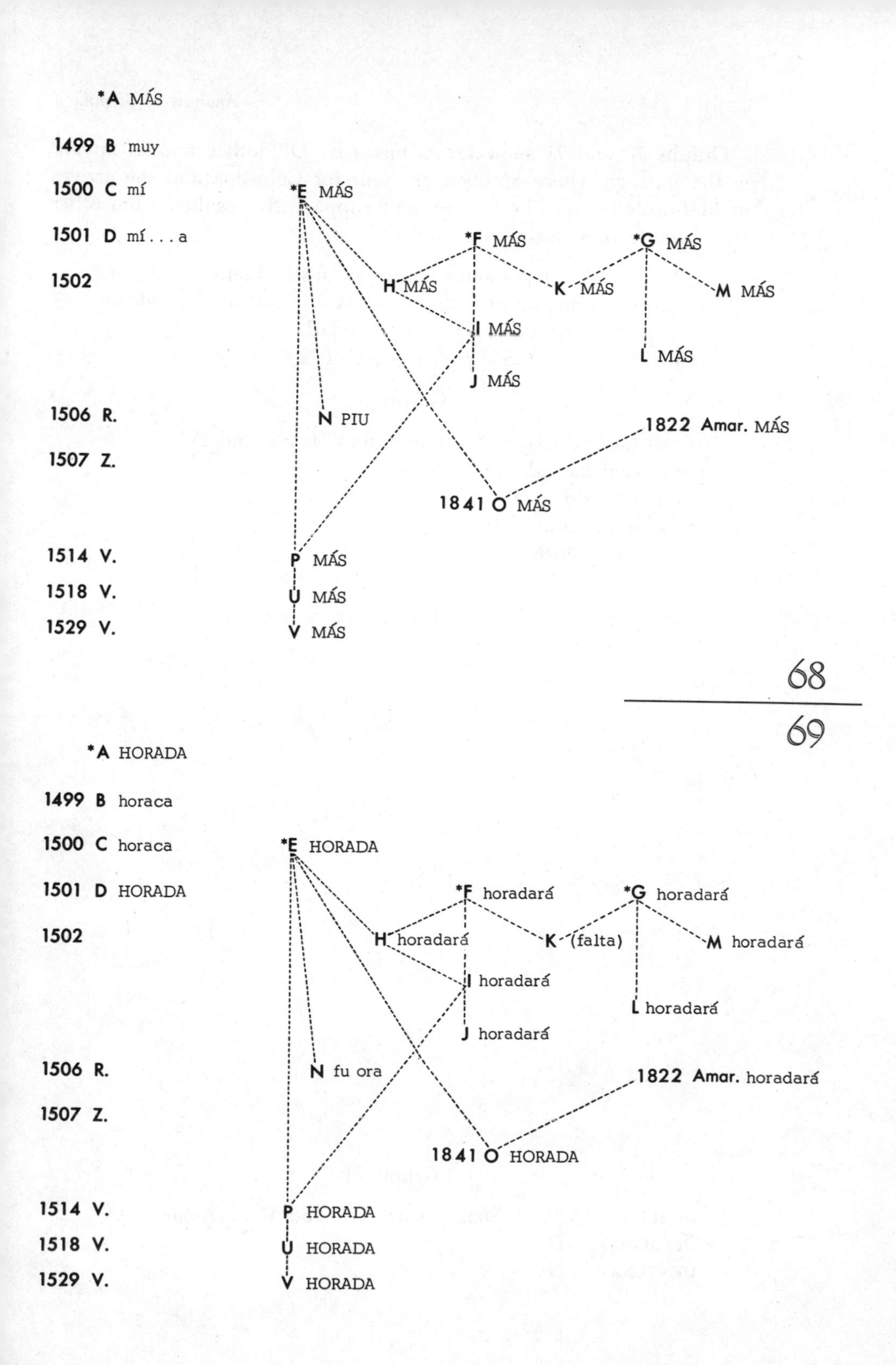

*A MÁS
1499 B muy
1500 C mí
1501 D mí . . . a
1502
*E MÁS
*F MÁS
*G MÁS
H MÁS
K MÁS
M MÁS
I MÁS
L MÁS
J MÁS
1506 R.
N PIU
1822 Amar. MÁS
1507 Z.
1841 O MÁS
1514 V.
P MÁS
1518 V.
U MÁS
1529 V.
V MÁS
68
69
*A HORADA
1499 B horaca
1500 C horaca
*E HORADA
1501 D HORADA
*F horadará
*G horadará
1502
H horadará
K (falta)
M horadará
I horadará
L horadará
J horadará
1506 R.
N fu ora
1822 Amar. horadará
1507 Z.
1841 O HORADA
1514 V.
P HORADA
1518 V.
U HORADA
1529 V.
V HORADA

Graphs 70 and 71 show errors made by D. Both examples appear in the passage where Melibea has sent for Celestina and she arrives at Melibea's home. The first example apparently resulted from other errors made previously by B and C.

> MEL. . . .¡O vieja sabia é honrrada, tú seas bienvenida! ¿Qué te parece, cómo ha *querido* mi DICHA é la fortuna ha rodeado que yo tuuiesse de tu saber necessidad, . . .
> *(Cej. II, X, 55, 11. 5–6 [52, 1. 3]; C–T, 183, 1. 14)*

Graph 70

| | |
|---|---|
| CÓMO HA QUESIDO | *A + Stemmas II, III, and IV |
| cómo que ha sido | BC |
| cómo ha sido | D |
| come a uolsuto | N |
| cómo ha querido | Amar. + O |

Graph 71

| | |
|---|---|
| DICHA | *ABC + Stemmas II, III, and IV + Amar. + O |
| desdicha | D |
| UENTURA | N |

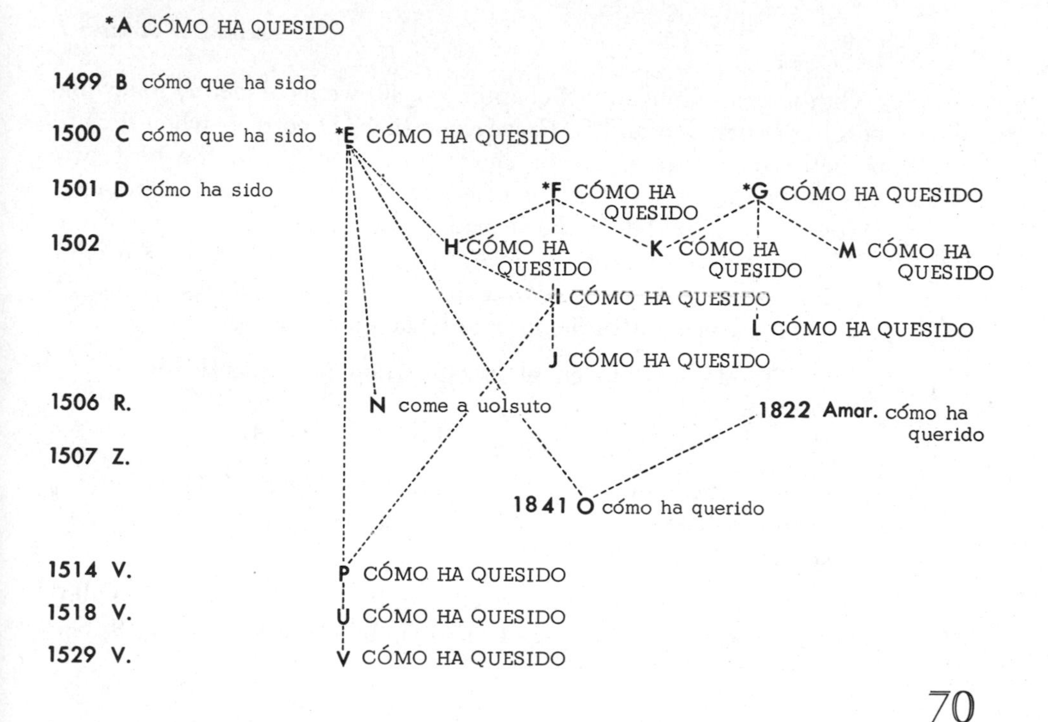
*A CÓMO HA QUESIDO
1499 B cómo que ha sido
1500 C cómo que ha sido
*E CÓMO HA QUESIDO
1501 D cómo ha sido
*F CÓMO HA QUESIDO
*G CÓMO HA QUESIDO
1502
H CÓMO HA QUESIDO
K CÓMO HA QUESIDO
M CÓMO HA QUESIDO
I CÓMO HA QUESIDO
L CÓMO HA QUESIDO
J CÓMO HA QUESIDO
1506 R.
N come a uolsuto
1822 Amar. cómo ha querido
1507 Z.
1841 O cómo ha querido
1514 V.
P CÓMO HA QUESIDO
1518 V.
U CÓMO HA QUESIDO
1529 V.
V CÓMO HA QUESIDO

70
71

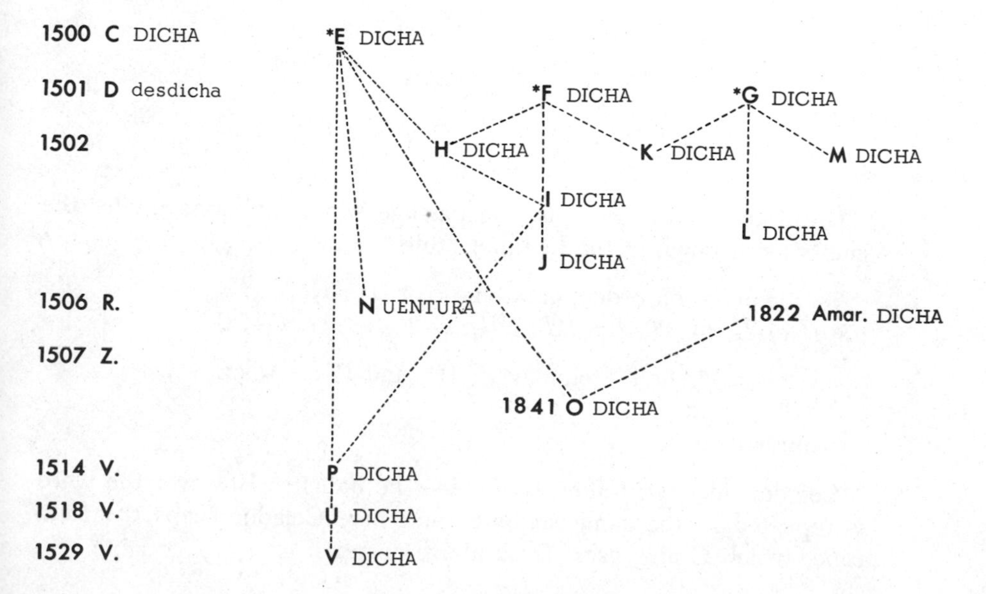
*A DICHA
1499 B DICHA
1500 C DICHA
*E DICHA
1501 D desdicha
*F DICHA
*G DICHA
1502
H DICHA
K DICHA
M DICHA
I DICHA
L DICHA
J DICHA
1506 R.
N UENTURA
1822 Amar. DICHA
1507 Z.
1841 O DICHA
1514 V.
P DICHA
1518 V.
U DICHA
1529 V.
V DICHA

On the first graphs in this chapter (48, 49) we have seen D following possible errors of B and C. However at times D corrects when B or C or both commit an error—as shown in Graph 69. In the next two graphs the same error, *cabo,* is made by B and C; in the first instance D follows B and C but in the second D corrects to CABE.

The variants on Graph 72 appear in a speech by Sempronio who has just been invited by Pármeno to a banquet at the home of Celestina. Pármeno asks Sempronio what Calisto is doing.

> —Allí está tendido en el estrado *cabo* la cama, donde le dexaste anoche.
> *(Cej. II, VIII, 17, 1. 1 [16, 1. 12]; C–T, 158, 1. 5)*

CABE *A + Stemmas II, III, and IV + Amar. + O
cabo BCD
sta sopra lo lecto del N

There is another example of CABE with the erroneous variant "cabo" in BCD in Cej. II, XII, 101, 1. 15 (95, 1. 4); C–T, 218, 1. 29. See Graph 167.

On Graph 73 the word is in a passage where Celestina invites the guests to sit down at the banquet table.

> . . . Ponéos en orden, cada vno CABE la suya; . . .
> *(Cej. II, IX, 29, 1. 9 [28, 1. 4]; C–T, 166, 11. 17–18)*

CABE *AD + Stemmas II, III, and IV + Amar. + O
cabo BC
apresso N

Cejador does not follow B nor does he italicize. However the word is repeated in the same sentence and here Cejador keeps the form *cabo,* which C also uses. D as above corrects.

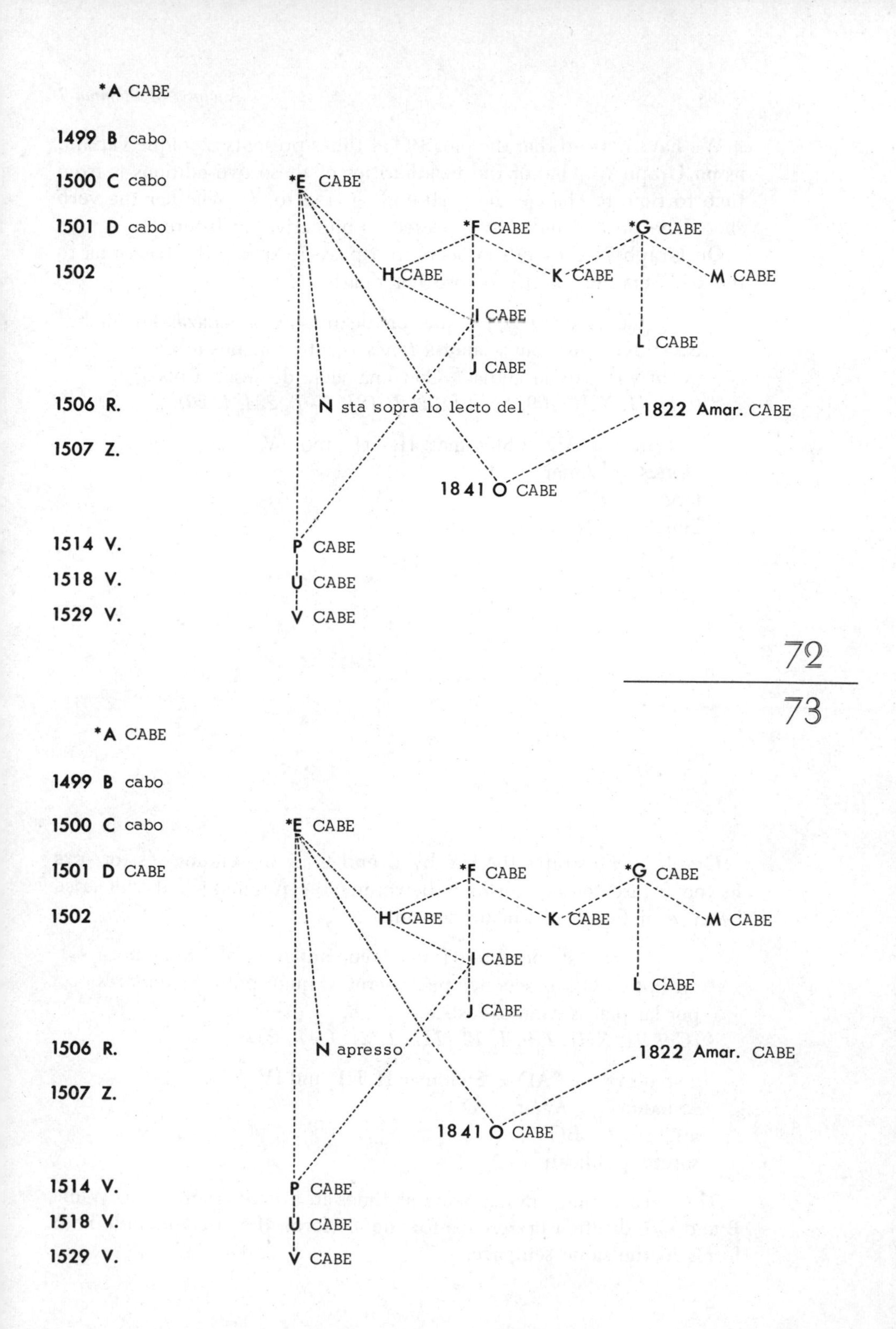
*A CABE
1499 B cabo
1500 C cabo
*E CABE
1501 D cabo
*F CABE
*G CABE
1502
H CABE
K CABE
M CABE
I CABE
L CABE
J CABE
1506 R.
N sta sopra lo lecto del
1822 Amar. CABE
1507 Z.
1841 O CABE
1514 V.
P CABE
1518 V.
U CABE
1529 V.
V CABE
*A CABE
1499 B cabo
1500 C cabo
*E CABE
1501 D CABE
*F CABE
*G CABE
1502
H CABE
K CABE
M CABE
I CABE
L CABE
J CABE
1506 R.
N apresso
1822 Amar. CABE
1507 Z.
1841 O CABE
1514 V.
P CABE
1518 V.
U CABE
1529 V.
V CABE

We have noticed that the pair BC at times presents a unique variant, as on Graph 73. One of the peculiarities of these two editions is from time to time to change the verb ending -ÉYS to -és, whether the verb should be present indicative, present subjunctive, or future.

On Graph 74 the verb appears in a passage spoken by Celestina to the two servants shortly before her death.

> . . . ¿Qué es esto? ¿Qué quieren dezir tales amenazas en mi casa? ¿Con una oueja mansa *tenés* vosotros manos é braueza? ¿Con vna gallina atada? ¿Con una vieja de sesenta años?
> *(Cej. II, XIII, 109, l. 14 [102, l. 18]; C–T, 224, l. 20)*

TENÉYS *AD + Stemmas II, III, and IV
TENÉIS Amar. + O
tenés BC
hauete N

Graph 75 illustrates the use by B and C of the ending -és for -ÉYS in the future tense. Calisto is bewailing the publicity that will arise because of the deaths of his servants.

> . . . ¡O mi triste nombre é fama, cómo andas al tablero de boca en boca! ¡O mis secretos más secretos, quán públicos *andarés* por las plaças é mercados!
> *(Cej. II, XIII, 119, l. 12 [111, l. 2]; C–T, 232, l. 11)*

ANDARÉYS *AD + Stemmas II, III, and IV
ANDARÉIS Amar. + O
andarés BC
sarete publicati N

The verb ending -ÉYS appears at times in a nonvariant form. While B and C indicate a preference for the -és form, they may include both forms in the same sentence.

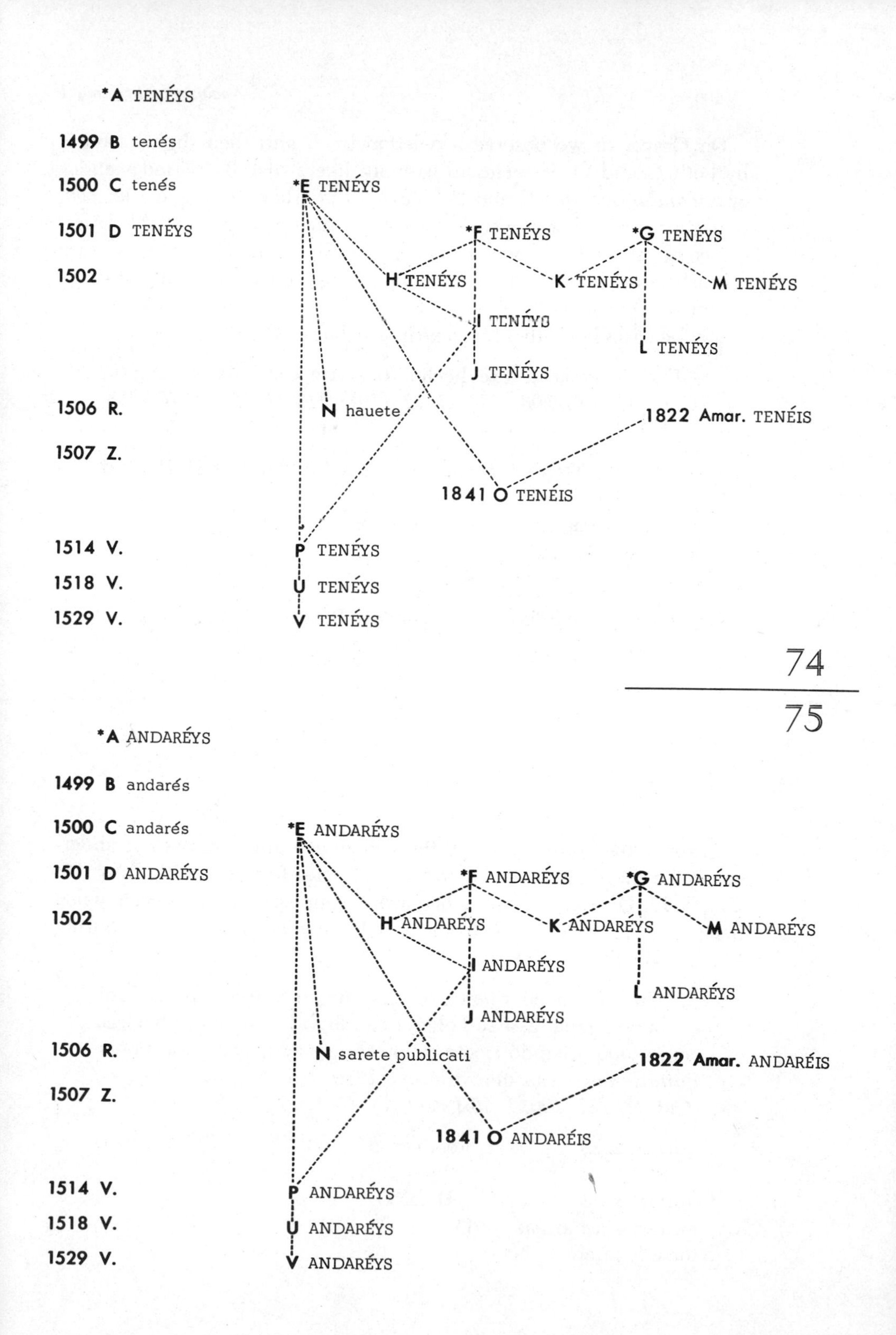
*A TENÉYS
1499 B tenés
1500 C tenés
*E TENÉYS
1501 D TENÉYS
*F TENÉYS
*G TENÉYS
1502
H TENÉYS
K TENÉYS
M TENÉYS
I TENÉYS
L TENÉYS
J TENÉYS
1506 R.
N hauete
1822 Amar. TENÉIS
1507 Z.
1841 O TENÉIS
1514 V.
P TENÉYS
1518 V.
U TENÉYS
1529 V.
V TENÉYS
74
75
*A ANDARÉYS
1499 B andarés
1500 C andarés
*E ANDARÉYS
1501 D ANDARÉYS
*F ANDARÉYS
*G ANDARÉYS
1502
H ANDARÉYS
K ANDARÉYS
M ANDARÉYS
I ANDARÉYS
L ANDARÉYS
J ANDARÉYS
1506 R.
N sarete publicati
1822 Amar. ANDARÉIS
1507 Z.
1841 O ANDARÉIS
1514 V.
P ANDARÉYS
1518 V.
U ANDARÉYS
1529 V.
V ANDARÉYS

On Graph 76 we observe a deletion by B and then slight changes by both C and D. It seems to us more likely that B omitted *mandar* or *a mandar* and that C and D followed B, perhaps adding *a* after *voy*, than that the author or corrector of the princeps edition of the Tragicomedia inserted the word *mandar* in the text. Therefore we are reconstructing both *A and *E by accepting a form which all witnesses except BCD support.

Melibea asks her father for some musical instruments.

> —Esso, hija mía, luego es hecho. YO LO VOY A MANDAR APAREJAR.
> *(Cej. II, XX, 206, ll. 11–12 [191, ll. 11–12]; C–T, 288, ll. 1–2)*

YO LO VOY A MANDAR APAREJAR   *A? + Stemmas II, III, and IV + Amar. + O
UOGLIO ANDAR AD FARLO APPARECCHIARE   N
yo lo voy aparejar   B
yo lo voy a aparejar   CD

Cejador in his edition does not follow B but italicizes MANDAR.

At times the editor of one of the sixteen-act editions does not understand the meaning of certain words and tries to improve the text. On Graph 77 D adds a word. The words appear in the speech when Sempronio reports to Calisto his and Pármeno's great bravery during his interview with Melibea.

> . . . Pues Pármeno, que te parecía que no te seruía hasta aquí de buena gana, assí se holgó, quando vido los de las hachas, como lobo, quando siente poluo de ganado, pensando poder *quitárleslas*, hasta que vido que eran muchos.
> *(Cej. II, XII, 100, l. 13 [94, l. 7]; C–T, 218, l. 9)*

QUITÁRSELAS   *A + Stemmas II and IV + *FIJ + Amar. + O
quitárles las   BC   (H falta)
quitarles las armas   D
torse la fame   N

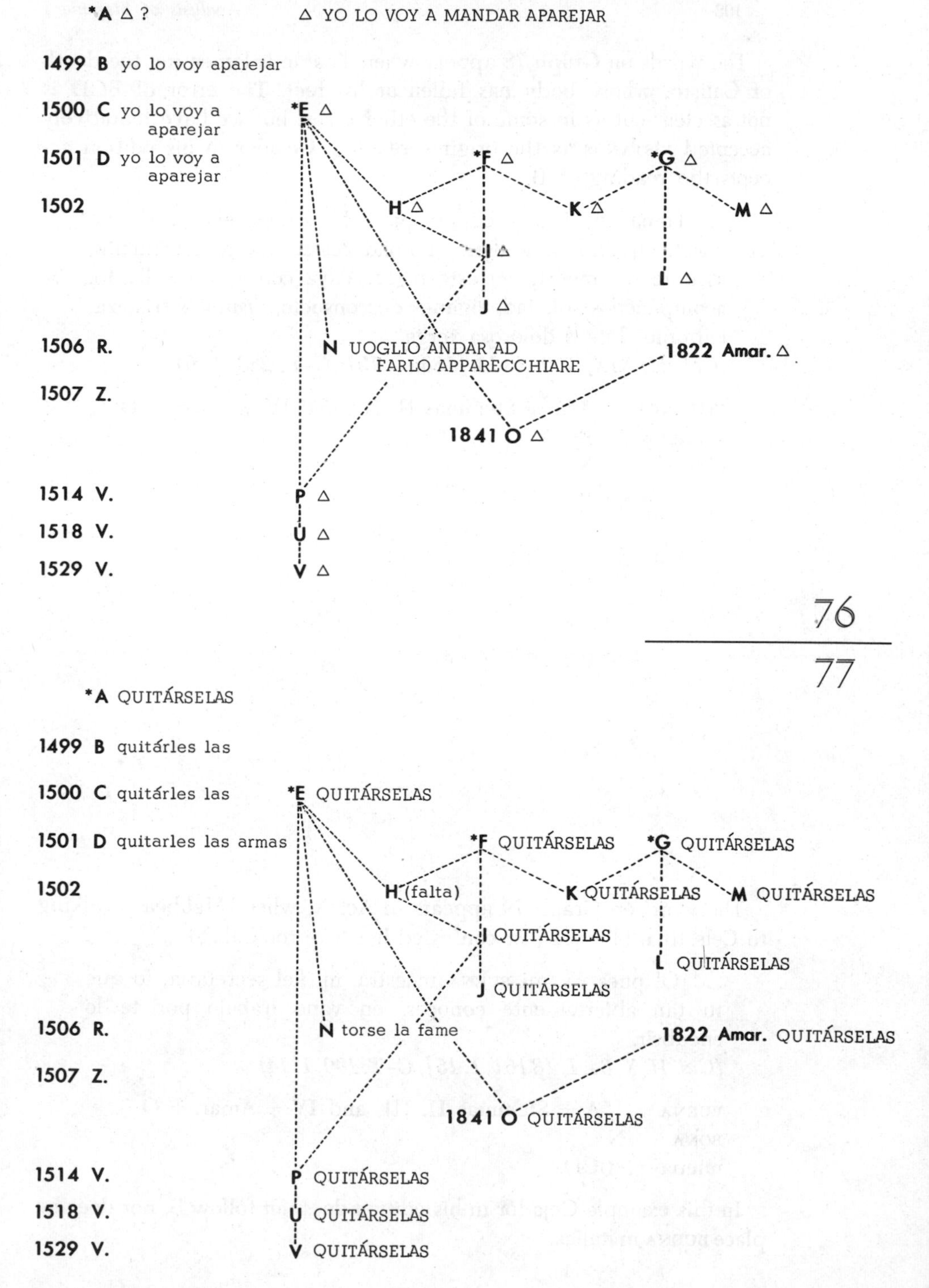
*A △ ?
△ YO LO VOY A MANDAR APAREJAR
1499 B yo lo voy aparejar
1500 C yo lo voy a aparejar
*E △
1501 D yo lo voy a aparejar
*F △
*G △
1502
H △
K △
M △
I △
L △
J △
1506 R.
N UOGLIO ANDAR AD FARLO APPARECCHIARE
1822 Amar. △
1507 Z.
1841 O △
1514 V.
P △
1518 V.
U △
1529 V.
V △
76
77
*A QUITÁRSELAS
1499 B quitárles las
1500 C quitárles las
*E QUITÁRSELAS
1501 D quitarles las armas
*F QUITÁRSELAS
*G QUITÁRSELAS
1502
H (falta)
K QUITÁRSELAS
M QUITÁRSELAS
I QUITÁRSELAS
L QUITÁRSELAS
J QUITÁRSELAS
1506 R.
N torse la fame
1822 Amar. QUITÁRSELAS
1507 Z.
1841 O QUITÁRSELAS
1514 V.
P QUITÁRSELAS
1518 V.
U QUITÁRSELAS
1529 V.
V QUITÁRSELAS

The words on Graph 78 appear when Tristán is lamenting the death of Calisto, whose body has fallen at his feet. The error of BCD is not as clear-cut as in some of the other cases, but we have tentatively accepted VÍSTANOS as the original reading. Cejador in his edition accepts the reading of B.

> . . . Toma tú, Sosia, dessos pies. Lleuemos el cuerpo de nuestro querido amo donde no padezca su honrra detrimento, avnque sea muerto en este lugar. Vaya con nosotros llanto, acompáñenos soledad, síganos desconsuelo, *visítenos* tristeza, cúbranos luto é dolorosa xerga.
> *(Cej. II, XIX, 200, 1. 14 [185, 1. 19]; C–T, 283, 1. 6)*

VÍSTANOS *A? + Stemmas II, III, and IV + Amar.+ O
visítenos BCD
(———) N

The word on Graph 79 appears in Act X, where Melibea is talking to Celestina. She has just confessed her love for Calisto.

> . . . ¡O! pues ya, mi BUENA maestra, mi fiel secretaria, lo que tú tan abiertamente conoces, en vano trabajo por te lo encubrir.
> *(Cej. II, X, 64, 1. 18 [61, 1. 15]; C–T, 190, 1. 14)*

BUENA *A + Stemmas II, III, and IV + Amar. + O
BONA N
nueua BCD

In this example Cejador in his edition does not follow B, nor does he place BUENA in italics.

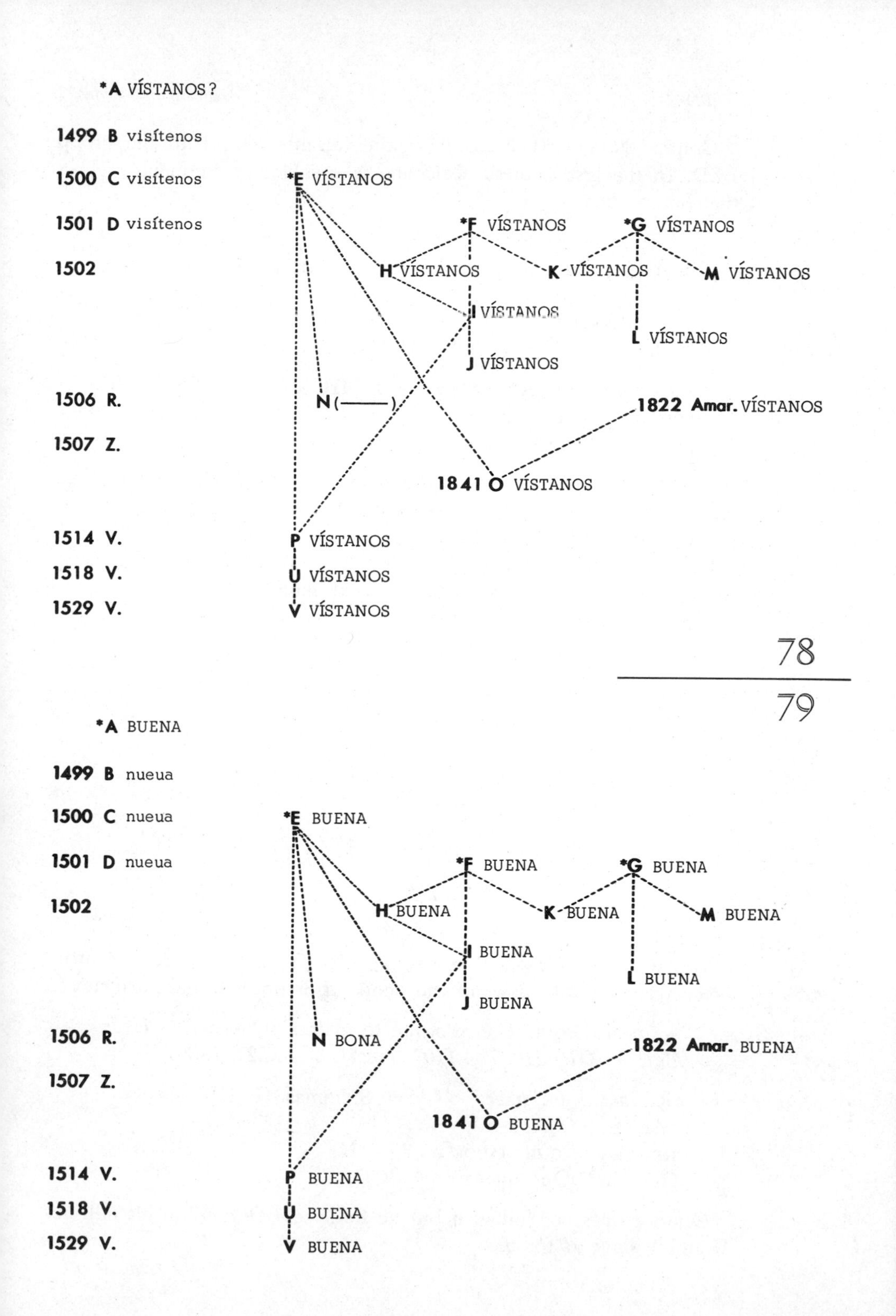

*A VÍSTANOS?
1499 B visítenos
1500 C visítenos
1501 D visítenos
1502
1506 R.
1507 Z.
1514 V.
1518 V.
1529 V.
*E VÍSTANOS
*F VÍSTANOS
*G VÍSTANOS
H VÍSTANOS
K VÍSTANOS
M VÍSTANOS
I VÍSTANOS
L VÍSTANOS
J VÍSTANOS
N (——)
1822 Amar. VÍSTANOS
1841 O VÍSTANOS
P VÍSTANOS
U VÍSTANOS
V VÍSTANOS
78
79
*A BUENA
1499 B nueua
1500 C nueua
1501 D nueua
1502
1506 R.
1507 Z.
1514 V.
1518 V.
1529 V.
*E BUENA
*F BUENA
*G BUENA
H BUENA
K BUENA
M BUENA
I BUENA
L BUENA
J BUENA
N BONA
1822 Amar. BUENA
1841 O BUENA
P BUENA
U BUENA
V BUENA

Graphs 80 and 81 illustrate again variants unique to the group BCD. In the first example Celestina is speaking to Pármeno a short time before she is killed.

> . . . Tan bien seré oyda, avnque muger, como vosotros, muy peynados. Déxame en mi casa con mi fortuna. É tú, Pármeno, NO PIENSES que soy tu catiua por saber mis secretos é mi passada vida . . . .
> *(Cej. II, XII, 109, l. 1 [102, l. 5]; C–T, 224, l.8)*

NO PIENSES *A? + Stemmas II, III, and IV + Amar. + O
non te pensar N
piensas BCD

In the above text again Cejador does not follow B nor italicize NO PIENSES. Celestina had said just before the above passage: ". . . E no pienses con tu yra maltratarme, que justicia ay para todos: a todos es ygual." It is possible that *E, influenced by the preceding words, made an error which was continued in all later editions.

The words on Graph 81 are spoken by Tristán when Sosia returns home weeping with news of the death of Sempronio and Pármeno.

> —¿QUÉ ES? ¿QUÉ HAS? ¿Porqué te matas? ¿Qué mal es éste?
> *(Cej. II, XIII, 116, l. 4 [107, l. 24]; C–T, 229, l. 30)*

¿QUÉ ES? ¿QUÉ HAS? *A? + Stemmas II, III, and IV + Amar. + O
CHE COSA E? CHE DIAUOL HAI? N
¿Qué has? ¿Qué quexas? BCD

Cejador does not follow B but he italicizes ¿*Qué es*? in his edition. U and V have AS for HAS.

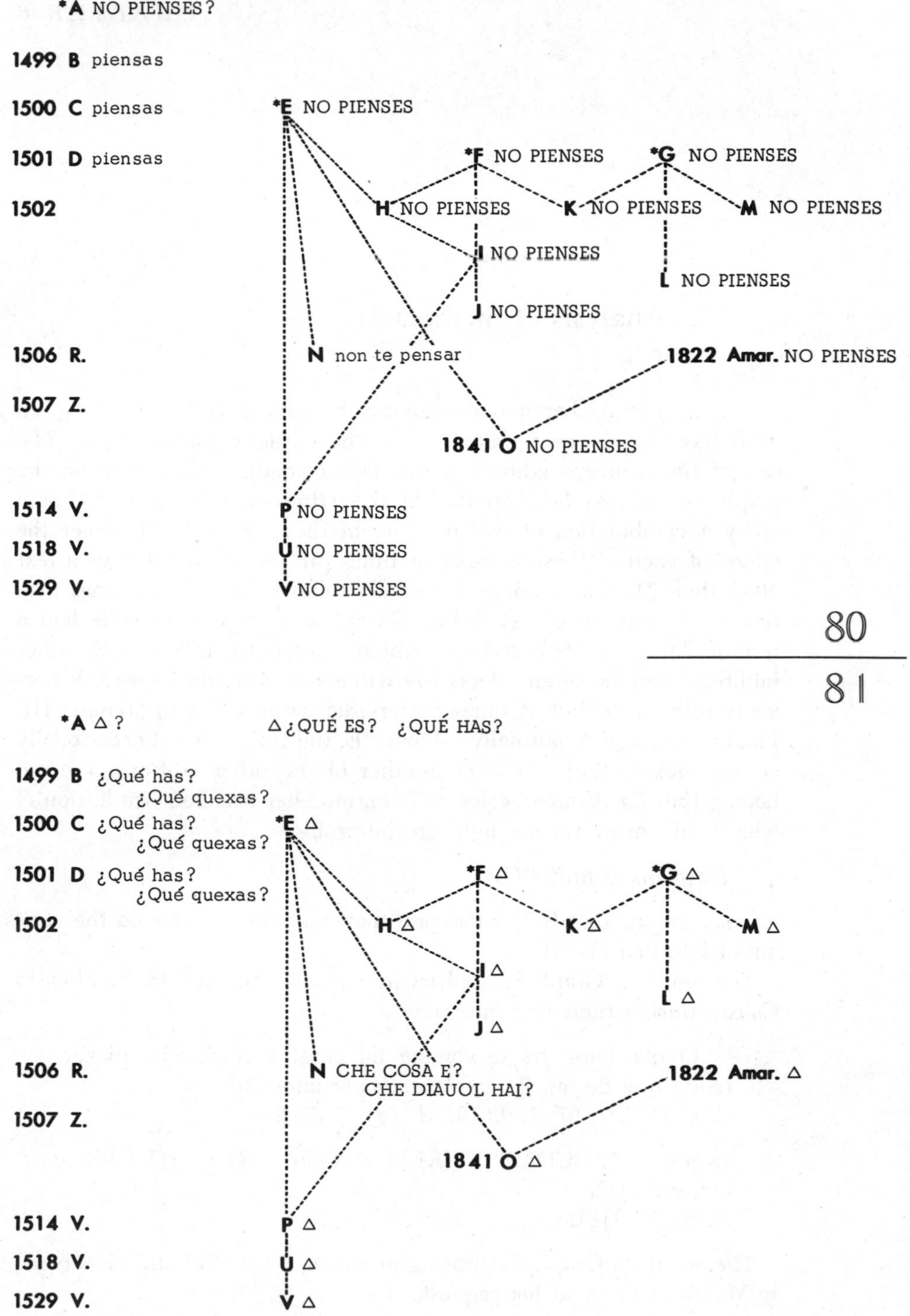

*A NO PIENSES?
1499 B piensas
1500 C piensas
*E NO PIENSES
1501 D piensas
*F NO PIENSES
*G NO PIENSES
1502
H NO PIENSES
K NO PIENSES
M NO PIENSES
I NO PIENSES
L NO PIENSES
J NO PIENSES
1506 R.
N non te pensar
1822 Amar. NO PIENSES
1507 Z.
1841 O NO PIENSES
1514 V.
P NO PIENSES
1518 V.
U NO PIENSES
1529 V.
V NO PIENSES
80
81
*A △ ?
△ ¿QUÉ ES? ¿QUÉ HAS?
1499 B ¿Qué has?
¿Qué quexas?
1500 C ¿Qué has?
¿Qué quexas?
*E △
1501 D ¿Qué has?
¿Qué quexas?
*F △
*G △
1502
H △
K △
M △
I △
L △
J △
1506 R.
N CHE COSA E?
CHE DIAUOL HAI?
1822 Amar. △
1507 Z.
1841 O △
1514 V.
P △
1518 V.
U △
1529 V.
V △

# CHAPTER 6

## Analysis of Stemma II

Let us begin our analysis of Stemma II by summing up what has already been stated about the editions composing it. The text of the princeps edition of the Tragicomedia represented on the graphs by *E may be supported by the witnesses of H or N or O or P or by a combination of two or more of these editions. However the editor of each of these editions at times prefers the reading of a text other than *E. For example H usually follows *F, only at times preferring the variant of *E. When Gorchs was preparing O, he had a text of Zaragoza 1507 at hand which apparently reflects *E rather faithfully, but he often selects the witness of Amarita instead. P normally follows *E but at times prefers the witness of I in Stemma III. Finally although N normally follows *E, the Italian word occasionally corresponds to that in one or another of the other editions. We are hoping that Dr. Emma Scoles will continue her excellent studies on N which will throw further light on the problem.

### *Editions P and PUV*

The six graphs that follow indicate that P at times preferred the variant of I to that of *E.

The word on Graph 82 appears in a speech directed by Melibea to Calisto during their first interview.

> —¡O por Dios, no se cometa tal cosa! Pero mucho plazer tengo que de tan fiel gente *andas* acompañado.
> *(Cej. II, XII, 97, 1. 22 [91, 1. 14]; C–T, 216, 1. 2)*

| | | |
|---|---|---|
| ANDES | *ABCD*E*F*GKLM + Amar. + O | (H falta) |
| UENGHI | N | |
| andas | IJPUV | |

The word on Graph 83 appears in Act X, when Celestina has come to Melibea's home at her request.

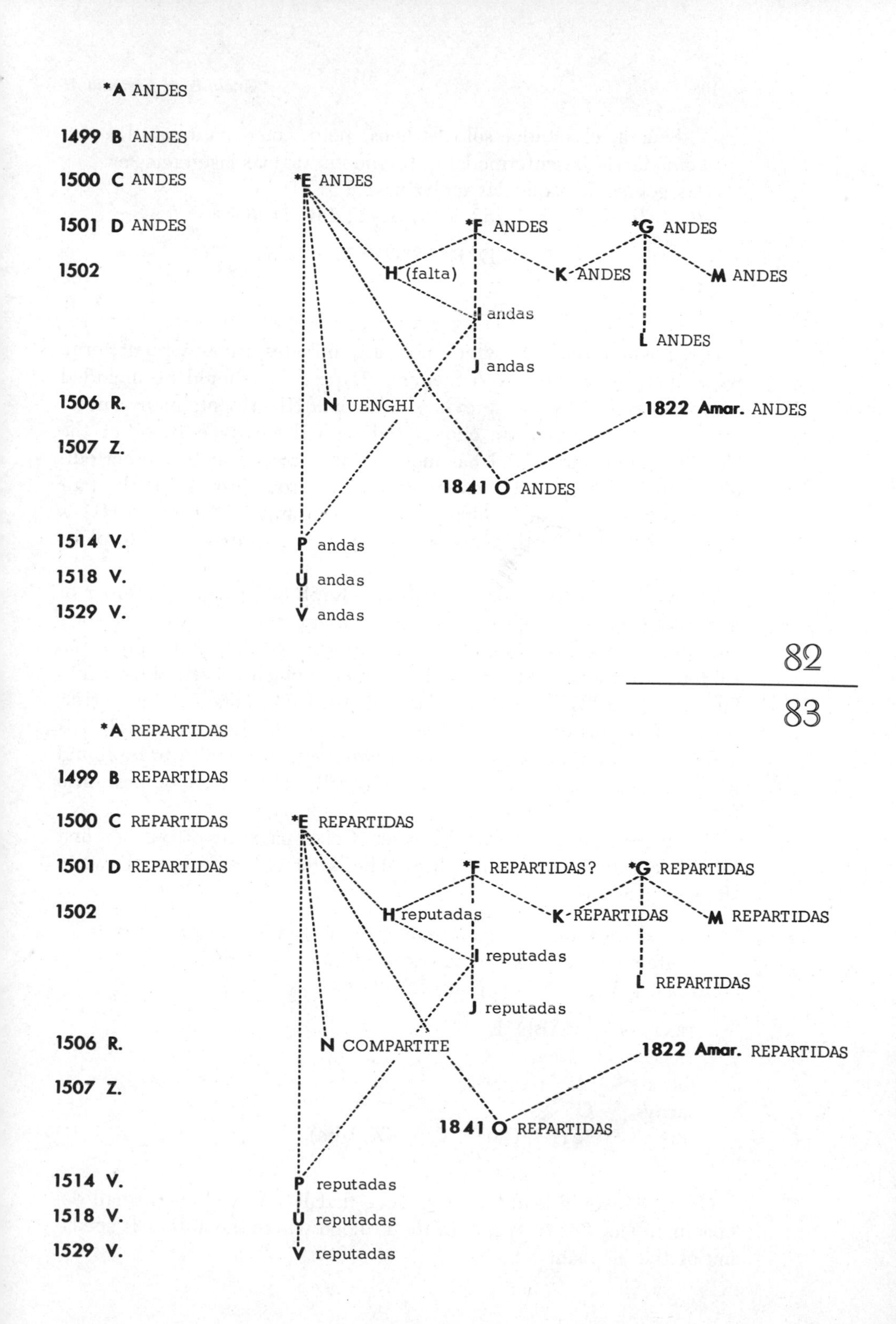
*A ANDES
1499 B ANDES
1500 C ANDES
1501 D ANDES
1502
1506 R.
1507 Z.
1514 V.
1518 V.
1529 V.
*E ANDES
*F ANDES
*G ANDES
H (falta)
K ANDES
M ANDES
I andas
L ANDES
J andas
N UENGHI
1822 Amar. ANDES
1841 O ANDES
P andas
U andas
V andas
82
83
*A REPARTIDAS
1499 B REPARTIDAS
1500 C REPARTIDAS
1501 D REPARTIDAS
1502
1506 R.
1507 Z.
1514 V.
1518 V.
1529 V.
*E REPARTIDAS
*F REPARTIDAS?
*G REPARTIDAS
H reputadas
K REPARTIDAS
M REPARTIDAS
I reputadas
L REPARTIDAS
J reputadas
N COMPARTITE
1822 Amar. REPARTIDAS
1841 O REPARTIDAS
P reputadas
U reputadas
V reputadas

—Señora, el sabidor solo es Dios; pero, como para salud é remedio de las enfermedades fueron REPARTIDAS las gracias en las gentes de hallar las melezinas, . . .
*(Cej. II, X, 56, 1. 7 [53, 1. 5]; C–T, 184, 11. 6–7)*

REPARTIDAS *ABCD*E*F?*GKLM + Amar. + O
COMPARTITE N
reputadas HIJPUV

It is possible that *F, which normally initiates a new variant form, when there is one, for both Stemmas III and IV, should be included here with HIJ. As stated previously Stemma III presents many knotty problems. Those who are acquainted with the early editions of the *Celestina* are aware that J has more unique errors than any other edition and that the pair IJ has many unique errors, just as has the pair BC in Stemma I. The number of unique variants in the group HIJ is somewhat limited. In this case we hesitate at the present time to place *F in this group.

The variants of the word TRATAR on Graph 84 present a number of interesting witnesses. C has a unique variant, *sacáys,* which supports our opinion that this edition is not the princeps edition of the Comedia. All four witnesses of Stemma III are *traéys,* which is carried over into Stemma IV in *G and M. K is lacking and L presents a unique error, *tratéys.* P in this case prefers the variant of I to *E even though it is an error. When the group HIJ has a witness which is also to be found in Stemma IV, including *G, we normally accept the witness also for *F.

The word appears in Act VI when Celestina is reporting her first interview with Melibea to Calisto. The latter is beside himself when she mentions the sash.

. . . ¡O mis manos! ¡con qué atreuimiento, con quán poco acatamiento tenéys y TRATÁYS la triaca de mi llaga!
*(Cej. I, VI, 224, 1. 1; C–T, 125, 1. 1)*

TRATÁYS *ABD*E
TRATÁIS Amar. + O
toccate N
sacáys C
traéys *FHIJ*GMPUV (K falta)
tratéys L

Graph 85 would lead one to believe that P observed even small details in I. The word appears in the Prólogo where the author is speaking of the elephant which

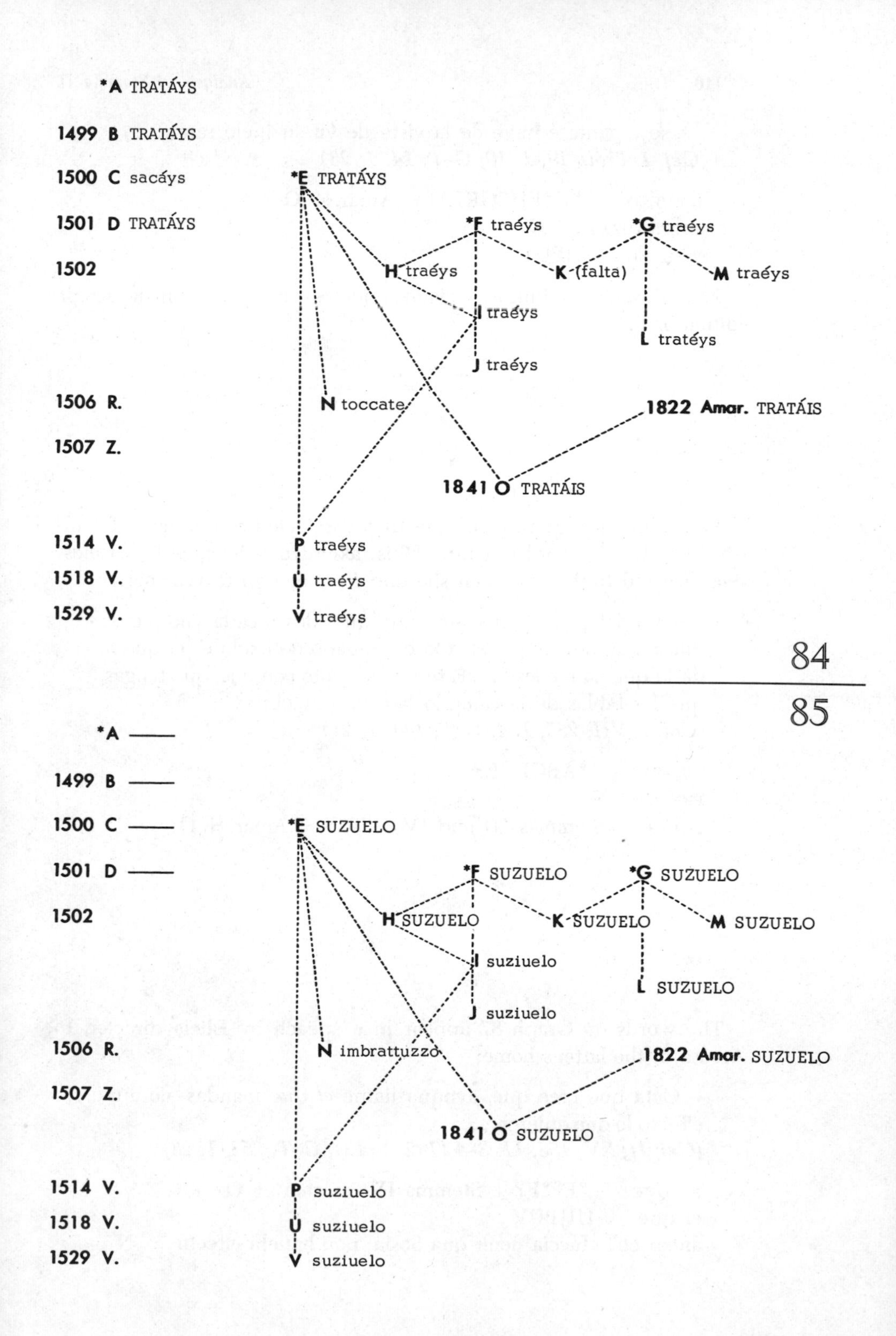
*A TRATÁYS
1499 B TRATÁYS
1500 C sacáys
*E TRATÁYS
1501 D TRATÁYS
*F traéys
*G traéys
1502
H traéys
K (falta)
M traéys
I traéys
L tratéys
J traéys
1506 R.
N toccate
1822 Amar. TRATÁIS
1507 Z.
1841 O TRATÁIS
1514 V.
P traéys
1518 V.
U traéys
1529 V.
V traéys
84
85
*A ——
1499 B ——
1500 C ——
*E SUZUELO
1501 D ——
*F SUZUELO
*G SUZUELO
1502
H SUZUELO
K SUZUELO
M SUZUELO
I suziuelo
L SUZUELO
J suziuelo
1506 R.
N imbrattuzzo
1822 Amar. SUZUELO
1507 Z.
1841 O SUZUELO
1514 V.
P suziuelo
1518 V.
U suziuelo
1529 V.
V suziuelo

. . . se espanta é huye de la vista de vn suziuelo ratón, . . .
*(Cej. I, Pról., 19, 1. 10; C–T, 14, 1. 25)*

SUZUELO *E*FH*GKLM + Amar. + O
imbrattuzzo N
suziuelo IJPUV

Since this is an addition, Cejador chooses the spelling in the Krapf edition or P.

Two additional graphs indicate that P selected the variant of I instead of *E. The word in Graph 86 is taken from the speech of Celestina directed to Areúsa when she and Pármeno go to visit her.

. . . é todos piensan que son muy queridos é cada vno piensa que no ay otro é que él solo es priuado é él solo es el que le da lo que ha menester. ¿É tú PIENSAS que con dos, que tengas, que las tablas de la cama lo han de descobrir?
*(Cej. I, VII, 255, 1. 4; C–T, 144, 1. 21)*

PIENSAS *ABCD*E?
PENSI N
temes Stemmas III and IV + PUV + Amar. + O

The words on Graph 87 appear in a speech by Elicia directed to Areúsa in the latter's home:

—Cata que creo que, avnque llame *el que* mandas, no aurá effecto lo que quieres, . . .
*(Cej. II, XV, 153, 11. 3–4 [142, 1. 13]; C–T, 253, 1. 28)*

AL QUE *E?*F? + Stemma IV + Amar. + O
el que HIJPUV
ancor ch'io faccia uenir qua Sosia, non hauera effecto N

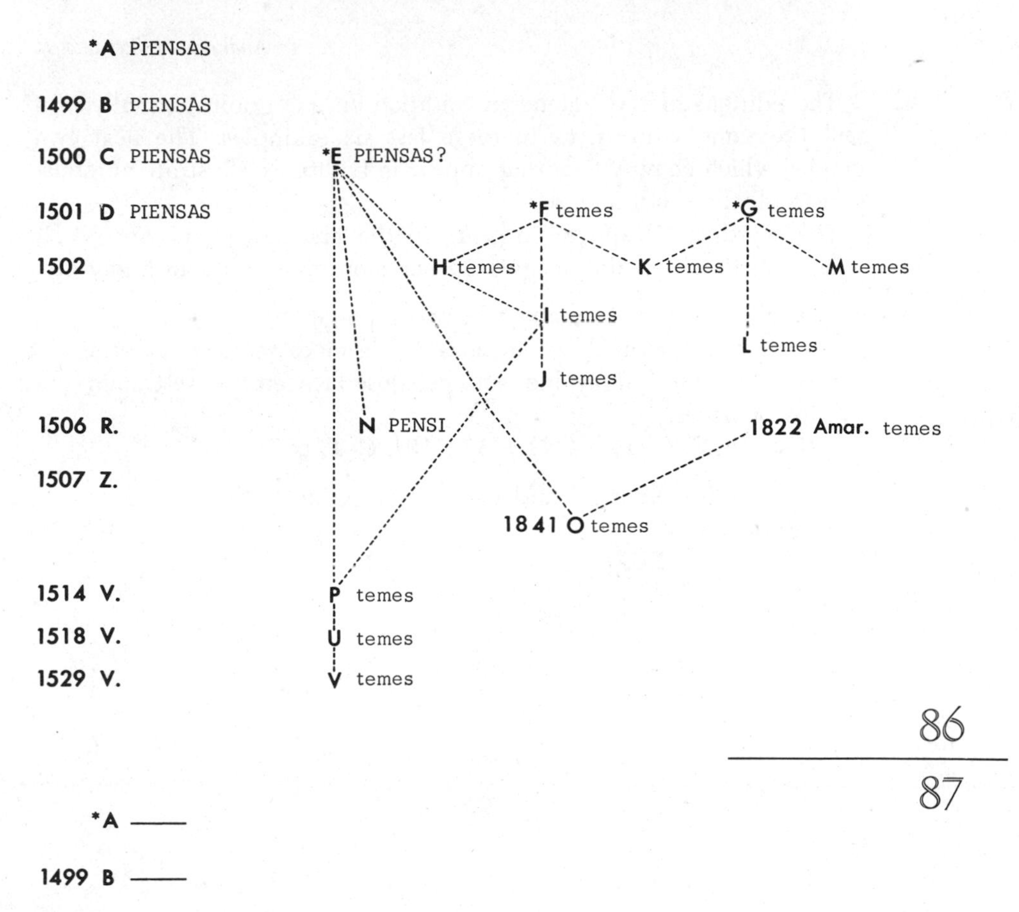
*A PIENSAS
1499 B PIENSAS
1500 C PIENSAS
1501 D PIENSAS
1502
*E PIENSAS?
*F temes
*G temes
H temes
K temes
M temes
I temes
L temes
J temes
1506 R.
N PENSI
1822 Amar. temes
1507 Z.
1841 O temes
1514 V.
P temes
1518 V.
U temes
1529 V.
V temes

86

87

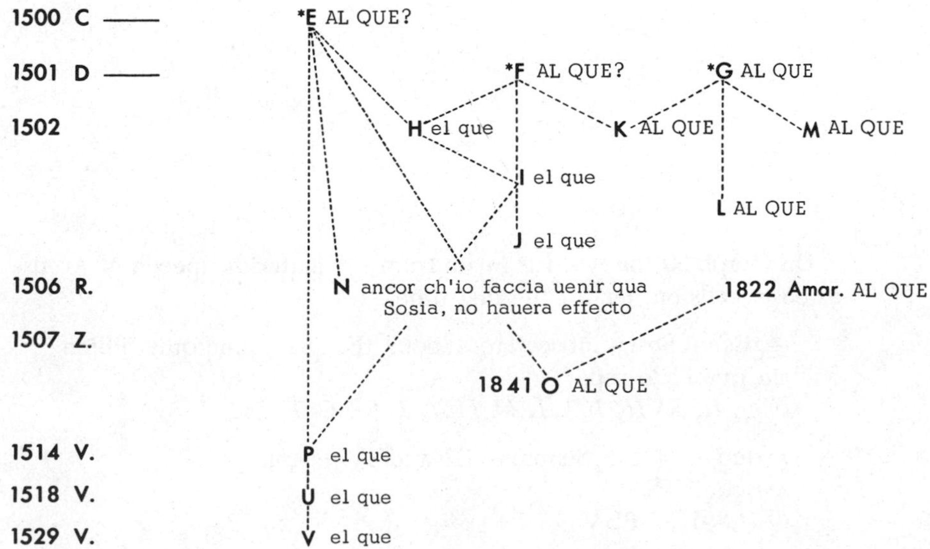
*A ——
1499 B ——
1500 C ——
1501 D ——
1502
*E AL QUE?
*F AL QUE?
*G AL QUE
H el que
K AL QUE
M AL QUE
I el que
L AL QUE
J el que
1506 R.
N ancor ch'io faccia uenir qua
Sosia, no hauera effecto
1822 Amar. AL QUE
1507 Z.
1841 O AL QUE
1514 V.
P el que
1518 V.
U el que
1529 V.
V el que

The editions of the Valencian tradition on our graph normally present the same witness, as in these last six examples. The next two graphs, which show words that appear in additions, illustrate an omission in all three editions.

The word on Graph 88 appears in the first speech in Act XVII, where Elicia is deciding to give up her mourning and lead a gay life.

> . . . viendo que los atauíos hazen la muger hermosa, avnque no lo sea, tornan de vieja moça é á la moça más. No es otra cosa la color é aluayalde, sino pegajosa LIGA en que se trauan los hombres.
> *(Cej. II, XVII, 167, 1. 11 [155, 1. 9]; C–T, 263, 1. 2)*

LIGA Stemmas III and IV + *E + Amar. + O
UISCHO N
(———) PUV

On Graph 89 the word is taken from the flattering speech of Areúsa as Sosia calls on her for the first time.

> —¿Es mi Sosia, mi secreto AMIGO? ¿El que yo me quiero bien sin que él lo sepa?
> *(Cej. II, XVII, 169, 1. 11 [157, 1. 8]; C–T, 264, 1. 5)*

AMIGO *E + Stemmas III and IV + Amar. + O
AMICO N
(———) PUV

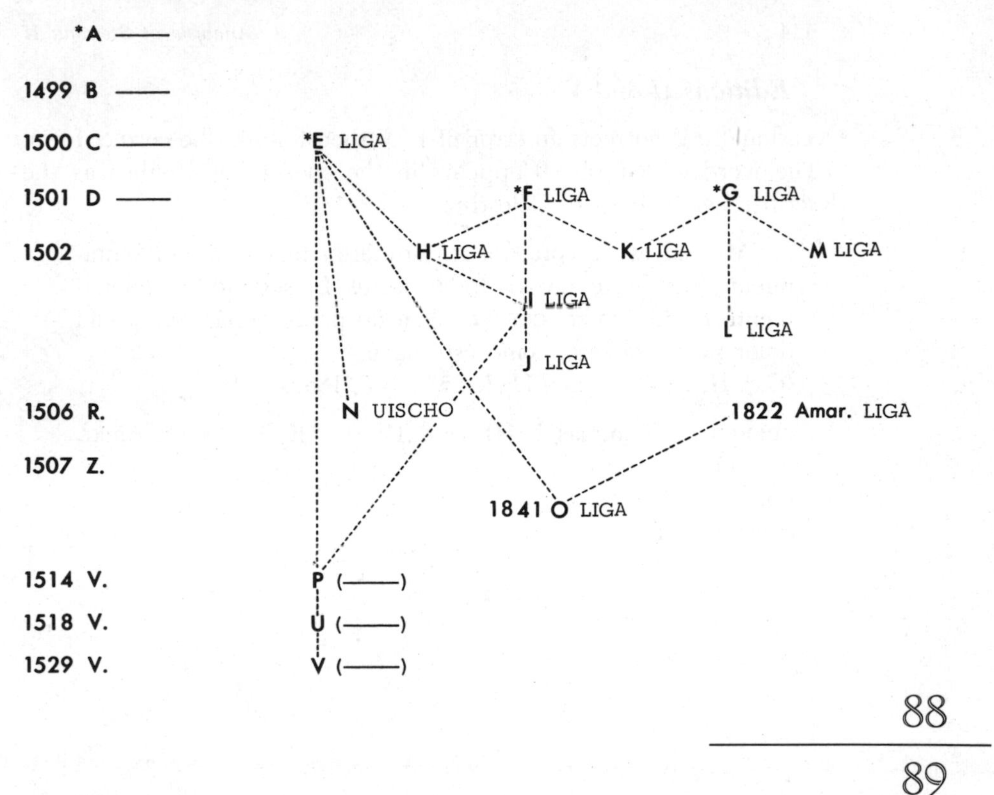

*A
1499 B
1500 C
1501 D
1502
1506 R.
1507 Z.
1514 V.
1518 V.
1529 V.
*E LIGA
*F LIGA
*G LIGA
H LIGA
K LIGA
M LIGA
I LIGA
L LIGA
J LIGA
N UISCHO
1822 Amar. LIGA
1841 O LIGA
P (——)
U (——)
V (——)


88

89

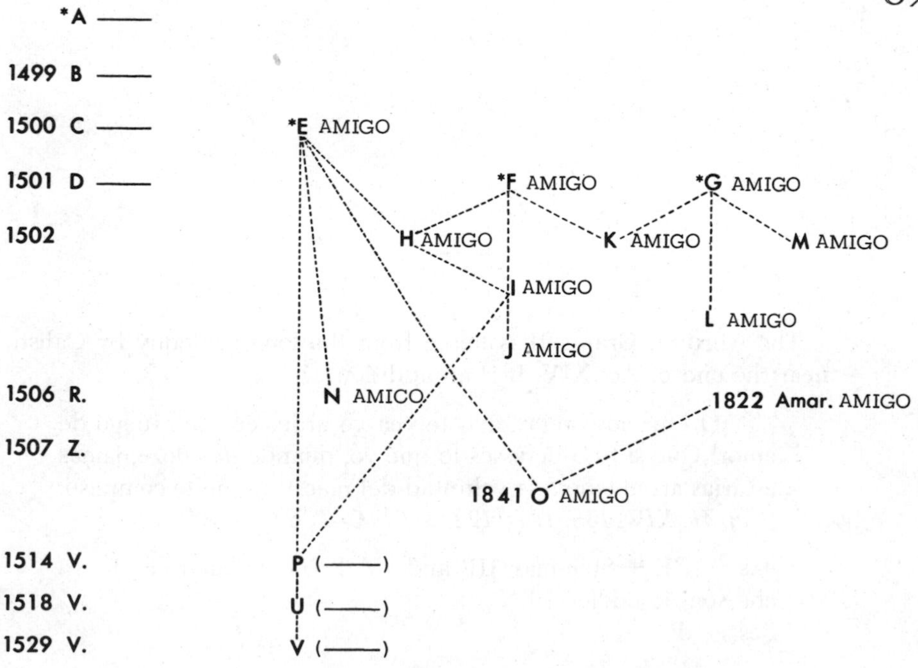

*A
1499 B
1500 C
1501 D
1502
1506 R.
1507 Z.
1514 V.
1518 V.
1529 V.
*E AMIGO
*F AMIGO
*G AMIGO
H AMIGO
K AMIGO
M AMIGO
I AMIGO
L AMIGO
J AMIGO
N AMICO
1822 Amar. AMIGO
1841 O AMIGO
P (——)
U (——)
V (——)

### *Editions U and V*

Occasionally U corrects an error of P. V then follows the correct form.
The word on Graph 90 appears in the speech by Melibea as she describes her feelings to Celestina.

> . . . Mi mal es de coraçón, la ysquierda teta es su aposentamiento, tiende sus rayos á todas partes. Lo segundo, es nueuamente nacido en mi CUERPO. Que no pensé jamás que podía dolor priuar el seso, como éste haze.
> *(Cej. II, X, 57, 1. 27 [54, 1. 25]; C–T, 185, 1. 14)*

CUERPO Stemmas I, III, and IV + *E + UV + Amar. + O
CORPO N
cuerdo P

The word on Graph 91 is taken from the long soliloquy by Calisto near the end of Act XIV. It is an addition.

> ' ' ' ¡O espacioso relox, avn te vea yo arder en biuo fuęgo de amor! Que si tú esperasses lo que yo, quando *des* doze, jamás estarías arrendado á la voluntad del maestro, que te compuso.
> *(Cej. II, XIV, 138, 1. 7 [128, 1. 6]; C–T, 243, 1. 35)*

DAS *E + Stemmas III and IV + UV + Amar. + O
che soni le dodici N
des P

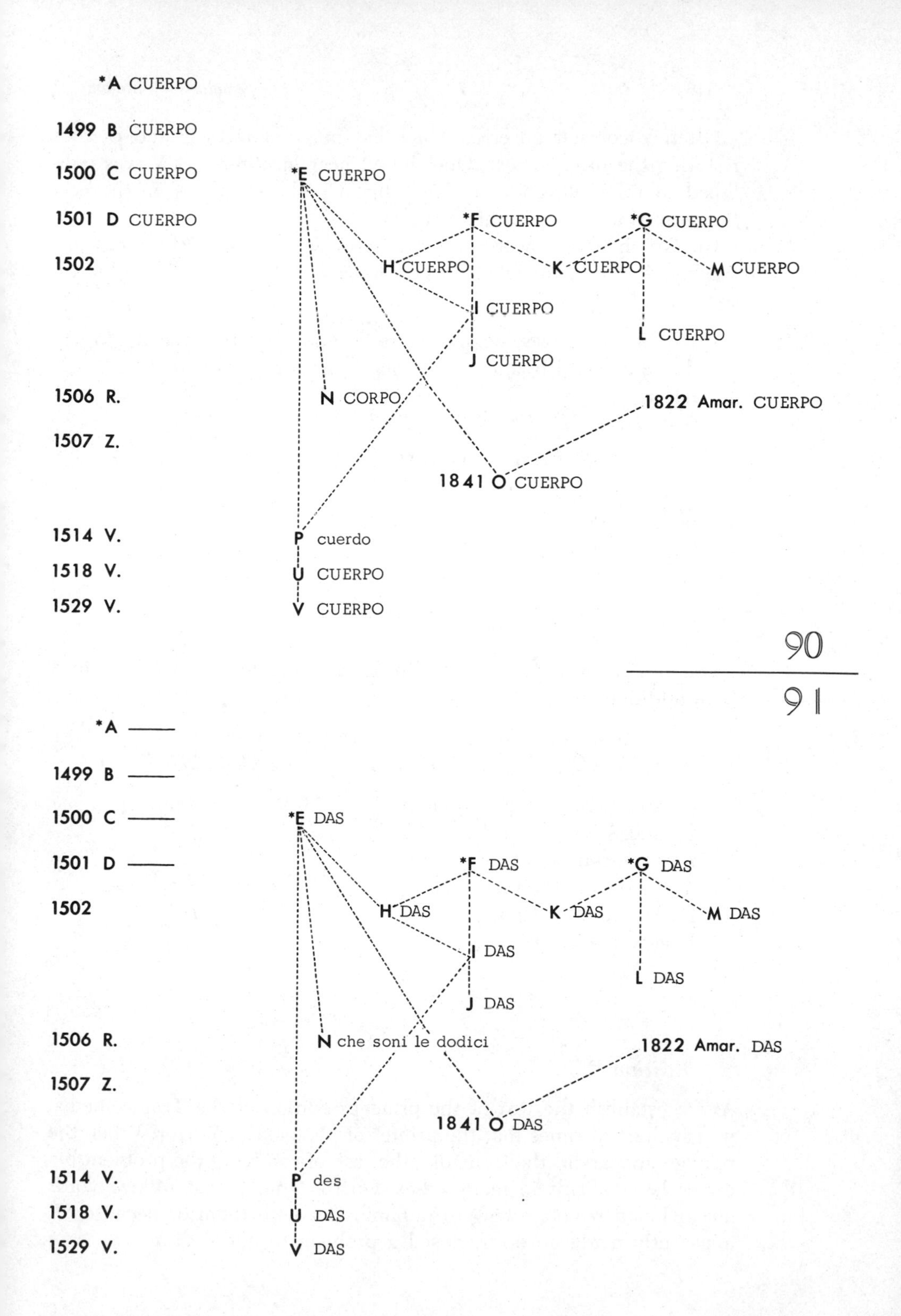
*A CUERPO
1499 B CUERPO
1500 C CUERPO
*E CUERPO
1501 D CUERPO
*F CUERPO
*G CUERPO
1502
H CUERPO
K CUERPO
M CUERPO
I CUERPO
L CUERPO
J CUERPO
1506 R.
N CORPO
1822 Amar. CUERPO
1507 Z.
1841 O CUERPO
1514 V.
P cuerdo
1518 V.
U CUERPO
1529 V.
V CUERPO
90
91
*A ——
1499 B ——
1500 C ——
*E DAS
1501 D ——
*F DAS
*G DAS
1502
H DAS
K DAS
M DAS
I DAS
L DAS
J DAS
1506 R.
N che soni le dodici
1822 Amar. DAS
1507 Z.
1841 O DAS
1514 V.
P des
1518 V.
U DAS
1529 V.
V DAS

Often V corrects an error which has been made by P and U, thus restoring the original text. One should bear in mind that V was published in 1529, eleven years later than U. The examples on the next two graphs are typographical errors.

On Graph 92 the word is taken from an addition. Elicia has just thanked Centurio for what he says he is willing to do. The latter answers:

> —¿Offrescer DIZES, señora? Yo te juro por el sancto martilogio de pe á pa, el braço me tiembla de lo que por ella entiendo hazer, . . .
> *(Cej. II, XVIII, 180, 1. 11 [167, 1. 4]; C–T, 271, 1. 21)*

DIZES *E*FHIJ*GLM + V (K falta)
DICES Amar. + O
di tu N
diez PU

Graph 93 shows the witnesses in the Argumento of Act XIX, which is an addition.

> . . . la qual salida fué causa que sus días PERESCIESSEN, . . .
> *(Cej. II, XIX, 187, 1. 12 [173, 11. 11–12]; C–T, 275, 1. 10)*

PERESCIESSEN *E + Stemma III + *GM (K falta)
PERECIESSEN L + V?
paresciessen PU
& fine de suoi giorni N
fenesciesen Amar.
feneciesen O

### *Edition *E*

As we establish the text of the princeps edition of the Tragicomedia, we conclude at times that the printer of *E makes an error. When the passage appears in the Comedia, the task of resolving the problem becomes less difficult in many cases. On the graphs that follow words are included which, owing to unfamiliarity with them or because *E apparently made an error, posed a problem to later editors.

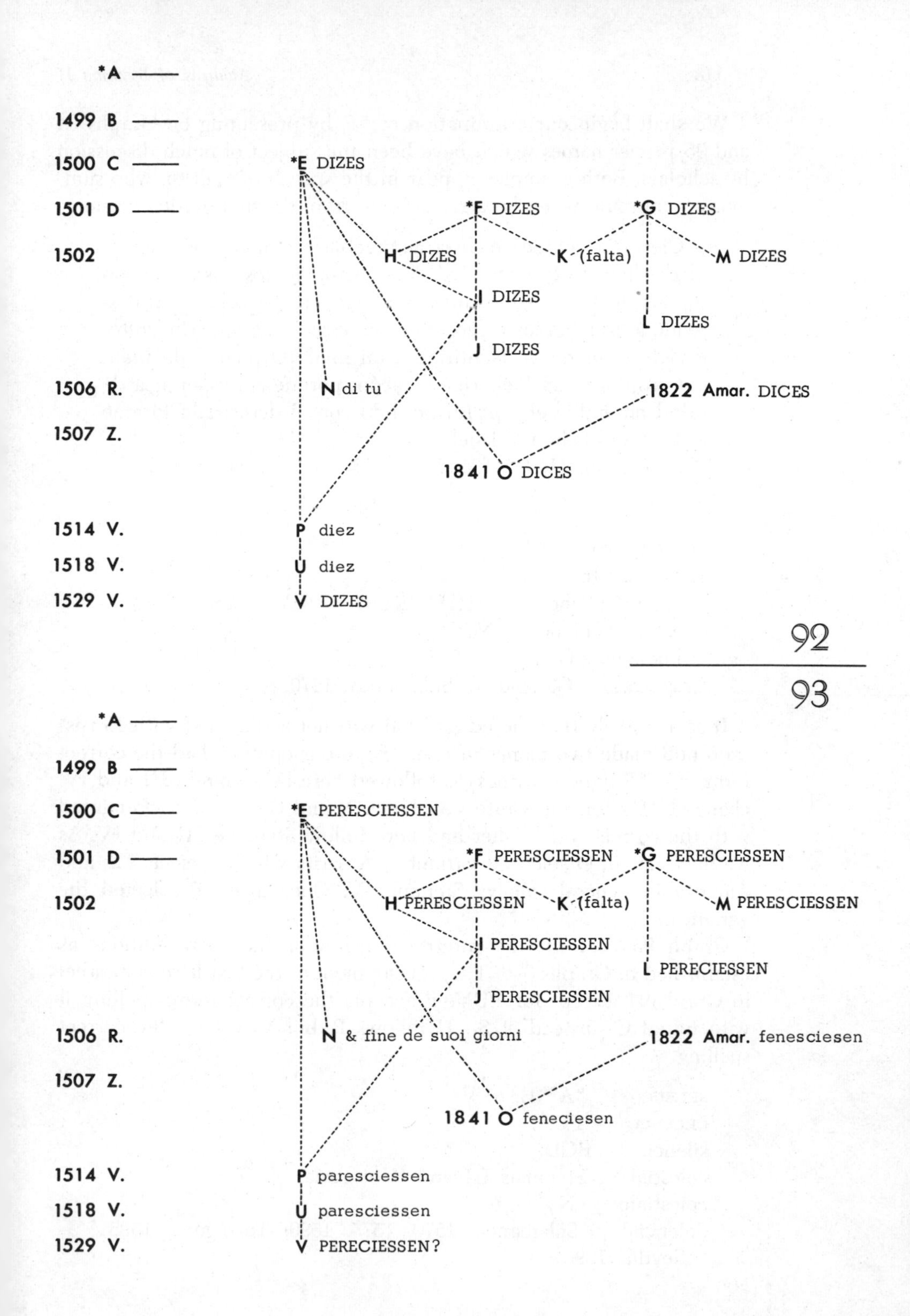

*A
1499 B
1500 C
1501 D
1502
1506 R.
1507 Z.
1514 V.
1518 V.
1529 V.
*E DIZES
*F DIZES
*G DIZES
H DIZES
K (falta)
M DIZES
I DIZES
L DIZES
J DIZES
N di tu
1822 Amar. DICES
1841 O DICES
P diez
U diez
V DIZES
92
93
*A
1499 B
1500 C
1501 D
1502
1506 R.
1507 Z.
1514 V.
1518 V.
1529 V.
*E PERESCIESSEN
*F PERESCIESSEN
*G PERESCIESSEN
H PERESCIESSEN
K (falta)
M PERESCIESSEN
I PERESCIESSEN
L PERECIESSEN
J PERESCIESSEN
N & fine de suoi giorni
1822 Amar. fenesciesen
1841 O feneciesen
P paresciessen
U paresciessen
V PERECIESSEN?

We shall begin our examination of *E by presenting on Graphs 94 and 95 proper names which have been the subject of much discussion by scholars. Both examples appear in the speech of Calisto, who summons Sempronio when he arrives home from the first garden scene.

> —Cierra la ventana é dexa la tiniebla acompañar al triste y al desdichado la ceguedad. Mis pensamientos tristes no son dignos de luz. ¡O bienauenturada muerte aquella, que desseada á los afligidos viene! ¡O si viniéssedes agora, *Hipócrates é Galeno,* médicos, ¿sentiríades mi mal? ¡O piedad de *silencio,* inspira en el Plebérico coraçón, porque sin esperança de salud no embie el espíritu perdido con el desastrado Píramo é de la desdichada Tisbe!
> *(Cej. I, I, 36, 11. 1–2 [35–36, 11. 13–1]; C–T, 25, 11. 1–2)*

Graph 94

ERASISTRATO *A?*E?
Eras y Crato BCD
Crato y Galieno *FHIJ*GKLM + PUV + Amar. + O
Creato & Galieno N
Hipócrates y Galeno Cej.
Erasistrato y Galieno Salamanca, 1570

It seems likely that the editor of B was not acquainted with Erasistrato and made two names of one. *E, in our opinion, had the correct form; but *F, whose witness is followed here by Stemmas III and IV, changed *E's form to Crato y Galieno. N and O were not acquainted with the correct form either and here follow Stemmas III and IV. As we have noted, O selects a variant of Amarita when it rejects *E, and Amarita in general follows Stemma IV. Once again P selected the variant of I.

Graph 95 confirms the interrelationship of the early editions as established in Graphs 3–6. The development of the text here is parallel to Graph 94, except for PUV. P accepts the correct form, spelling it with initial C- instead of S-. U follows P, but V restores the correct spelling.

SELEUCO *A?*E? + V
CELEUCO PU
silencio BCD
celestial Stemmas III and IV + Amar. + O
celestiale N
Seleucial Salamanca, 1570, 1575, 1590; Tarragona, 1595; Sevilla, 1596

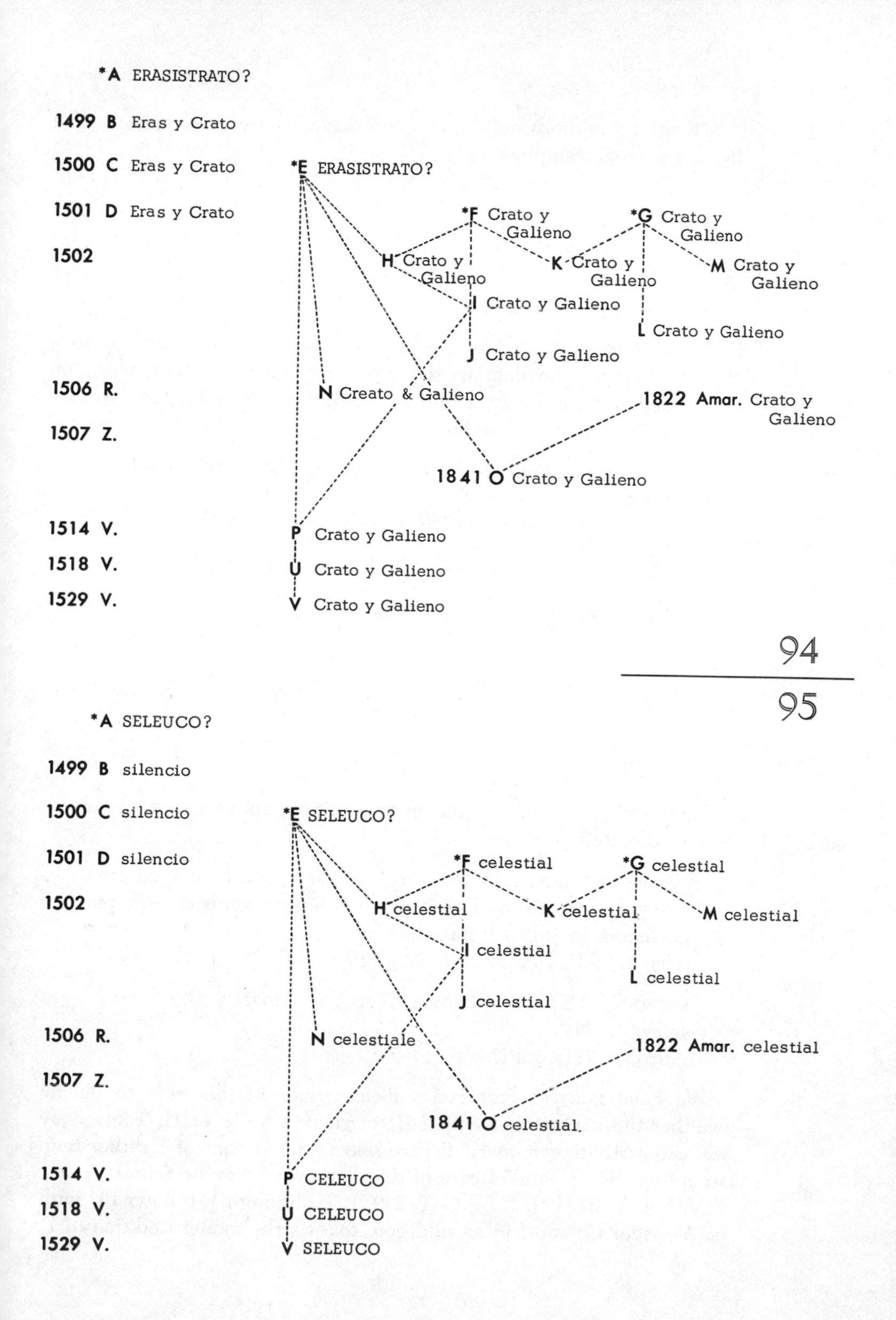
*A ERASISTRATO?
1499 B Eras y Crato
1500 C Eras y Crato
1501 D Eras y Crato
1502
*E ERASISTRATO?
*F Crato y Galieno
*G Crato y Galieno
H Crato y Galieno
K Crato y Galieno
M Crato y Galieno
I Crato y Galieno
L Crato y Galieno
J Crato y Galieno
1506 R.
N Creato & Galieno
1822 Amar. Crato y Galieno
1507 Z.
1841 O Crato y Galieno
1514 V.
P Crato y Galieno
1518 V.
U Crato y Galieno
1529 V.
V Crato y Galieno
94
95
*A SELEUCO?
1499 B silencio
1500 C silencio
1501 D silencio
*E SELEUCO?
*F celestial
*G celestial
1502
H celestial
K celestial
M celestial
I celestial
L celestial
J celestial
1506 R.
N celestiale
1822 Amar. celestial
1507 Z.
1841 O celestial.
1514 V.
P CELEUCO
1518 V.
U CELEUCO
1529 V.
V SELEUCO

A few later editions not on the graph have been included above. The list is far from complete.

The next two graphs illustrate that at times P prefers initial ç- to s, thus supporting the data in the preceding summary. The word on Graph 96 appears in an addition, when Sosia is informing Areúsa about Calisto's visits to Melibea.

> . . . Ni menos auía de yr cada noche, que aquel officio no *çufre* cotidiana visitación.
> *(Cej. II, XVI, 173, l. 9 [160, l. 24]; C–T, 266, l. 7)*

SUFRE *E + Stemmas III and IV + Amar. + O
patisce N
çufre PUV

The word on Graph 97, also in an addition, appears in a speech by Areúsa directed to Elicia.

> . . . no te fatigues tú tanto, que cegarás llorando. Que creo que poca ventaja me lleuas en sentimiento y verás con quanta paciencia lo *çuffro* y passo.
> *(Cej. II, XV, 148, l. 19 [138, l. 10]; C–T, 251, l. 19)*

SUFRO *E*F? + Stemma IV + V + Amar. + O
soffro N
çufro HIJ + PU

We have not yet gathered sufficient data in this case to decide whether the variant in Stemma III originated in *F or H. Tentatively we are attributing it to H. P here selects the variant of I rather than accepting *E. A parallel case of the same word may be found in Cej., XIV, 144, l. 10 (134, l. 5); C–T, 249, l. 7, although V follows PU with ç-. As usual Cejador, in an addition, follows the modern edition of P.

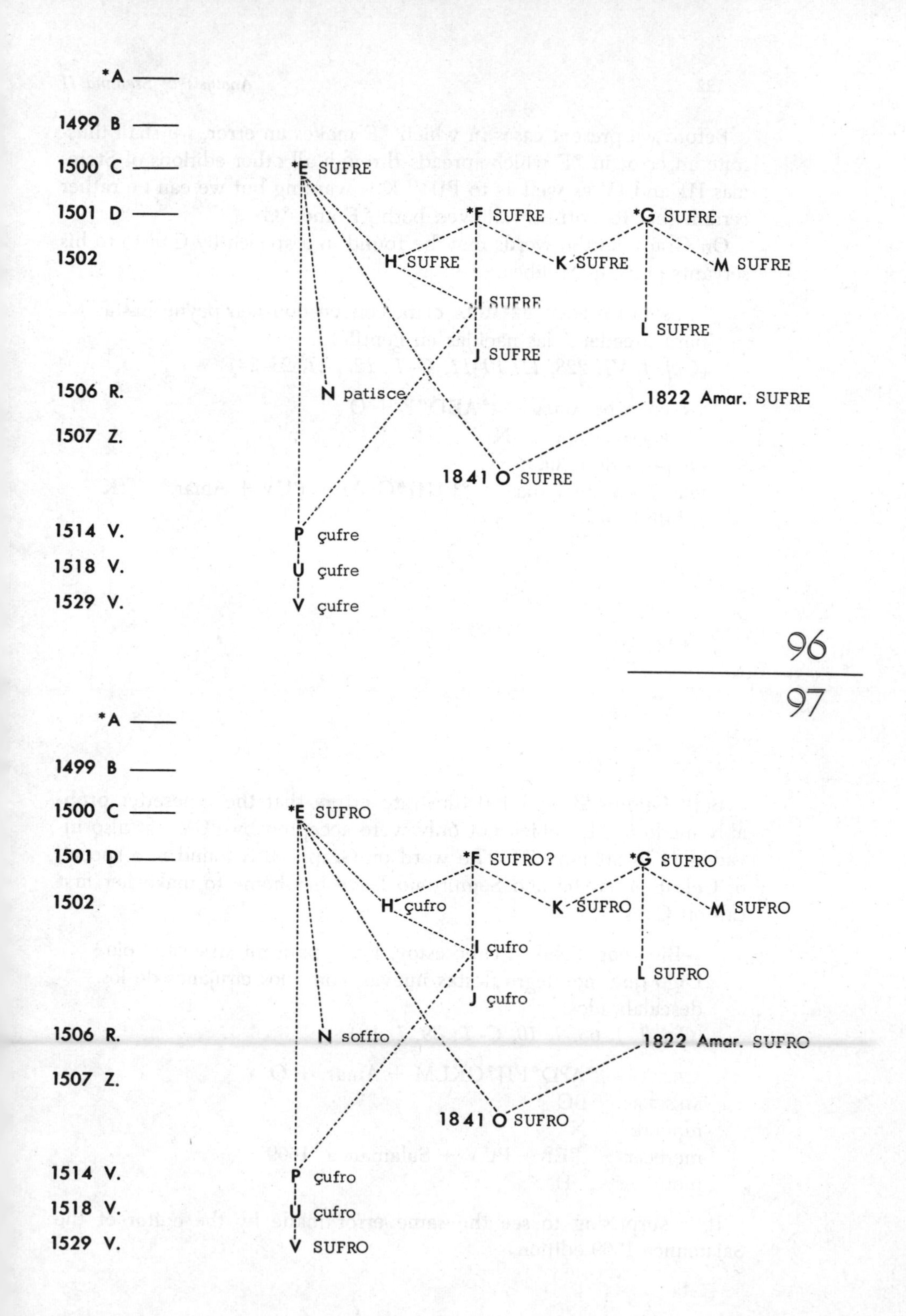
*A
1499 B
1500 C
1501 D
1502
1506 R.
1507 Z.
1514 V.
1518 V.
1529 V.
*E SUFRE
*F SUFRE
*G SUFRE
H SUFRE
K SUFRE
M SUFRE
I SUFRE
L SUFRE
J SUFRE
N patisce
1822 Amar. SUFRE
1841 O SUFRE
P çufre
U çufre
V çufre
96
97
*A
1499 B
1500 C
1501 D
1502
1506 R.
1507 Z.
1514 V.
1518 V.
1529 V.
*E SUFRO
*F SUFRO?
*G SUFRO
H çufro
K SUFRO
M SUFRO
I çufro
L SUFRO
J çufro
N soffro
1822 Amar. SUFRO
1841 O SUFRO
P çufro
U çufro
V SUFRO

Before we present cases in which *E makes an error, we shall illustrate an error in *F which spreads through all other editions of Stemmas III and IV as well as to PUV. K is wanting but we can be rather certain that its witness followed both *F and *G.

On Graph 98 the words may be found in a speech by Calisto to his servants praising Melibea.

> . . . solo VN POCO DE AGUA clara con vn eburneo peyne basta para exceder á las nacidas en gentileza.
> *(Cej. I, VI, 228, 11. 10–11; C–T, 127, 11. 23–24)*

VN POCO DE AGUA *ABD*E + O
UN POCO DAQUA N
en poco de agua C
vna poca de agua *FHIJ*GLM + PUV + Amar. (K falta)

Both Graphs 99 and 100 illustrate errors that the typesetter probably made in *E, which not only were accepted by PUV but also invaded H in Stemma III. The word on Graph 99 is found in a speech of Celestina as she and Sempronio leave her home to make her first call on Calisto.

> —Bien has dicho, al cabo estoy. Basta para mí MESCER el ojo. Digo que me alegro destas nuevas, como los cirujanos de los descalabrados.
> *(Cej. I, I, 65, 1. 10; C–T, 39, 1. 18)*

MECER *A?D*FIJ*GKLM + Amar. + O
MESCER BC
mouere N
merecer *E? + PUV + Salamanca, 1569
merescer H

It is surprising to see the same error made by the editor of the Salamanca 1569 edition.

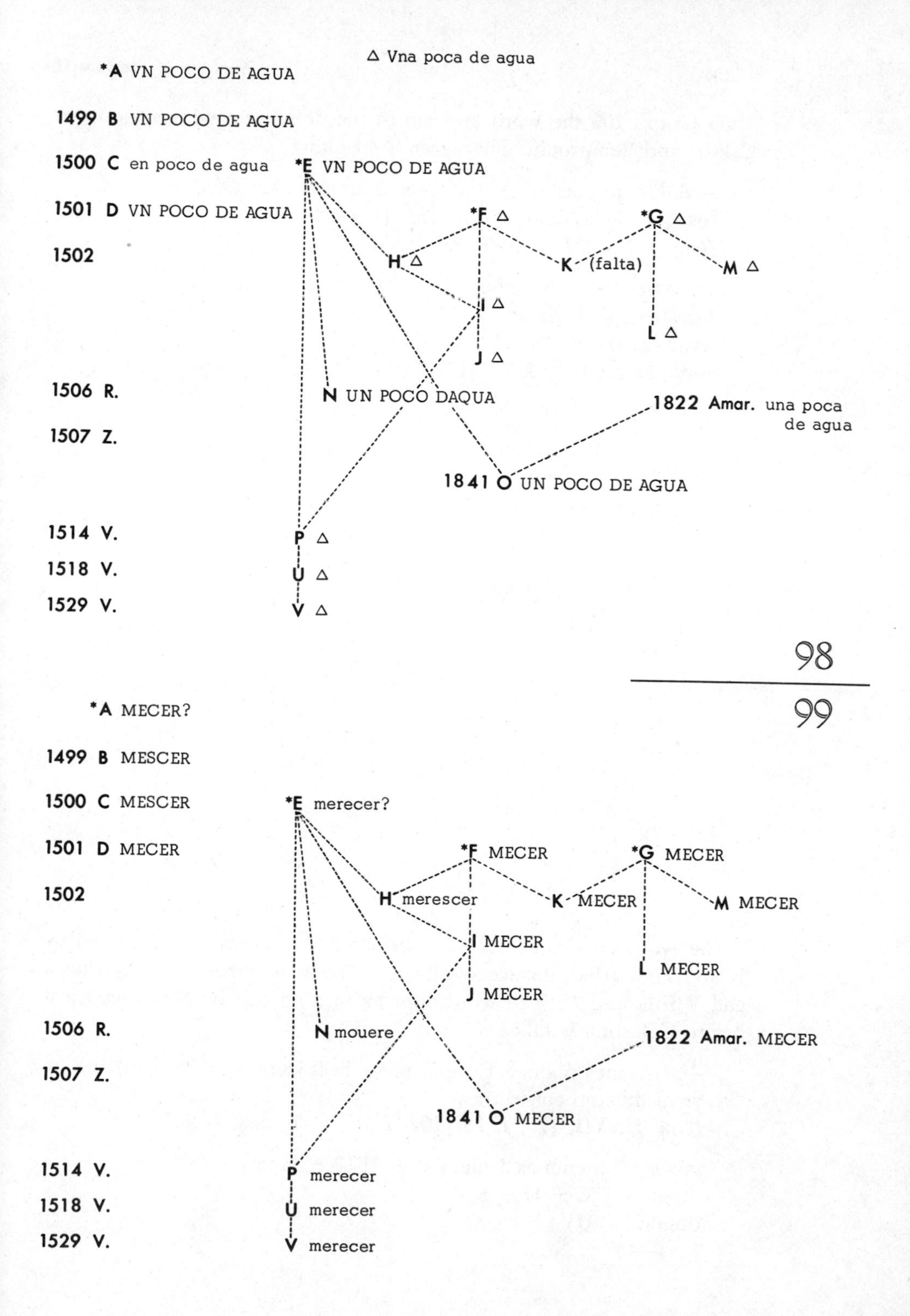
△ Vna poca de agua
*A VN POCO DE AGUA
1499 B VN POCO DE AGUA
1500 C en poco de agua
*E VN POCO DE AGUA
1501 D VN POCO DE AGUA
*F △
*G △
1502
H △
K (falta)
M △
I △
L △
J △
1506 R.
N UN POCO DAQUA
1822 Amar. una poca de agua
1507 Z.
1841 O UN POCO DE AGUA
1514 V.
P △
1518 V.
U △
1529 V.
V △
98
99
*A MECER?
1499 B MESCER
1500 C MESCER
*E merecer?
1501 D MECER
*F MECER
*G MECER
1502
H merescer
K MECER
M MECER
I MECER
L MECER
J MECER
1506 R.
N mouere
1822 Amar. MECER
1507 Z.
1841 O MECER
1514 V.
P merecer
1518 V.
U merecer
1529 V.
V merecer

On Graph 100 the word appears in the debate on women between Calisto and Sempronio. The latter is speaking.

> —A los que las vencieron querría que REMEDASSES, que no á los que dellas fueron vencidos. Huye de sus engaños.
> *(Cej. I, I, 51, 1. 4; C–T, 31, 1. 23)*

| | |
|---|---|
| REMEDASSES | Stemma I + *FIJ + Stemma IV |
| REMEDASES | Amar. + O |
| assimigliassi | N |
| remediasses | *E? + H + PUV |

The word on Graph 101 is an error of *E, which was accepted by H and P. U tried, unsuccessfully, to correct the error by using *dueña* and V followed U. The word appears in a speech by Sempronio just before Celestina is killed.

> —¿Rufianes ó qué? Esperá, DOÑA hechizera, que yo te haré yr al infierno con cartas.
> *(Cej. II, XII, 110, 1. 25 [104, 1. 3]; C–T, 225, 1. 20)*

| | |
|---|---|
| DOÑA | Stemmas I and IV + *FIJ + Amar. + O |
| duna | *E + H + P |
| dueña | UV |
| (———) | N |

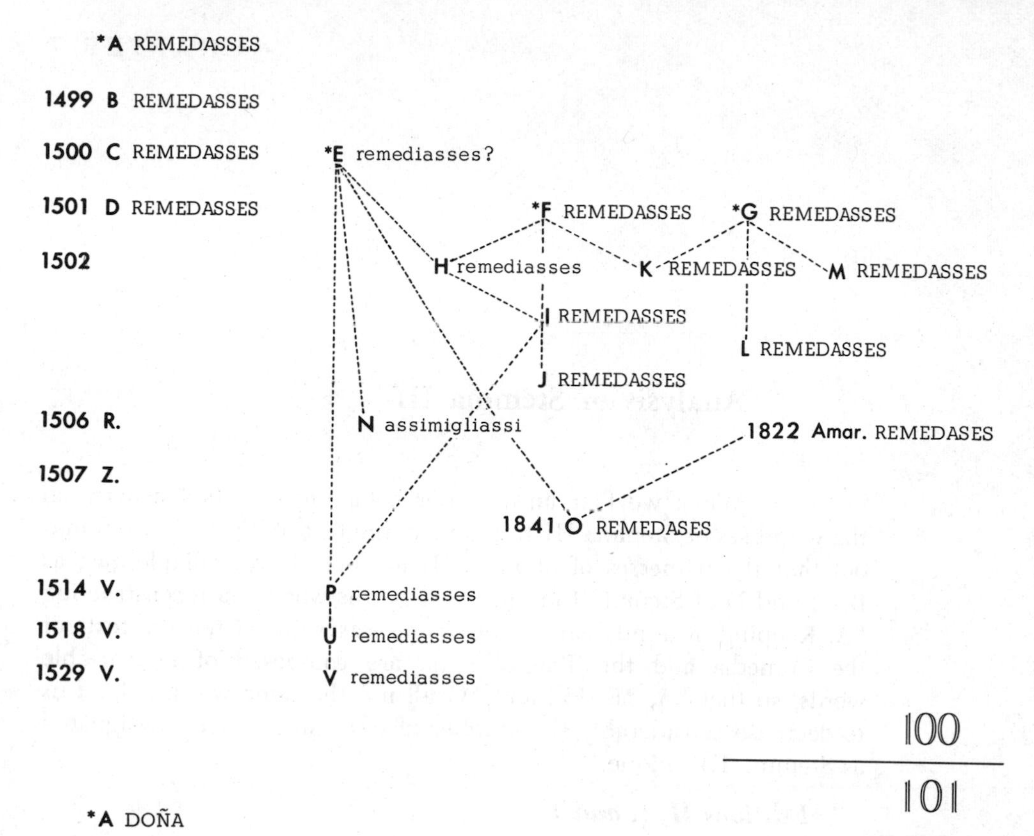
*A REMEDASSES
1499 B REMEDASSES
1500 C REMEDASSES
*E remediasses?
1501 D REMEDASSES
*F REMEDASSES
*G REMEDASSES
1502
H remediasses
K REMEDASSES
M REMEDASSES
I REMEDASSES
L REMEDASSES
J REMEDASSES
1506 R.
N assimigliassi
1822 Amar. REMEDASES
1507 Z.
1841 O REMEDASES
1514 V.
P remediasses
1518 V.
U remediasses
1529 V.
V remediasses





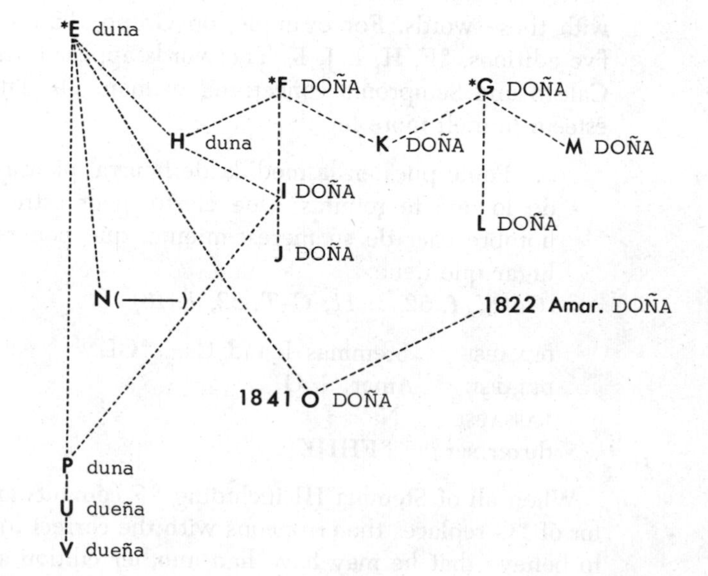
*A DOÑA
1499 B DOÑA
1500 C DOÑA
*E duna
1501 D DOÑA
*F DOÑA
*G DOÑA
1502
H duna
K DOÑA
M DOÑA
I DOÑA
L DOÑA
J DOÑA
1506 R.
N(——)
1822 Amar. DOÑA
1507 Z.
1841 O DOÑA
1514 V.
P duna
1518 V.
U dueña
1529 V.
V dueña

CHAPTER 7

# Analysis of Stemma III

When we first finished our collation we relied heavily on the witnesses of Stemma III to establish the text of *F. Soon we found out that the witnesses of Stemma III are not always reliable, just as B, C, and D of Stemma I are not always trustworthy in reconstructing *A. Keeping in mind that in about nine cases out of ten the texts of the Comedia and the Tragicomedia are composed of nonvariable words, so that *A, *E, *F, and *G all use the same word, helped us to decrease considerably the number of cases we formerly designated as Stemma III unique.

### *Editions H, I, and J*

However, when the group HIJ of Stemma III and K of Stemma IV have the same word or words, we normally establish the text of *F with these words. For example, on Graph 102 an error occurs in all five editions, *F, H, I, J, K. The words appear in the debate between Calisto and Sempronio concerning women. The latter tells Calisto to esteem himself more highly.

> . . . Ponte pues en la medida de honrra, piensa ser más digno de lo que te reputas. Que cierto, peor estremo es DEXARSE hombre caer de su merescimiento, que ponerse en más alto lugar que deue.
> *(Cej. I, I, 52, 1. 11; C–T, 32, 1. 16)*

| | |
|---|---|
| DEXARSE | Stemmas I and II + *GLM |
| DEJARSE | Amar. + O |
| LASSARSE | N |
| dexar ser | *FHIJK |

When all of Stemma III including *F commits an error but the editor of *G replaces the erroneous with the correct form, it seems logical to believe that he may have had another edition at hand besides *F.

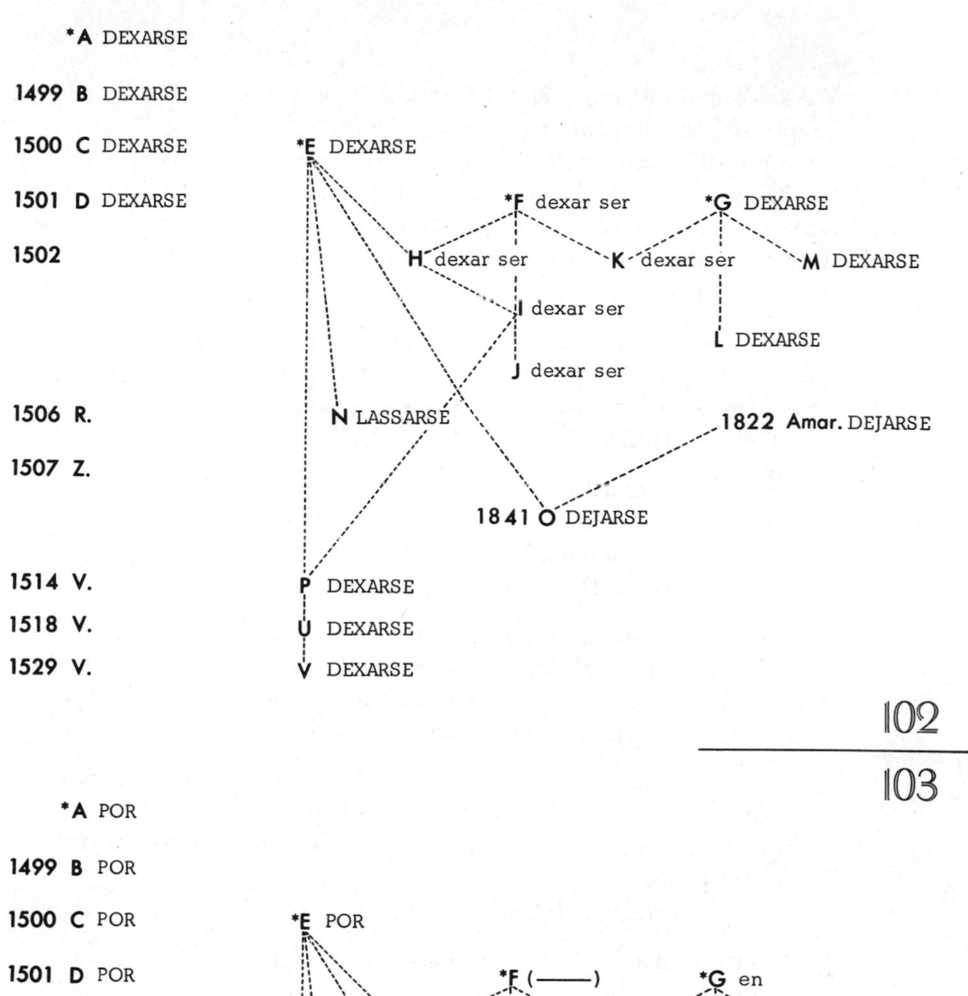


102

---

103

*A POR

1499 B POR

1500 C POR

1501 D POR

1502

1506 R.

1507 Z.

1514 V.

1518 V.

1529 V.

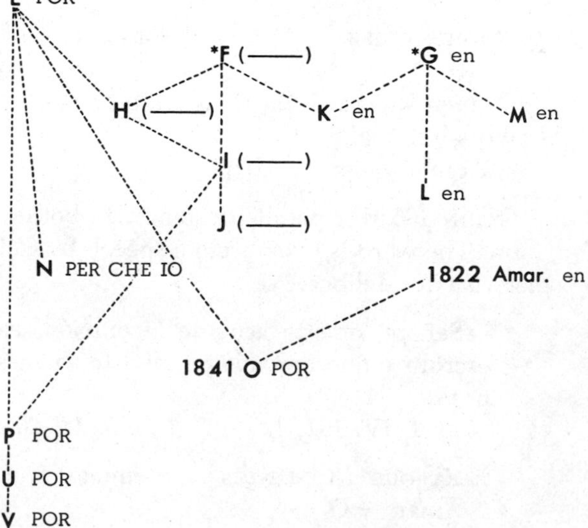

We shall find out more about Stemma IV in the next chapter, but on Graph 102 this appears to be true.

Graph 103 would indicate that *G either did not have any edition but *F or, if he did have another, decided to reject the witness and replace it with a variant of his own. The word appears in a speech where Celestina suggests to Pármeno that he should have a girl just as Sempronio has.

> —E avnque lo viua [engañada], no me pena mucho, que también lo hago por amor de Dios é POR verte solo en tierra agena é más por aquellos huessos de quien te me encomendó.
> *(Cej. I, VII, 236, 1. 23; C–T, 133, 1. 27)*

POR Stemmas I and II + O
PER CHE IO N
(———) Stemma III
en Stemma IV + Amar.

Graph 104 illustrates the problem of the source of the error in Stemma III. In this case K does not support the error and we are attributing it to H; it was then accepted in turn by I and by J. The word appears in the Carta in the preliminary materials.

> . . . Ví que no tenía su firma del auctor, el qual, según algunos dizen, fué Juan de Mena, é según otros, Rodrigo Cota; pero QUIEN QUIER que fuesse, es digno de recordable memoria por la sotil inuención, . . .
> *(Cej. I, Carta, 6, 1. 1: C–T, 4, 1. 10)*

QUIEN QUIER *AC + Stemmas II and IV + *F? + Amar. + O
quien quiera D (B falta)
qual si uoglia N
a quien quier HIJ

Graph 105 is a parallel instance; in both cases *G uses the correct form. The word is taken from a speech by Celestina as she leaves after her visit to Melibea.

> —Señora, que te acuerde la oración, PARA QUE LA MANDES escriuir é que aprenda de mí á tener mesura en el tiempo de tu yra, . . .
> *(Cej. I, IV, 191, 1. 10; C–T, 100, 11. 20–21)*

PARA QUE LA MANDES Stemmas I, II, and IV + *F? + Amar. + O

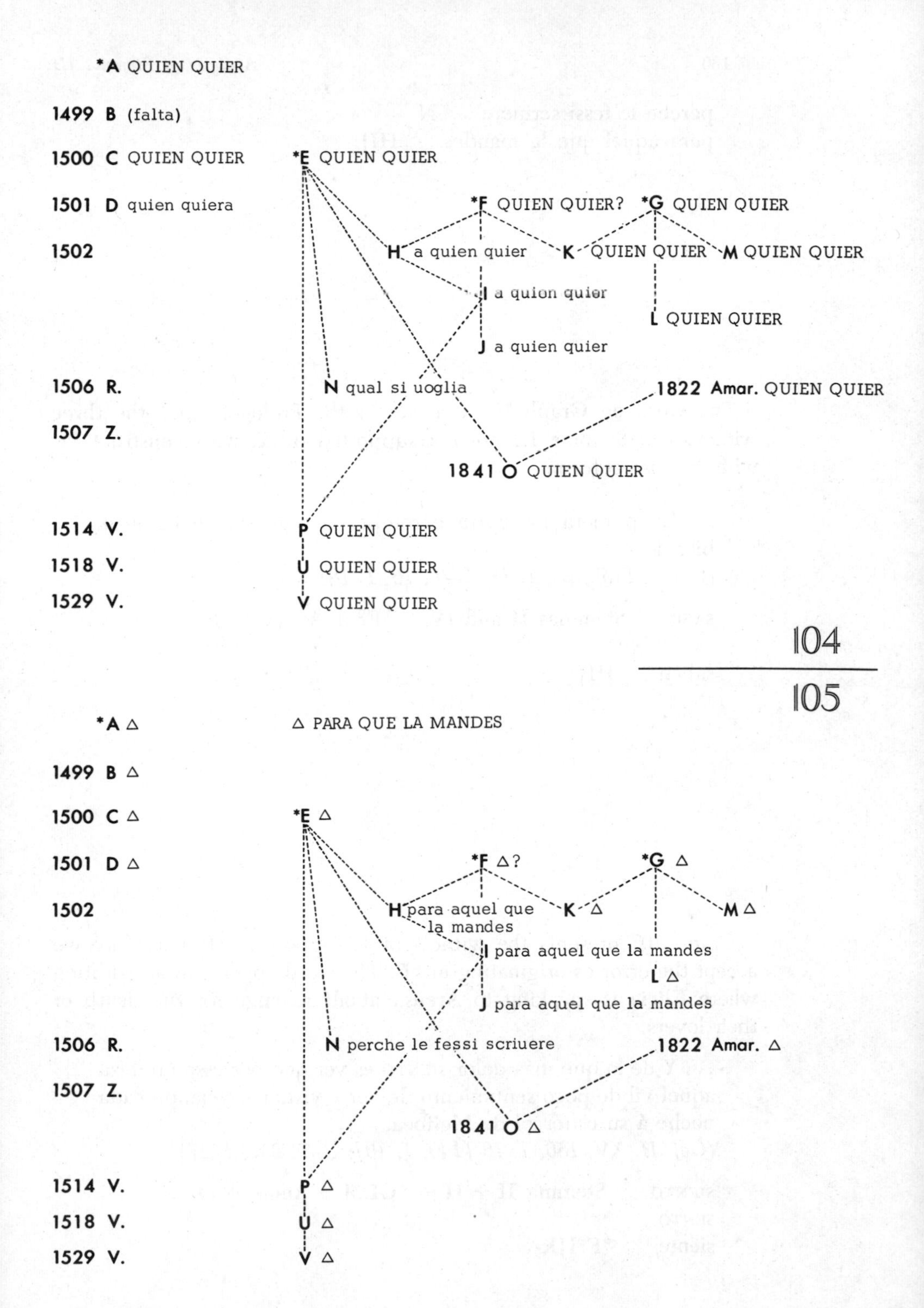
*A QUIEN QUIER
1499 B (falta)
1500 C QUIEN QUIER
*E QUIEN QUIER
1501 D quien quiera
*F QUIEN QUIER?
*G QUIEN QUIER
1502
H a quien quier
K QUIEN QUIER
M QUIEN QUIER
I a quion quier
L QUIEN QUIER
J a quien quier
1506 R.
N qual si uoglia
1822 Amar. QUIEN QUIER
1507 Z.
1841 O QUIEN QUIER
1514 V.
P QUIEN QUIER
1518 V.
U QUIEN QUIER
1529 V.
V QUIEN QUIER
104
105
*A △
△ PARA QUE LA MANDES
1499 B △
1500 C △
*E △
1501 D △
*F △?
*G △
1502
H para aquel que la mandes
K △
M △
I para aquel que la mandes
L △
J para aquel que la mandes
1506 R.
N perche le fessi scriuere
1822 Amar. △
1507 Z.
1841 O △
1514 V.
P △
1518 V.
U △
1529 V.
V △

perche le fessi scriuere N
para aquel que la mandes HIJ

The word on Graph 106 appears in the Prólogo. Since the three witnesses of Stemma III are not supported by K, we reconstruct *F with the correct form.

> . . . La primera los borra é rompe; la segunda no los SABE bien leer.
> *(Cej. I, Pról., 23, 1. 18; C–T, 16, 1. 18)*

SABE Stemmas II and IV + *F? + Amar. + O
SA N
saben HIJ

Graph 107 presents the witness of K supporting IJ. Therefore we accept the error as originating in *F. The word appears in an addition where Elicia is speaking to Areúsa about revenge for the death of their lovers.

> . . . Y de lo que más dolor SIENTO es ver que por esso no dexa aquel vil de poco sentimiento de ver y visitar festejando cada noche á su estiércol de Melibea, . . .
> *(Cej. II, XV, 150, 1. 16 [140, 1. 10]; C–T, 252, 1. 17)*

SIENTO Stemma II + H + *GLM + Amar. + O
SENTO N
siente *F?IJK

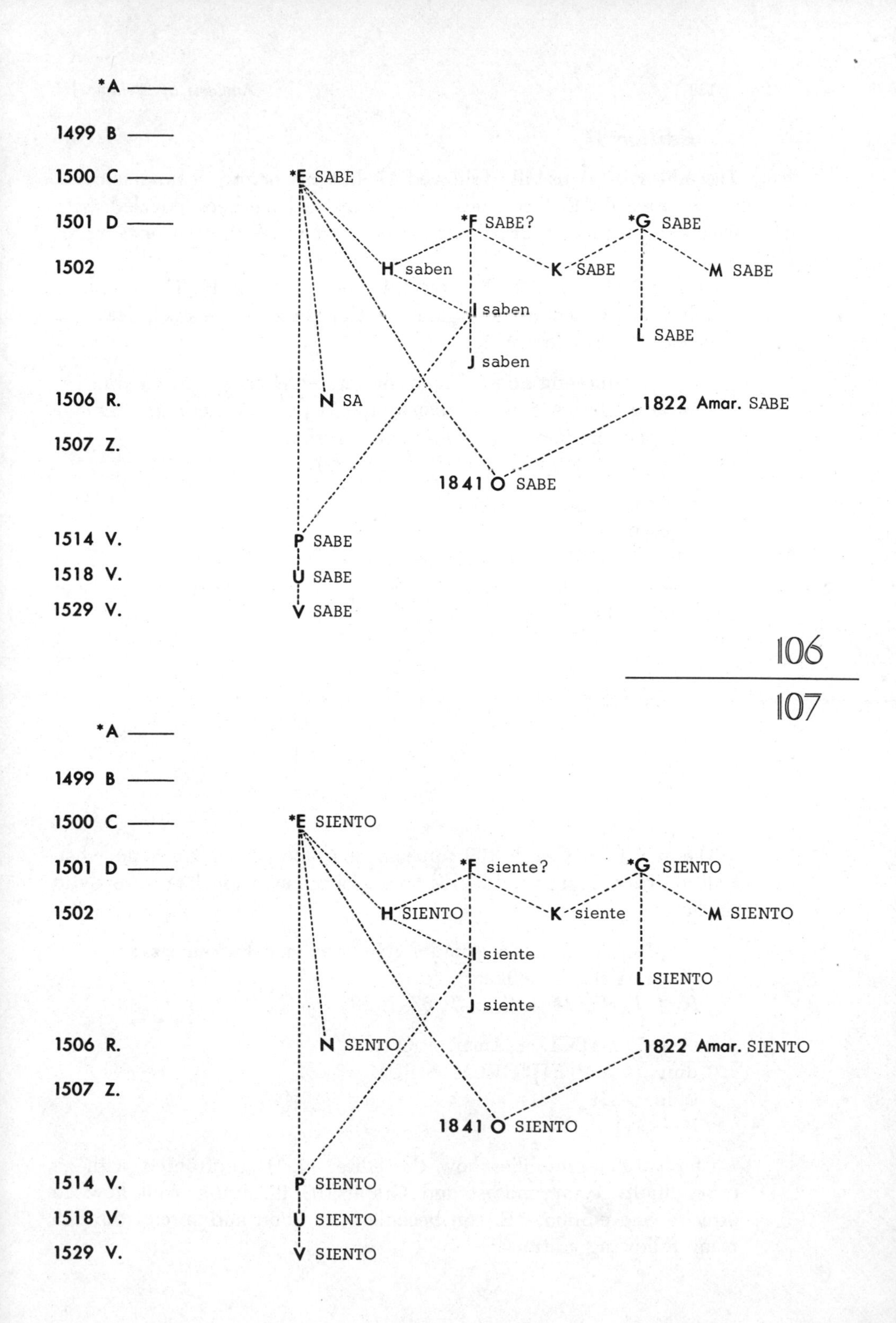
*A
1499 B
1500 C
1501 D
1502
1506 R.
1507 Z.
1514 V.
1518 V.
1529 V.
*E SABE
*F SABE?
*G SABE
H saben
K SABE
M SABE
I saben
L SABE
J saben
N SA
1822 Amar. SABE
1841 O SABE
P SABE
U SABE
V SABE
106
107
*A
1499 B
1500 C
1501 D
1502
1506 R.
1507 Z.
1514 V.
1518 V.
1529 V.
*E SIENTO
*F siente?
*G SIENTO
H SIENTO
K siente
M SIENTO
I siente
L SIENTO
J siente
N SENTO
1822 Amar. SIENTO
1841 O SIENTO
P SIENTO
U SIENTO
V SIENTO

### *Edition H*

The editor of H usually followed *F but from time to time selected the witness of *E. Occasionally he seems to have been puzzled as to which variant to accept, and creates a variant of his own or compromises.

Graphs 108 and 109 illustrate this peculiarity of H. The word on Graph 108 appears in the speech of Celestina as she takes leave of Melibea after her first visit.

> . . . que aprenda de mí á tener mesura en el tiempo de tu yra, en la qual yo vsé lo que SE DIZE: que del ayrado es de apartar por poco tiempo, del enemigo por mucho.
> *(Cej. I, IV, 191, 1. 12; C–T, 100, 1. 22)*

SE DIZE Stemmas I and II
SE DICE N + O
dizen *FIJ + Stemma IV
dicen Amar.
dize H

The word on Graph 109 appears in a speech by Pármeno when Calisto orders him to saddle his horse. Pármeno is speaking directly to the horse.

> . . . ¿Rehincháys, DON cauallo? ¿No basta vn celoso en casa? . . . ¿O barruntás á Melibea?
> *(Cej. I, II, 124, 1. 7; C–T, 67, 1. 26)*

DON *ABCD + Amar. + O
dun *E?*FIJ*GKLM + PUV
duin H
(———) N

Graph 108 exemplifies how the editor of H, confronted with an error, finally compromises; and Graph 109 illustrates well how an error in one edition, *E, can become a tradition and spread through many following editions.

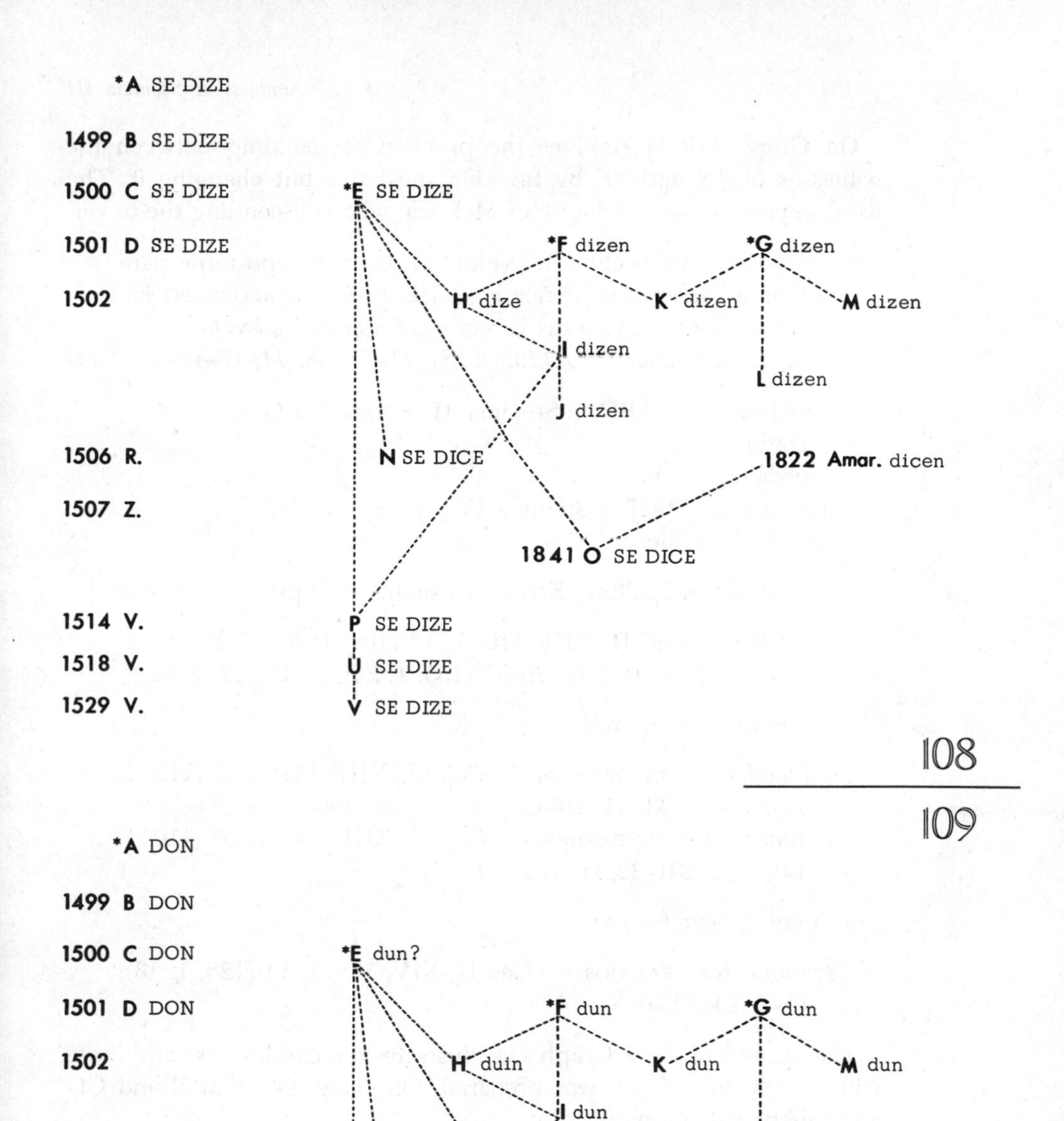


108

109

*A DON
1499 B DON
1500 C DON
1501 D DON
1502
1506 R.
1507 Z.
1514 V.
1518 V.
1529 V.
*E dun?
*F dun
*G dun
H duin
K dun
M dun
I dun
L dun
J dun
N (——)
1822 Amar. DON
1841 O DON
P dun
U dun
V dun

On Graph 110 H resolves the problem of deciding between the witnesses of *E and *F by favoring the latter but changing it. The word appears in the soliloquy of Melibea, who is ascending the tower.

> . . . Todo se ha hecho á mi voluntad. Buen tiempo terné para contar á Pleberio mi señor la causa de mi ya ACORDADO fin. Gran sinrazón hago á sus canas, gran ofensa á su vegez.
> *(Cej. II, XX, 207, l. 11 [192, l. 8]; C–T, 288, ll. 17–18)*

ACORDADO *ABD + Stemma II + Amar. + O
cortado H
acordando C
acortado *FIJ + Stemma IV
mio desiato fine N

H is careless in spelling. Erroneous single -r- is preferred to double:

*boracho*——Cej. II, XIII, 116, l. 12 (108, l. 5); C–T, 230, l. 5 and II, XVII, 167, ll. 26–27 (155, l. 24); C–T, 263, l. 14.

-r- is omitted at times:

*esfoçados* for ESFORÇADOS——Cej. II, XIII, 121, l. 7 (112, l. 17); C–T, 233, ll. 10–11.
*entambos* for ENTRAMBOS——Cej. II, XIII, 118, l. 26 (110, l. 14); C–T, 231–32, ll. 32 and l.

-o- may appear for -A:

*trabojos* for TRABAJOS——Cej. II, XIV, 138, l. 14 (128, l. 13); C–T, 244, l. 6.

The witness of H on Graph 111 illustrates the carelessness and haste with which this edition was prepared. One may note that B and CD also misspelled the word.

The word is taken from Pleberio's lament as he addresses the World:

> . . . me pareces vn LABERINTO de errores, . . .
> *(Cej. II, XXI, 219, l. 9 [204, l. 5]; C–T, 296, l. 22)*

LABERINTO *A + Stemmas II and IV + *FIJ + Amar. + N + O
labarinto B
laborinto CD
labernito H

Cejador does not follow B.

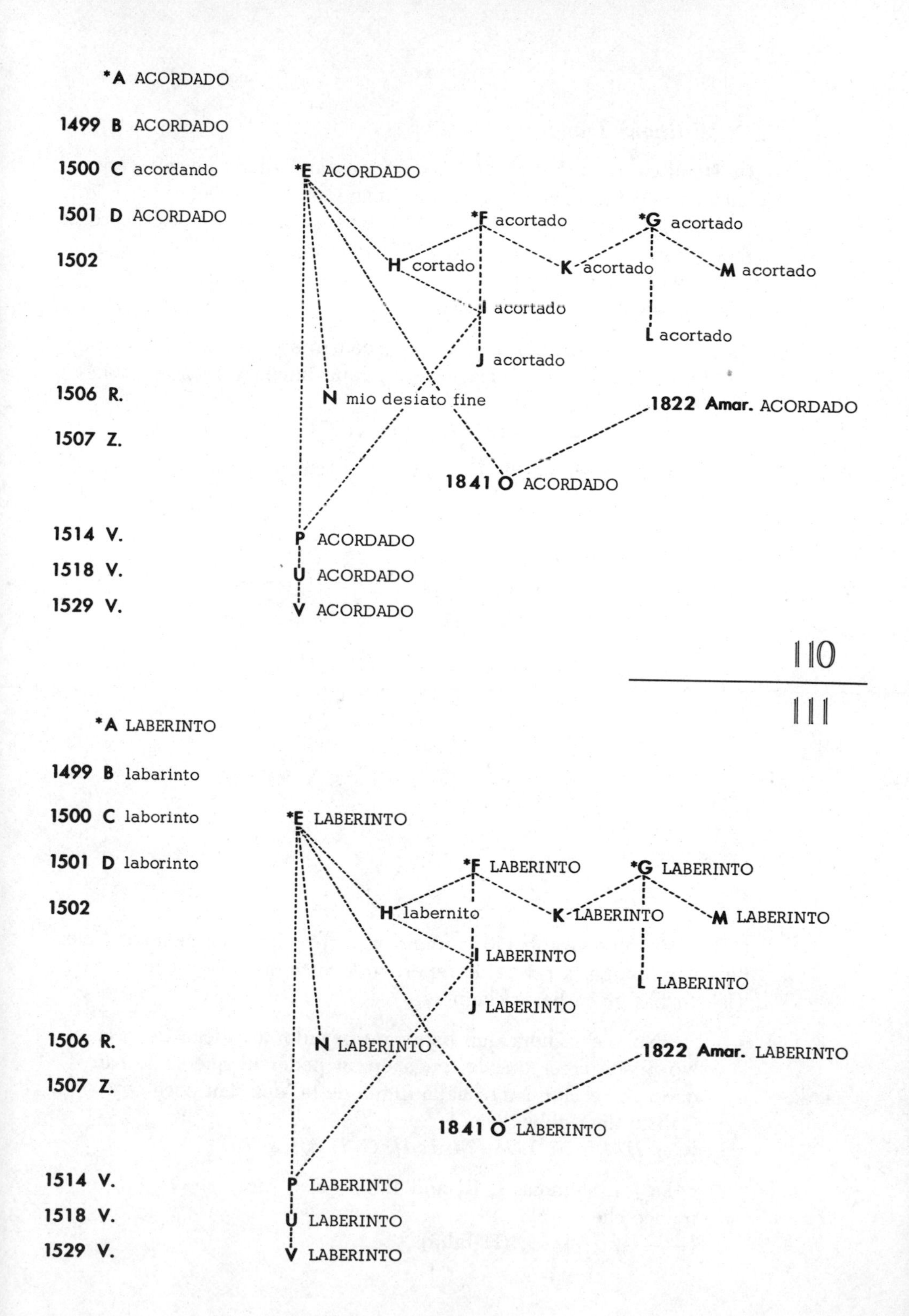
*A ACORDADO
1499 B ACORDADO
1500 C acordando
1501 D ACORDADO
1502
*E ACORDADO
*F acortado
*G acortado
H cortado
K acortado
M acortado
I acortado
L acortado
J acortado
1506 R.
N mio desiato fine
1822 Amar. ACORDADO
1507 Z.
1841 O ACORDADO
1514 V.
P ACORDADO
1518 V.
U ACORDADO
1529 V.
V ACORDADO
110
111
*A LABERINTO
1499 B labarinto
1500 C laborinto
1501 D laborinto
1502
*E LABERINTO
*F LABERINTO
*G LABERINTO
H labernito
K LABERINTO
M LABERINTO
I LABERINTO
L LABERINTO
J LABERINTO
1506 R.
N LABERINTO
1822 Amar. LABERINTO
1507 Z.
1841 O LABERINTO
1514 V.
P LABERINTO
1518 V.
U LABERINTO
1529 V.
V LABERINTO

### *Editions I and J*

In Stemma III, although H is capricious and therefore not very reliable, I and J have more errors, and many of these seem to be unique to this pair. On Graphs 112 and 113 the fate of *como* in the hands of the editors or printers of I and J is illustrated.

The word on Graph 112 appears in the speech by Areúsa as Celestina and Pármeno arrive to visit her.

> —¡Válala el diablo á esta vieja, con qué viene COMO huestantigua á tal hora! Tía, señora, ¿qué buena venida es ésta tan tarde?
> *(Cej. I, VII, 247, 1. 12; C–T, 139, 1. 27)*

COMO Stemmas I, II, and IV + *FH + Amar. + N + O
coma IJ

The word on Graph 113 is found in a speech by Pármeno as Celestina has brought a favorable report to Calisto on her visit to Melibea. Calisto has given her a chain.

> . . . No vee la hora que hauer despegado la cadena de casa. No puede creer que la tenga en su poder ni que se la han dado de verdad. No se halla digna de tal don, tan poco COMO Calisto de Melibea.
> *(Cej. II, XI, 77, 1. 18 [74, 1. 4]; C–T, 201, 1. 16)*

COMO Stemmas I, II, and IV + *F + Amar. + O
manco che N
(———) IJ (H falta)

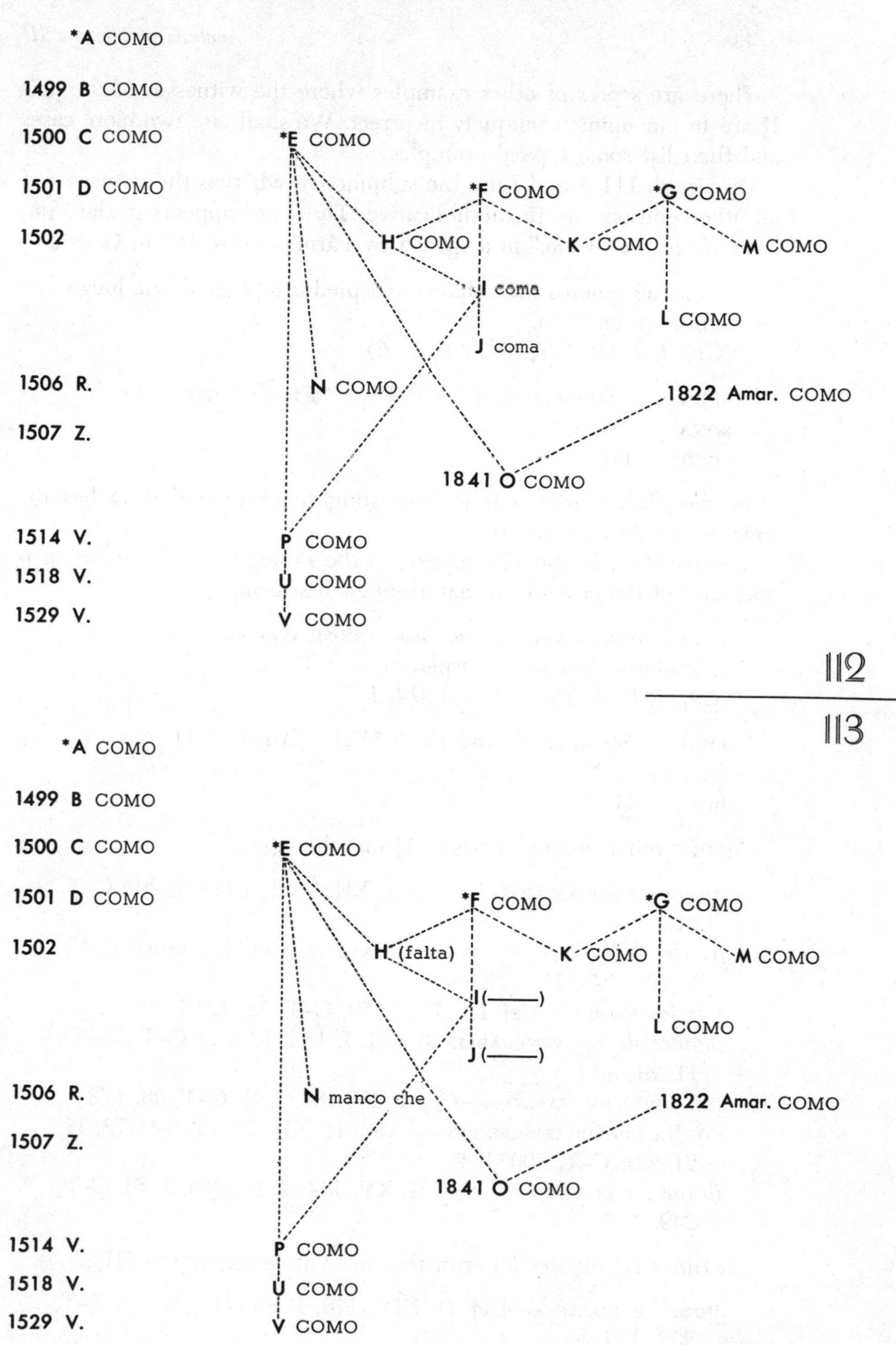
*A COMO
1499 B COMO
1500 C COMO
1501 D COMO
1502
1506 R.
1507 Z.
1514 V.
1518 V.
1529 V.
*E COMO
*F COMO
*G COMO
H COMO
K COMO
M COMO
I coma
J coma
L COMO
N COMO
1822 Amar. COMO
1841 O COMO
P COMO
U COMO
V COMO
112
113
*A COMO
1499 B COMO
1500 C COMO
1501 D COMO
1502
1506 R.
1507 Z.
1514 V.
1518 V.
1529 V.
*E COMO
*F COMO
*G COMO
H (falta)
K COMO
M COMO
I (——)
J (——)
L COMO
N manco che
1822 Amar. COMO
1841 O COMO
P COMO
U COMO
V COMO

There are scores of other examples where the witnesses of the pair IJ are in our opinion uniquely incorrect. We shall cite two more cases and then list some typical examples.

On Graph 114, I and J use the subjunctive whereas the witnesses of all other editions are in the indicative. The word appears in the "*Sinfonía de la puta vieja*," in a speech by Pármeno directed to Calisto.

> . . . ¿Qué quieres más, sino si vna piedra topa con otra, luego SUENA ¿puta vieja?
> *(Cej. I, I, 69, 1. 7; C–T, 41, 1. 6)*

SUENA Stemmas I, II, and IV + *FH + Amar. + O
SONA N
suene IJ

In the above citation it is interesting to observe that D has the unique variant *toca* for TOPA.

The word on Graph 115 appears in the Prólogo where the author is speaking of the cruelties of nature in each season.

> . . . El verano vemos que nos aquexa con calor demasiado, el inuierno con FRÍO y aspereza: . . .
> *(Cej. I, Pról., 18, 1. 2; C–T, 14, 1. 7)*

FRÍO Stemmas II and IV + *FH + Amar. + O
FREDDO N
firio IJ

Among other unique errors of IJ may be cited:

*animosos* for ÁNIMOS——Cej. II, XII, 98, 1. 1 (91, 1. 20); C–T, 216, 1. 8
*os de defendays* for OS DEFENDAYS——Cej. I, Acrostics, 13, 1. 12; C–T, 11, 1. 2
*por* for PEOR——Cej. I, I, 52, 1. 10; C–T, 32, 1. 15
*venecable* for VENERABLE——Cej. I, I, 111, 1. 2; C–T, 58–59, 11. 29 and 1
*tan tanto* for TANTO——Cej. I, IV, 187, 1. 2; C–T, 98, 1. 8
*confession* for CONCESSION——Cej. II, XII, 76, 11. 8–9 (72, 11. 21–22); C–T, 200, 1. 20
*llorar* for LLORARÁ——Cej. II, XV, 144, 1. 10 (134, 1. 5); C–T, 249, 1. 7

At times H initiates an error that has witnesses only in HIJ:

*goza* for GOZAR——Cej. II, XIV, 126, 1. 28 (117, 1. 20); C–T, 238, 1. 1

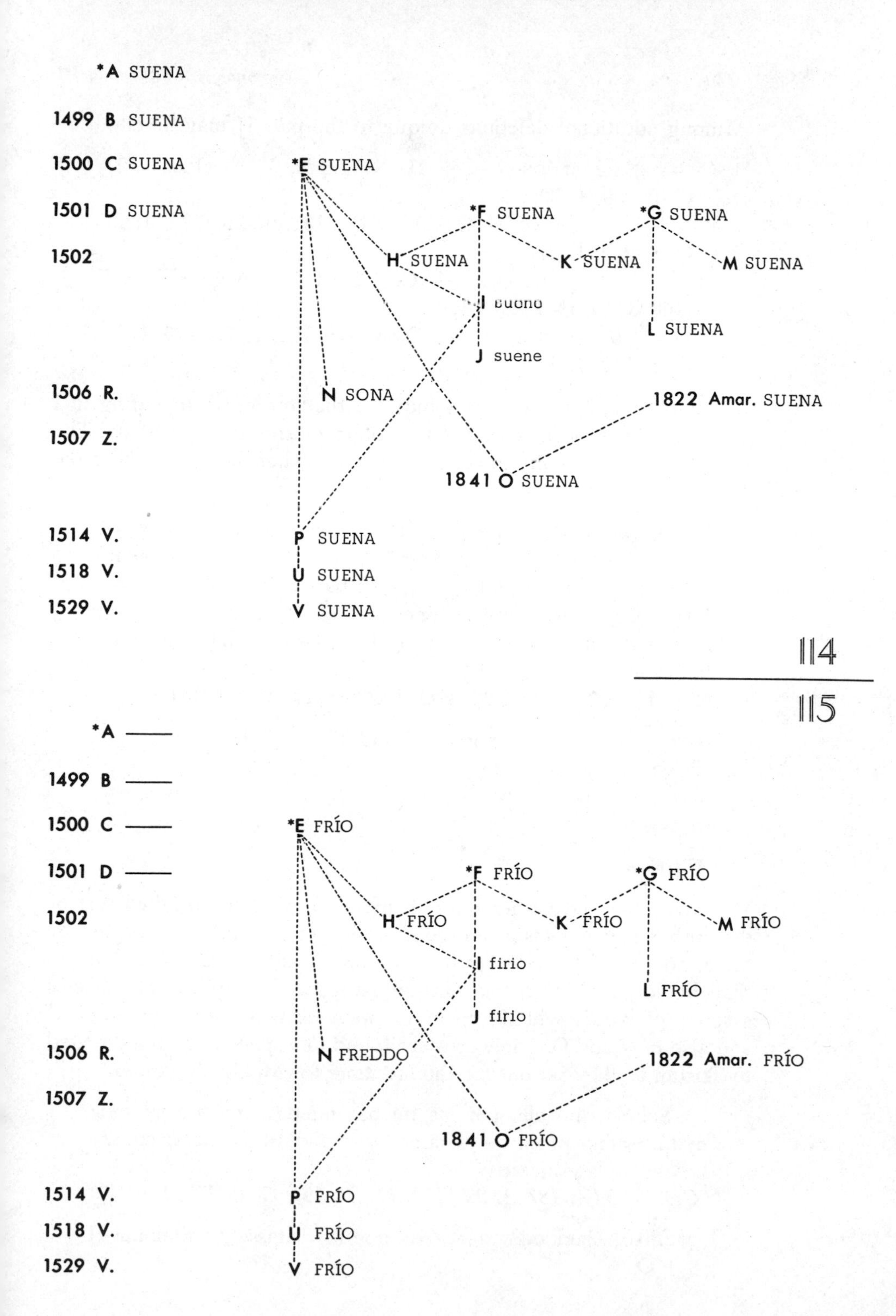
*A SUENA
1499 B SUENA
1500 C SUENA
*E SUENA
1501 D SUENA
*F SUENA
*G SUENA
1502
H SUENA
K SUENA
M SUENA
I buono
L SUENA
J suene
1506 R.
N SONA
1822 Amar. SUENA
1507 Z.
1841 O SUENA
1514 V.
P SUENA
1518 V.
U SUENA
1529 V.
V SUENA
114
115
*A ——
1499 B ——
1500 C ——
*E FRÍO
1501 D ——
*F FRÍO
*G FRÍO
1502
H FRÍO
K FRÍO
M FRÍO
I firio
L FRÍO
J firio
1506 R.
N FREDDO
1822 Amar. FRÍO
1507 Z.
1841 O FRÍO
1514 V.
P FRÍO
1518 V.
U FRÍO
1529 V.
V FRÍO

Among additional deletions unique to the pair IJ may be cited:

(———) for SEÑOR——Cej. II, XIV, 129, 1. 10 (120, 1. 1); C–T, 239, 1. 20
(———) for OGAÑO——Cej. II, XIV, 131, 1. 20 (122, 1. 2); C–T, 240, 1. 21
el (———) for EL QUAL——Cej. II, XVIII, Arg., 177, 1. 7 (164, 1. 7); C–T, 269, 1. 5
(———) for SEÑORA——Cej. II, XVIII, 178, 1. 11 (165, 1. 7); C–T, 270, 1. 17

On Graph 116 the witnesses indicate that the error appearing in I and J may have been committed by other editors independently. The word is taken from the lament of Pleberio when he is attacking the World.

> ... yo por triste esperiencia lo contaré, como á quien las ventas é compras de tu engañosa feria no prósperamente sucedieron, como aquel, que mucho ha fasta agora callado tus falsas propiedades, por no encender con odio tu yra, porque no me SECASSES sin tiempo esta flor, que este día echaste de tu poder.
> *(Cej. II, XXI, 218, 1. 26 [203, 1. 20]; C–T, 296, 1. 15)*

SECASSES *A + Stemmas II and IV + *FH
SECASES Amar. + O
NON MI SECASSI N
sacasses BCDIJ

### *Edition *F*

We have observed earlier that *F often changes the original text of the author and creates a new form which many times is accepted by the editors of all the editions in Stemmas III and IV. Graph 117 shows that the editor of *F, either through haplography or purposely, deletes a series of words which appear in previous witnesses of Stemma II and also in N and O. The words are found in a speech of Sosia directed to Tristán as they set out for the last time for Melibea's garden.

> ... Sabrás que ella por las buenas nueuas, que de mí auía oydo, estaua presa de mi amor y EMBIÓME Á ELICIA, ROGÁNDOME que la visitasse.
> *(Cej. II, XIX, 187, 1. 22 [173, 11. 21–22]; C–T, 276, 1. 6)*

EMBIÓME Á ELICIA, ROGÁNDOME que la visitasse Stemma II + O

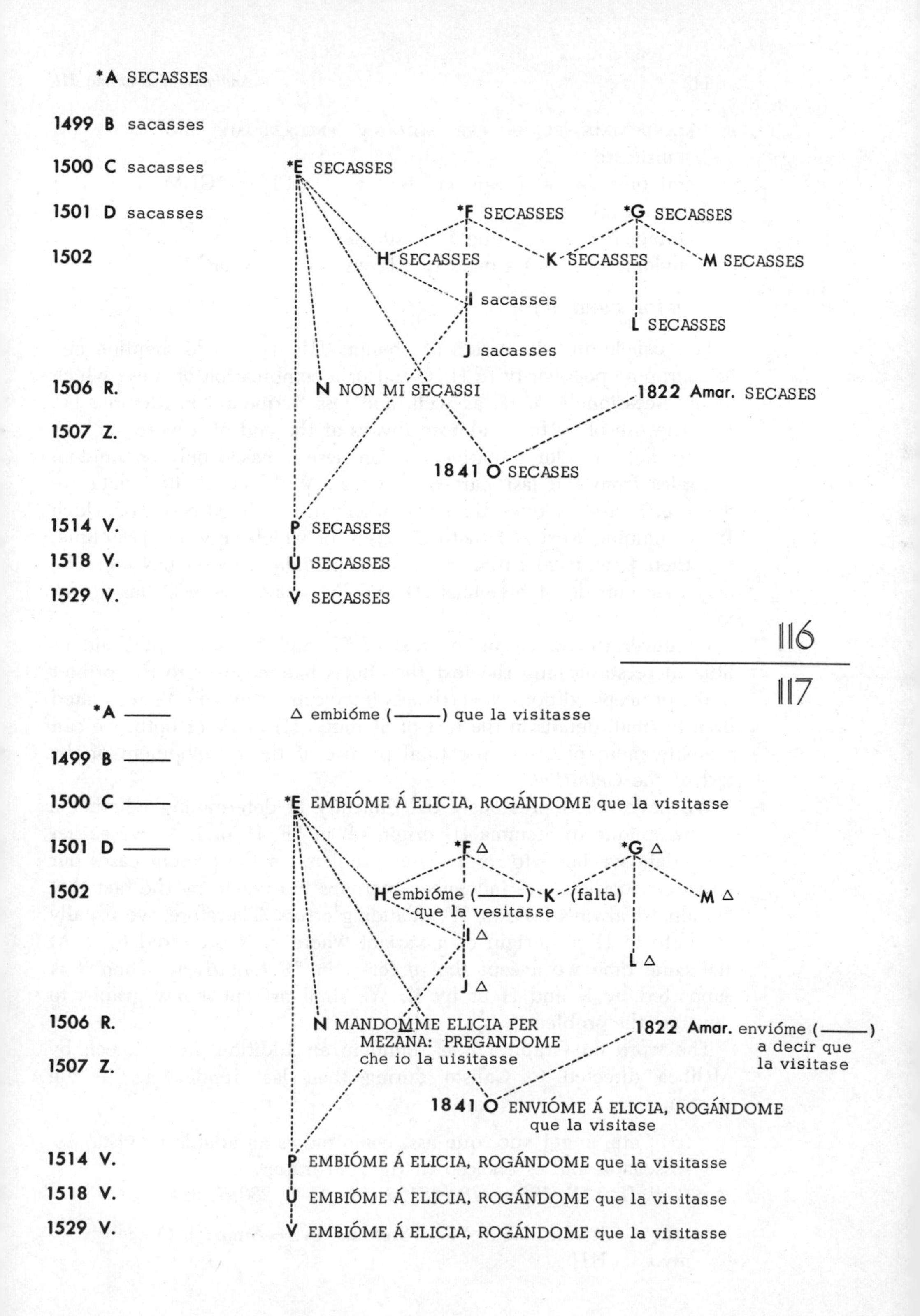
*A SECASSES
1499 B sacasses
1500 C sacasses
*E SECASSES
1501 D sacasses
*F SECASSES
*G SECASSES
1502
H SECASSES
K SECASSES
M SECASSES
I sacasses
L SECASSES
J sacasses
1506 R.
N NON MI SECASSI
1822 Amar. SECASES
1507 Z.
1841 O SECASES
1514 V.
P SECASSES
1518 V.
U SECASSES
1529 V.
V SECASSES
116
117
*A ——
△ embióme (——) que la visitasse
1499 B ——
1500 C ——
*E EMBIÓME Á ELICIA, ROGÁNDOME que la visitasse
1501 D ——
*F △
*G △
1502
H embióme (——) que la vesitasse
K (falta)
M △
I △
L △
J △
1506 R.
N MANDOMME ELICIA PER MEZANA: PREGANDOME che io la uisitasse
1822 Amar. envióme (——) a decir que la visitase
1507 Z.
1841 O ENVIÓME Á ELICIA, ROGÁNDOME que la visitase
1514 V.
P EMBIÓME Á ELICIA, ROGÁNDOME que la visitasse
1518 V.
U EMBIÓME Á ELICIA, ROGÁNDOME que la visitasse
1529 V.
V EMBIÓME Á ELICIA, ROGÁNDOME que la visitasse

MANDOMME ELICIA PER MEZANA, PREGANDOME che io la uisitasse N
embióme (———) que la visitasse *FIJ + *GLM (K falta)
embióme (———) que la vesitasse H
envióme (———) a decir que la visitase Amar.

*-y for -I and -i- for -Y-*

Before concluding discussion of Stemma III, we should mention one orthographic peculiarity of H, I, or J or a combination of these which occurs occasionally in K as well, and less frequently in Stemma IV. It is the use of -y for -I almost always at the end of a word such as *my, ty, ny,* etc. Our tentative opinion here is based only on random examples from the last part of the text. With our limited data we find that H uses -y more than any other edition: in 34 cases, of which 12 are unique. Next is I, with 27 cases, of which only one is unique; and then J, with 20 cases and one error, *muy* where I has *my*. The only case outside of Stemmas III and IV is one where D has *ny* for NI.

Whatever the words in the text of *F and *G were, they aid us little in reestablishing the text that Rojas handed over to the printer of the princeps edition. Nevertheless if we can resolve problems related even to small details in the text of Stemmas III or IV or both, we can evaluate more precisely the total picture of the development of the text of the *Celestina*.

We have noted previously the difficulty in determining whether a variant unique to Stemma III originates in *F, H, or I. As we gather more data we hope to resolve this problem. In the present cases our tentative decisions are influenced, perhaps too much, by the fact that *G almost always follows *F, including errors. Therefore, we usually attribute to H the origin of a variant where -y is preferred to -I. At the same time we accept the *-y* for -I in *F tentatively when it is supported by K and H or by K. We shall present a few graphs to illustrate the problems.

The word on Graph 118 is found in an addition, in a speech by Melibea directed to Calisto during their last rendezvous in the garden.

. . . Cata, ángel MÍO, que assí como me es agradable tu vista sossegada, me es enojoso tu riguroso trato; . . .
*(Cej. II, XIX, 195, 1. 18 [181, 1. 14]; C–T, 280, 1. 21)*

MÍO Stemma II + *F + Stemma IV + Amar. + O
myo HIJ

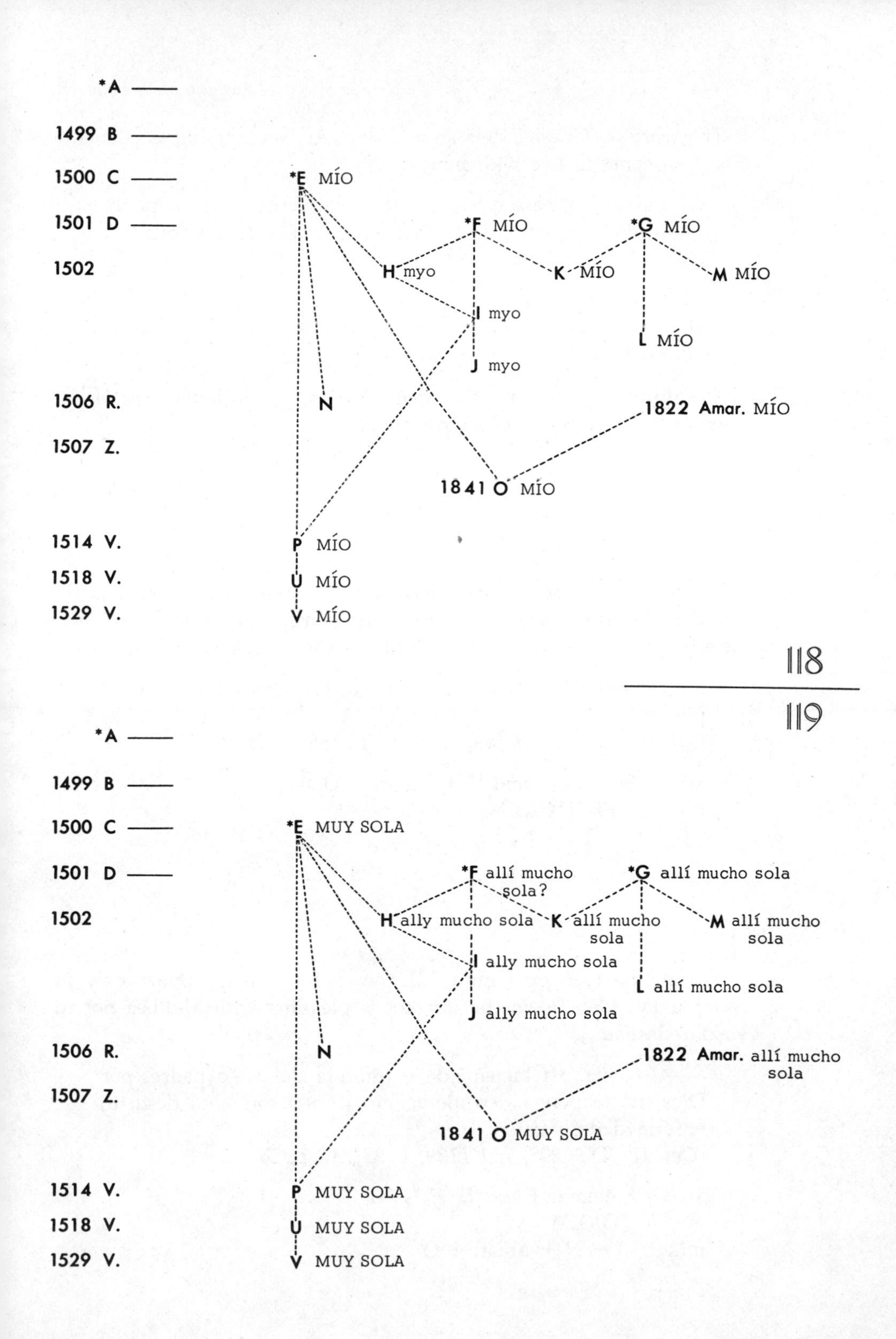
*A
1499 B
1500 C
1501 D
1502
1506 R.
1507 Z.
1514 V.
1518 V.
1529 V.
*E MÍO
*F MÍO
*G MÍO
H myo
K MÍO
M MÍO
I myo
L MÍO
J myo
N
1822 Amar. MÍO
1841 O MÍO
P MÍO
U MÍO
V MÍO
118
119
*A
1499 B
1500 C
1501 D
1502
1506 R.
1507 Z.
1514 V.
1518 V.
1529 V.
*E MUY SOLA
*F allí mucho sola?
*G allí mucho sola
H ally mucho sola
K allí mucho sola
M allí mucho sola
I ally mucho sola
L allí mucho sola
J ally mucho sola
N
1822 Amar. allí mucho sola
1841 O MUY SOLA
P MUY SOLA
U MUY SOLA
V MUY SOLA

The word on Graph 119 is an addition; Areúsa is trying to persuade Elicia to come to live with her.

> . . . Passa á mi casa tu ropa é alhajas é vente á mi compañía, que estarás MUY SOLA é la tristeza es amiga de la soledad.
> *(Cej. II, XV, 152, 1. 7 [141, 1. 18]; C–T, 253, 1. 13)*

MUY SOLA Stemma II + O
ally mucho sola HIJ
allí mucho sola *F? + Stemma IV + Amar.

The group HIJ presents the witness *my* for MI in both cases of the possessive adjective in the above passage.

In a few cases the -y for -I may be found throughout Stemmas III and IV. The word on Graph 120 appears in a speech by Melibea when Celestina visits her at her request. She is speaking about Calisto.

> . . . ¿Qué le deuo yo á él? ¿Qué le soy á cargo? ¿Qué ha hecho por MÍ?
> *Cej. II, X, 62, 1. 11 [59, 1. 7]; C–T, 188, 1. 25)*

MÍ Stemmas I and II + Amar. + O
my *FHIJ*GKLM

As may be seen on Graph 121 the -y for -I may appear only in Stemma IV. Pleberio in the last act is pleading with Melibea not to yield to despair.

> ——— Hija, MI bienamada é querida del viejo padre, por Dios, no te ponga desesperación el cruel tormento desta tu enfermedad é passión, . . .
> *(Cej. II, XXI, 205, 1. 1 [189, 1. 25]; C–T, 287, 1. 4)*

MI Stemmas I and II + *FHI
my *GKLM
mía J + N + Amar. + O

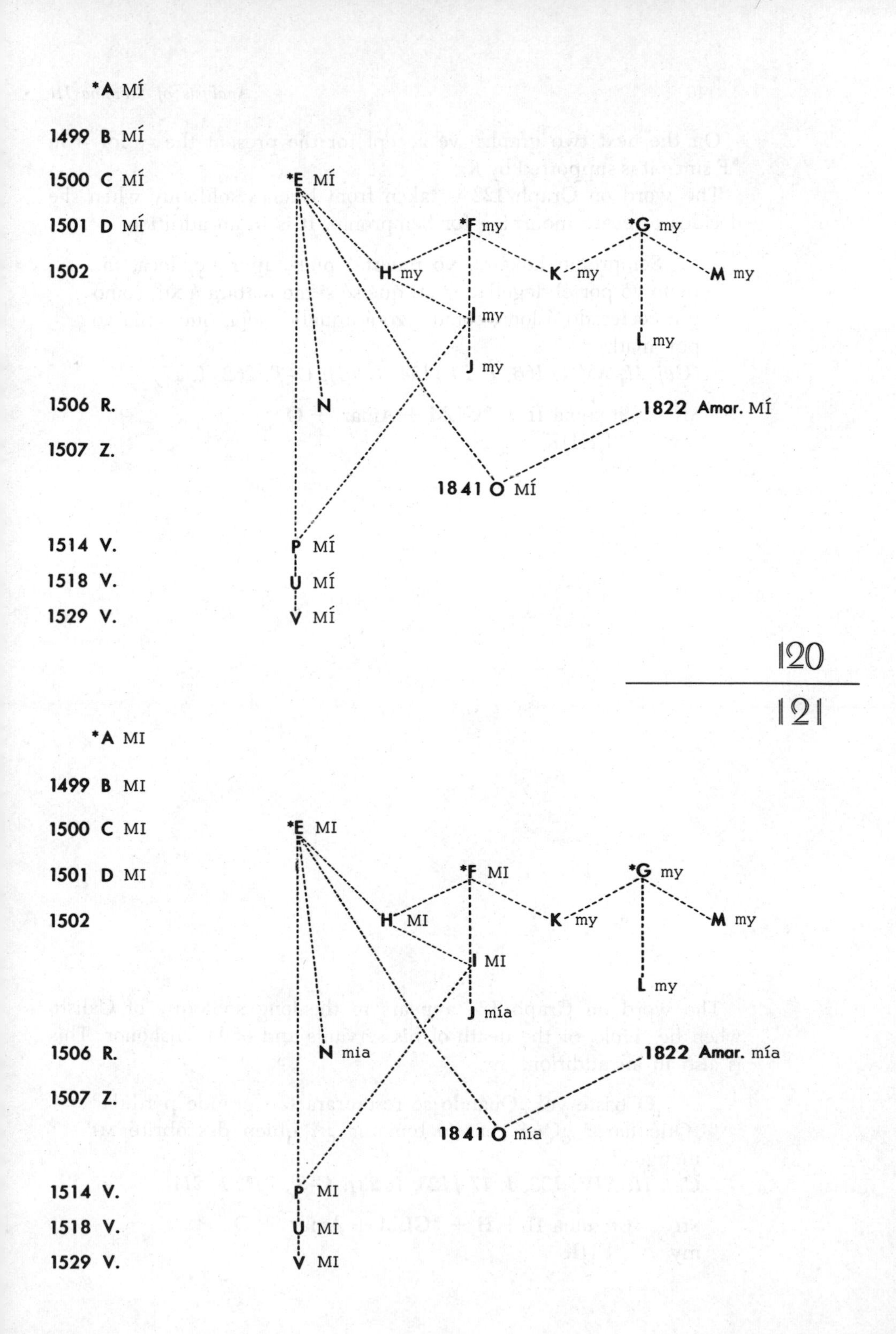
*A MÍ
1499 B MÍ
1500 C MÍ
*E MÍ
1501 D MÍ
*F my
*G my
1502
H my
K my
M my
I my
L my
J my
1506 R.
N
1822 Amar. MÍ
1507 Z.
1841 O MÍ
1514 V.
P MÍ
1518 V.
U MÍ
1529 V.
V MÍ
*A MI
1499 B MI
1500 C MI
*E MI
1501 D MI
*F MI
*G my
1502
H MI
K my
M my
I MI
L my
J mía
1506 R.
N mia
1822 Amar. mía
1507 Z.
1841 O mía
1514 V.
P MI
1518 V.
U MI
1529 V.
V MI

On the next two graphs we accept for the present the -y for -I in *F since it is supported by K.

The word on Graph 122 is taken from Elicia's soliloquy when she decides to cease mourning for Sempronio. It is in an addition.

> ... Sempronio holgara, yo muerta; pues, ¿porqué, loca, me peno yo por él degollado? ¿É qué sé si me matara á MÍ, como era acelerado é loco, como hizo á aquella vieja, que tenía yo por madre?
> *(Cej. II, XVII, 166, l. 14 [154, l. 13]; C–T, 262, l. 17)*

MÍ Stemma II + *GLM + Amar. + O
my *FHIJK

The word on Graph 123 appears in the long soliloquy of Calisto when he thinks of the death of his servants and of his dishonor. This is also in an addition.

> ... ¡O triste yo! ¿Quándo se restaurará tan grande pérdida? ¿Qué haré? ¿Qué consejo tomaré? ¿A quien descobriré MI mengua?
> *Cej. II, XIV, 133, l. 17 [123, l. 23]; C–T, 241, l. 21)*

MI Stemma II + H + *GLM + Amar. + O
my *FIJK

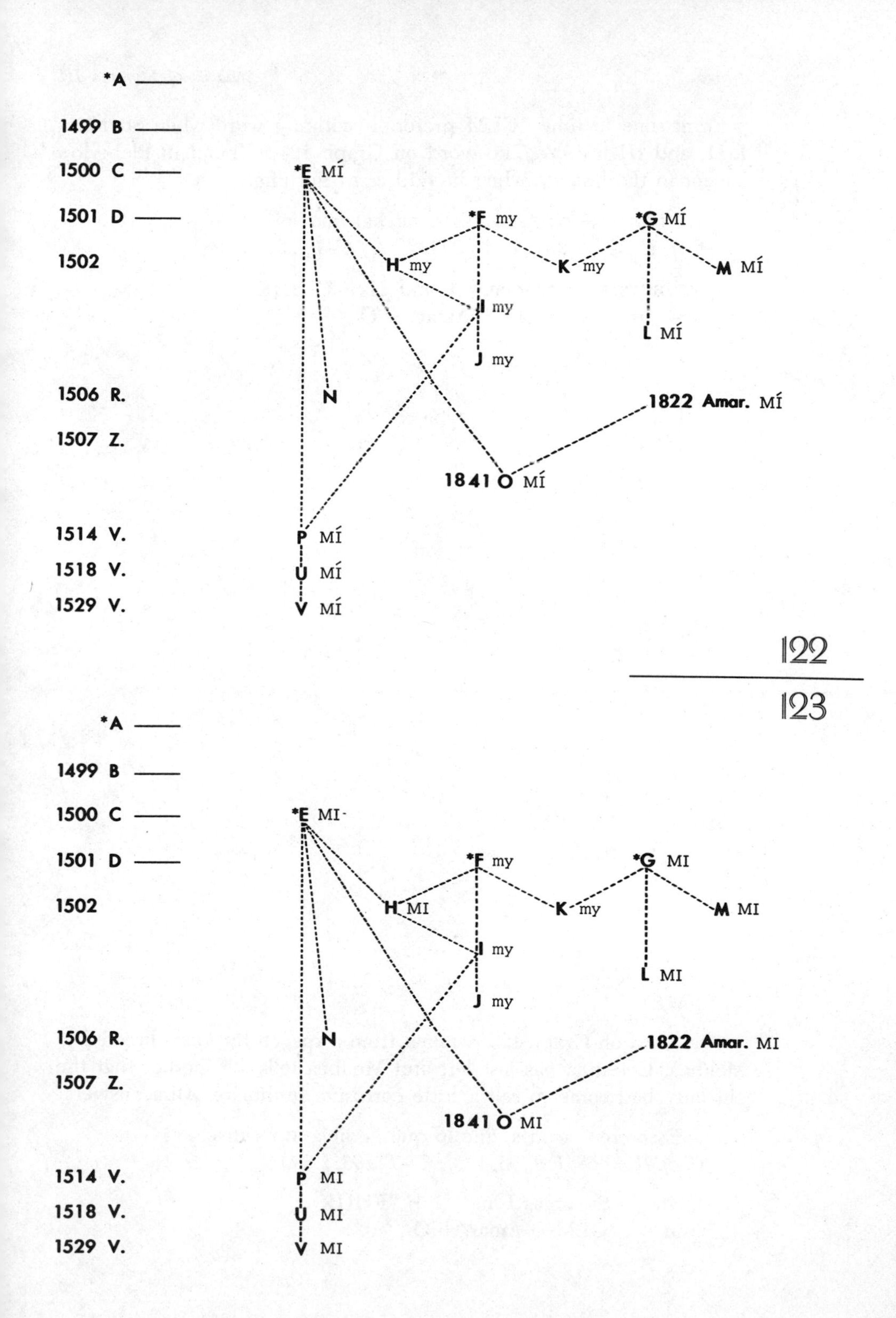

*A
1499 B
1500 C
1501 D
1502
1506 R.
1507 Z.
1514 V.
1518 V.
1529 V.
*E MÍ
*F my
*G MÍ
H my
K my
M MÍ
I my
L MÍ
J my
N
1822 Amar. MÍ
1841 O MÍ
P MÍ
U MÍ
V MÍ
122
123
*A
1499 B
1500 C
1501 D
1502
1506 R.
1507 Z.
1514 V.
1518 V.
1529 V.
*E MI-
*F my
*G MI
H MI
K my
M MI
I my
L MI
J my
N
1822 Amar. MI
1841 O MI
P MI
U MI
V MI

From time to time *GLM prefer -i- within a word when Stemmas I, II, and III use -Y-. The word on Graph 124 is found in Pleberio's lament in the last act when he addresses Fortune.

> . . . ¿Por qué no DESTRUYSTE mi patrimonio?
> *Cej. II, XXI, 218, 1. 8 [203, 1. 2]; C–T, 295, 1. 28)*

DESTRUYSTE Stemmas I and II + *FHIJK
destruiste *GLM + Amar. + O

The word on Graph 125 is taken from a speech by Alisa directed to Melibea. Celestina has just left and Melibea tells her mother that the old lady had come to sell a little corrosive sublimate. Alisa answers:

> —Esso creo yo más, que lo que la vieja RUYN dixo.
> *(Cej. II, X, 68, 1. 9 [65, 1. 5]; C—T, 193, 1. 11)*

RUYN Stemmas I and II + *FHIJK
ruin *GLM + Amar. + O

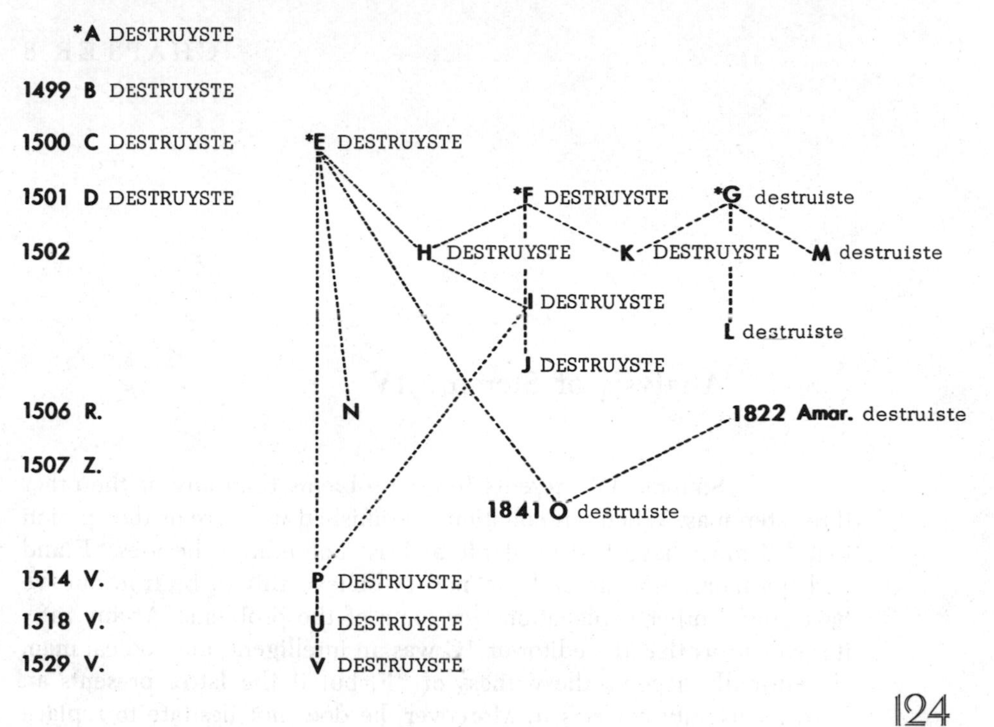
*A DESTRUYSTE
1499 B DESTRUYSTE
1500 C DESTRUYSTE
1501 D DESTRUYSTE
1502
1506 R.
1507 Z.
1514 V.
1518 V.
1529 V.
*E DESTRUYSTE
*F DESTRUYSTE
*G destruiste
H DESTRUYSTE
K DESTRUYSTE
M destruiste
I DESTRUYSTE
L destruiste
J DESTRUYSTE
N
1822 Amar. destruiste
1841 O destruiste
P DESTRUYSTE
U DESTRUYSTE
V DESTRUYSTE



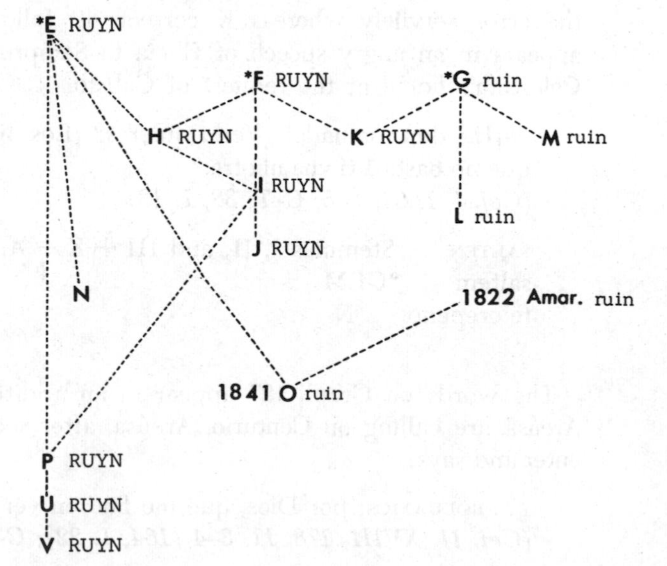
*A RUYN
1499 B RUYN
1500 C RUYN
1501 D RUYN
1502
1506 R.
1507 Z.
1514 V.
1518 V.
1529 V.
*E RUYN
*F RUYN
*G ruin
H RUYN
K RUYN
M ruin
I RUYN
L ruin
J RUYN
N
1822 Amar. ruin
1841 O ruin
P RUYN
U RUYN
V RUYN

# Analysis of Stemma IV

Stemma IV presents fewer problems than any of the other three stemmas. When our collation was finished we were of the opinion that *G must have had available at least one edition besides *F and perhaps more. We are still inclined to believe this to be true but we have found other explanations for some of the problems. At any rate, it seems to us that the editor of *G was an intelligent, methodical man. He normally accepts the witness of *F, but if the latter presents an error he usually corrects it. Moreover, he does not hesitate to replace a word of the text with one of his own choosing if he believes the latter to be more appropriate.

Graph 126 represents only a small typographical error, but interesting, as even the slightest errors can be, in studying the attitude of editors towards errors in their basic text. In this case L and M follow the error servilely whereas K corrects it, following *F. The word appears in an angry speech of Elicia to Sempronio when he goes to Celestina's home at the request of Calisto.

> —¡Ha don maluado! ¿Verla quieres? ¡Los ojos se te SALTEN!, que no basta á tí vna ni otra.
> *(Cej. I, I, 63, 1. 5; C–T, 38, 1. 13)*

SALTEN Stemmas I, II, and III + K + Amar. + O
saltem *GLM
te crepeno N

The words on Graph 127 appear in an addition where Elicia and Areúsa are calling on Centurio. Areúsa, after seeing him, is afraid to enter and says:

> . . . BOLUAMOS, por Dios, que me fino en ver tan mal gesto.
> *(Cej. II, XVIII, 178, 11. 3–4 [164, 1. 22]; C–T 270, 1. 11)*

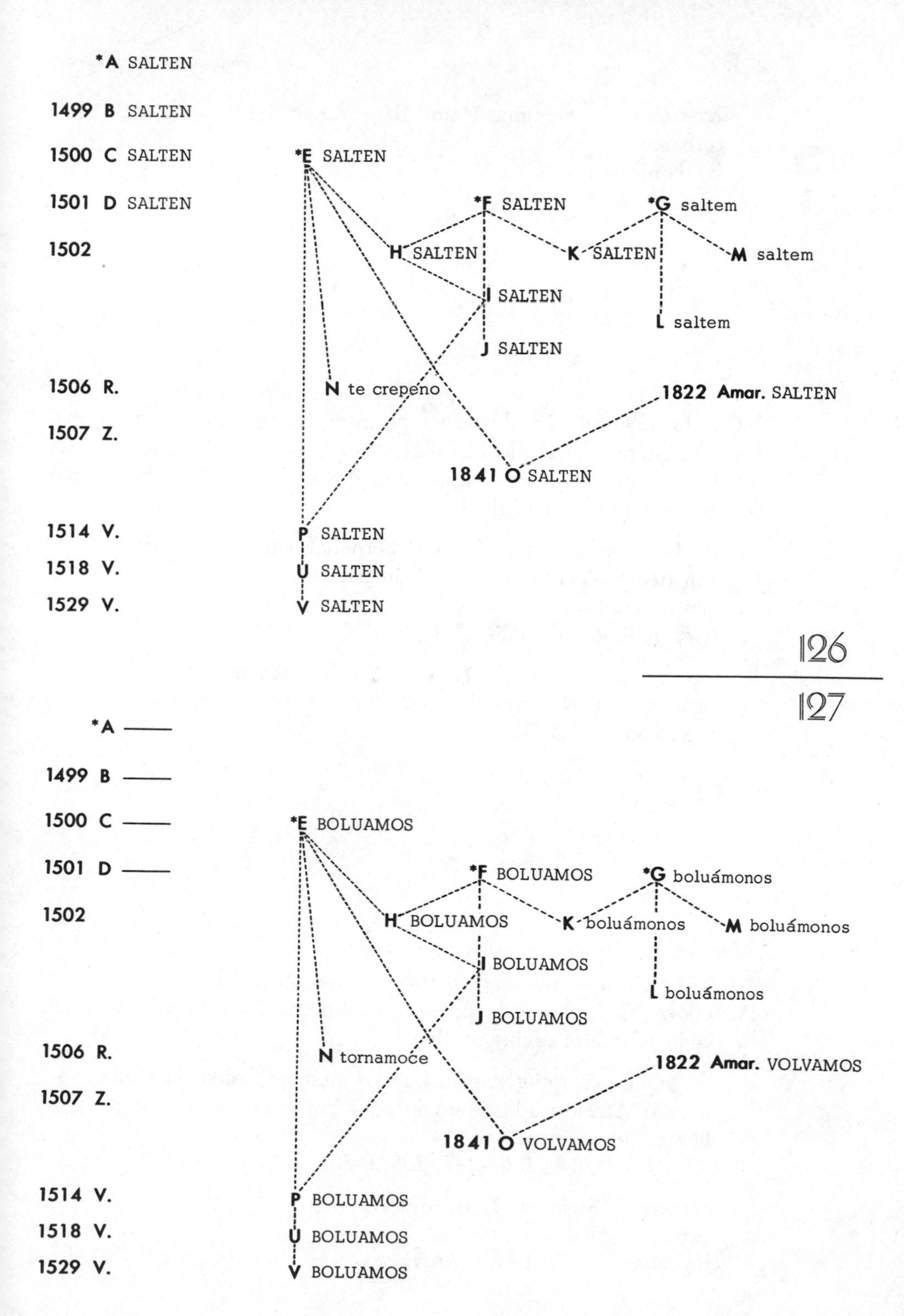
*A SALTEN
1499 B SALTEN
1500 C SALTEN
1501 D SALTEN
1502
1506 R.
1507 Z.
1514 V.
1518 V.
1529 V.
*E SALTEN
*F SALTEN
*G saltem
H SALTEN
K SALTEN
M saltem
I SALTEN
L saltem
J SALTEN
N te crepeno
1822 Amar. SALTEN
1841 O SALTEN
P SALTEN
U SALTEN
V SALTEN
126
127
*A ——
1499 B ——
1500 C ——
1501 D ——
1502
1506 R.
1507 Z.
1514 V.
1518 V.
1529 V.
*E BOLUAMOS
*F BOLUAMOS
*G boluámonos
H BOLUAMOS
K boluámonos
M boluámonos
I BOLUAMOS
L boluámonos
J BOLUAMOS
N tornamoce
1822 Amar. VOLVAMOS
1841 O VOLVAMOS
P BOLUAMOS
U BOLUAMOS
V BOLUAMOS

| | |
|---|---|
| BOLUAMOS | Stemmas II and III + Amar. + O |
| tornamoce | N |
| boluámonos | *GKLM |

Graphs 128 and 129 illustrate two more changes from the original text. On Graph 128 L and M follow *G whereas K selects the correct words from *F. The words appear in the Prólogo where the eternal conflict in nature is described.

> . . . los vientos entre sí traen perpetua guerra, los tiempos con tiempos contienden é litigan entre sí, VNO A VNO é todos contra nosotros.
> *(Cej. I, Pról.; 17, 1. 28; C–T, 14, 1. 6)*

| | |
|---|---|
| VNO A VNO | Stemmas II and III + K + Amar. + O |
| ogni cosa | N |
| cada vno | *GLM |

Graph 129 indicates that all three of the other editions of Stemma IV follow *G. The word appears in a speech to Pármeno in which Celestina tells him of his mother.

> . . . ¿Qué más quieres, sino que los mesmos diablos la hauían miedo? Atemorizados é espantados los tenía con las CRUDAS bozes, que les daua.
> *(Cej. I, VII, 240, 1. 6; C–T, 135, 1. 15)*

| | |
|---|---|
| CRUDAS | Stemmas I, II, and III + O |
| CRUDE | N |
| turbadas | *GKLM + Amar. |

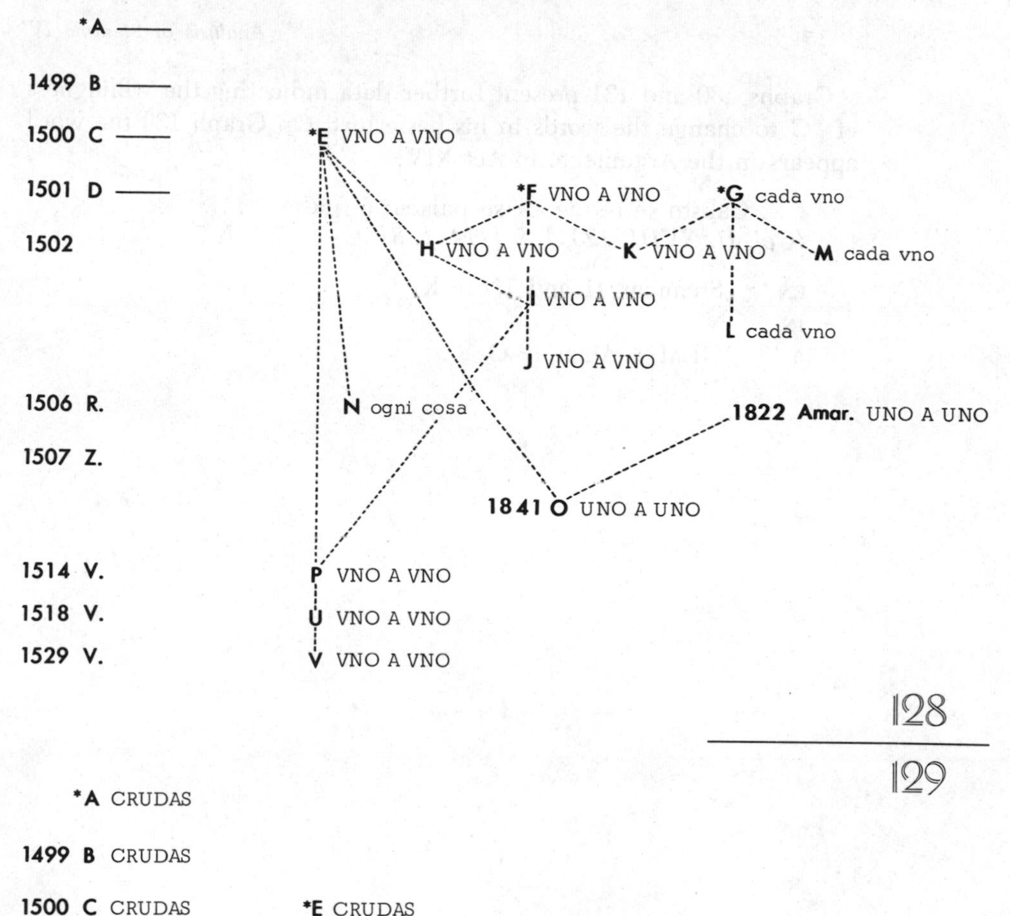

*A
1499 B
1500 C
1501 D
1502
1506 R.
1507 Z.
1514 V.
1518 V.
1529 V.
*E VNO A VNO
*F VNO A VNO
*G cada vno
H VNO A VNO
K VNO A VNO
M cada vno
I VNO A VNO
L cada vno
J VNO A VNO
N ogni cosa
1822 Amar. UNO A UNO
1841 O UNO A UNO
P VNO A VNO
U VNO A VNO
V VNO A VNO


128

129

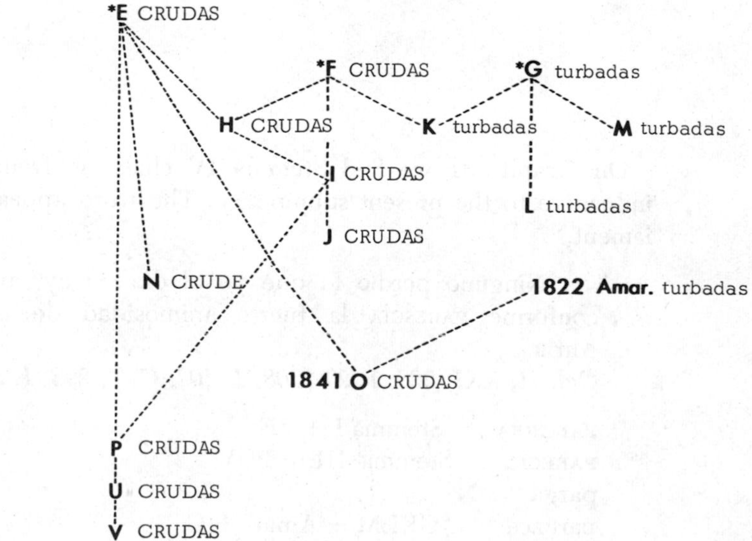

*A CRUDAS
1499 B CRUDAS
1500 C CRUDAS
1501 D CRUDAS
1502
1506 R.
1507 Z.
1514 V.
1518 V.
1529 V.
*E CRUDAS
*F CRUDAS
*G turbadas
H CRUDAS
K turbadas
M turbadas
I CRUDAS
L turbadas
J CRUDAS
N CRUDE
1822 Amar. turbadas
1841 O CRUDAS
P CRUDAS
U CRUDAS
V CRUDAS

Graphs 130 and 131 present further data indicating the willingness of *G to change the words in his basic text. On Graph 130 the word appears in the Argumento to Act XIV:

> . . . Calisto se retrae EN su palacio é quéxase . . .
> *(Cej. II, XVIII, 123, 1. 9 [114, 1. 8]; C–T, 235, 1. 7)*

EN Stemmas II and III + K
IN N
a *GLM + Amar. + O

On Graph 131 we find Stemma IV changing from the imperfect indicative to the present subjunctive. The word appears in Pleberio's lament.

> . . . Ninguno perdió lo que yo el día de oy, avnque algo conforme PARESCÍA la fuerte animosidad de Lambas de Auria, . . .
> *Cej. II, XXI, 223, 1. 20 [208, 1. 10]; C–T, 298, 1. 23)*

PARESCÍA Stemma I + *E
PARECÍA Stemma III + PUV
parga N
parezca *GKLM + Amar. + O

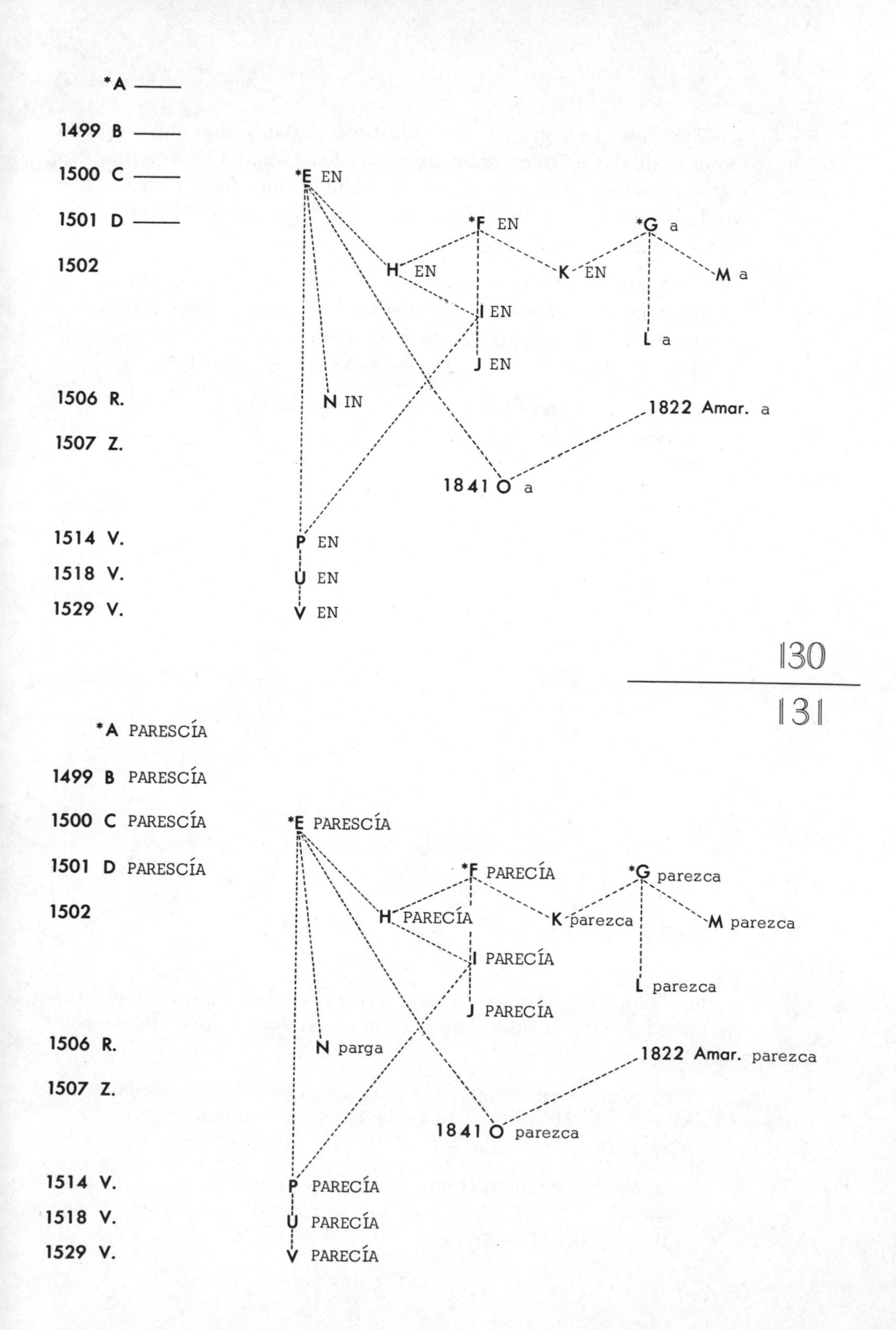
*A
1499 B
1500 C
1501 D
1502
1506 R.
1507 Z.
1514 V.
1518 V.
1529 V.
*E EN
*F EN
*G a
H EN
K EN
M a
I EN
L a
J EN
N IN
1822 Amar. a
1841 O a
P EN
U EN
V EN
130
131
*A PARESCÍA
1499 B PARESCÍA
1500 C PARESCÍA
1501 D PARESCÍA
1502
1506 R.
1507 Z.
1514 V.
1518 V.
1529 V.
*E PARESCÍA
*F PARECÍA
*G parezca
H PARECÍA
K parezca
M parezca
I PARECÍA
L parezca
J PARECÍA
N parga
1822 Amar. parezca
1841 O parezca
P PARECÍA
U PARECÍA
V PARECÍA

The next two graphs also illustrate variants that have spread through all the editions of Stemma IV. On Graph 132 Amarita, unwilling to accept the variant, chooses the correct form instead. The words are taken from the Argumento of Act VII, where Celestina and Pármeno visit Areúsa.

> . . . Tráele Pármeno á memoria la promessa, que le hiziera, de le fazer auer á Areúsa, qu'él mucho amaua. VÁNSE á casa de Areúsa. Queda ay la noche Pármeno.
> *(Cej. I, VII, 231, 1. 7; C–T, 129, 1. 5)*

VÁNSE Stemmas I, II, and III + Amar. + O
insieme sen andorno N
váse *GKLM

On Graph 133 the words are spoken by Celestina as she visits Melibea for the first time. The portion of her speech given below is an addition.

> . . . ¡Ea!, buen amigo, ¡tener rezio! Agora es mi tiempo o NUNCA. No la dexes, lléuamela de aquí á quien digo.
> *(Cej. I, IV, 163, 1. 10; C–T, 85, 1. 8)*

O NUNCA Stemmas II and III + O
(———) N
¡ea! *GKLM + Amar.

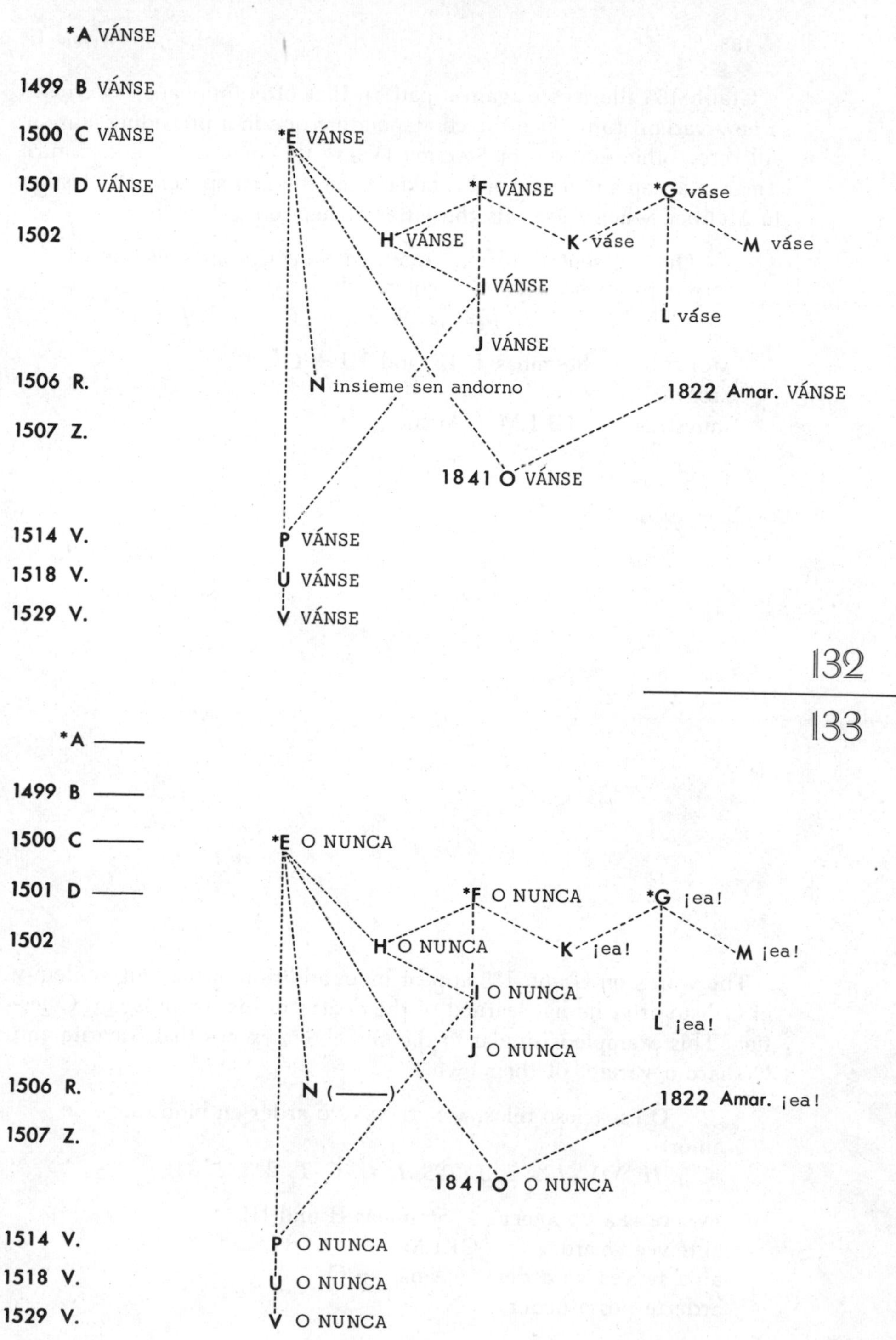
*A VÁNSE
1499 B VÁNSE
1500 C VÁNSE
*E VÁNSE
1501 D VÁNSE
*F VÁNSE
*G váse
1502
H VÁNSE
K váse
M váse
I VÁNSE
L váse
J VÁNSE
1506 R.
N insieme sen andorno
1822 Amar. VÁNSE
1507 Z.
1841 O VÁNSE
1514 V.
P VÁNSE
1518 V.
U VÁNSE
1529 V.
V VÁNSE
132
133
*A ——
1499 B ——
1500 C ——
*E O NUNCA
1501 D ——
*F O NUNCA
*G ¡ea!
1502
H O NUNCA
K ¡ea!
M ¡ea!
I O NUNCA
L ¡ea!
J O NUNCA
1506 R.
N (——)
1822 Amar. ¡ea!
1507 Z.
1841 O O NUNCA
1514 V.
P O NUNCA
1518 V.
U O NUNCA
1529 V.
V O NUNCA

Graph 134 illustrates again a pattern that often appears. *G creates a new variant to replace the corresponding one in a preceding edition. All three other editions of Stemma IV use this new word, and in turn Amarita accepts it. The word is taken from the first speech of Celestina to Melibea when she visits the latter at her request.

> —¿Qué es, señora, tu mal, que assí MUESTRA las señas de su tormento en las coloradas colores de tu gesto?
> *(Cej. II, X, 55, l. 12 [52, ll. 9–10]; C–T, 183, l. 19)*

MUESTRA  Stemmas I, II, and III + O
MOSTRA  N
muestras  *GKLM + Amar.

The words on Graph 135 appear in an addition in the long soliloquy of Calisto after he has learned of the deaths of his servants and Celestina. This example is similar to the one above except that Amarita and O share a variant of their own.

> . . . ¡O espacioso relox, AV́N TE VEA YO arder en biuo fuego de amor!
> *(Cej. II, XIV, 138, l. 5 [128, l. 4]; C–T, 243, l. 34)*

AV́N TE VEA YO ARDER  Stemmas II and III
ante vea yo arder  *GKLM
aína te vea yo arder  Amar. + O
arderte possa ueder  N

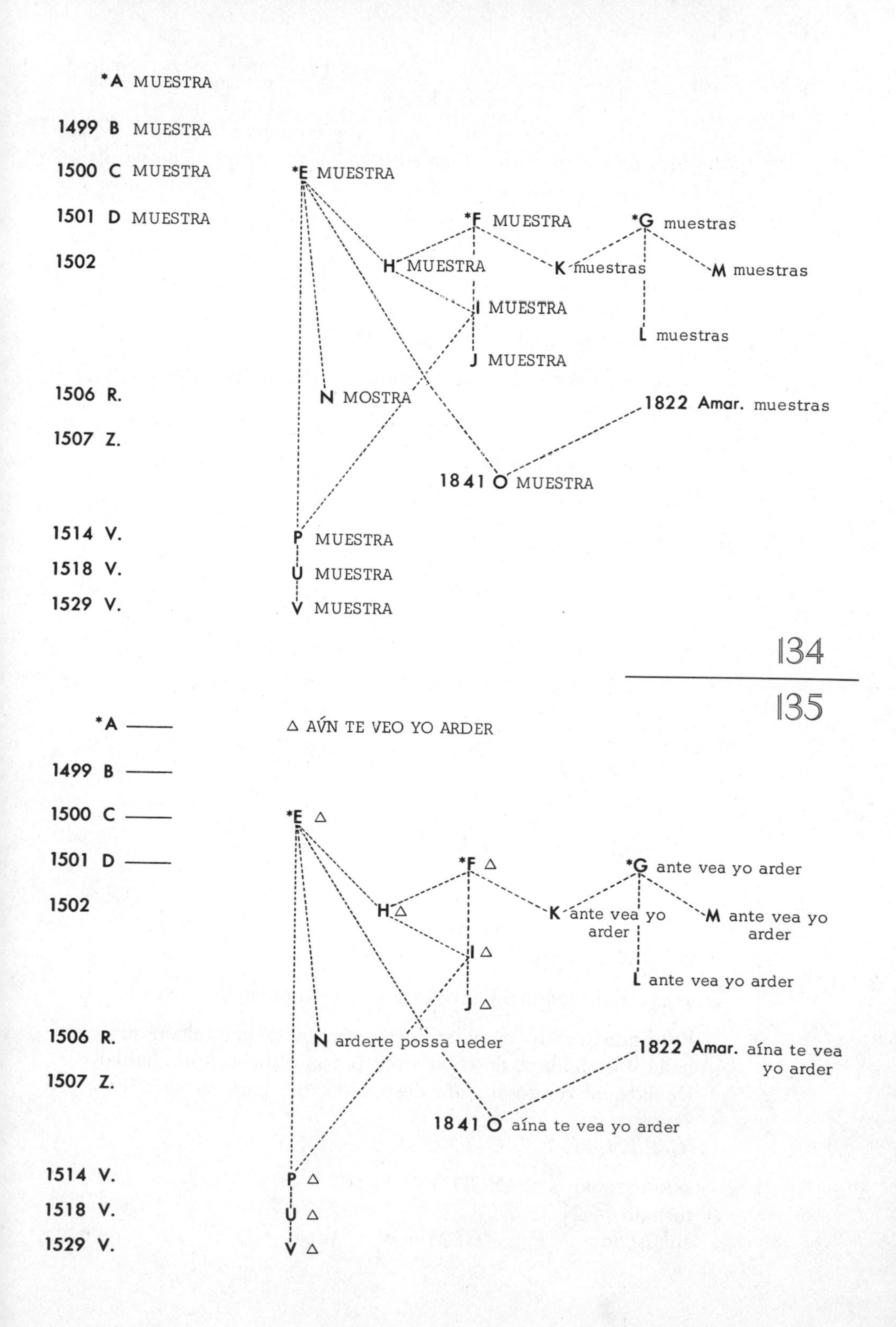
*A MUESTRA
1499 B MUESTRA
1500 C MUESTRA
*E MUESTRA
1501 D MUESTRA
*F MUESTRA
*G muestras
1502
H MUESTRA
K muestras
M muestras
I MUESTRA
L muestras
J MUESTRA
1506 R.
N MOSTRA
1822 Amar. muestras
1507 Z.
1841 O MUESTRA
1514 V.
P MUESTRA
1518 V.
U MUESTRA
1529 V.
V MUESTRA
134
135
*A ——
△ AV́N TE VEO YO ARDER
1499 B ——
1500 C ——
*E △
1501 D ——
*F △
*G ante vea yo arder
1502
H △
K ante vea yo arder
M ante vea yo arder
I △
L ante vea yo arder
J △
1506 R.
N arderte possa ueder
1822 Amar. aína te vea yo arder
1507 Z.
1841 O aína te vea yo arder
1514 V.
P △
1518 V.
U △
1529 V.
V △

At times the variant of some or all the editions of Stemma IV appears also in one or more other editions on the graph. The words on Graph 136 appear in a speech of Celestina directed to Alisa during her first visit.

> . . . Dios la dexe gozar su noble juuentud é florida mocedad, que es el tiempo en que más plazeres é mayores deleytes SE ALCANÇARÁN.
> *(Cej. I, IV, 164, 11. 14–15; C–T, 86, 1. 1)*

SE ALCANÇARÁN *ABC + Stemmas II and III + K
se alcanzará O
se alcançan D + *GLM
se alcanzan Amar.
si prende N

The word on Graph 137 appears in the Argumento of Act I.

> Entrando Calisto en una huerta empós de un falcón suyo, halló y á Melibea, de cuyo amor preso, començole de hablar. De la qual rigorosamente despedido, fué para su casa muy SANGUSTIADO.
> *(Cej. I, I, 31, 1. 7; C–T, 21, 1. 6)*

SANGUSTIADO *ABCD*EPU*FIJK
turbato N
angustiado H + *GLM + V + Amar. + O

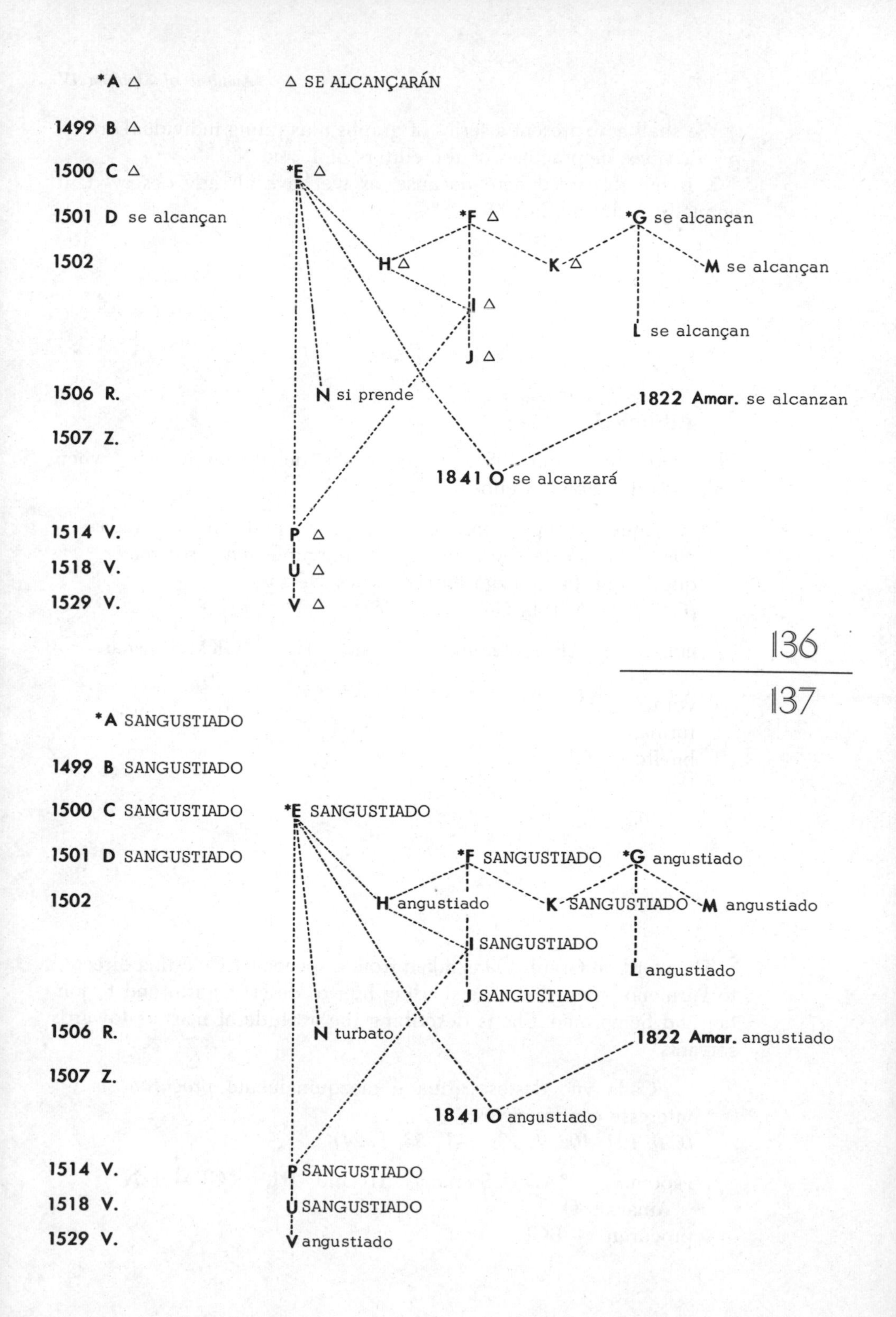
*A △
△ SE ALCANÇARÁN
1499 B △
1500 C △
*E △
1501 D se alcançan
*F △
*G se alcançan
1502
H △
K △
M se alcançan
I △
L se alcançan
J △
1506 R.
N si prende
1822 Amar. se alcanzan
1507 Z.
1841 O se alcanzará
1514 V.
P △
1518 V.
U △
1529 V.
V △
136
137
*A SANGUSTIADO
1499 B SANGUSTIADO
1500 C SANGUSTIADO
*E SANGUSTIADO
1501 D SANGUSTIADO
*F SANGUSTIADO
*G angustiado
1502
H angustiado
K SANGUSTIADO
M angustiado
I SANGUSTIADO
L angustiado
J SANGUSTIADO
1506 R.
N turbato
1822 Amar. angustiado
1507 Z.
1841 O angustiado
1514 V.
P SANGUSTIADO
1518 V.
U SANGUSTIADO
1529 V.
V angustiado

We shall now present a series of graphs illustrating individual errors, peculiarities, or practices of the editors of L and M.

K is not discussed here because, as we have already observed, it normally follows either *F or *G.

## *Edition L*

The word on Graph 138 appears in the debate on women, when Calisto is describing Melibea.

> . . . Aquella proporción, que veer yo no pude, no sin duda por el BULTO de fuera juzgo incomparablemente ser mejor, que la que Páris juzgó entre las tres Deesas.
> *(Cej. I, I, 56, 1. 6; C–T, 34, 1. 16)*

BULTO *AB + Stemmas II and III + *GKM + Amar. + O
VULTO D
forma N
buelto CL

The word on Graph 139 is taken from a speech by Celestina directed to Pármeno when she is persuading him to desert Calisto and to join her and Sempronio. She is describing the attitude of masters towards servants.

> . . . Cada vno destos catiua é mezquinamente *procuran* su interesse con los suyos.
> *(Cej. I, I, 102, 1. 13; C–T, 53, 1. 24)*

PROCURA *AD + Stemmas II and III + *GKM + N + Amar. + O
procuran BCL

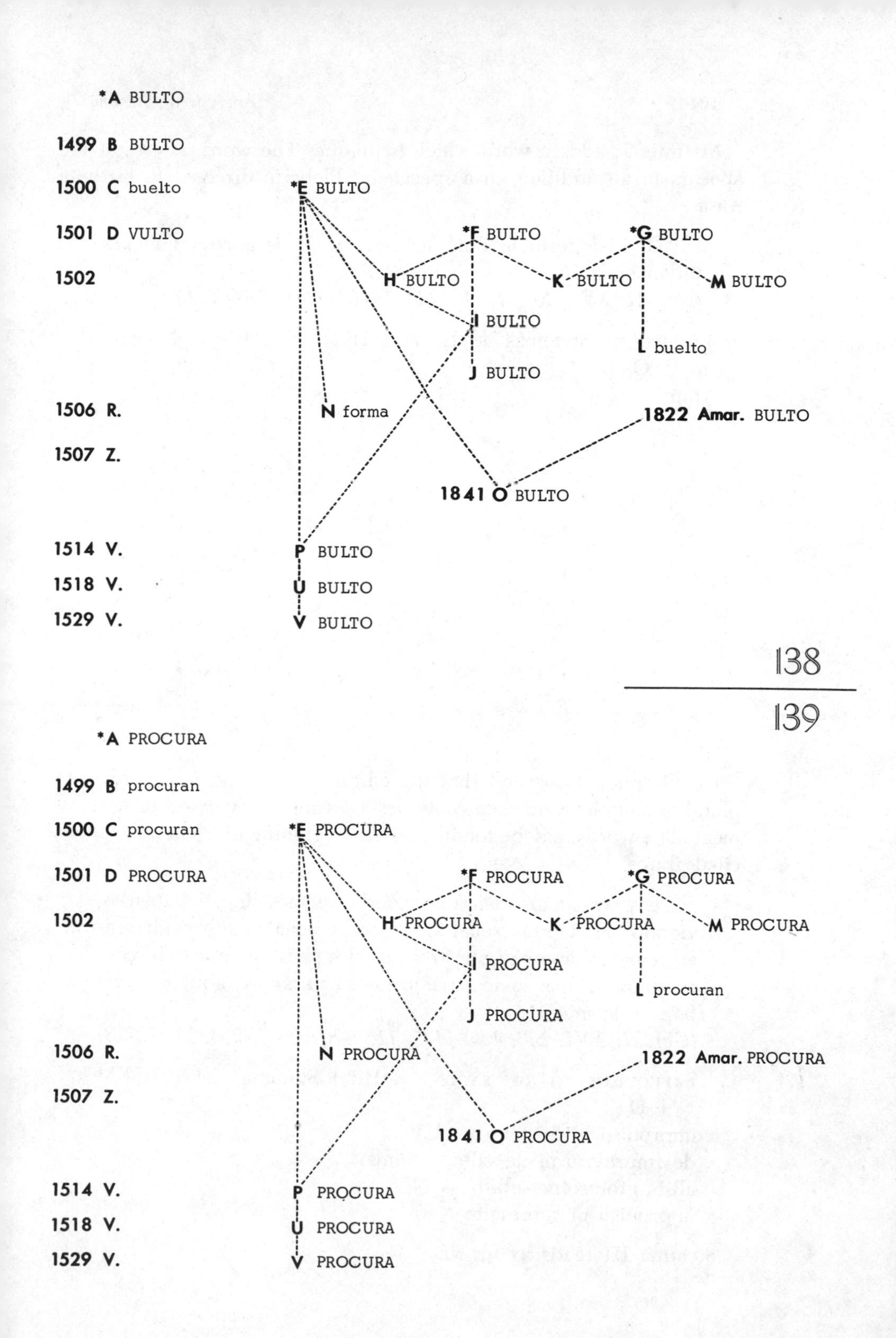
*A BULTO
1499 B BULTO
1500 C buelto
*E BULTO
1501 D VULTO
*F BULTO
*G BULTO
1502
H BULTO
K BULTO
M BULTO
I BULTO
L buelto
J BULTO
1506 R.
N forma
1822 Amar. BULTO
1507 Z.
1841 O BULTO
1514 V.
P BULTO
1518 V.
U BULTO
1529 V.
V BULTO
138
139
*A PROCURA
1499 B procuran
1500 C procuran
*E PROCURA
1501 D PROCURA
*F PROCURA
*G PROCURA
1502
H PROCURA
K PROCURA
M PROCURA
I PROCURA
L procuran
J PROCURA
1506 R.
N PROCURA
1822 Amar. PROCURA
1507 Z.
1841 O PROCURA
1514 V.
P PROCURA
1518 V.
U PROCURA
1529 V.
V PROCURA

At times L adds a word which is unique. The word on Graph 140 appears in an addition, in a speech by Pleberio directed to his wife Alisa.

> . . . De todo esto la dotó natura. Qualquiera cosa que nos pidan hallarán ——— bien complida.
> *(Cej. II, XVI, 157, 1. 16 [146, 1. 13]; C–T, 257, 1. 5)*

——— Stemmas I, II, and III + *GKM + N + Amar. + O

tan L

On Graph 141 we find that the editor of L changes a word from plural to singular, and then continues, creating a new word or replacement. The words may be found near the beginning of Pleberio's speech cited above.

> . . . E pues somos inciertos quándo auemos de ser llamados, viendo tan ciertas señales, deuemos echar nuestras baruas en remojo é aparejar nuestros fardeles para andar este forçoso camino: no nos tome IMPROUISOS NI DE SALTO aquella cruel boz de la muerte.
> *(Cej. II, XVI, 156, 1. 9 [145, 11. 7–8]; C–T, 256, 11. 12–13)*

IMPROUISOS NI DE SALTO *EP + Stemma III + *GKM + O

improuiso ni de salto UV

de improviso ni de salto Amar.

all improuiso ne subito N

improuiso ni sobresalto L

Stemma III reads NY for NI.

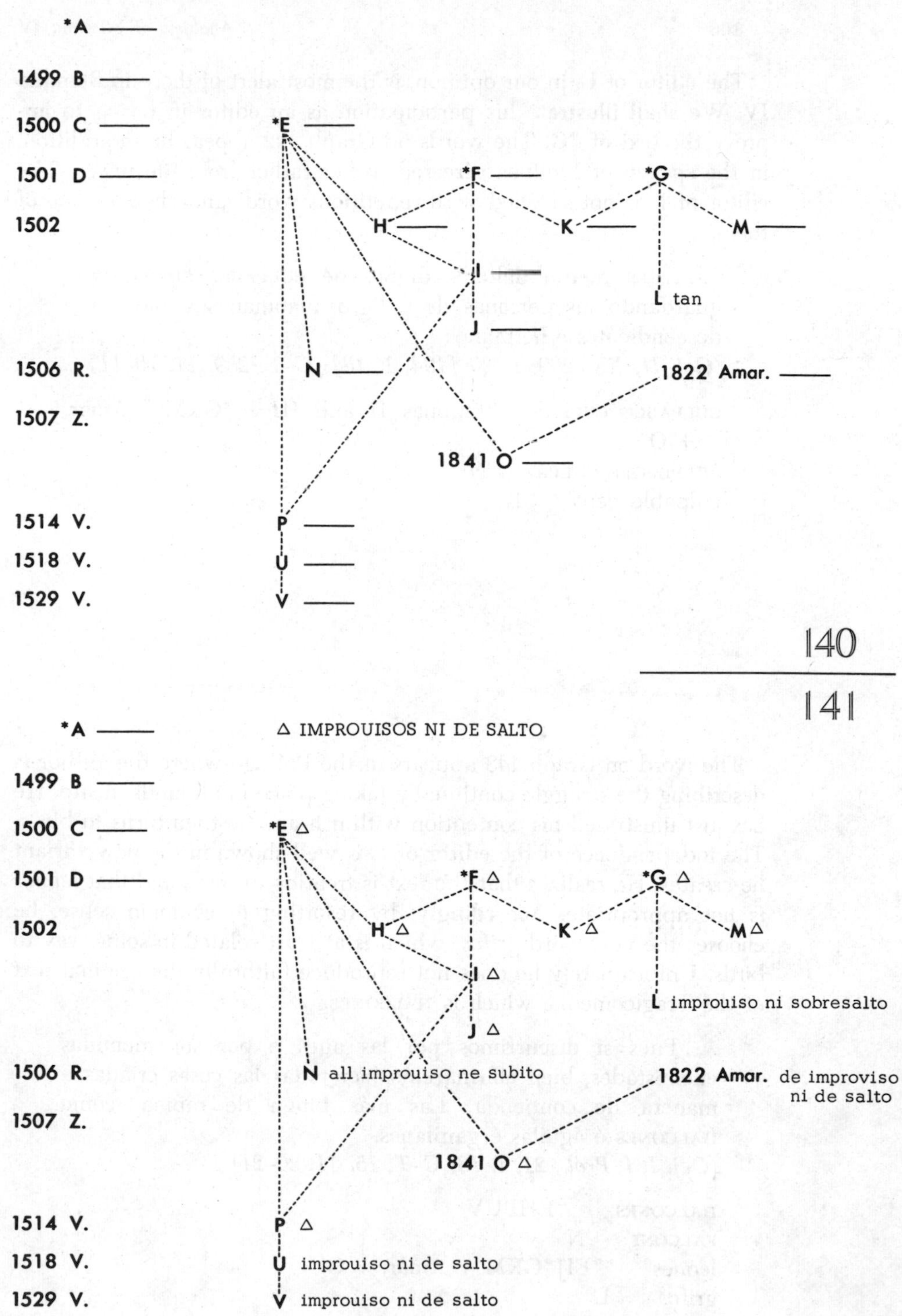

*A
1499 B
1500 C
*E
1501 D
*F
*G
1502
H
K
M
I
L tan
J
1506 R.
N
1822 Amar.
1507 Z.
1841 O
1514 V.
P
1518 V.
U
1529 V.
V
140
141
*A
△ IMPROUISOS NI DE SALTO
1499 B
1500 C
*E △
1501 D
*F △
*G △
1502
H △
K △
M △
I △
L improuiso ni sobresalto
J △
1506 R.
N all improuiso ne subito
1822 Amar.
de improviso ni de salto
1507 Z.
1841 O △
1514 V.
P △
1518 V.
U improuiso ni de salto
1529 V.
V improuiso ni de salto

The editor of L, in our opinion, is the most alert of those in Stemma IV. We shall illustrate his participation as an editor in trying to improve the text of *G. The words on Graph 142 appear in an addition, in the speech of Melibea directed to her father from the tower. The editor of L is not satisfied with repetitious words and changes one of them.

> . . . Estos fueron delictos dignos de CULPABLE CULPA, que, guardando sus personas de peligro, matauan sus mayores é descendientes é hermanos.
> *(Cej. II, XX, 209, 1. 20 [194, 1. 13]; C–T, 289, 11. 10–11)*

CULPABLE CULPA Stemmas II and III + *GKM + Amar. + O
CULPEUOLE CULPA N
culpable pena L

The word on Graph 143 appears in the Prólogo where the author is describing the struggle continually taking place in all kinds of life. He has just illustrated his contention with fish and he then turns to birds. The independence of the editor of L is well shown in the new variant he creates. He realizes that the text is treating of birds and that *leones* is not appropriate. Accordingly, by resorting to common sense, he chooses the new word *grifos,* which is at least related in some way to birds. Unfortunately he does not reproduce faithfully the original text of the Tragicomedia, which is HALCONES.

> . . . Pues si discurrimos por las aues é por sus menudas enemistades, bien affirmaremos ser todas las cosas criadas a manera de contienda. Las más biuen de rapina, como HALCONES é águilas é gauilanes.
> *(Cej. I, I, Pról., 21, 1. 16; C–T, 15, 11. 20–21)*

HALCONES *EHPUV
FALCONI N
leones *FIJ*GKM + Amar. + O
grifos L

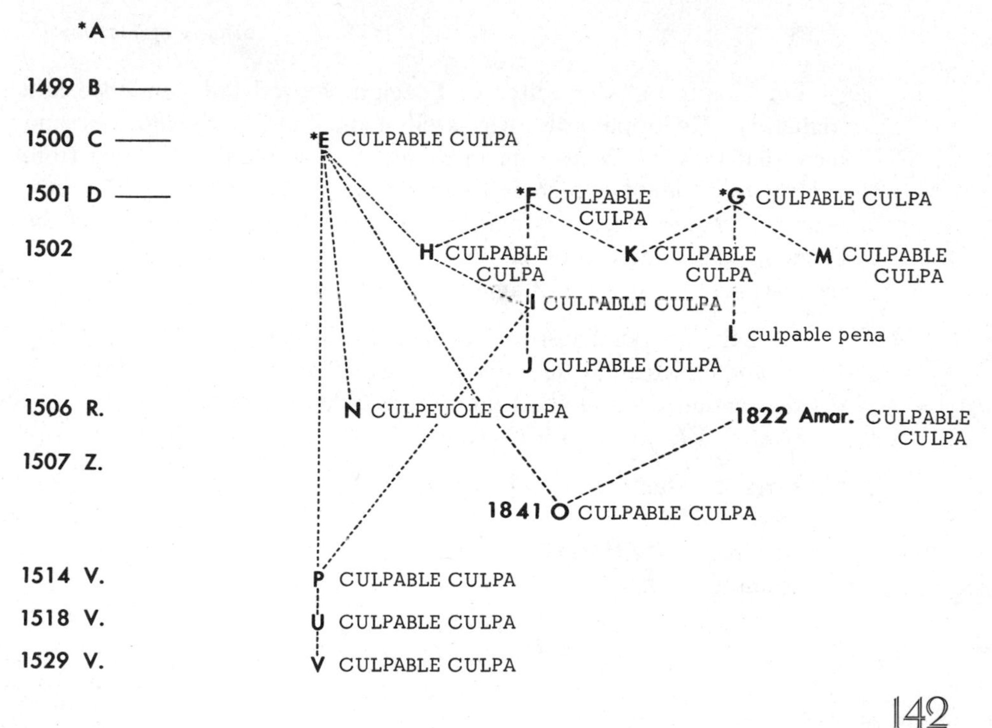
*A
1499 B
1500 C
1501 D
1502
1506 R.
1507 Z.
1514 V.
1518 V.
1529 V.
*E CULPABLE CULPA
*F CULPABLE CULPA
*G CULPABLE CULPA
H CULPABLE CULPA
K CULPABLE CULPA
M CULPABLE CULPA
I CULPABLE CULPA
L culpable pena
J CULPABLE CULPA
N CULPEUOLE CULPA
1822 Amar. CULPABLE CULPA
1841 O CULPABLE CULPA
P CULPABLE CULPA
U CULPABLE CULPA
V CULPABLE CULPA

142
———
143

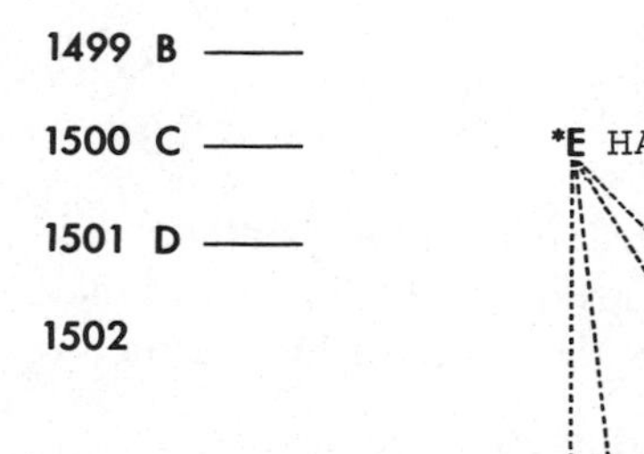
*A
1499 B
1500 C
1501 D
1502
1506 R.
1507 Z.
1514 V.
1518 V.
1529 V.

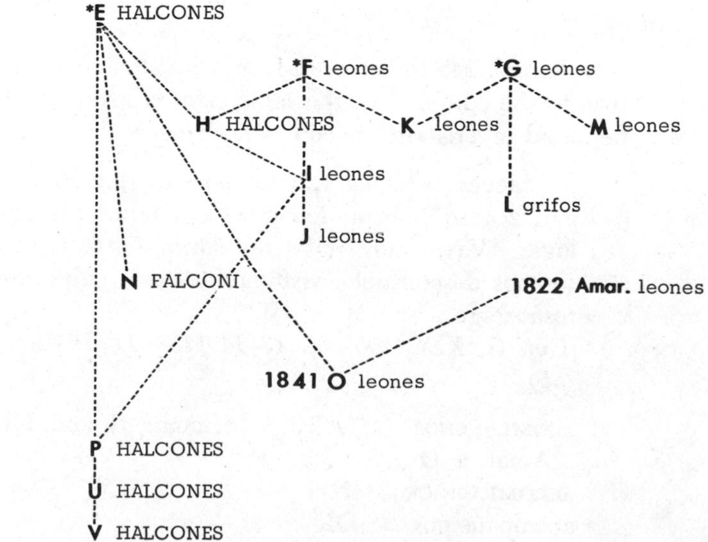
*E HALCONES
*F leones
*G leones
H HALCONES
K leones
M leones
I leones
L grifos
J leones
N FALCONI
1822 Amar. leones
1841 O leones
P HALCONES
U HALCONES
V HALCONES

On Graph 144 the editor of L again showed independence and originality. He apparently was well acquainted with *refranes* and knew that most of them were in rhyme. So he changed the text from *se viste* to *se ianta,* which is the form we find in Correas. However again the change does not reflect the original text of the author of the Tragicomedia. The words come from a speech by Sempronio as he and Pármeno begin to plot against Celestina.

> —¿Callarás, por Dios, o te echaré dende con el diablo? Que si anda rodeando su vestido, haze bien, pues tiene dello necessidad. Que el abad de dó canta, de allí VISTE.
> *(Cej. I, VI, 205, 1. 11; C–T, 113, 1. 10)*

VISTE Stemmas I and II + H + O
UESTE N
se viste *FIJ*GKM + Amar.
se ianta L

On Graph 145 the error in L may be attributed to the printer rather than to the editor since the same error crops out in D. The word may be found in Tristán's speech as he laments the death of his master.

> . . . Lleuemos el cuerpo de nuestro querido amo donde no padezca su honrra detrimento, avnque sea muerto en este lugar. Vaya con nosotros llanto, ACOMPÁÑENOS soledad, síganos desconsuelo, visítenos tristeza, cúbranos luto é dolorosa xerga.
> *(Cej. II, XIX, 200, 11. 13–14 [185, 11. 18–19]; C–T, 283, 1. 5)*

ACOMPÁÑENOS *ABC + Stemmas II and III + *GKM + Amar. + O
ACCOMPAGNICE N
acompañemos DL

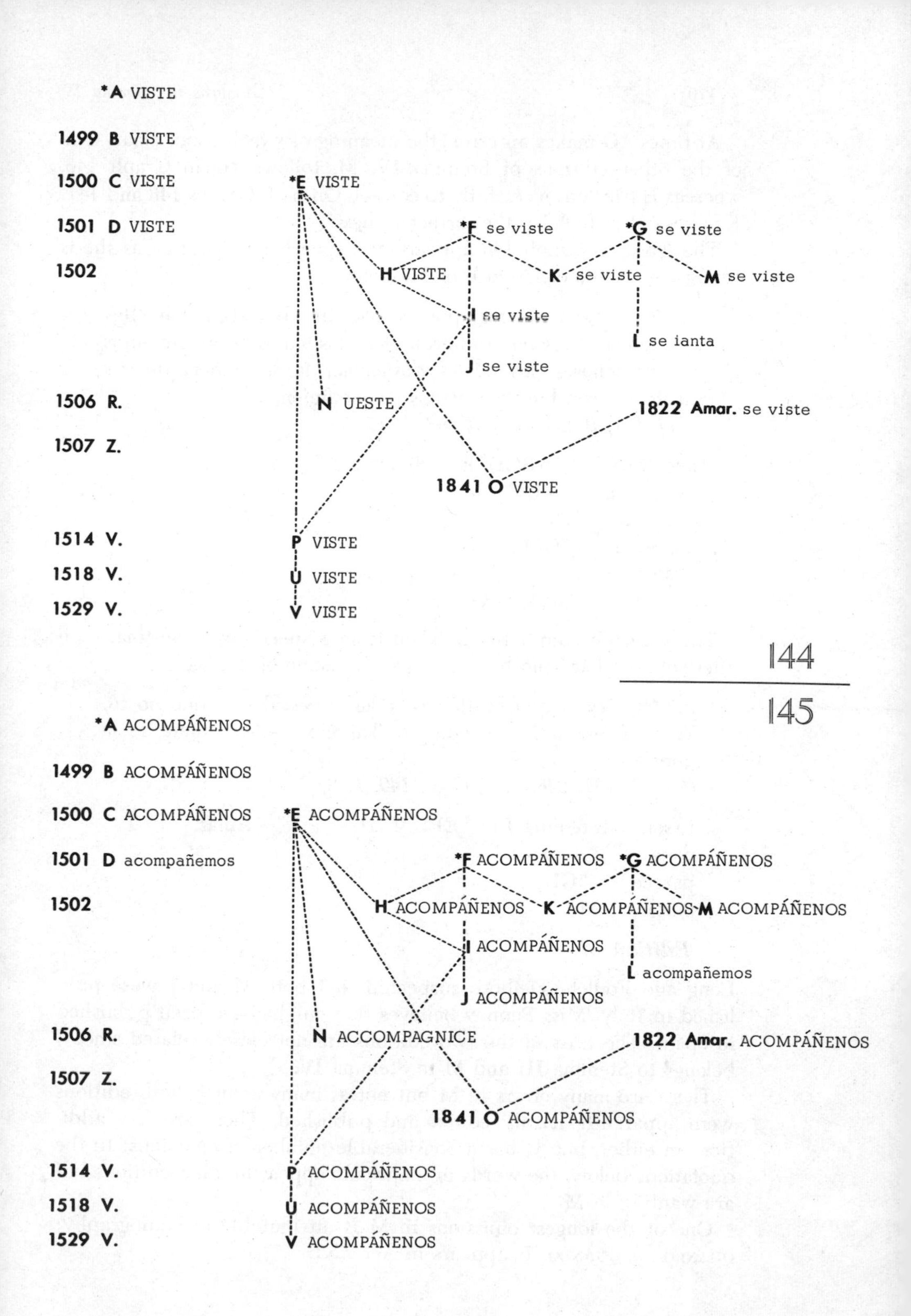

*A VISTE
1499 B VISTE
1500 C VISTE
1501 D VISTE
1502
1506 R.
1507 Z.
1514 V.
1518 V.
1529 V.
*E VISTE
*F se viste
*G se viste
H VISTE
K se viste
M se viste
I se viste
L se ianta
J se viste
N UESTE
1822 Amar. se viste
1841 O VISTE
P VISTE
U VISTE
V VISTE
144
145
*A ACOMPÁÑENOS
1499 B ACOMPÁÑENOS
1500 C ACOMPÁÑENOS
1501 D acompañemos
1502
1506 R.
1507 Z.
1514 V.
1518 V.
1529 V.
*E ACOMPÁÑENOS
*F ACOMPÁÑENOS
*G ACOMPÁÑENOS
H ACOMPÁÑENOS
K ACOMPÁÑENOS
M ACOMPÁÑENOS
I ACOMPÁÑENOS
L acompañemos
J ACOMPÁÑENOS
N ACCOMPAGNICE
1822 Amar. ACOMPÁÑENOS
1841 O ACOMPÁÑENOS
P ACOMPÁÑENOS
U ACOMPÁÑENOS
V ACOMPÁÑENOS

At times *G makes an error, the meaning of which is not clear. One of the other editions of Stemma IV, M, follows *G in Graph 146, whereas L tries unsuccessfully to correct. On both Graphs 146 and 147. K follows *F, which has the correct witness.

The word on Graph 146 appears in a speech by Celestina as she is trying to win the confidence of Pármeno.

> . . . É tú gana amigos que es cosa durable. Ten con ellos constancia. No viuas en flores. Dexa los vanos prometimientos de los señores, los cuales *deshechan* la substancia de sus siruientes con huecos é vanos prometimientos.
> *(Cej. I, I, 102, 1. 1; C–T, 53, 1. 15)*

DESECHAN *ABCD*E + Stemma III + K
deshechan PUV
scacciano N
dessecan *GM
dessean L
desecan Amar. + O

The word on Graph 147 is taken from a speech by Celestina, soon after she and Pármeno have reached the home of Areúsa.

> . . . Otro es el que ha de llorar las necessidades, que no tú. Yerua PASCE quien lo cumple. Tal vida quien quiera se la quería.
> *(Cej. I, VII, 248, 1. 2; C–T, 140, 1. 2)*

PASCE Stemma I + *EPU*FHIJK + N + Amar.
pace V + O
parece *GL
parce M

### *Edition M*

Long ago Foulché-Delbosc suspected that both M and J were published in Italy. Miss Penney believes they might have been published in Spain. The texts of the two editions are not closely related since J belongs to Stemma III and M to Stemma IV.

There are many errors in M but not as many as in J. Both editions were apparently hastily edited and published. There are few additions in either, but M has a considerable number of omissions. In the quotations below, the words in majuscule appear in other editions but are wanting in M.

One of the longest omissions in M is attributable to haplography: QUANDO . . . QUANDO. It appears in Act XXI:

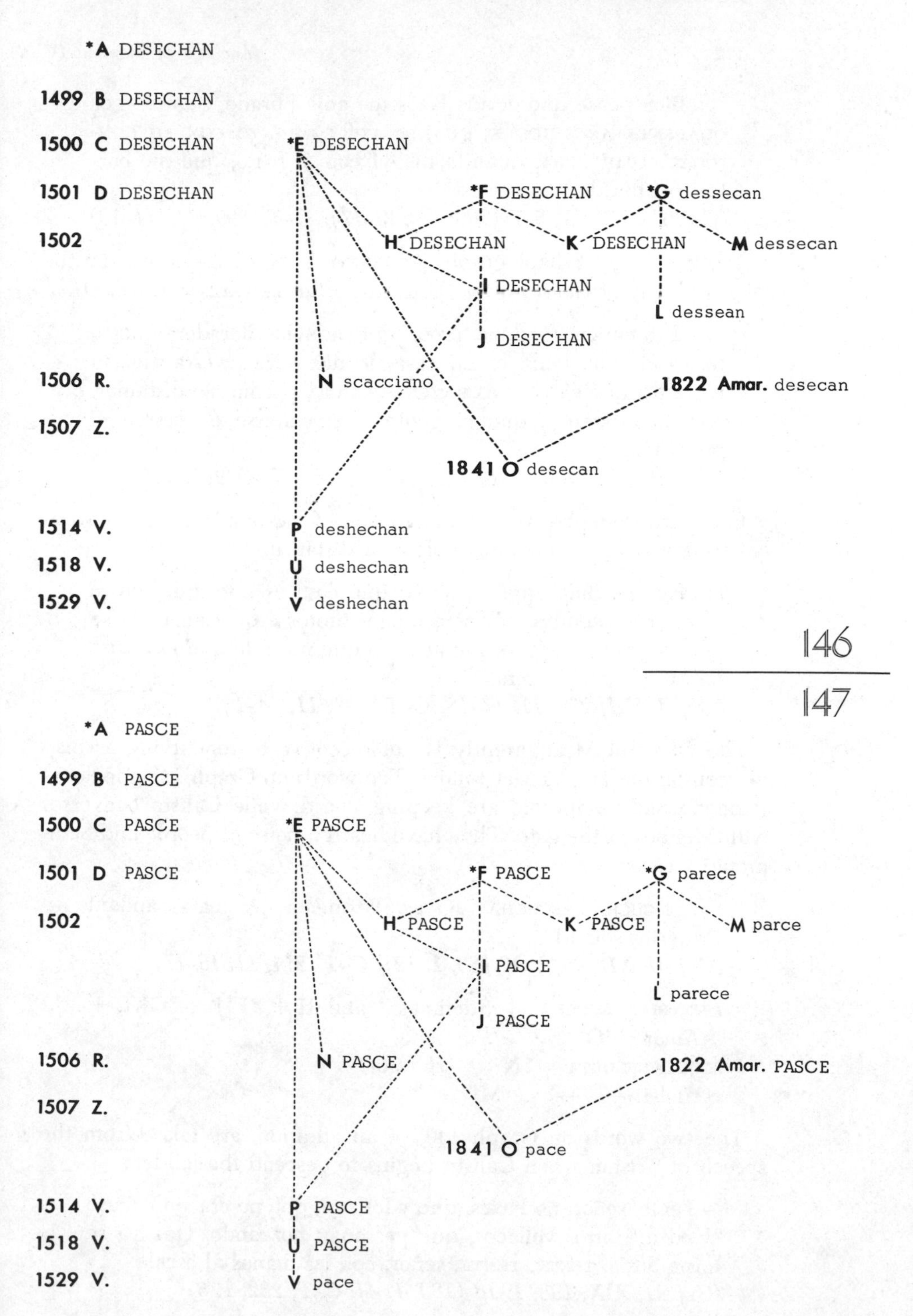
*A DESECHAN
1499 B DESECHAN
1500 C DESECHAN
*E DESECHAN
1501 D DESECHAN
*F DESECHAN
*G dessecan
1502
H DESECHAN
K DESECHAN
M dessecan
I DESECHAN
L dessean
J DESECHAN
1506 R.
N scacciano
1822 Amar. desecan
1507 Z.
1841 O desecan
1514 V.
P deshechan
1518 V.
U deshechan
1529 V.
V deshechan
146
147
*A PASCE
1499 B PASCE
1500 C PASCE
*E PASCE
1501 D PASCE
*F PASCE
*G parece
1502
H PASCE
K PASCE
M parce
I PASCE
L parece
J PASCE
1506 R.
N PASCE
1822 Amar. PASCE
1507 Z.
1841 O pace
1514 V.
P PASCE
1518 V.
U PASCE
1529 V.
V pace

> . . . Bien pensé que de tus lazos me auía librado, QUANDO LOS QUARENTA AÑOS TOQUÉ, QUANDO FUÍ CONTENTO CON MI CONJUGAL COMPAÑERA, quando me ví con el fruto, que me cortaste el día de oy.
> *(Cej. II, 225, ll. 5–7 [209, ll. 15–17]; C–T, 299, ll. 11–13)*

Another case of haplography—POR NO . . . POR NO—occurs in the long soliloquy of Calisto after the death of his servants and Celestina.

> . . . E también se deue creer que aquella lloradera moça, que Celestina tenía en su casa, le dió rezia priessa con su triste llanto é él, POR NO HAZER BULLICIO, por no me disfamar, por no esperar á que la gente se leuantasse é oyessen el pregón, . . .
> *(Cej. II, XIV, 136, l. 14 [126, ll. 15–16]; C–T, 243, l. 2)*

In a third example—LO QUE . . . LO QUE—Celestina is using her wiles on Areúsa as Pármeno watches from a distance.

> . . . Paresce, hija, que no sé yo qué cosa es esto, que nunca ví estar vn hombre con vna muger juntos é que jamás passé por ello ni gozé de lo que gozas é que no sé lo que PASSAN É LO QUE dizen é hazen.
> *(Cej. I, VII, 259, ll. 17–18; C–T, 147, ll. 14–15)*

The editor of M apparently is not receptive to repetitions, as may be seen on the graphs that follow. The words on Graph 148 appear as Pármeno and Sempronio are keeping guard while Calisto converses with Melibea at the gate. They have heard a noise of people and Sempronio wishes to run away.

> . . . ¡ESCUCHA, ESCUCHA! ¿Oyes, Pármeno? ¡A malas andan! ¡Muertos somos!
> *(Cej. II, XII, 95, l. 16 [89, l. 12]; C–T, 214, ll. 16–17)*

ESCUCHA, ESCUCHA     Stemmas I and II + *FIJ + *GKL + Amar. + O
SCOLTA, SCOLTA     N     (H falta)
escucha (———)     M

The two words on Graph 149, in an addition, are taken from the speech of Tristán when Calisto begins to descend the ladder.

> —Tente, señor, no baxes, que ydos son; que no era sino Traso el coxo é otros vellacos, que passauan bozeando. Que ya se torna Sosia. TENTE, TENTE, señor, con las manos al escala.
> *(Cej. II, XIX, 198, l. 16 [184, l. 4]; C–T, 282, l. 6)*

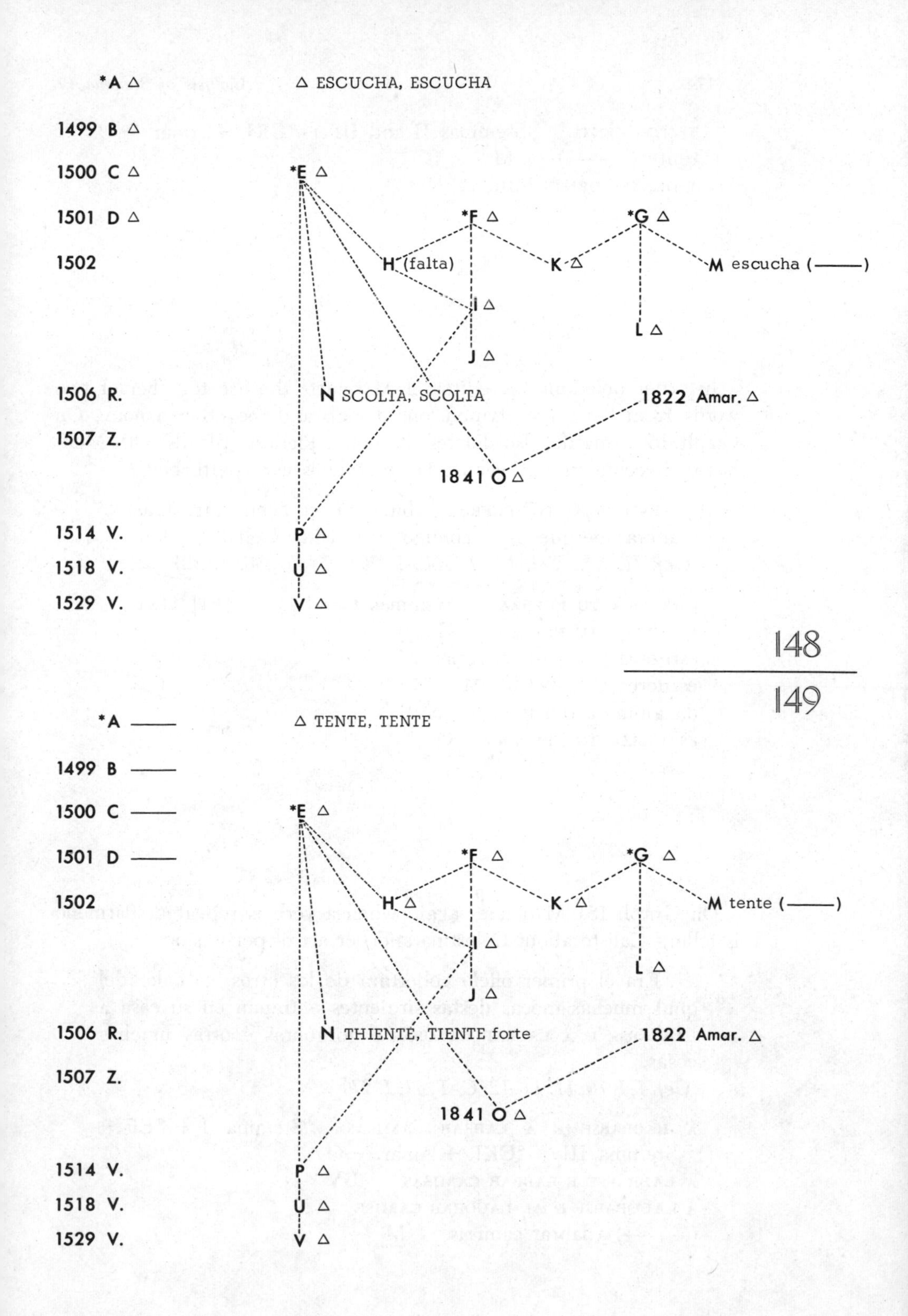
*A △
△ ESCUCHA, ESCUCHA
1499 B △
1500 C △
*E △
1501 D △
*F △
*G △
1502
H (falta)
K △
M escucha (——)
I △
L △
J △
1506 R.
N SCOLTA, SCOLTA
1822 Amar. △
1507 Z.
1841 O △
1514 V.
P △
1518 V.
U △
1529 V.
V △
148
149
*A ——
△ TENTE, TENTE
1499 B ——
1500 C ——
*E △
1501 D ——
*F △
*G △
1502
H △
K △
M tente (——)
I △
L △
J △
1506 R.
N THIENTE, TIENTE forte
1822 Amar. △
1507 Z.
1841 O △
1514 V.
P △
1518 V.
U △
1529 V.
V △

TENTE, TENTE Stemmas II and III + *GKL + Amar. + O
tente (———) M
THIENTE, TIENTE forte N

In other deletions the editor of M rejects the use together of two words from the same etymon, one a verb and the other a noun. On Graph 150 Amarita also deletes the noun. Pleberio pleads with Melibea to become strong because her mother is very perturbed.

> . . . ESFUERÇA TU FUERÇA, abiua tu coraçon, arréziate de manera que puedas tú comigo yr á visitar á ella.
> *(Cej. II, XX, 204, l. 20 [189, l. 20]; C–T, 286, l. 22)*

ESFUERÇA TU FUERZA Stemmas I and II + *FIJ*GKL
ESFUERÇA TU FUERZA H
esfuerza (———) Amar.
esfuerça (———) M
da animo a tua forza N
ESFUERZA TU FUERZA O

On Graph 151 M deletes again when a verb is repeated. Pármeno is telling Calisto about Celestina and her art of persuasion.

> . . . Era el primer oficio cobertura de los otros, so color del qual muchas moças destas siruientes entrauan en su casa Á LABRARSE É Á LABRAR CAMISAS é gorgueras é otras muchas cosas.
> *(Cej. I, I, 70, ll. 11–12; C–T, 41, l. 27)*

Á LABRARSE É Á LABRAR CAMISAS Stemma I + *EP + Stemma III + *GKL + Amar. + O
Á LABRARSE É LABRAR CAMISAS UV
A LAUORARSE & AL LAUORAR CAMISE N
(———) a labrar camisas M

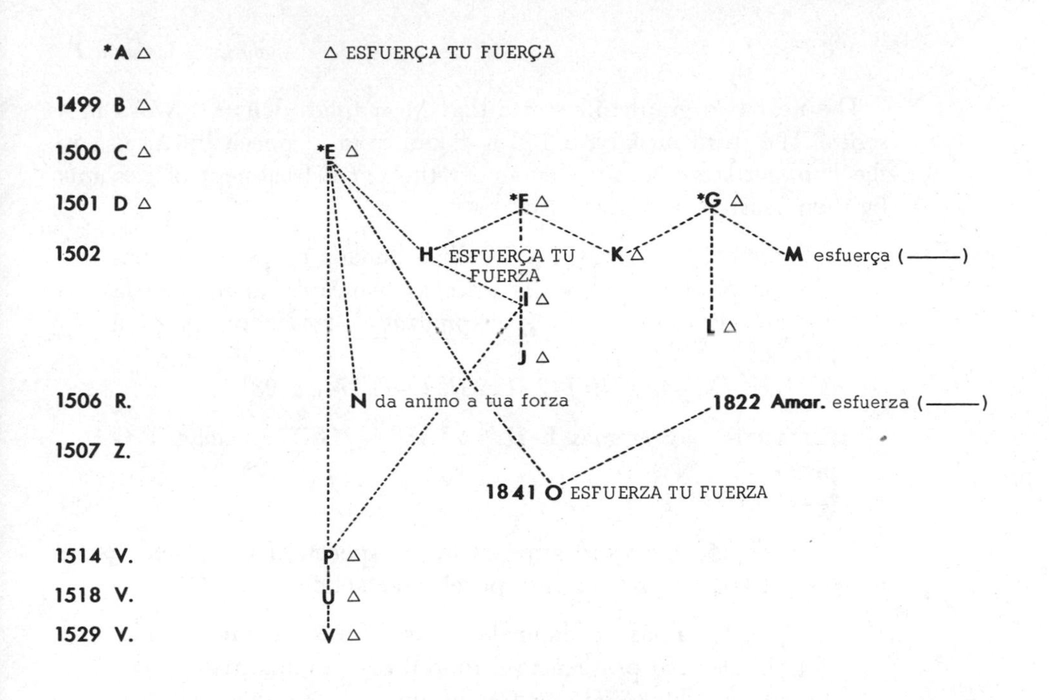
*A △
△ ESFUERÇA TU FUERÇA
1499 B △
1500 C △
*E △
1501 D △
*F △
*G △
1502
H ESFUERÇA TU FUERZA
K △
M esfuerça (——)
I △
L △
J △
1506 R.
N da animo a tua forza
1822 Amar. esfuerza (——)
1507 Z.
1841 O ESFUERZA TU FUERZA
1514 V.
P △
1518 V.
U △
1529 V.
V △

150

151

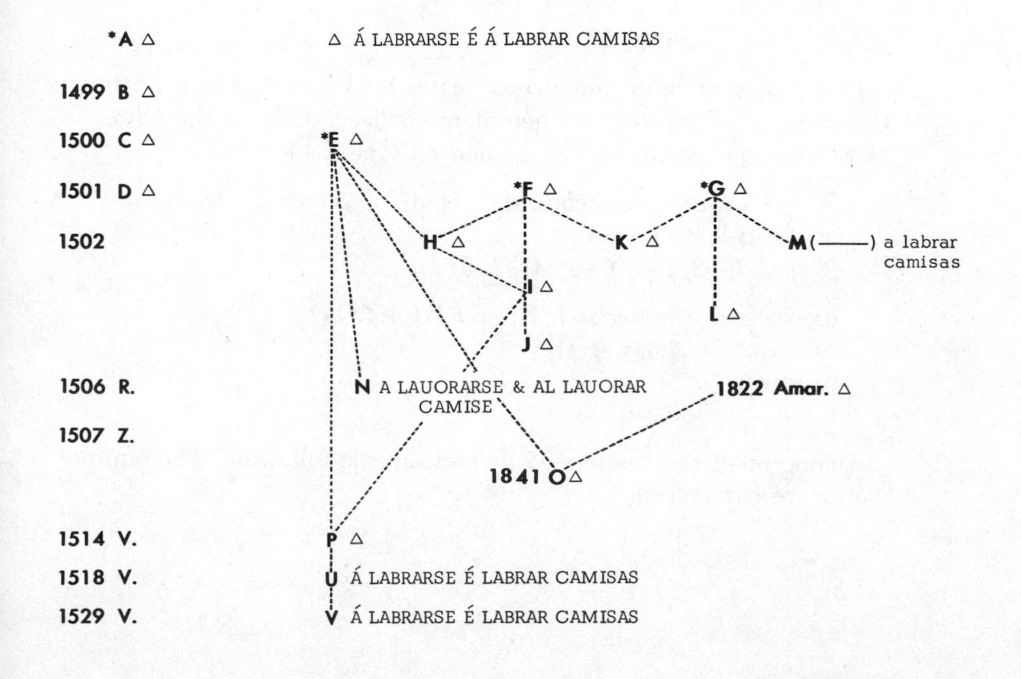
*A △
△ Á LABRARSE É Á LABRAR CAMISAS
1499 B △
1500 C △
*E △
1501 D △
*F △
*G △
1502
H △
K △
M (——) a labrar camisas
I △
L △
J △
1506 R.
N A LAUORARSE & AL LAUORAR CAMISE
1822 Amar. △
1507 Z.
1841 O△
1514 V.
P △
1518 V.
U Á LABRARSE É LABRAR CAMISAS
1529 V.
V Á LABRARSE É LABRAR CAMISAS

The next two graphs illustrate that M at times deletes a word in a series. The word on Graph 152 is taken from a speech by Areúsa in the banquet scene as she denounces the harsh treatment of servants by their masters and mistresses.

> . . . Ven acá, mala muger, la gallina hauada no paresce: pues búscala presto; si nó, en la primera blanca de tu soldada la contaré. E tras esto mill chapinazos é PELLIZCOS, palos é açotes.
> *(Cej. II, IX, 44, 1. 10 [42, 1. 23]; C–T, 174, 1. 23)*

| | |
|---|---|
| PELLIZCOS | Stemmas I, II, and III + *GKL + Amar. + O |
| pizzichi | N |
| (———) | M |

On Graph 153 the word appears in the speech of Sempronio as he tongue-lashes Pármeno for his speech and actions.

> . . . Que tú fablas en daño de todos é yo a ninguno ofendo. ¡O! ¡Intolerable pestilencia é mortal te consuma, rixoso, EMBIDIOSO, maldito! Toda esta es la amistad, que con Celestina é comigo hauías concertado?
> *(Cej. I, VI, 207, 1. 9; C–T, 114, 1. 11)*

| | | |
|---|---|---|
| EMBIDIOSO | Stemmas I and II + *GL | |
| ENBIDIOSO | H | |
| E*m*BIDIOSO | *FIJ | |
| ENVIDIOSO | Amar. + O | |
| INUIDIOSO | N | |
| (———) | M | (K falta) |

In a series of brief statements made by Pármeno when he hears Celestina tell Sempronio of her plans to fleece Calisto, the editor of M deletes the last statement, as seen on Graph 154:

> . . . ¡O Calisto desauenturado, abatido, ciego! . . . Deshecho es, vencido es, CAYDO ES . . . .
> *(Cej. I, I, 92, 1. 9; C–T, 48, 1. 2)*

| | |
|---|---|
| CAYDO ES | Stemmas I, II, and III + *GKL |
| CAIDO ES | Amar. + O |
| CADUTO E | N |
| (———) | M |

Among other cases where M deletes are the following. The omitted words are capitalized.

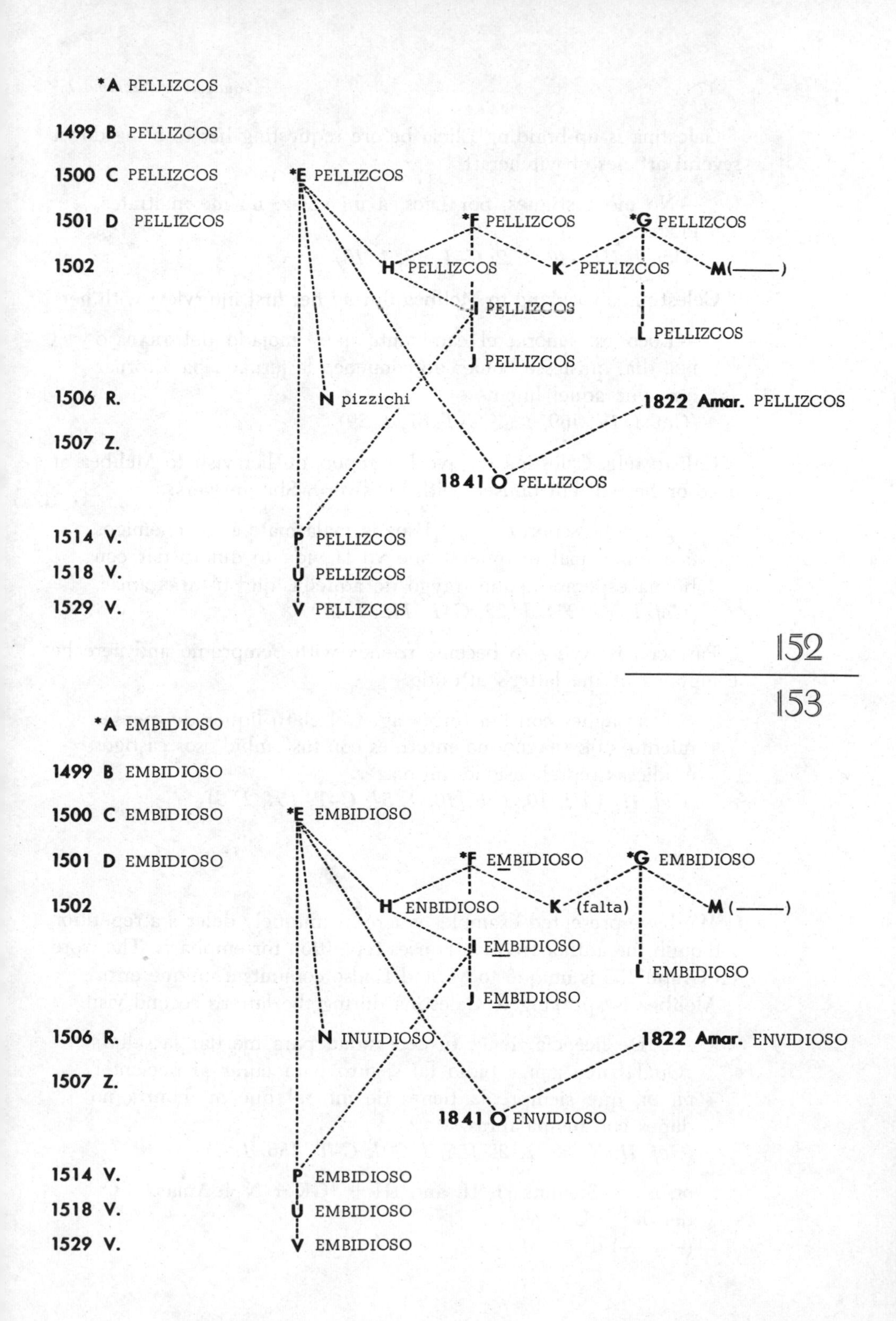
*A PELLIZCOS
1499 B PELLIZCOS
1500 C PELLIZCOS
*E PELLIZCOS
1501 D PELLIZCOS
*F PELLIZCOS
*G PELLIZCOS
1502
H PELLIZCOS
K PELLIZCOS
M(——)
I PELLIZCOS
L PELLIZCOS
J PELLIZCOS
1506 R.
N pizzichi
1822 Amar. PELLIZCOS
1507 Z.
1841 O PELLIZCOS
1514 V.
P PELLIZCOS
1518 V.
U PELLIZCOS
1529 V.
V PELLIZCOS
152
153
*A EMBIDIOSO
1499 B EMBIDIOSO
1500 C EMBIDIOSO
*E EMBIDIOSO
1501 D EMBIDIOSO
*F EMBIDIOSO
*G EMBIDIOSO
1502
H ENBIDIOSO
K (falta)
M (——)
I EMBIDIOSO
L EMBIDIOSO
J EMBIDIOSO
1506 R.
N INUIDIOSO
1822 Amar. ENVIDIOSO
1507 Z.
1841 O ENVIDIOSO
1514 V.
P EMBIDIOSO
1518 V.
U EMBIDIOSO
1529 V.
V EMBIDIOSO

Celestina is up-braiding Elicia before requesting her to bring down several articles of witchcraft:

> —No me castigues, por Dios, á mi vejez; no me maltrates, ELICIA.
> *(Cej. I, III, 146, l. 2; C–T, 77, l. 16)*

Celestina is speaking to Melibea during her first interview with her:

> —Loco es, señora, el caminante que, enojado del TRABAJO DEL día, quisiesse boluer de comienço la jornada para tornar otra vez aquel lugar.
> *(Cej. I, IV, 169, l. 4; C–T, 87, l. 29)*

Calisto tells Celestina to give her report on her visit to Melibea at once or he will kill himself with his sword. She answers:

> —¿Espada, señor, o qué? ¡Espada mala mate á tus enemigos é á quien mal te quiere! que yo la vida te quiero dar con buena esperança, que traygo de aquella, que tú MÁS amas.
> *(Cej. I, VI, 204, l. 22; C–T, 112, l. 27)*

Pármeno is trying to become friends with Sempronio and here he complains of the latter's attitude:

> . . . no agües con tan turbia agua el claro liquor del pensamiento, QUE TRAYGO, no enturuies con tus embidiosos castigos é odiosas reprehensiones mi plazer.
> *(Cel. II, VIII, 10, l. 8 [10, l. 5]; C–T, 154, l. 3)*

We have presented examples where M uniquely deletes a repetition although the author frequently uses repetition for emphasis. The word on Graph 155 is unique to M, and L also commits a unique error.

Melibea is speaking to Celestina during the latter's second visit.

> . . . ¿De licencia tienes tú necessidad para me dar la salud? ¿Quál físico jamás pidió tal seguro para curar al paciente? DÍ, DÍ, que siempre la tienes de mí, tal que mi honrra no dañes con tus palabras.
> *(Cej. II, X, 58, l. 22 [55, l. 20]; C–T, 186, l. 3)*

| | |
|---|---|
| DÍ, DÍ | Stemmas I, II, and III + *GK + N + Amar. + O |
| de, dí | L |
| (———) dí | M |

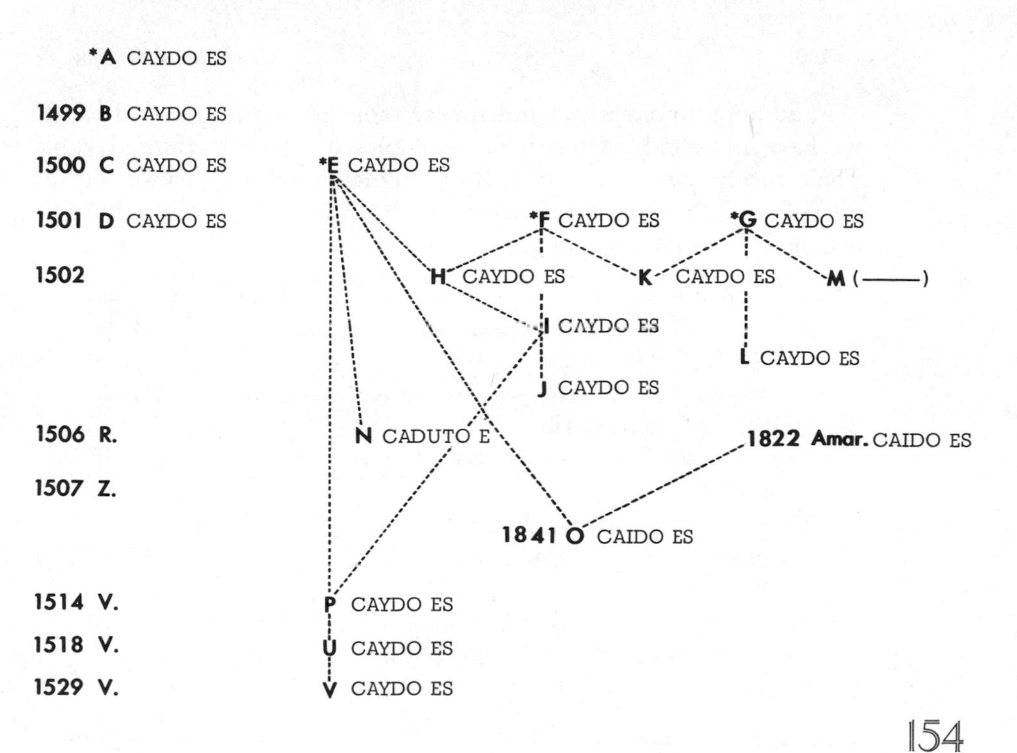


154
155

*A DÍ, DÍ

1499 B DÍ, DÍ

1500 C DÍ, DÍ

1501 D DÍ, DÍ

1502

1506 R.

1507 Z.

1514 V.

1518 V.

1529 V.

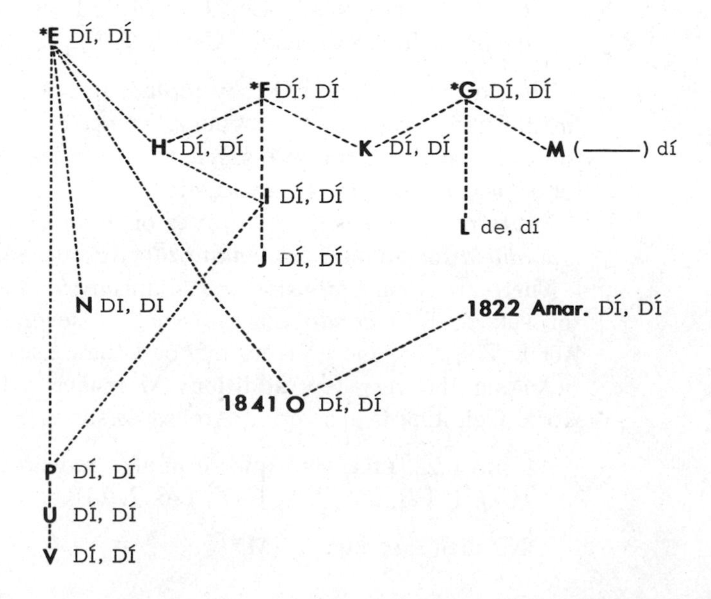

In addition to omissions and substitutions of words, many of which we have not cited, M has other examples of careless editorial work. Their nature contributed to making Foulché-Delbosc believe that M as well as J (N of his filiation) was printed in Italy. Below are a few instances from among many:

*primiera* for PRIMERA—Cej. I, III, 137, 1. 19; C–T, 74, 1. 27; Cej. I, VI, 225, 1. 18; C–T, 125, 1. 29; Cej. I, VII, 242, 11. 2–3; C–T, 136, 1. 20
*sieruientes* for SIRUIENTES—Cej. II, XX, 211, 1. 7 (195, 11. 25–26); C–T, 290, 1. 12
*ligieramente* for LIGERAMENTE—Cej. I, I, 71, 11. 3–4; C–T, 42, 1. 6
*tiengo* for TENGO—Cej. I, I, 86, 1. 10; C–T, 44, 1. 29
*miserabile* for MISERABLE—Cej. I, I, 52, 1. 2; C–T, 32, 11. 9–10
*impossibile* for IMPOSSIBLE—Cej. I, I, 58, 1. 11; C–T, 35, 1. 23
*quale* for QUAL—Cej. I, I, 56, 1. 14; C–T, 34, 1. 24; Cej. I, I, 35, 1. 6 (35, 1. 3); C–T 24, 1. 20

Many words have -ti- instead of -CI-: *Lucretia, pacientia, estationes, innocentia, licentia, gratias, presentia, magnificentia, manificentia, prouidentia.*

At times one syllable of a word is sheared off:

*albarra* for ALBARRANA—Cej. I, I, 79, 1. 13; C–T, 44, 1. 7
*tengas* for DETENGAS—Cej. I, I, 64, 1. 15; C–T, 39, 1. 7
*desperes* for DESESPERES—Cej. I, I, 57, 1. 16; C–T, 35, 1. 10

The vowels A, E, and O may replace one another: *donda* for DONDE, *fua* for FUÉ, *pessible* for POSSIBLE, *manester* for MENESTER, *manedas* for MONEDAS, *antos* for ANTES, *major* for MEJOR, *rozon* for RAZÓN, *agoro* for AGORA, *ramano* for ROMANO, etc.

M often presents *u for* N, *n for* U, or *e for* C: *uo* for NO, *qne* for QUE, *ignoraneia* for IGNORANCIA, *enlantrillo* for CULANTRILLO, etc.

There are some Latinisms or Italianisms: *quam* for QUÁN, *pregonam* for PREGONAN, *secundo* for SEGUNDO; *et* several times, especially in Act I. There are more errors in Act I than elsewhere.

Among the very few additions M makes is the following, of one word. Celestina is answering Areúsa as she talks to Pármeno.

—NO DIZE, HIJA, sino que se huelga mucho con tu amistad.
*(Cej. I, VII, 258, 1. 7; C–T, 146, 1. 15)*

No dize *esso* hija M

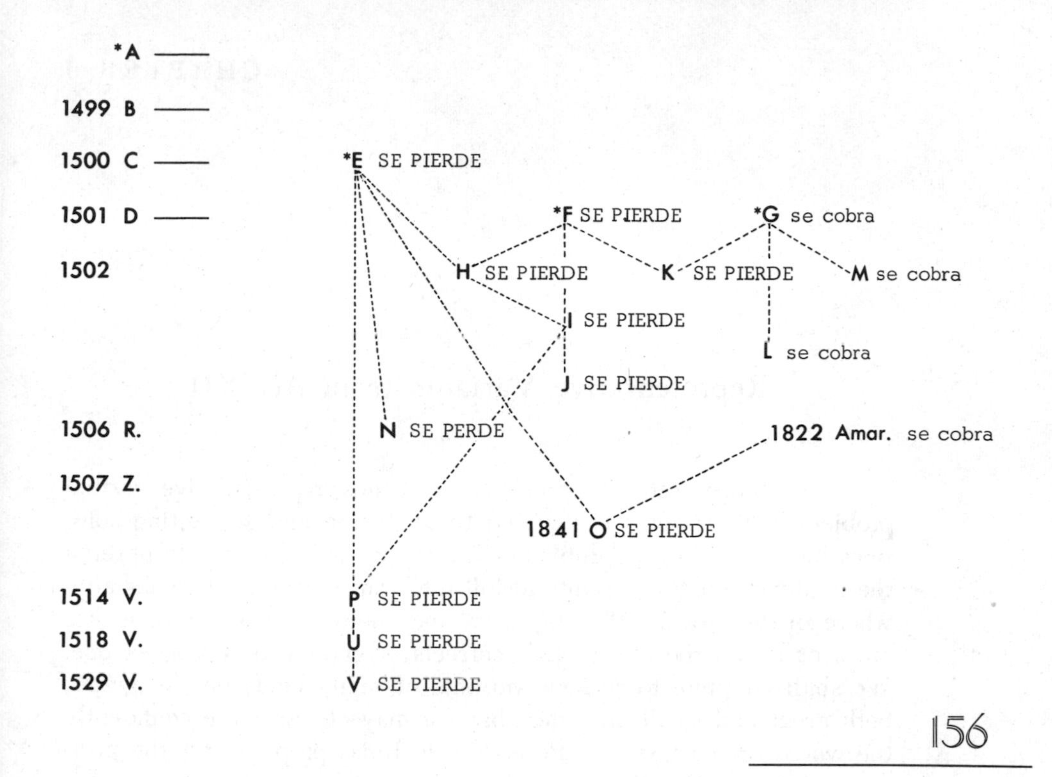


Although there are many deviations in L and M, the reader should bear in mind that these two editions normally follow *G closely and that K does so too except when drawing on *F instead of *G.

The word on Graph 156 appears in an addition. Areúsa asks Elicia to send Sosia to her so that she may plot vengeance for the death of their lovers. *GLM and Amarita replace the words.

> . . . Passa á mi casa tu ropa é alhajas é vente á mi compañía, que estarás muy sola é la tristeza es amiga de la soledad. Con nueuo amor oluidarás los viejos. Vn hijo que nasce restaura la falta de tres finados. Con nueuo sucessor SE PIERDE la alegre memoria é plazeres perdidos del passado.
> *(Cej. II, XV, 152, l. 10 [141, l. 21]; C–T, 253, l. 16)*

SE PIERDE  Stemmas II and III + K + O
SE PERDE  N
se cobra  *GLM + Amar.

# CHAPTER 9

# Representative Variants from Act XII

Since Act XII presents numerous representative textual problems, this chapter is devoted to analyzing and suggesting solutions for some of these problems. The reader will continue to observe the tendency for the variants to fall into four principal stemmas anywhere in the text. On the graphs we may note when an editor makes an error or, on the other hand, corrects or endeavors to correct one. We shall continue to present variants of many kinds on the graph, both great and small, in order that we may choose more confidently the words of the text that Fernando de Rojas prepared for the princeps edition of the Tragicomedia.

The first error of any edition in Act XII occurs at the beginning in the subtitle "Argumento del DOZENO Auto," where *F erroneously uses *dezeno* for DOZENO. The error is accepted by the three witnesses of Stemma III, HIJ, and is followed by *G, which in turn is reflected in KLM. Both N and O are correct—as well as Amarita, who may have followed the correction as found in Osmont, 1633. The distribution of the variants may be seen on Graph 157.

*(Cej. II, XII, 81, 1. 3 [76, 1. 3]; C–T, 203, 1. 1)*

| | |
|---|---|
| DOZENO | *ABCD*EPUV |
| DUODECIMO | N |
| DOCENO | Amar. + O |
| dezeno | *FHIJ*GKLM |

The error on Graph 158 may perhaps be attributed to the printers rather than to the editors, but it is possible that the latter or even the correctors are to blame. The two words TÚ and TU together were probably confusing, so that the same error was committed independently in three editions: B, P, and L. As often occurs, CD follow B and UV follow P. The words are directed to Calisto by Melibea near the close of their rendezvous at the gate.

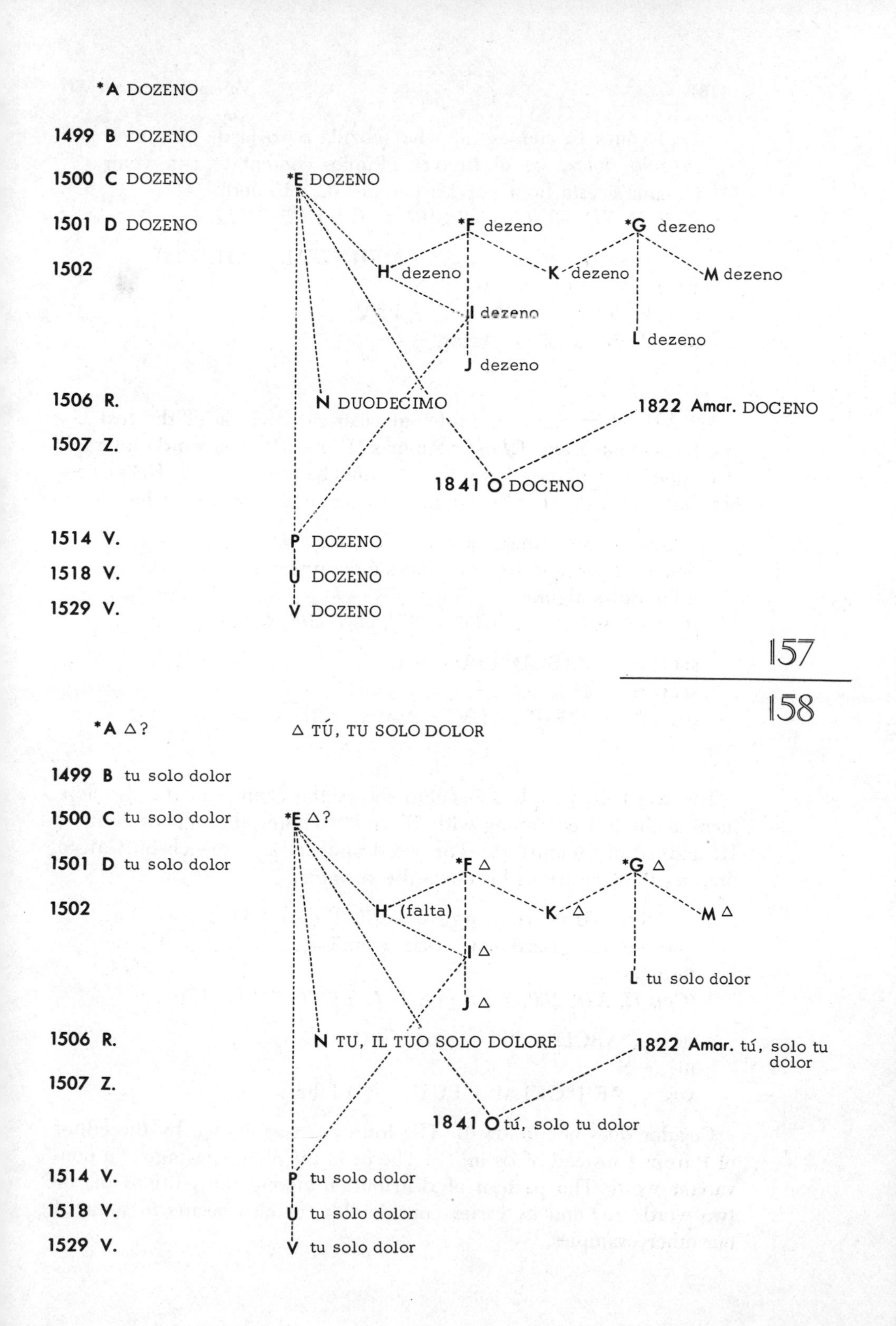
*A DOZENO
1499 B DOZENO
1500 C DOZENO
1501 D DOZENO
1502
*E DOZENO
*F dezeno
*G dezeno
H dezeno
K dezeno
M dezeno
I dezeno
L dezeno
J dezeno
1506 R.
N DUODECIMO
1822 Amar. DOCENO
1507 Z.
1841 O DOCENO
1514 V.
P DOZENO
1518 V.
U DOZENO
1529 V.
V DOZENO
157
158
*A △?
△ TÚ, TU SOLO DOLOR
1499 B tu solo dolor
1500 C tu solo dolor
*E △?
1501 D tu solo dolor
*F △
*G △
1502
H (falta)
K △
M △
I △
L tu solo dolor
J △
1506 R.
N TU, IL TUO SOLO DOLORE
1822 Amar. tú, solo tu dolor
1507 Z.
1841 O tú, solo tu dolor
1514 V.
P tu solo dolor
1518 V.
U tu solo dolor
1529 V.
V tu solo dolor

. . . É pues tú sientes tu pena senzilla é yo la de entramos, *tu solo dolor,* yo el tuyo é el mío, conténtate con venir mañana á esta hora por las paredes de mi huerto.
*(Cej. II, XII, 93, ll. 11–12 [87, l. 11]; C–T, 213, l. 1)*

TÚ, TU SOLO DOLOR *A?*E?*FIJ*GKM (H falta)
TU, IL TUO SOLO DOLORE N
tu solo dolor BCD + L + PUV
tú, solo tu dolor Amar. + O

Act XII offers many examples of clear-cut division of the text between Stemmas I and II and Stemmas III and IV. The word on Graph 159 appears in a speech by Calisto directed to Melibea. He assures her that he is safe, for his courageous servants will protect him.

—Señora, no temas, que á buen SEGURO vengo. Los míos deuen de ser, que son unos locos é desarman á quantos passan é huyríales alguno.
*(Cej. II, XII, 97, l. 7 [90, l. 27]; C–T, 215, l. 20)*

SEGURO *ABCD*EPUV + O
SECURO N
recaudo *FIJ*GKLM + Amar. (H falta)

The word on Graph 160 again shows the change in the development of the text beginning with *F and extending throughout Stemma III and all of Stemma IV. The word appears in a speech by Calisto praising the bravery of his cowardly servants.

. . . Fijos, en mucho cargo *vos* soy. Rogad á Dios por salud, que yo os galardonaré más conplidamente vuestro buen seruicio.
*(Cej. II, XII, 100, l. 22 [94, l. 16]; C–T, 218, l. 17)*

os *ABCD + *E + Amar. + O
ui N
vos *FIJ*GKLM + PUV (H falta)

Cejador does not follow B. The form *vos* was chosen by the editor of P from I instead of os in *E. The *os* in the above passage is a nonvariant word. The pattern of distribution among the editions of the two words *vos* and *os* varies considerably, as also occurs in some of our other examples.

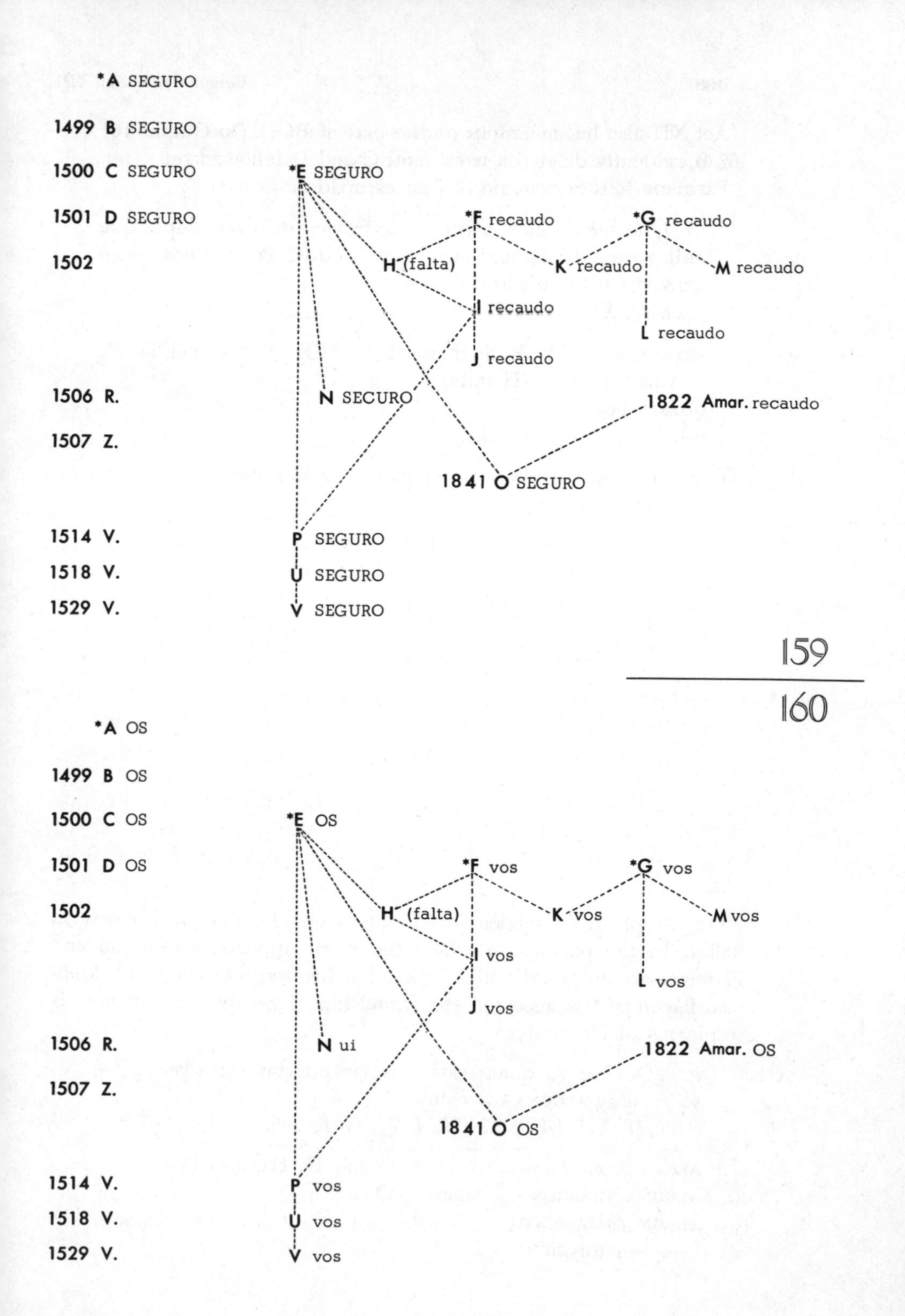
*A SEGURO
1499 B SEGURO
1500 C SEGURO
*E SEGURO
1501 D SEGURO
*F recaudo
*G recaudo
1502
H (falta)
K recaudo
M recaudo
I recaudo
L recaudo
J recaudo
1506 R.
N SECURO
1822 Amar. recaudo
1507 Z.
1841 O SEGURO
1514 V.
P SEGURO
1518 V.
U SEGURO
1529 V.
V SEGURO
159
160
*A OS
1499 B OS
1500 C OS
*E OS
1501 D OS
*F vos
*G vos
1502
H (falta)
K vos
M vos
I vos
L vos
J vos
1506 R.
N ui
1822 Amar. OS
1507 Z.
1841 O OS
1514 V.
P vos
1518 V.
U vos
1529 V.
V vos

Act XII also has omissions on the part of BCD. On Graphs 161 and 162 B evidently deleted a word, and C and D followed suit.

Pármeno tells Sempronio of past escapades.

> . . . Que nueue años seruí á los frayles de Guadalupe, que mill vezes nos apuñeáuamos yo é otros. Pero nunca como ESTA VEZ houe miedo de morir.
> *(Cej. II, XII, 96, 1. 17 [90, 1. 13]; C–T, 215, 1. 8)*

ESTA VEZ *A + Stemma II + *FIJ + Stemma IV + Amar. + O (H falta)
QUESTA UOLTA N
ésta (———) BCD

Cejador does not follow B nor place VEZ in italics.

On Graph 162 Cejador inserts the word ALGUNA in his text in italics. In the passage in which the word appears, Sempronio and Pármeno are on guard while Calisto has his first interview with Melibea. Pármeno has accepted the friendship of Sempronio and now is suspicious of his master.

> . . . ¿Qué sé yo quién está tras las puertas cerradas? ¿Qué sé yo si ay ALGUNA trayción?
> *(Cej. II, XII, 84, 1. 13 [79, 1. 7]; C–T, 206, 1. 28)*

ALGUNA TRAYCIÓN *A + Stemmas II, III, and IV
ALGUNA TRAICIÓN Amar. + O
ALCUN TRADIMENTO N
(———) trayción BCD

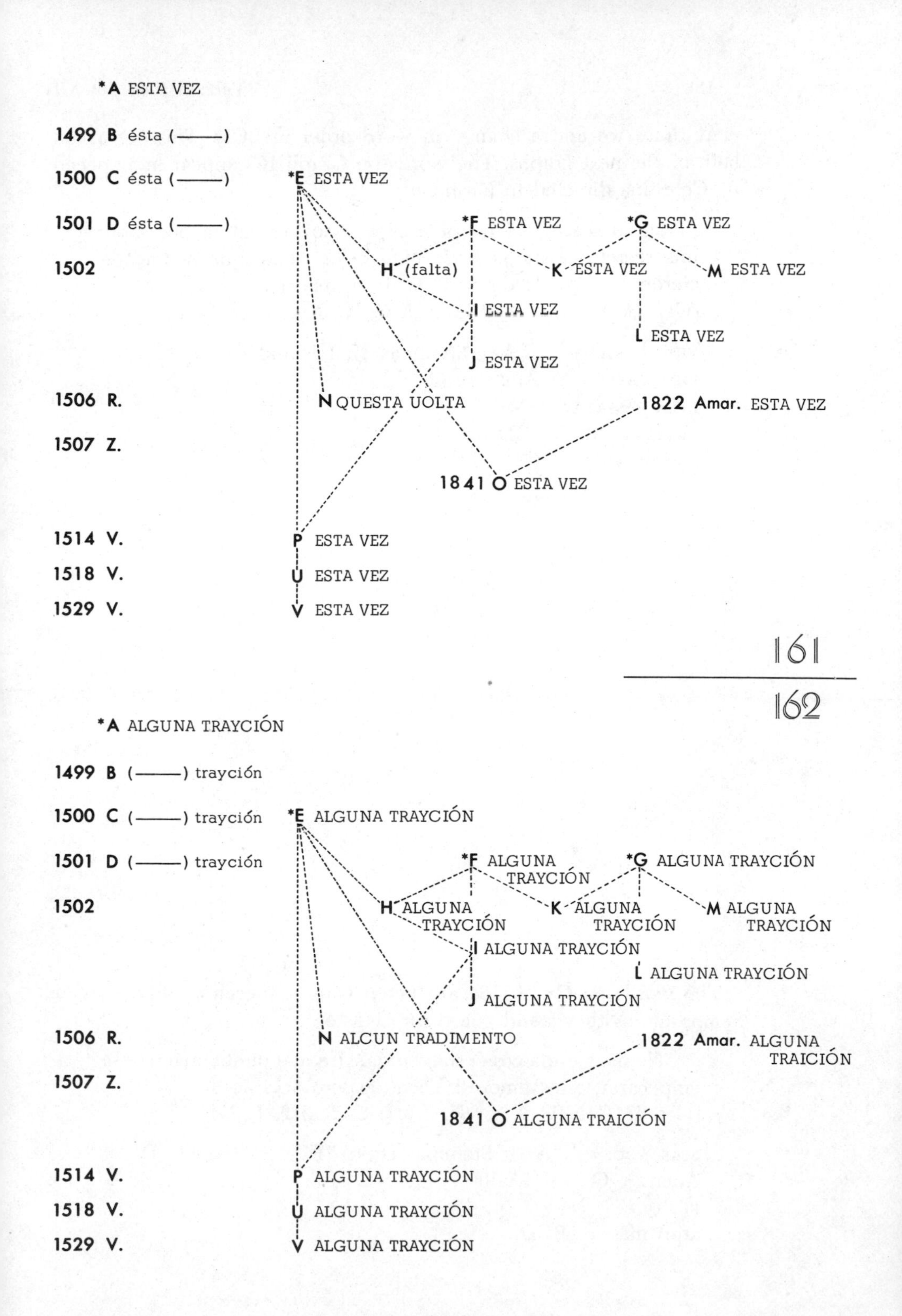

*A ESTA VEZ
1499 B ésta (——)
1500 C ésta (——)
*E ESTA VEZ
1501 D ésta (——)
*F ESTA VEZ
*G ESTA VEZ
1502
H (falta)
K ESTA VEZ
M ESTA VEZ
I ESTA VEZ
L ESTA VEZ
J ESTA VEZ
1506 R.
N QUESTA UOLTA
1822 Amar. ESTA VEZ
1507 Z.
1841 O ESTA VEZ
1514 V.
P ESTA VEZ
1518 V.
U ESTA VEZ
1529 V.
V ESTA VEZ
161
162
*A ALGUNA TRAYCIÓN
1499 B (——) trayción
1500 C (——) trayción
*E ALGUNA TRAYCIÓN
1501 D (——) trayción
*F ALGUNA TRAYCIÓN
*G ALGUNA TRAYCIÓN
1502
H ALGUNA TRAYCIÓN
K ALGUNA TRAYCIÓN
M ALGUNA TRAYCIÓN
I ALGUNA TRAYCIÓN
L ALGUNA TRAYCIÓN
J ALGUNA TRAYCIÓN
1506 R.
N ALCUN TRADIMENTO
1822 Amar. ALGUNA TRAICIÓN
1507 Z.
1841 O ALGUNA TRAICIÓN
1514 V.
P ALGUNA TRAYCIÓN
1518 V.
U ALGUNA TRAYCIÓN
1529 V.
V ALGUNA TRAYCIÓN

At times we find a change in word order in BCD. This occurs on both of the next graphs. The words on Graph 163 appear in a speech by Celestina directed to Pármeno.

> . . . É tú, Pármeno, no pienses que soy tu catiua por saber mis secretos é mi *passada vida* é los casos, que nos acaescïeron á mí é á la desdichada de tu madre.
> *(Cej. II, XII, 109, 1. 2 [102, 1. 6]; C–T, 224, 11. 9–10)*

| | |
|---|---|
| VIDA PASSADA | *A + Stemmas II, III, and IV |
| VIDA PASADA | Amar. + O |
| UITA PASSATA | N |
| passada vida | BD |
| pasada vida | C |

The words on Graph 164 are taken from a speech by Pármeno to Sempronio as they stand guard for Calisto.

> . . . No me agrada cosa esta venida. ¡En mal punto creo que se empeçaron estos amores! Yo no espero MÁS AQUÍ.
> *(Cej. II, XII, 93, 1. 4 [87, 1. 4]; C–T, 212, 1. 25)*

MÁS AQUÍ *A + Stemma II + *FIJ + Stemma IV + Amar. + O (H falta)
PIU QUI N
aquí más BCD

*A VIDA PASSADA

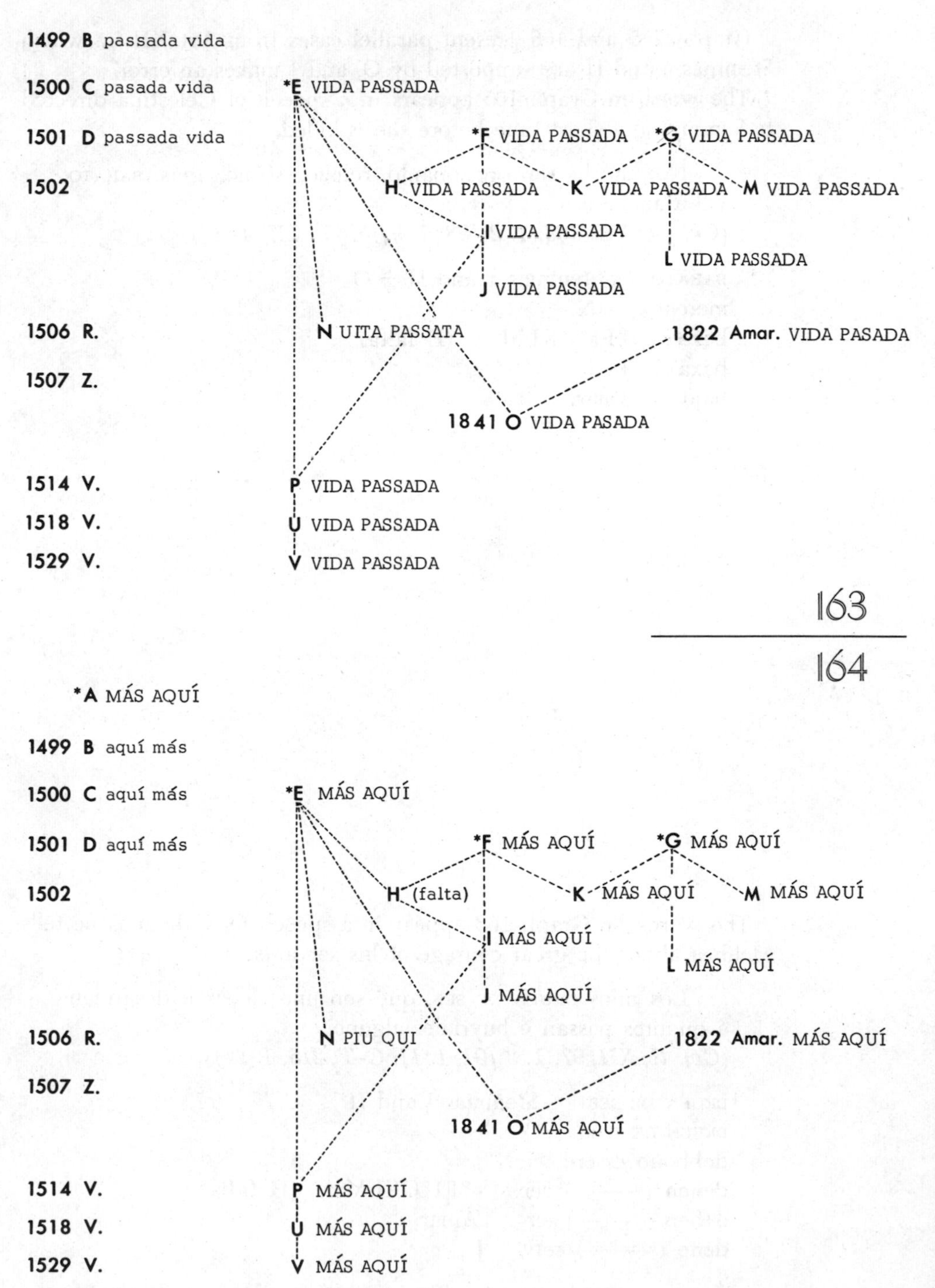
1499 B passada vida
1500 C pasada vida
*E VIDA PASSADA
1501 D passada vida
*F VIDA PASSADA
*G VIDA PASSADA
1502
H VIDA PASSADA
K VIDA PASSADA
M VIDA PASSADA
I VIDA PASSADA
L VIDA PASSADA
J VIDA PASSADA
1506 R.
N UITA PASSATA
1822 Amar. VIDA PASADA
1507 Z.
1841 O VIDA PASADA
1514 V.
P VIDA PASSADA
1518 V.
U VIDA PASSADA
1529 V.
V VIDA PASSADA
163
164
*A MÁS AQUÍ
1499 B aquí más
1500 C aquí más
*E MÁS AQUÍ
1501 D aquí más
*F MÁS AQUÍ
*G MÁS AQUÍ
1502
H (falta)
K MÁS AQUÍ
M MÁS AQUÍ
I MÁS AQUÍ
L MÁS AQUÍ
J MÁS AQUÍ
1506 R.
N PIU QUI
1822 Amar. MÁS AQUÍ
1507 Z.
1841 O MÁS AQUÍ
1514 V.
P MÁS AQUÍ
1518 V.
U MÁS AQUÍ
1529 V.
V MÁS AQUÍ

Graphs 165 and 166 present parallel cases from Act XII, in which Stemmas I and II are supported by O, and J makes an error.

The word on Graph 165 appears in a speech of Celestina directed to Sempronio a short time before she is killed.

> . . . No ha de ser oro quanto reluze; si nó, más BARATO valdría.
> *(Cej. II, XII, 105, 1. 2 [98, 1. 9]; C–T, 221, 1. 14)*

BARATO Stemmas I and II + O
mercato N
baxo *FI*GKLM (H falta)
baxa J
bajo Amar.

The words on Graph 166 appear in a speech by Calisto as he tells Melibea about the great courage of his servants.

> . . . Los míos DEUEN DE SER, que son unos locos é desarman á quantos passan é huyríales alguno.
> *(Cej. II, XII, 97, 1. 8 [91, 1. 1]; C–T, 215, 1. 21)*

DEUEN DE SER Stemmas I and II
DEBEN DE SER O
debbono essere N
deuen (———) ser *FI*GKLM (H falta)
deben (———) ser Amar.
deue (———) ser J

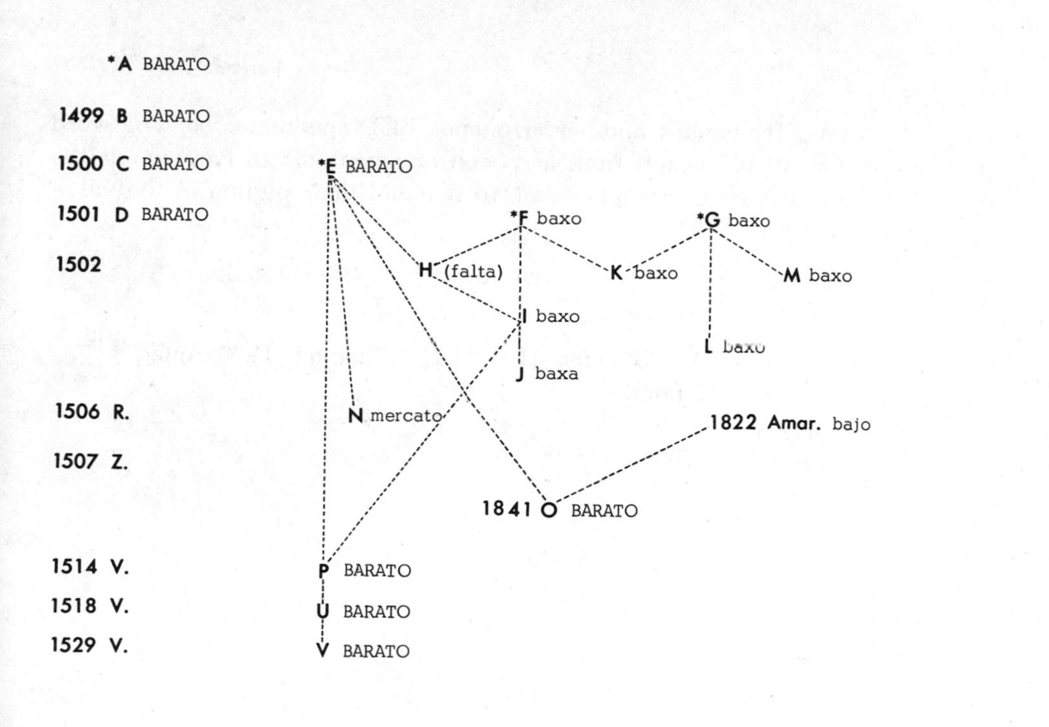
*A BARATO
1499 B BARATO
1500 C BARATO
*E BARATO
1501 D BARATO
*F baxo
*G baxo
1502
H (falta)
K baxo
M baxo
I baxo
L baxo
J baxa
1506 R.
N mercato
1822 Amar. bajo
1507 Z.
1841 O BARATO
1514 V.
P BARATO
1518 V.
U BARATO
1529 V.
V BARATO

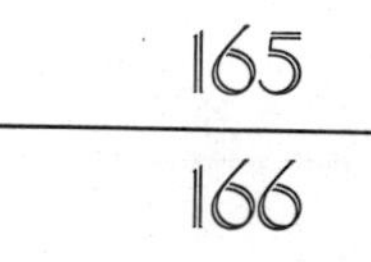
165
166

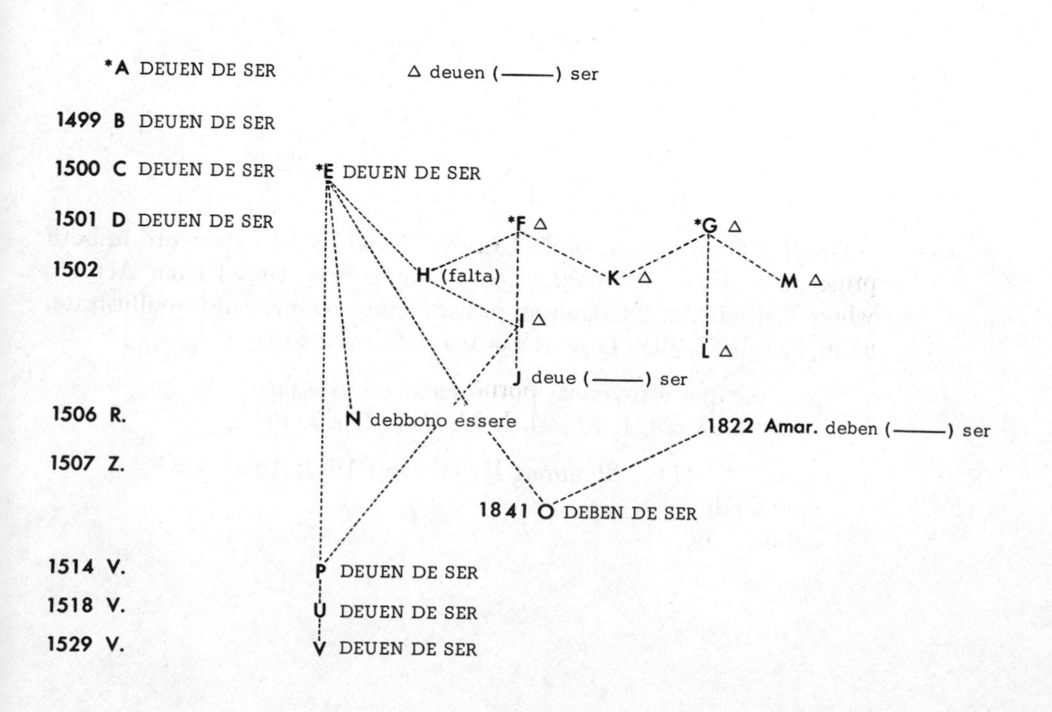
*A DEUEN DE SER
△ deuen (——) ser
1499 B DEUEN DE SER
1500 C DEUEN DE SER
*E DEUEN DE SER
1501 D DEUEN DE SER
*F △
*G △
1502
H (falta)
K △
M △
I △
L △
J deue (——) ser
1506 R.
N debbono essere
1822 Amar. deben (——) ser
1507 Z.
1841 O DEBEN DE SER
1514 V.
P DEUEN DE SER
1518 V.
U DEUEN DE SER
1529 V.
V DEUEN DE SER

Act XII contains another erroneous BCD spelling, *cabo*. The word on Graph 167 comes from a speech of Sempronio to Pármeno as the two approach Celestina's home to demand their portion of the value of the chain.

—¡Ce! ¡ce! Calla, que duerme *cabo* esta ventanilla.
*(Cej. II, XII, 101, 1. 15 [95, 1. 4]; C–T, 218, 1. 29)*

CABE *A + Stemma II + *FIJ + Stemma IV + Amar. + O (H falta)
appresso N
cabo BCD

Graph 168 illustrates, as do Graphs 72 and 73, that the word in both princeps editions was CABE. The example here comes from Act IX, where Celestina at the banquet praises wine. We present it to illustrate, as in Graph 73, that D at times corrects *cabo* to CABE.

. . . yo, que estoy sola, porné *cabo* mí este jarro . . . .
*(Cej. II, IX, 29, 1. 10 [28, 1. 5]; C–T, 166, 1. 18)*

CABE *AD + Stemmas II, III, and IV + Amar. + O
apresso di N
cabo BC

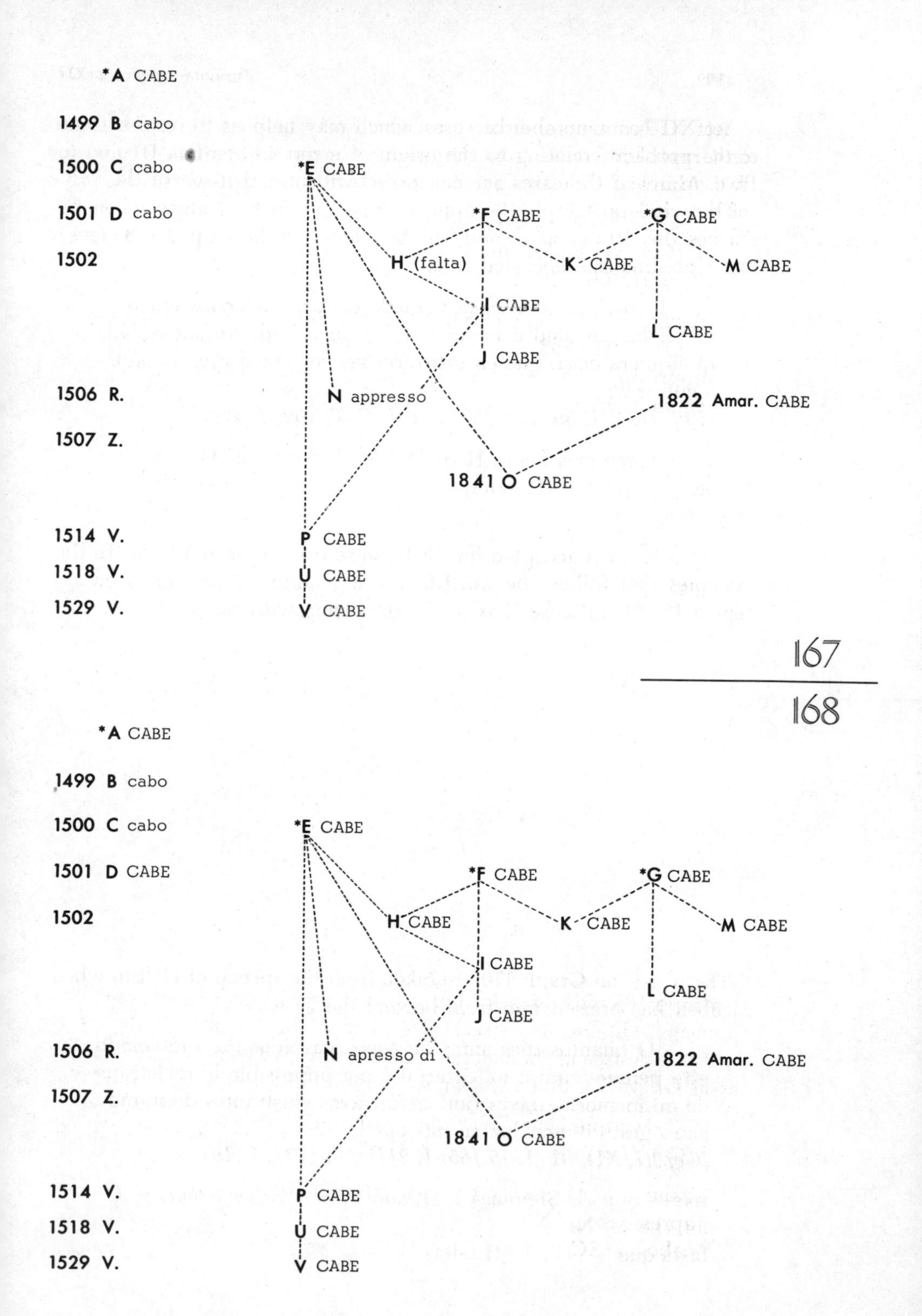
*A CABE
1499 B cabo
1500 C cabo
*E CABE
1501 D cabo
*F CABE
*G CABE
1502
H (falta)
K CABE
M CABE
I CABE
L CABE
J CABE
1506 R.
N appresso
1822 Amar. CABE
1507 Z.
1841 O CABE
1514 V.
P CABE
1518 V.
U CABE
1529 V.
V CABE
167
168
*A CABE
1499 B cabo
1500 C cabo
*E CABE
1501 D CABE
*F CABE
*G CABE
1502
H CABE
K CABE
M CABE
I CABE
L CABE
J CABE
1506 R.
N apresso di
1822 Amar. CABE
1507 Z.
1841 O CABE
1514 V.
P CABE
1518 V.
U CABE
1529 V.
V CABE

Act XII has a number of cases which may help us to resolve some of the problems relating to the origin of errors in Stemma III and to PUV. Many of the cases are concerned with initial H- versus f-.

The word on Graph 169 appears in a speech by Calisto when he reaches the gate at night and Melibea does not show up. He believes that Celestina has deceived him.

> . . . Pero el triste que, desarmado é sin proueer los engaños é celadas, se vino á meter por las puertas de TU seguridad, qualquiera cosa, que en contrario vea, es razón que me atormente . . . .
> *(Cej. II, XII, 89, 1. 8 [83, 1. 19]; C–T, 209, 1. 27)*

TU Stemmas I and II + *GLM + Amar. + O
su FIJK (H falta)
TUA N

The word *su* is accepted for *F because it is supported by K. In the examples that follow the word in I and J normally has not been accepted for *F because K is not a supporting witness.

The words on Graph 170 are taken from the speech of Calisto when Melibea has praised him from beyond the gate.

> . . . ¡O quántos días antes de agora passados me fué venido este pensamiento á mi coraçón é por impossible le rechaçaua de mi memoria, HASTA QUE ya los rayos ylustrantes de tu muy claro gesto dieron luz en mis ojos . . . .
> *(Cej. II, XII, 91, 1. 15 [85, 1. 21]; C–T, 211, 1. 19)*

HASTA QUE Stemmas I, II, and IV + *F? + Amar. + O
fin che N
fasta que IJ (H falta)

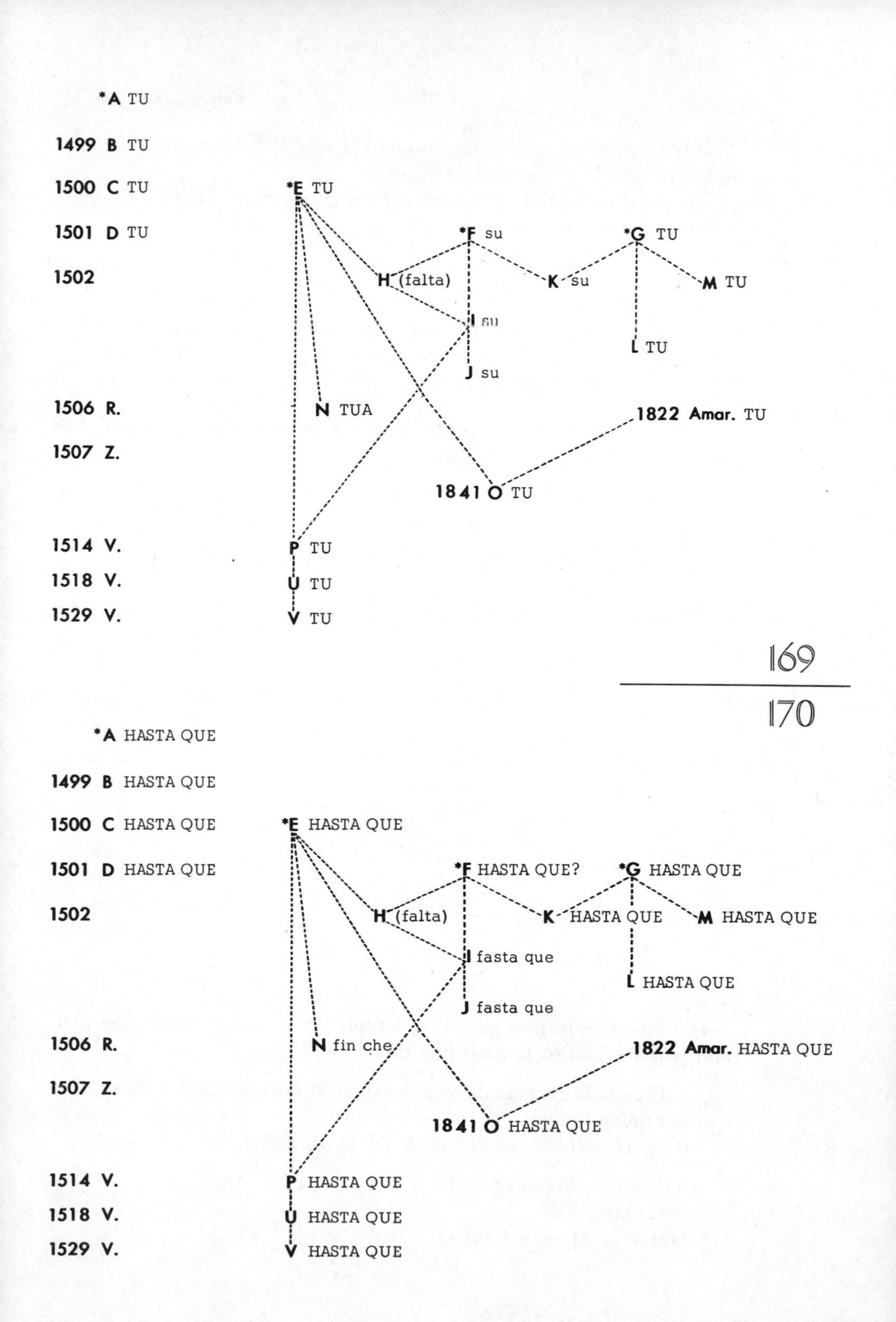

*A TU
1499 B TU
1500 C TU
1501 D TU
1502
1506 R.
1507 Z.
1514 V.
1518 V.
1529 V.
*E TU
*F su
*G TU
H (falta)
K su
M TU
I su
L TU
J su
N TUA
1822 Amar. TU
1841 O TU
P TU
U TU
V TU
169
170
*A HASTA QUE
1499 B HASTA QUE
1500 C HASTA QUE
1501 D HASTA QUE
1502
1506 R.
1507 Z.
1514 V.
1518 V.
1529 V.
*E HASTA QUE
*F HASTA QUE?
*G HASTA QUE
H (falta)
K HASTA QUE
M HASTA QUE
I fasta que
L HASTA QUE
J fasta que
N fin che
1822 Amar. HASTA QUE
1841 O HASTA QUE
P HASTA QUE
U HASTA QUE
V HASTA QUE

Three examples, including Graphs 171 and 172, illustrate the use of initial H- and f- in the verb HABLAR.

The word on Graph 171 is taken from a speech by Melibea directed to Lucrecia as Calisto reaches the gate.

—¡Loca, HABLA passo! Mira bien si es él.
*(Cej. II, XII, 88, 1. 3 [82, 1. 14]; C–T, 208, 1. 29)*

HABLA Stemmas I, II, and IV + *F? + Amar. + O
parla N
fabla IJ (H falta)

The verb appears in the plural in a speech of Sempronio directed to Pármeno as they stand guard.

—Salido deue auer Melibea. Escucha, que HABLAN quedito.
*(Cej. II, XII, 87, 1. 13 [81, 1. 18]; C–T, 208, 1. 15)*

HABLAN Stemmas I, II, and IV + *F? + Amar. + O
parlano N
fablan IJ (H falta)

The infinitive form appears on Graph 172. Calisto reaches the gate and is perturbed to find no one there.

—Este bullicio más de vna persona lo haze. Quiero HABLAR, sea quien fuere.
*(Cej. II, XII, 87, 1. 20 [82, 1. 7]; C–T, 208, 1. 23)*

HABLAR Stemmas I, II, and IV + *F? + Amar. + O
chiamare N
fablar IJ (H falta)

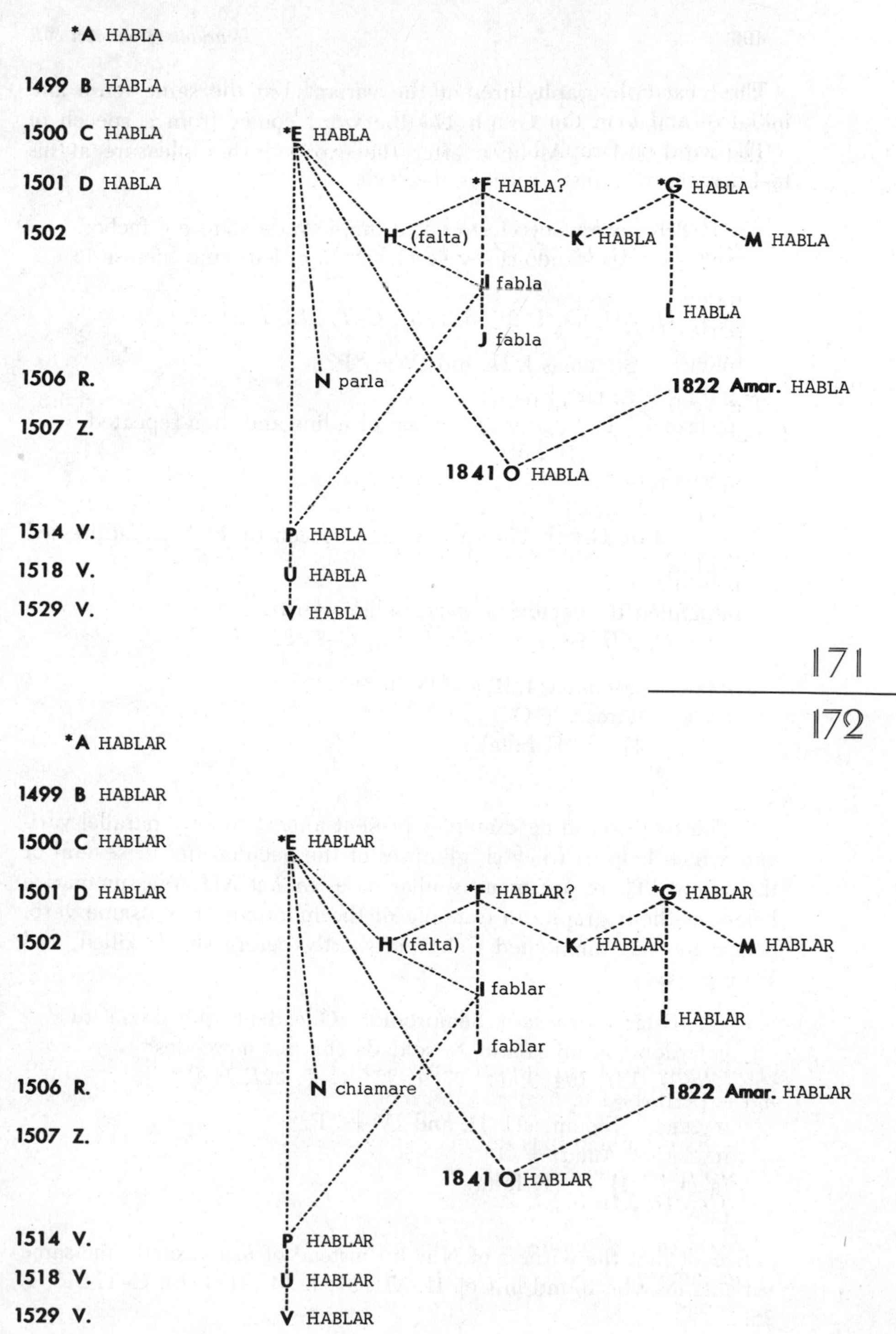

*A HABLA
1499 B HABLA
1500 C HABLA
*E HABLA
1501 D HABLA
*F HABLA?
*G HABLA
1502
H (falta)
K HABLA
M HABLA
I fabla
L HABLA
J fabla
1506 R.
N parla
1822 Amar. HABLA
1507 Z.
1841 O HABLA
1514 V.
P HABLA
1518 V.
U HABLA
1529 V.
V HABLA
171
172
*A HABLAR
1499 B HABLAR
1500 C HABLAR
*E HABLAR
1501 D HABLAR
*F HABLAR?
*G HABLAR
1502
H (falta)
K HABLAR
M HABLAR
I fablar
L HABLAR
J fablar
1506 R.
N chiamare
1822 Amar. HABLAR
1507 Z.
1841 O HABLAR
1514 V.
P HABLAR
1518 V.
U HABLAR
1529 V.
V HABLAR

The next two graphs present the variants, in the same tense and person, of HAZER. On Graph 173 the word comes from a speech of Calisto directed to Melibea after she expresses her pleasure at his arrival.

> . . . Pero, como soy cierto de tu limpieza de sangre é fechos, me estoy remirando si soy yo Calisto, á quien tanto bien se le HAZE.
> *(Cej. II, XII, 92, 1. 2 [86, 1. 5]; C–T, 212, 1. 2)*

HAZE    Stemmas I, II, and IV + *F?
HACE    Amar. + O
fa-faze    I    (*fa* is at the end of a line and then repeated.)
faze    J    (H falta)
fa    N

The word on Graph 174 appears in a speech by Pleberio addressed to Melibea.

> —¿Quién da patadas é HAZE bullicio en tu cámara?
> *(Cej. II, XII, 98, 1. 21 [92, 1. 13]; C–T, 216, 1. 28)*

HAZE    Stemmas I, II, and IV + *F?
HACE    Amar. + O
faze    IJ    (H falta)
fa    N

The two preceding examples present almost exactly parallel variants which help us to catch glimpses of the peculiarities of several of the editors. There are many similar cases in Act XII. We summarize below, without graph, an example of the infinitive of the same verb. Sempronio has threatened Celestina shortly before she is killed, and she replies:

> . . . ¿Estás en tu seso, Sempronio? ¿Qué tiene que HAZER tu galardón con mi salario, tu soldada con mis mercedes?
> *(Cej II, XII, 104, 1. 14 [97, 1. 22]; C–T, 221, 1. 4)*

HAZER    Stemmas I, II, and IV + *F?
HACER    Amar. + O
fazer    IJ    (H falta)
fare    N

Except that the witness of N is *far* instead of *fare,* exactly the same variants may be found in Cej. II, XII, 97, 1. 14 (91, 1. 6); C–T, 215, 1. 26:

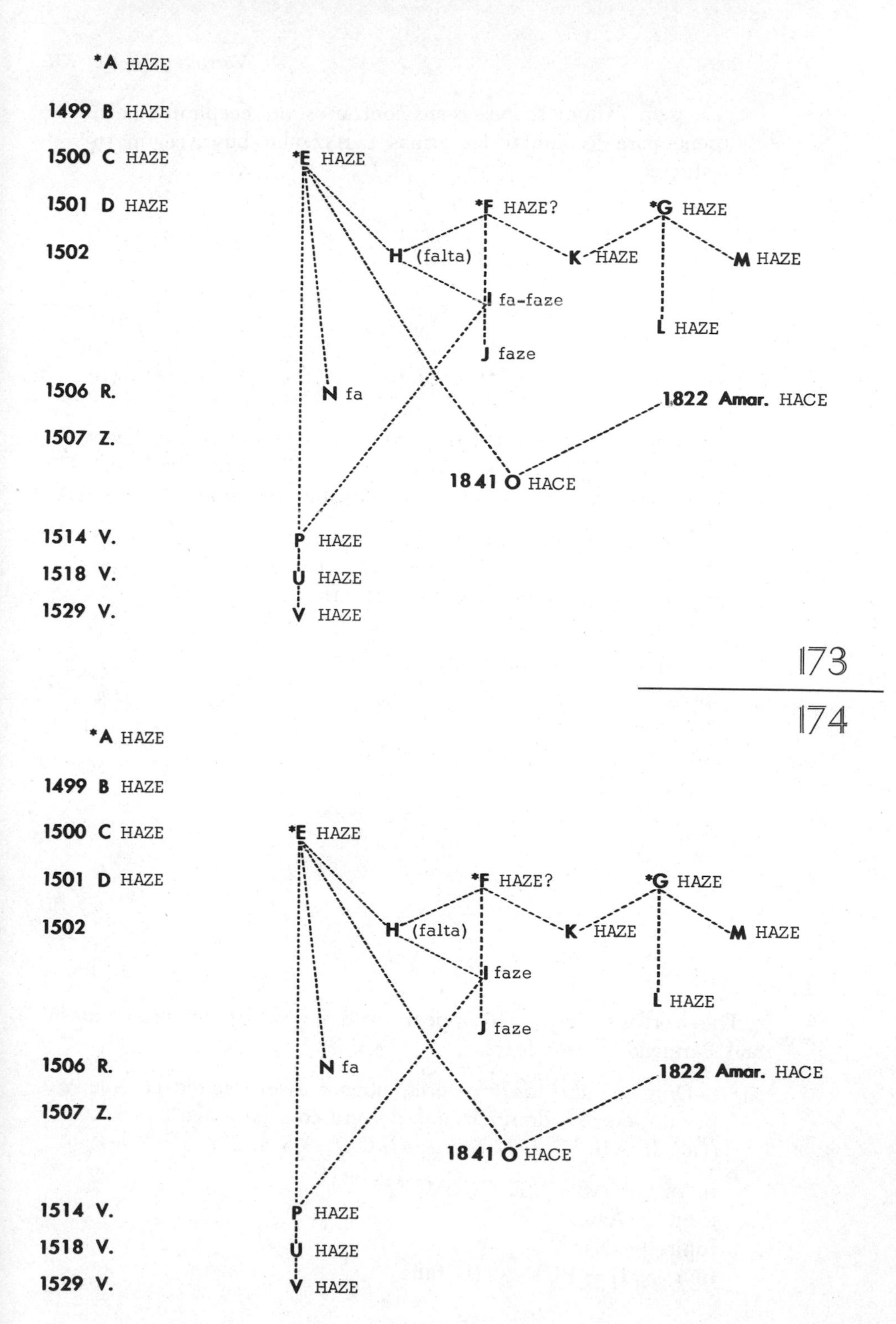
*A HAZE
1499 B HAZE
1500 C HAZE
1501 D HAZE
1502
1506 R.
1507 Z.
1514 V.
1518 V.
1529 V.
*E HAZE
*F HAZE?
*G HAZE
H (falta)
K HAZE
M HAZE
I fa-faze
L HAZE
J faze
N fa
1822 Amar. HACE
1841 O HACE
P HAZE
U HAZE
V HAZE
173
174
*A HAZE
1499 B HAZE
1500 C HAZE
1501 D HAZE
1502
1506 R.
1507 Z.
1514 V.
1518 V.
1529 V.
*E HAZE
*F HAZE?
*G HAZE
H (falta)
K HAZE
M HAZE
I faze
L HAZE
J faze
N fa
1822 Amar. HACE
1841 O HACE
P HAZE
U HAZE
V HAZE

. . . pero, avnque sean seys sus contrarios, no recebirán mucha pena para les quitar las armas é HAZERlos huyr, según su esfuerço.

The variants on the next two graphs illustrate the filiation between I and P which was discussed in Chapter 6. The word on Graph 175 is taken from a speech by Pármeno as he and Sempronio stand guard.

. . . Que nuestro amo, si es sentido, no temo que se escapará de manos desta gente de Pleberio, para podernos después demandar cómo lo HEZIMOS é incusarnos el huyr.
*(Cej. II, XII, 86, 1. 8 [81, 1. 5]; C–T, 208, 1. 4)*

HEZIMOS *ABCD*E*GKLM + *F?
HICIMOS O
HECIMOS Amar.
fezimos IJ + PUV (H falta)

The word on Graph 176 appears in a speech by Sempronio as he and Pármeno express fear.

—Dios nos libre de traydores, no nos ayan tomado la calle por do tenemos de HUYR; que de otra cosa no tengo temor.
*(Cej. II, XII, 87, 1. 17 [82, 1. 4]; C–T, 208, 1. 20)*

HUYR *ABCD*E*GKLM*F?
HUIR Amar. + O
fugire N
fuyr IJ + PUV (H falta)

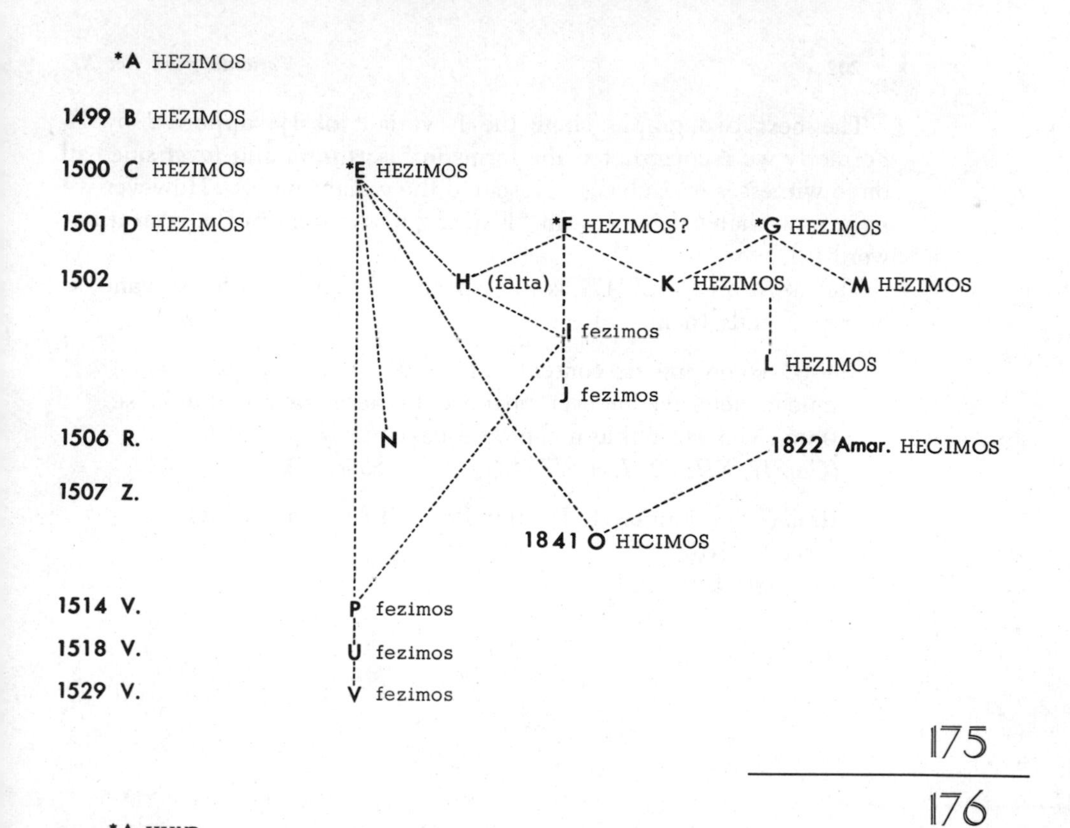


*A HUYR

1499 B HUYR

1500 C HUYR

1501 D HUYR

1502

1506 R.

1507 Z.

1514 V.

1518 V.

1529 V.

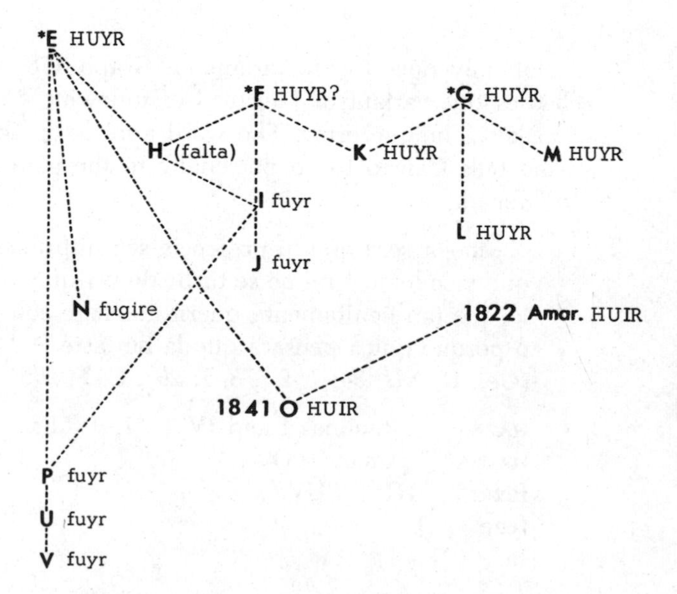

The next two graphs show the f- variant of IJ supported by H. Formerly we reconstructed the forms in *F as *faría* and *fazer* since all three witnesses in each case presented the variant with f-. However we have now changed f- to H- in *F owing to the data in the nonvariant word list.

The word on Graph 177 is in a speech by Calisto to his servants as he reprimands them.

> —¡O cómo me descontenta el oluido en los moços! De mi mucho acuerdo en esta noche é tu descuydar é oluido se HARÍA vna razonable memoria é cuydado.
> *(Cej. II, XII, 82, 1. 3 [77, 1. 1]; C–T, 205, 1. 5)*

HARÍA   Stemmas I, II, and IV + *F? + Amar. + O
faría   HIJ
se porria far   N

Not only does the f- variant on Graph 178 originate in H, but P chooses this variant of I instead of following *E. U and V follow P. J makes a unique error. The word appears in the speech where Pármeno tells Calisto to go personally to the gate lest Melibea become frightened.

> . . . mejor será que tu presencia sea su primer encuentro, porque viéndome á mí no se turbe de ver que de tantos es sabido lo que tan ocultamente quería HAZER é con tanto temor faze ó porque quiçá pensará que la burlaste.
> *(Cej. II, XII, 84, 1. 2 [78, 1. 20]; C–T, 206, 1. 19)*

HAZER   Stemmas I and IV + *E + *F?
HACER   Amar. + O
fazer   HI + PUV
feze   J
fa   N

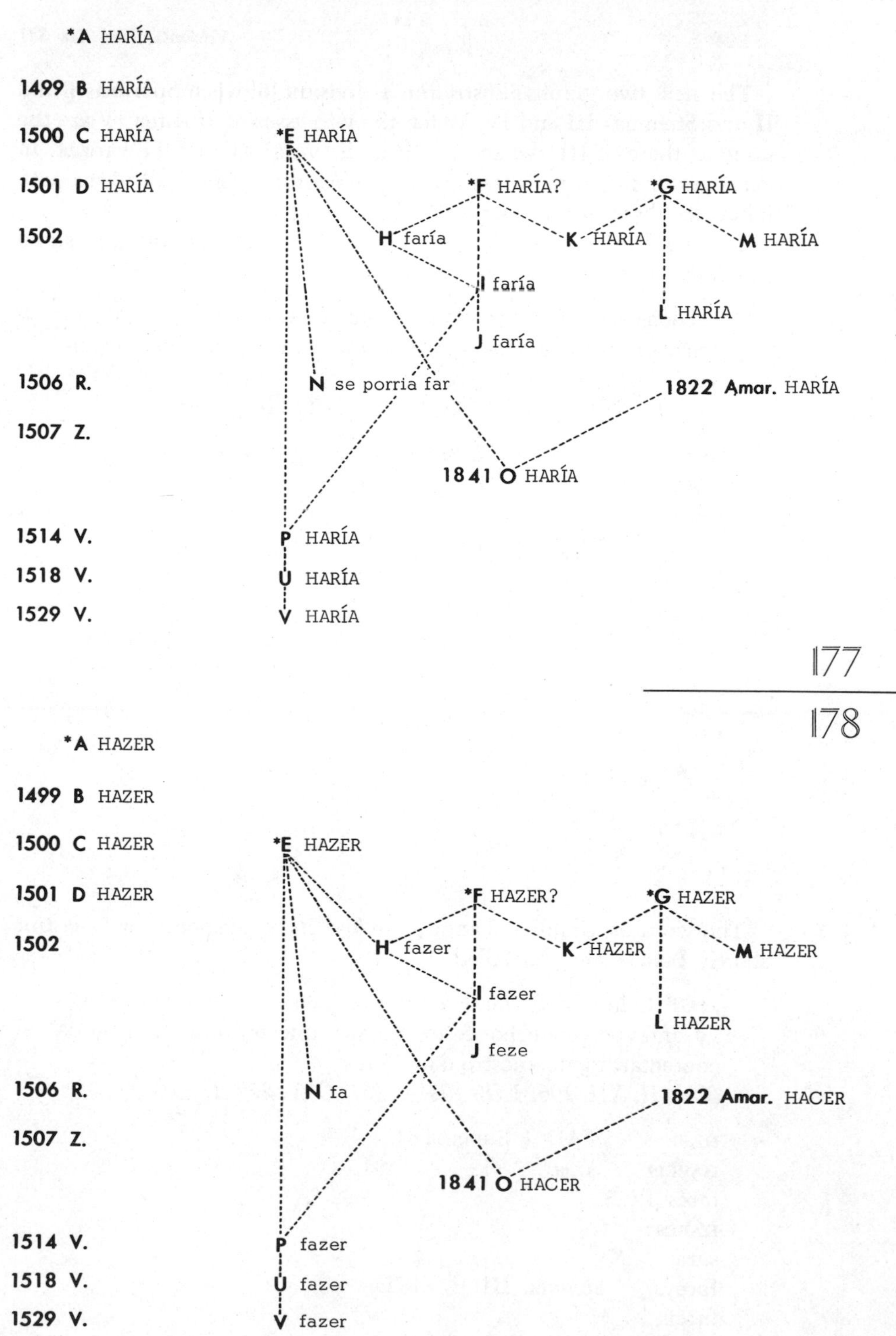

*A HARÍA
1499 B HARÍA
1500 C HARÍA
1501 D HARÍA
1502
1506 R.
1507 Z.
1514 V.
1518 V.
1529 V.
*E HARÍA
*F HARÍA?
*G HARÍA
H faría
K HARÍA
M HARÍA
I faría
L HARÍA
J faría
N se porria far
1822 Amar. HARÍA
1841 O HARÍA
P HARÍA
U HARÍA
V HARÍA
177
178
*A HAZER
1499 B HAZER
1500 C HAZER
1501 D HAZER
1502
1506 R.
1507 Z.
1514 V.
1518 V.
1529 V.
*E HAZER
*F HAZER?
*G HAZER
H fazer
K HAZER
M HAZER
I fazer
L HAZER
J feze
N fa
1822 Amar. HACER
1841 O HACER
P fazer
U fazer
V fazer

The next two graphs illustrate the division between Stemmas I and II and Stemmas III and IV. When the witnesses of Stemma IV are the same as those of III, we accept *F as the originator of the variant. In instances of H- versus f-, we usually place in majuscule all forms with initial H-, disregarding variations in spelling.

The word on Graph 179 is in a speech by Sempronio as they stand guard and Pármeno asks him about the stones.

> —Todas las vertí por yr más liuiano. Que harto tengo que lleuar en estas coraças, que me HIZISTE vestir por importunidad; . . .
> *(Cej. II, XII, 95, l. 14 [89, l. 10]; C–T, 214, l. 14)*

HEZISTE *ACD + Stemma II
HECISTE Amar. + O
HIZISTE B
feziste *FIJ + Stemma IV (H falta)
hai facta N

The word on Graph 180 appears at the end of a speech by Celestina shortly before she was killed.

> . . . É todo esto, de buen amor, porque holgastes que houiesse yo antes el prouecho destos passos, que no otra. É si no os contentardes, de vuestro daño *farés.*
> *(Cej. II, XII, 106, l. 19 [99, l. 25]; C–T, 222, l. 16)*

HARÉYS *AD + Stemma II
HARÉIS Amar. + O
farés B
HARÉS C
sara N
faréys Stemma III + *GKL
faréis M

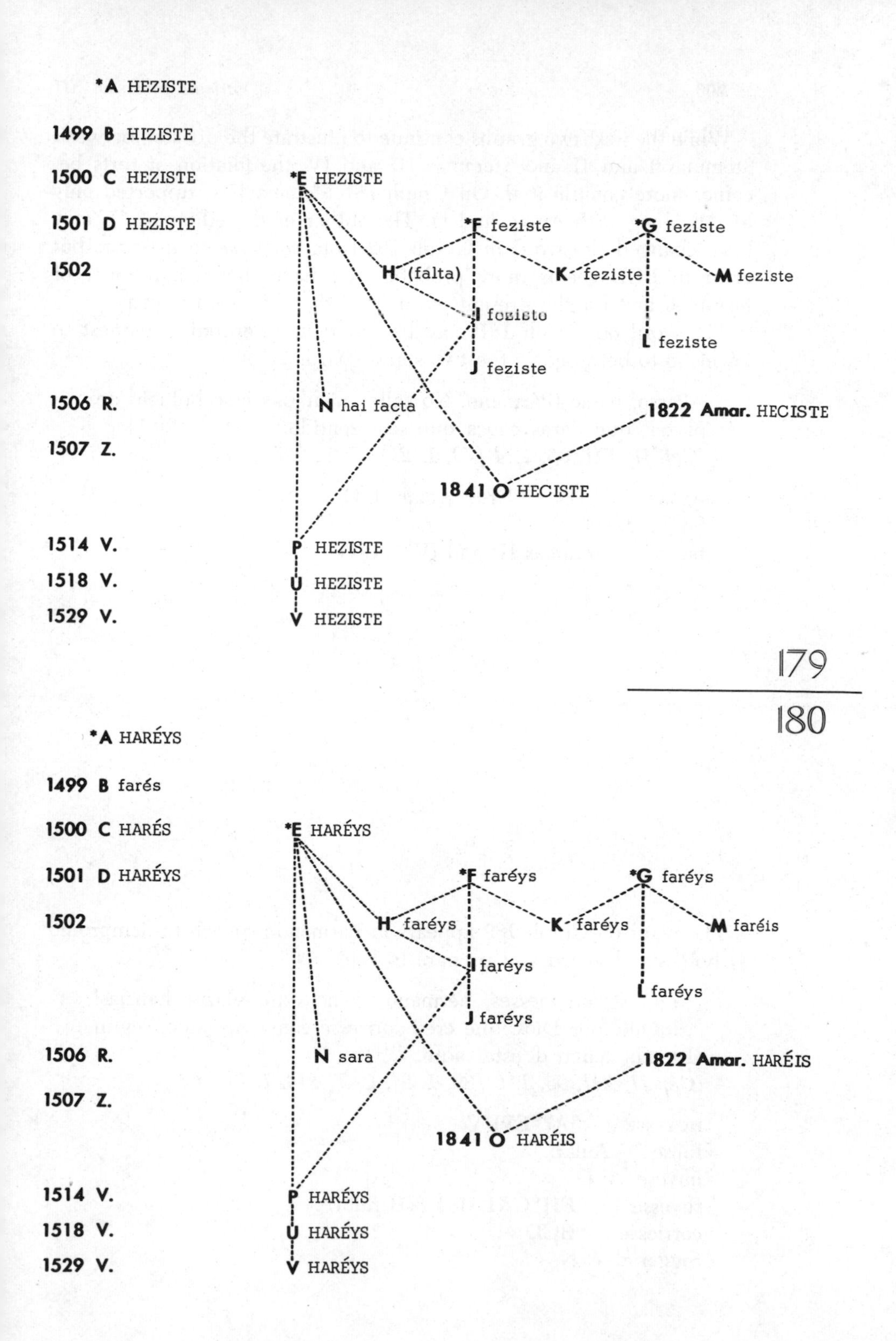
*A HEZISTE
1499 B HIZISTE
1500 C HEZISTE
1501 D HEZISTE
1502
1506 R.
1507 Z.
1514 V.
1518 V.
1529 V.
*E HEZISTE
*F feziste
*G feziste
H (falta)
K feziste
M feziste
I feziste
L feziste
J feziste
N hai facta
1822 Amar. HECISTE
1841 O HECISTE
P HEZISTE
U HEZISTE
V HEZISTE
179
180
*A HARÉYS
1499 B farés
1500 C HARÉS
1501 D HARÉYS
1502
1506 R.
1507 Z.
1514 V.
1518 V.
1529 V.
*E HARÉYS
*F faréys
*G faréys
H faréys
K faréys
M faréis
I faréys
L faréys
J faréys
N sara
1822 Amar. HARÉIS
1841 O HARÉIS
P HARÉYS
U HARÉYS
V HARÉYS

While the next two graphs continue to illustrate the division between Stemmas I and II and Stemmas III and IV, the filiation of texts becomes more complicated. On Graph 181 Stemma I is supported only by *E along with Amar. and O. The author or the editor of *E may have changed the word in Graph 182 from *corriesse* to HUYESSE, but error in BCD seems more probable; we have shown a number of instances and for the present we believe that *A was HUYESSE.

The word on Graph 181 may be found in Sempronio's request to Pármeno to be quiet, as the two stand guard.

> —Passo, passo, Pármeno. No saltes ni HAGAS esse bollicio de plazer, que darás causa que seas sentido.
> *(Cej. II, XII, 85, 1. 4 [79, 1. 21]; C–T, 207, 1. 11)*

HAGAS *ABCD*E? + Amar. + O
far N
fagas Stemmas III and IV + PUV

The word on Graph 182 appears in Parmeno's speech to Sempronio as both stand guard and prepare to flee.

> . . . ¡O si me viesses, hermano, como estó, plazer haurías! . . . ¡Que, por Dios, que creo *corriesse* como vn gamo, según el temor tengo d' estar aquí.
> *(Cej. II, XII, 95, 1. 6 [89, 1. 2]; C–T, 214, 1. 7)*

HUYESSE *A?*EPUV
fuese Amar.
huyese O
fuyesse *FIJ*GKLM (H falta)
corriesse BCD
fuggeria N

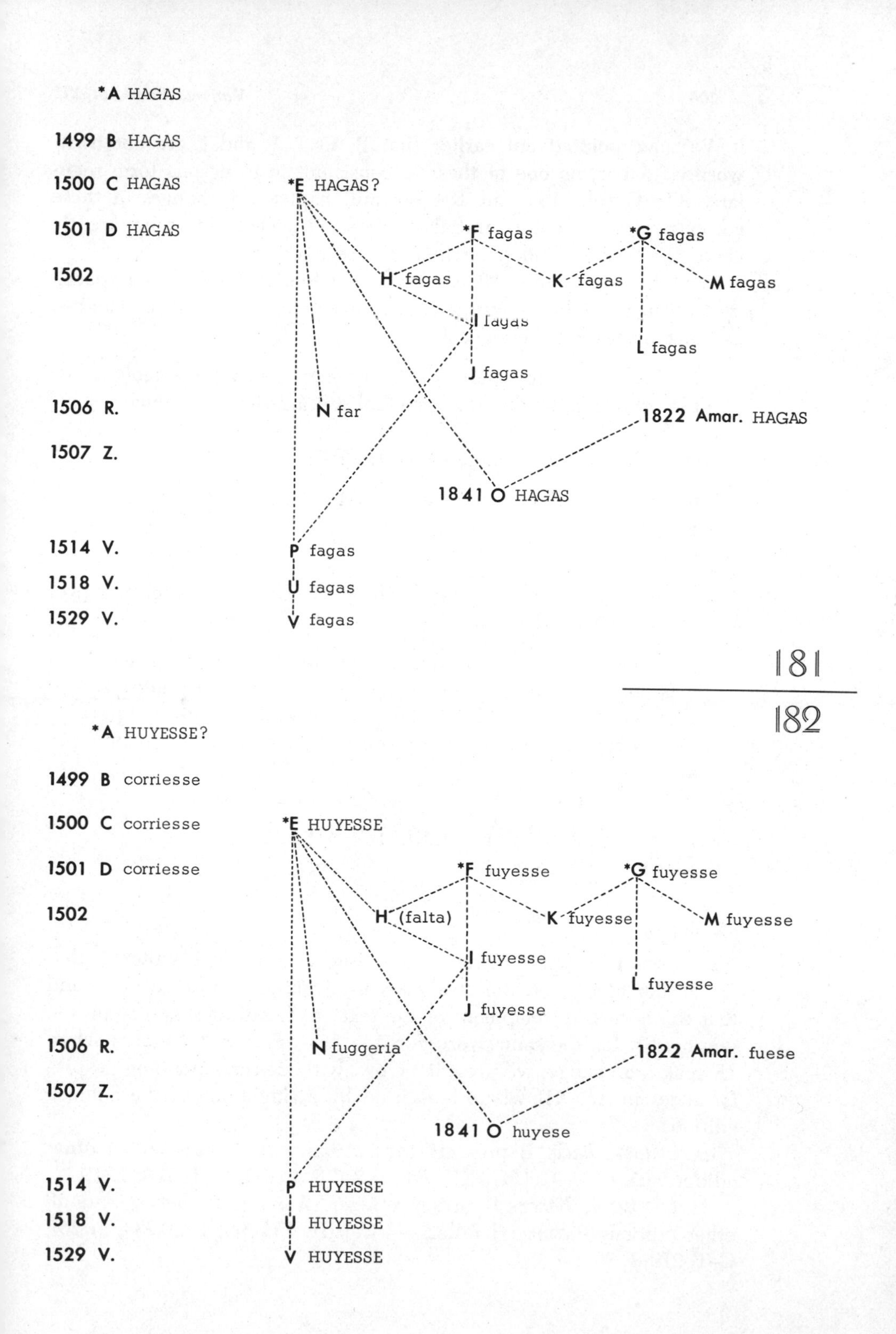
*A HAGAS
1499 B HAGAS
1500 C HAGAS
1501 D HAGAS
1502
*E HAGAS?
*F fagas
*G fagas
H fagas
K fagas
M fagas
I fagas
L fagas
J fagas
1506 R.
N far
1822 Amar. HAGAS
1507 Z.
1841 O HAGAS
1514 V.
P fagas
1518 V.
U fagas
1529 V.
V fagas
181
182
*A HUYESSE?
1499 B corriesse
1500 C corriesse
*E HUYESSE
1501 D corriesse
*F fuyesse
*G fuyesse
1502
H (falta)
K fuyesse
M fuyesse
I fuyesse
L fuyesse
J fuyesse
1506 R.
N fuggeria
1822 Amar. fuese
1507 Z.
1841 O huyese
1514 V.
P HUYESSE
1518 V.
U HUYESSE
1529 V.
V HUYESSE

We have pointed out earlier that B, C, I, J, and P are not trustworthy; that is, no one of these is consistent in using one form regularly. On Graphs 183 and 184 we find haphazard changes in these editions with respect to initial H- versus f-. The editors apparently made the changes independently of one another.

The word on Graph 183 is used as a noun. It appears in a speech by Calisto to Melibea during their conversation at the gate. Melibea has just manifested her love for him.

> . . . Pero, como soy cierto de tu limpieza de sangre é *fechos*, me estoy remirando si soy yo Calisto, á quien tanto bien se le haze.
> *(Cej. II, XII, 91, 1. 28 [86, 1. 4]; C–T, 212, 1. 1)*

HECHOS *ACD*EPUV*F*GKLM + Amar. + O
fechos B + IJ (H falta)
(———) N

The word on Graph 184 may be found in Calisto's speech just preceding the one cited above.

> . . . ¿Qué lengua será bastante para te dar yguales gracias á la sobrada é incomparable merced, que en este punto, de tanta congoxa para mí, me has quesido HAZER en querer que vn tan flaco é indigno hombre pueda gozar de tu suauíssimo amor?
> *(Cej. II, XII, 91, 1. 2 [85, 1. 8]; C–T, 211, 1. 7)*

HAZER *ABD*E*FIJ*GKLM (H falta)
HACER Amar. + O
usare N
fazer C + PUV

In order to support further our opinion, stated in Chapter 4, that the author always or almost always used initial H- instead of f-, and that the normal development of the text of the editions as seen on the graph calls for the same word for *A, *E, *F, and *G except when *F makes a change, we present below, without corresponding graphs, instances in Act XII where f- is used by a single one of the Spanish editions.

HAZE, *faze, hace.* B presents *faze,* Amar. + O *hace,* and all other editions HAZE.——Cej. II, XII, 84, 1. 2 (78, 1. 21); C–T, 206, 1. 19.

HAZER, *fazer, hacer.* B presents *fazer,* Amar. + O *hacer,* and all other editions HAZER. (H falta.)——Cej. II, XII, 90, 1. 20 (84, 1. 28); C–T, 210, 1. 28.

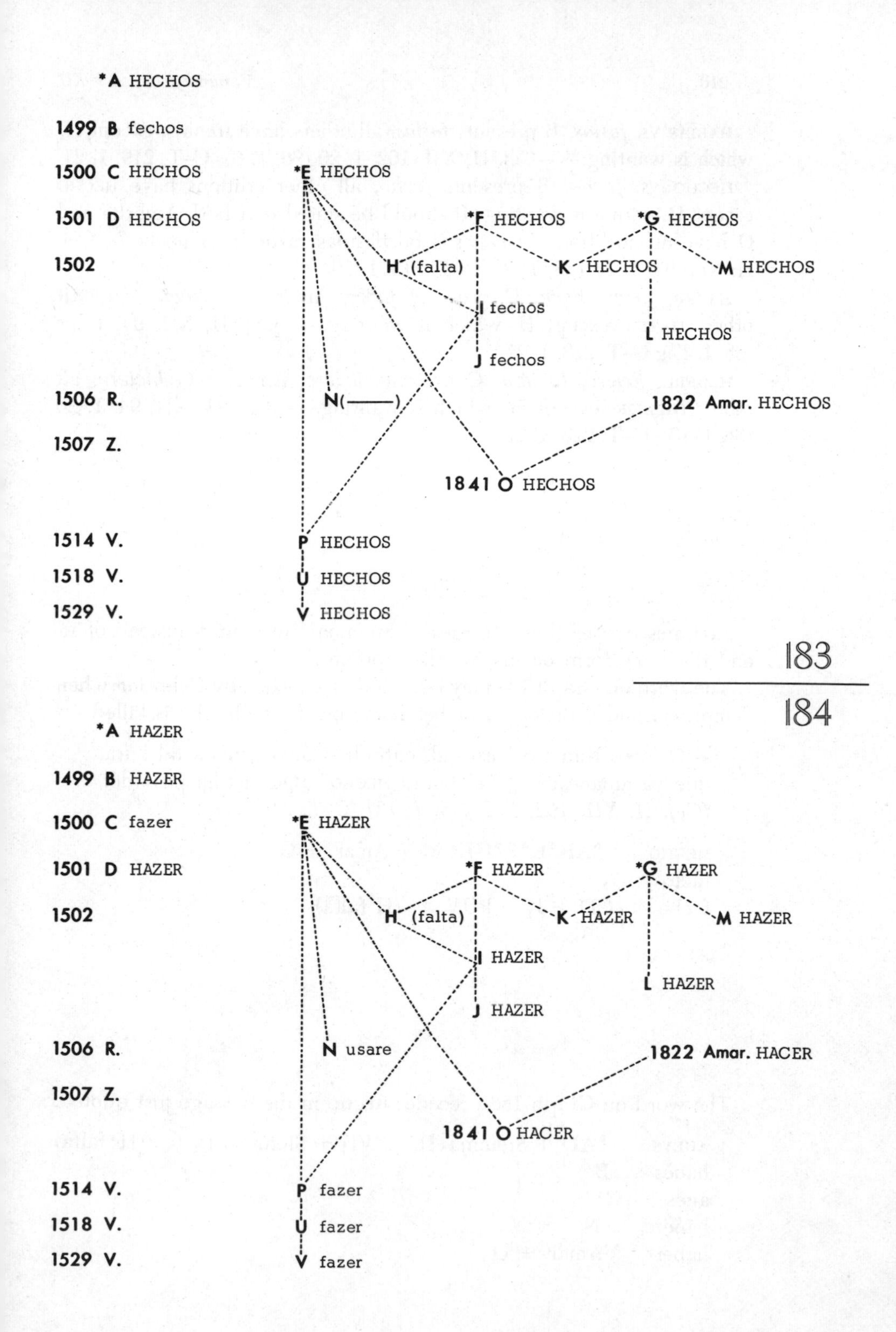
*A HECHOS
1499 B fechos
1500 C HECHOS
*E HECHOS
1501 D HECHOS
*F HECHOS
*G HECHOS
1502
H (falta)
K HECHOS
M HECHOS
I fechos
L HECHOS
J fechos
1506 R.
N(——)
1822 Amar. HECHOS
1507 Z.
1841 O HECHOS
1514 V.
P HECHOS
1518 V.
U HECHOS
1529 V.
V HECHOS
183
184
*A HAZER
1499 B HAZER
1500 C fazer
*E HAZER
1501 D HAZER
*F HAZER
*G HAZER
1502
H (falta)
K HAZER
M HAZER
I HAZER
L HAZER
J HAZER
1506 R.
N usare
1822 Amar. HACER
1507 Z.
1841 O HACER
1514 V.
P fazer
1518 V.
U fazer
1529 V.
V fazer

HARÍAS vs. *farías.* B presents *farías;* all others have HARÍAS, except H, which is wanting.——Cej. II, XII, 102, 1. 20 (96, 1. 6); C–T, 219, 1. 21.

HECHO vs. *fecho.* B presents *fecho;* all other editions have HECHO except H, which is wanting. It should be stated that both Amarita and O have an addition: "y con sus falsificadas razones ha hecho."—Cej. II, XII, 94, 1. 11 (88, 1. 9); C–T, 213, 1. 20.

HAZER, *fazer, hace.* C presents *fazer,* Amar. + O *hacer,* and all others HAZER, except H, which is wanting.——Cej. II, XII, 94, 1. 19 (88, 1. 17); C–T, 213, 1. 27.

HIZIERE, *fiziere, hiciere.* C presents *fiziere,* Amar. + O *hiciere;* all others HIZIERE, except H, which is wanting.——Cej. II, XII, 94, 1. 20 (88, 1. 18); C–T, 213, 1. 27.

At times two of the witnesses of Stemma I present f- instead of H- and the same form occurs in other editions.

The word on Graph 185 may be found in a speech by Celestina when Sempronio and Calisto call at her home on the night she is killed.

> —¡O locos trauiesos! Entrad, entrad. ¿Cómo venís á tal hora, que ya amanesce? ¿Qué haués HECHO? ¿Qué os ha passado?
> *(Cej. II, XII, 102, 1. 2 [95, 1. 13]; C–T, 219, 11. 6–7)*

HECHO *AB*E*F*GKLM + Amar. + O
facto N
fecho CD + IJ + PUV (H falta)

The word on Graph 186 precedes HECHO in the passage just quoted.

AUÉYS *AD + Stemma II + *FIJ + Stemma IV (H falta)
haués B
aués C
hauete N
habéis Amar. + O

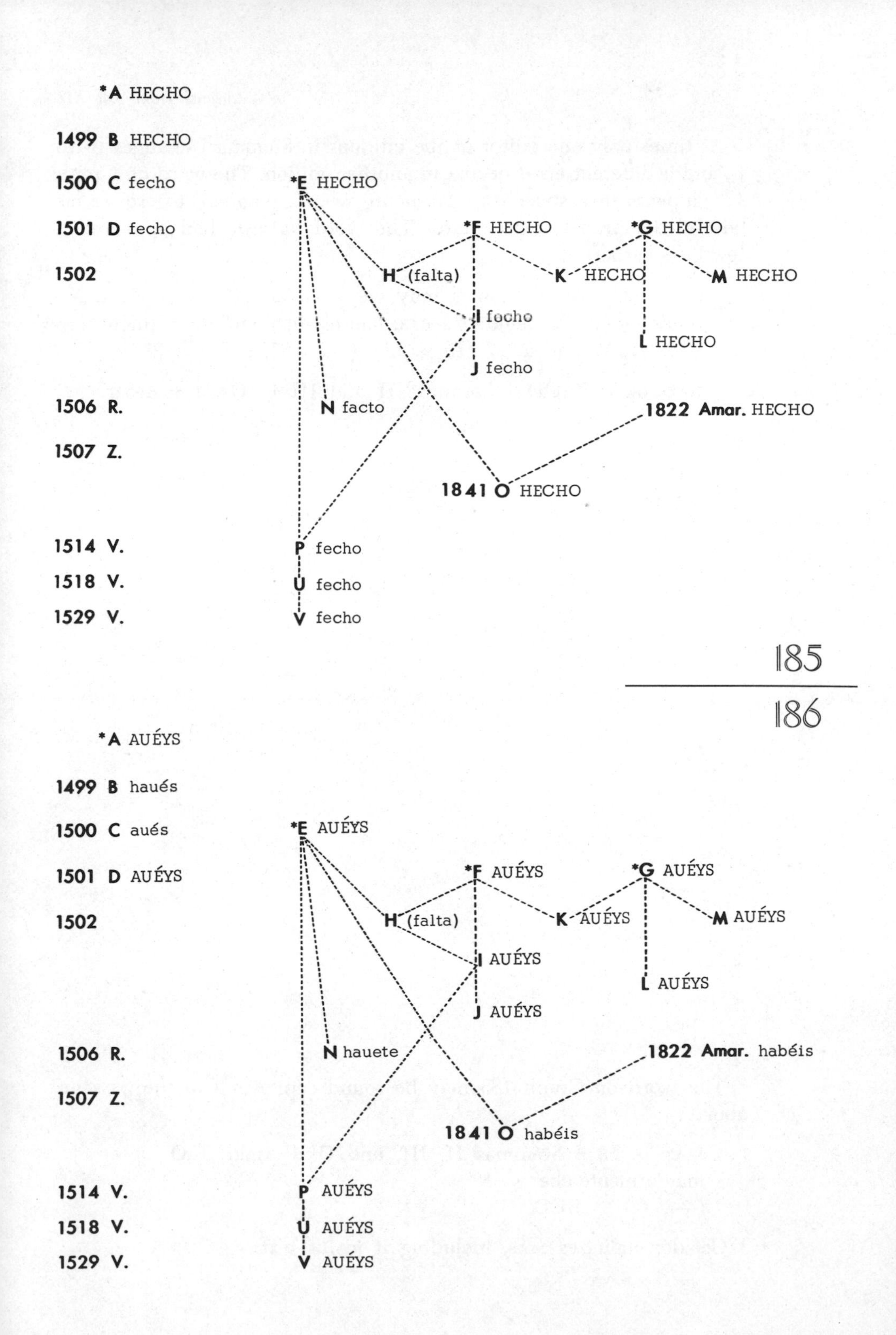
*A HECHO
1499 B HECHO
1500 C fecho
*E HECHO
1501 D fecho
*F HECHO
*G HECHO
1502
H (falta)
K HECHO
M HECHO
I focho
L HECHO
J fecho
1506 R.
N facto
1822 Amar. HECHO
1507 Z.
1841 O HECHO
1514 V.
P fecho
1518 V.
U fecho
1529 V.
V fecho
185
186
*A AUÉYS
1499 B haués
1500 C aués
*E AUÉYS
1501 D AUÉYS
*F AUÉYS
*G AUÉYS
1502
H (falta)
K AUÉYS
M AUÉYS
I AUÉYS
L AUÉYS
J AUÉYS
1506 R.
N hauete
1822 Amar. habéis
1507 Z.
1841 O habéis
1514 V.
P AUÉYS
1518 V.
U AUÉYS
1529 V.
V AUÉYS

At times only one editor of the editions in Stemma I changes H- to f-, and a different error occurs in another edition. The word on Graph 187 appears in a speech by Pármeno, who is planning to escape, as he and Sempronio stand guard. The word *burlaste* had appeared a few lines earlier.

> . . . É MÁS avn no somos muy ciertos dezir verdad la vieja. No sepas *fablar*, Pármeno: ¡sacarte han el alma, sin saber quién!
> *(Cej. II, XII, 84, 1. 17 [79, 1. 11]; C–T, 207, 1. 3)*

HABLAR *ACD + Stemmas II and III + *GKM + Amar. + O
fablar B
burlar L
parlar N

The word on Graph 188 may be found capitalized in the passage above.

MÁS *A + Stemmas II, III, and IV + Amar. + O
magiormente che N
(———) BCD

Cejador italicizes MÁS, including it in his text.

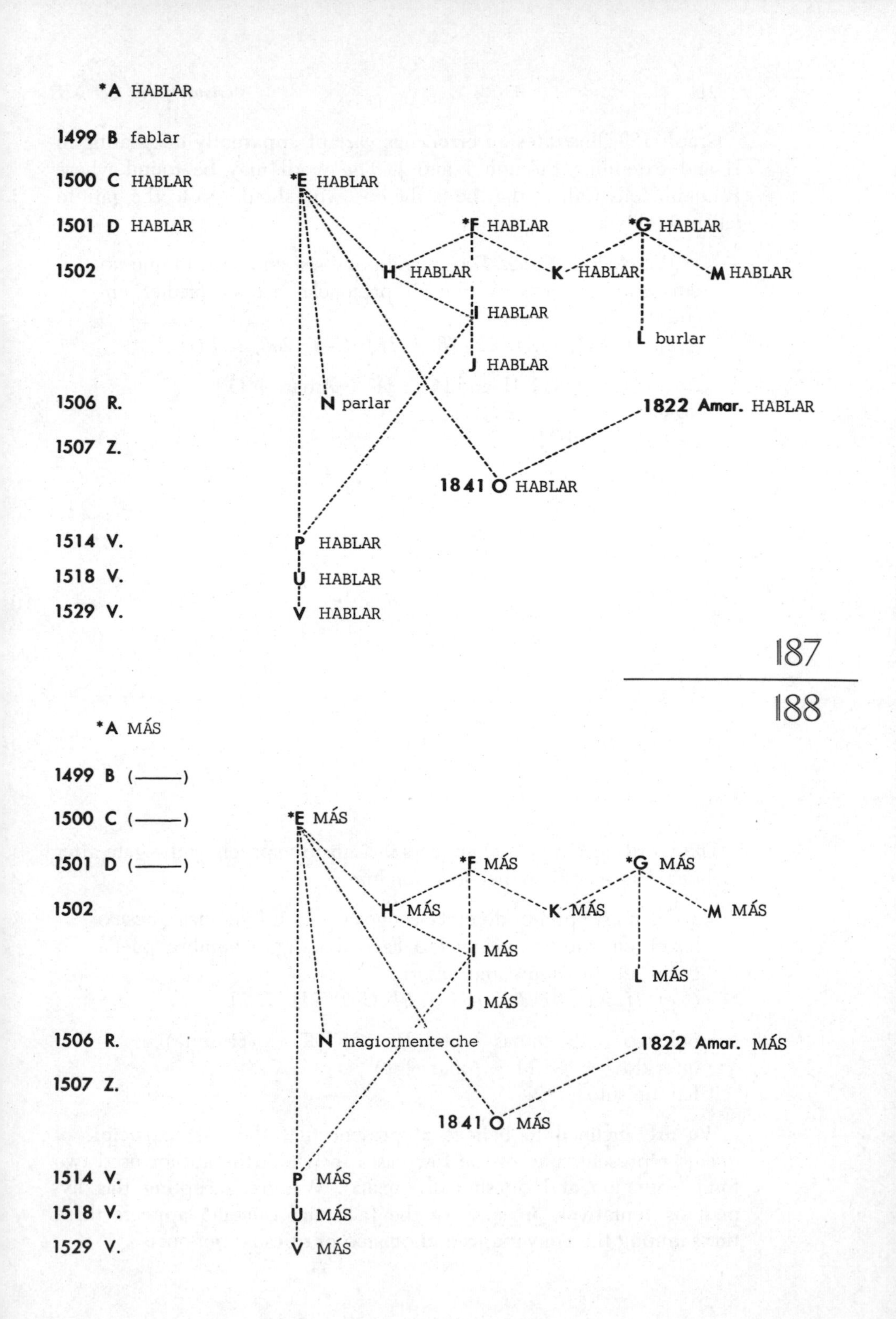
*A HABLAR
1499 B fablar
1500 C HABLAR
*E HABLAR
1501 D HABLAR
*F HABLAR
*G HABLAR
1502
H HABLAR
K HABLAR
M HABLAR
I HABLAR
L burlar
J HABLAR
1506 R.
N parlar
1822 Amar. HABLAR
1507 Z.
1841 O HABLAR
1514 V.
P HABLAR
1518 V.
U HABLAR
1529 V.
V HABLAR
187
188
*A MÁS
1499 B (——)
1500 C (——)
*E MÁS
1501 D (——)
*F MÁS
*G MÁS
1502
H MÁS
K MÁS
M MÁS
I MÁS
L MÁS
J MÁS
1506 R.
N magiormente che
1822 Amar. MÁS
1507 Z.
1841 O MÁS
1514 V.
P MÁS
1518 V.
U MÁS
1529 V.
V MÁS

Graph 189 illustrates an erroneous variant apparently originating in H and extending through I and J. The word may be found where Pármeno tells Calisto that he is the one who should go to the gate to talk to Melibea.

> —¿Yo, señor? Nunca Dios mande que sea en dañar lo que NO concerté; mejor será que tu presencia sea su primer encuentro, . . .
> *(Cej. II, XII, 83, l. 22 [78, l. 17]; C–T, 206, l. 16)*

NO Stemmas I, II, and IV + *F + Amar. + O
NON N
(———) HIJ

The word on Graph 190 appears in Calisto's speech at the gate after Melibea has confessed her love for him.

> ¿. . . en este punto, de tanta congoxa para mí, me has QUESIDO hazer en querer que vn tan flaco é indigno hombre pueda gozar de tu suauíssimo amor?
> *(Cej. II, XII, 91, l. 2 [85, l. 8]; C–T, 211, l. 7)*

QUESIDO Stemmas I and II + *FIJK (H falta)
querido *GLM + Amar. + O
hai uolsuto N

We are inclined to believe at present that the past participle of *querer* represents one of the few cases in which the author used two forms, QUERIDO and QUESIDO or QUISIDO. We are accepting this hypothesis tentatively in spite of the fact that QUERIDO appears three times among the nonvariants and QUISIDO or QUESIDO not once.

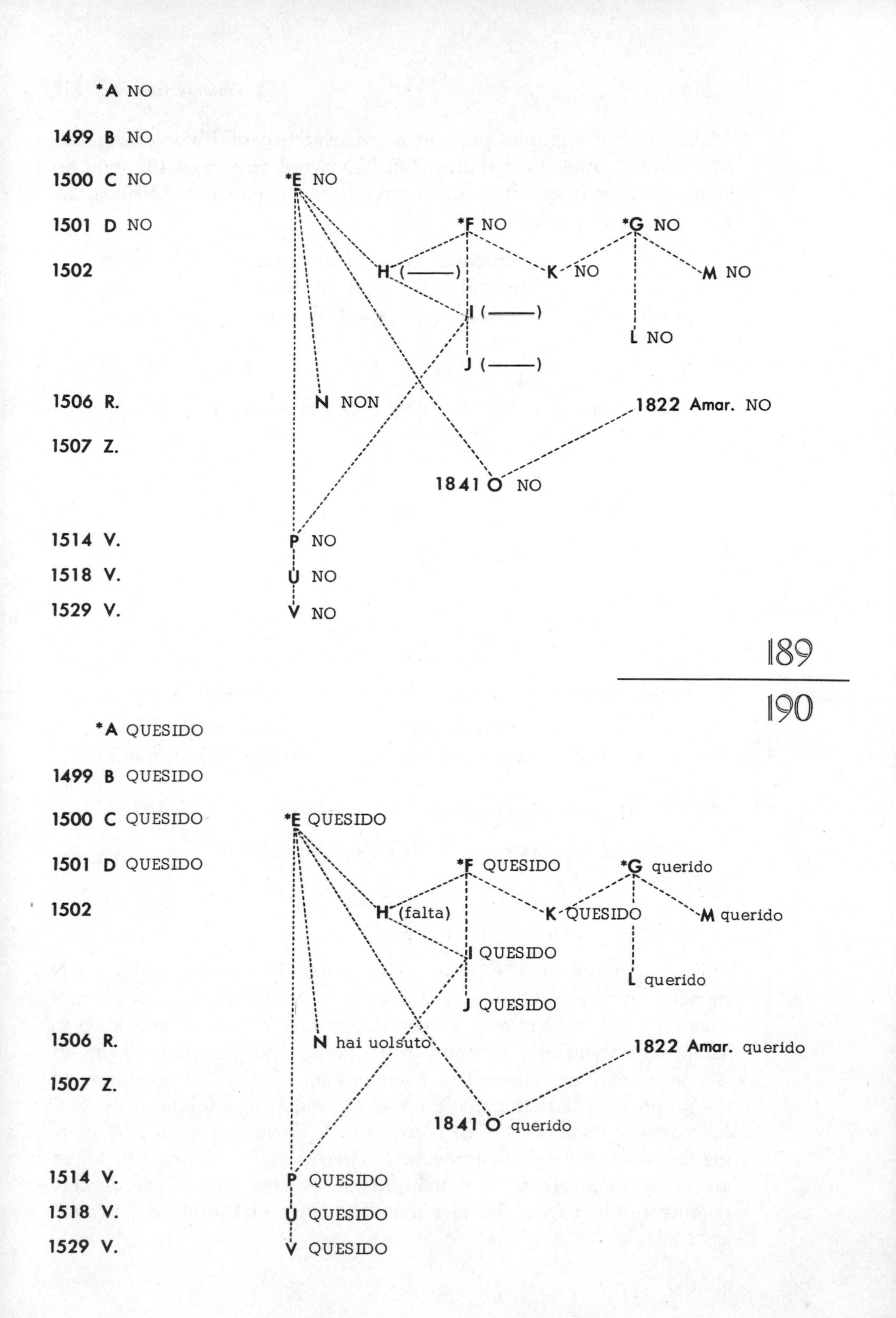
*A NO
1499 B NO
1500 C NO
*E NO
1501 D NO
*F NO
*G NO
1502
H (——)
K NO
M NO
I (——)
L NO
J (——)
1506 R.
N NON
1822 Amar. NO
1507 Z.
1841 O NO
1514 V.
P NO
1518 V.
U NO
1529 V.
V NO
189
190
*A QUESIDO
1499 B QUESIDO
1500 C QUESIDO
*E QUESIDO
1501 D QUESIDO
*F QUESIDO
*G querido
1502
H (falta)
K QUESIDO
M querido
I QUESIDO
L querido
J QUESIDO
1506 R.
N hai uolsuto
1822 Amar. querido
1507 Z.
1841 O querido
1514 V.
P QUESIDO
1518 V.
U QUESIDO
1529 V.
V QUESIDO

The next two graphs provide more evidence of P's selecting the witness of I rather than that of *E. The word on Graph 191 may be found in Calisto's speech in the interview at the gate after Melibea has spoken harshly to him.

> . . . ¿A qué me mandaste aquí venir, para que me fuese mostrado el disfauor, el entredicho, la desconfiança, el ODIO, por la mesma boca desta que tiene las llaues de mi perdición é gloria?
> *(Cej. II, XII, 89, 1. 21 [84, 1. 7]; C–T, 210, 1. 9)*

ODIO Stemma I + *E + *F *GKLM + Amar. + O
oydo IJPUV (H falta)
(———) N

The words on Graph 192 occur in an addition, in Pármeno's speech as he and Sempronio stand guard while Calisto is at the gate.

> . . . Pues más locura sería esperar pelea con *enemigo,* que no *ama* tanto la vitoria é vencimiento, como la continua guerra é contienda.
> *(Cej. II, XII, 94, 11. 27–28 [88, 11. 25–26]; C–T, 214, 1. 1)*

ENEMIGOS . . . AMAN *E?*F?*GKLM + Amar.
INIMICI . . . AMANO N
enemigo . . . aman IJ (H falta)
enemigo . . . ama PUV + O

Our suggestion for *E is tentative primarily because, although N supports this form, O does not. This may be one of those few cases where O follows neither *E nor Amarita. Pármeno is speaking to Sempronio about the servants of Pleberio, and the plural form of "servants" may be reflected in *enemigos* in *E. Our interpretation of the graph then is that I made an error, which was followed by J. P followed I instead of *E, but corrected the obvious error of I by placing the noun and verb in agreement. Then U and V followed P. There are many more errors in P than Krapf realized and a considerable number resulted from the fact that the editor of P utilized I as well as *E.

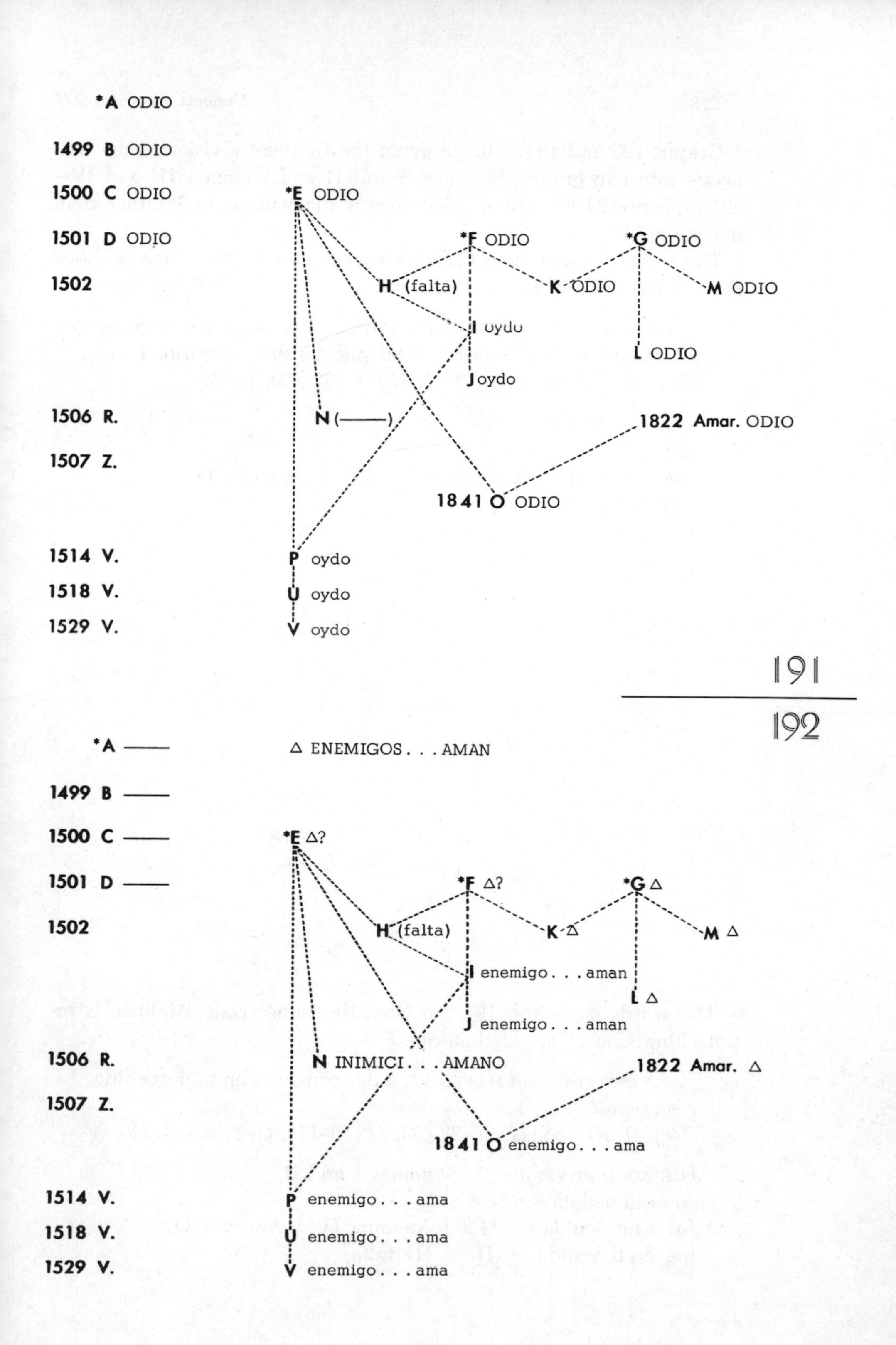
*A ODIO
1499 B ODIO
1500 C ODIO
*E ODIO
1501 D ODIO
*F ODIO
*G ODIO
1502
H (falta)
K ODIO
M ODIO
I oydo
L ODIO
J oydo
1506 R.
N (——)
1822 Amar. ODIO
1507 Z.
1841 O ODIO
1514 V.
P oydo
1518 V.
U oydo
1529 V.
V oydo
191
192
*A ——
△ ENEMIGOS . . . AMAN
1499 B ——
1500 C ——
*E △?
1501 D ——
*F △?
*G △
1502
H (falta)
K △
M △
I enemigo . . . aman
L △
J enemigo . . . aman
1506 R.
N INIMICI . . . AMANO
1822 Amar. △
1507 Z.
1841 O enemigo . . . ama
1514 V.
P enemigo . . . ama
1518 V.
U enemigo . . . ama
1529 V.
V enemigo . . . ama

Graphs 193 and 194 indicate again the frequent division of the witnesses into two groups, Stemmas I and II and Stemmas III and IV—although in 193 the editor of P selects the witness in I rather than the one in *E.

The word is taken from Calisto's speech at the gate when Melibea has reproached him for his boldness.

> . . . PERO el triste que, desarmado á sin proueer los engaños é celadas, se vino á meter por las puertas de tu seguridad, . . .
> *(Cej. II, XII, 89, 1. 6 [38, 1. 17]; C–T, 209, 1. 25)*

PERO  A?BCD + *E?
MA  N
pues  *FIJ + Stemma IV + PUV + Amar. + O
(H falta)

The words on Graph 194 are from the same scene. Melibea is reproaching Calisto for his boldness.

> . . . A esto FUÉ AQUÍ MI VENIDA, a dar concierto en tu despedida é mi reposo.
> *(Cej. II, XII, 88, 11. 27–28 [83, 11. 10–11]; C–T, 209, 1. 19)*

FUÉ AQUÍ MI VENIDA  Stemmas I and II
son qui uenuta  N
fuí aquí venida  *F? + Stemma IV + Amar. + O
fué aquí venida  IJ  (H falta)

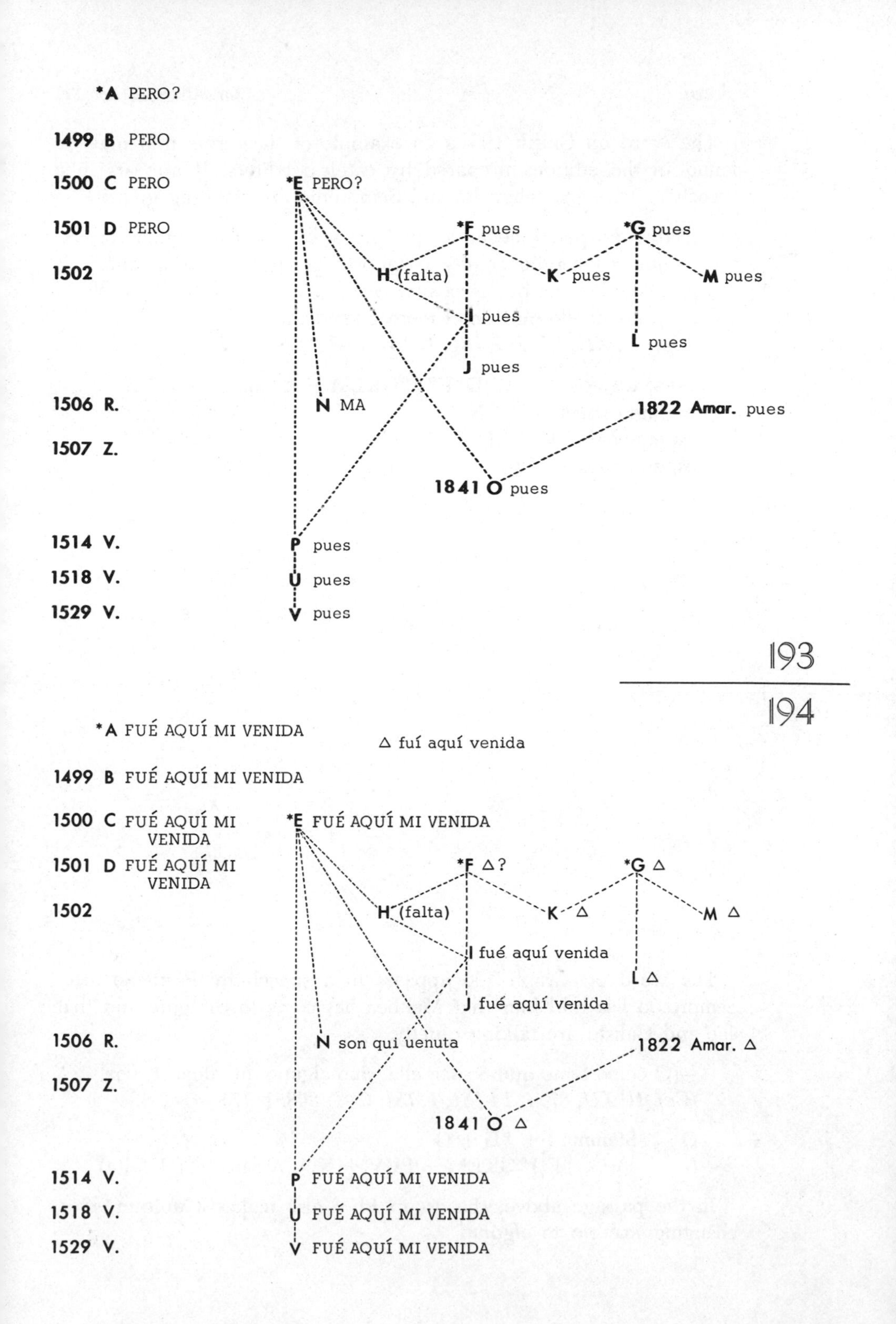

*A PERO?
1499 B PERO
1500 C PERO
*E PERO?
1501 D PERO
*F pues
*G pues
1502
H (falta)
K pues
M pues
I pues
L pues
J pues
1506 R.
N MA
1822 Amar. pues
1507 Z.
1841 O pues
1514 V.
P pues
1518 V.
U pues
1529 V.
V pues
193
194
*A FUÉ AQUÍ MI VENIDA
△ fuí aquí venida
1499 B FUÉ AQUÍ MI VENIDA
1500 C FUÉ AQUÍ MI VENIDA
*E FUÉ AQUÍ MI VENIDA
1501 D FUÉ AQUÍ MI VENIDA
*F △?
*G △
1502
H (falta)
K △
M △
I fué aquí venida
L △
J fué aquí venida
1506 R.
N son qui uenuta
1822 Amar. △
1507 Z.
1841 O △
1514 V.
P FUÉ AQUÍ MI VENIDA
1518 V.
U FUÉ AQUÍ MI VENIDA
1529 V.
V FUÉ AQUÍ MI VENIDA

The word on Graph 195 is an example of the errors that may be found in the editions prepared by careless editors. It appears in a speech of Pármeno when he and Sempronio are standing guard.

—Ninguno podrá negar lo que por sí se muestra. Manifiesto es que con vergüença el vno del otro, por no ser odiosamente acusado de couarde, ESPERÁRAMOS aquí la muerte con nuestro amo, no siendo más de él merecedor della.
*(Cej. II, XII, 87, 1. 9 [81, 1. 15]; C–T, 208, 1. 12)*

ESPERÁRAMOS *ABD*E*F*GKLM + Amar. + O
hariamo spectata N
esperamos C + IJ (H falta)
esperaremos PUV

The word on Graph 196 appears in a speech by Pármeno after Sempronio has told him that Melibea has come to the gate and that she and Calisto are talking quietly.

—¡O cómo temo que no sea ella, sino alguno que finja su voz!
*(Cej. II, XII, 87, 1. 14 [81, 1. 15]; C–T, 208, 1. 17)*

O Stemma I + *E + O
(———) *FIJ*GKLM + PUV + N + Amar. (H falta)

In the passage above, the group PUV also makes a unique error, changing ALGUNO to *alguna*.

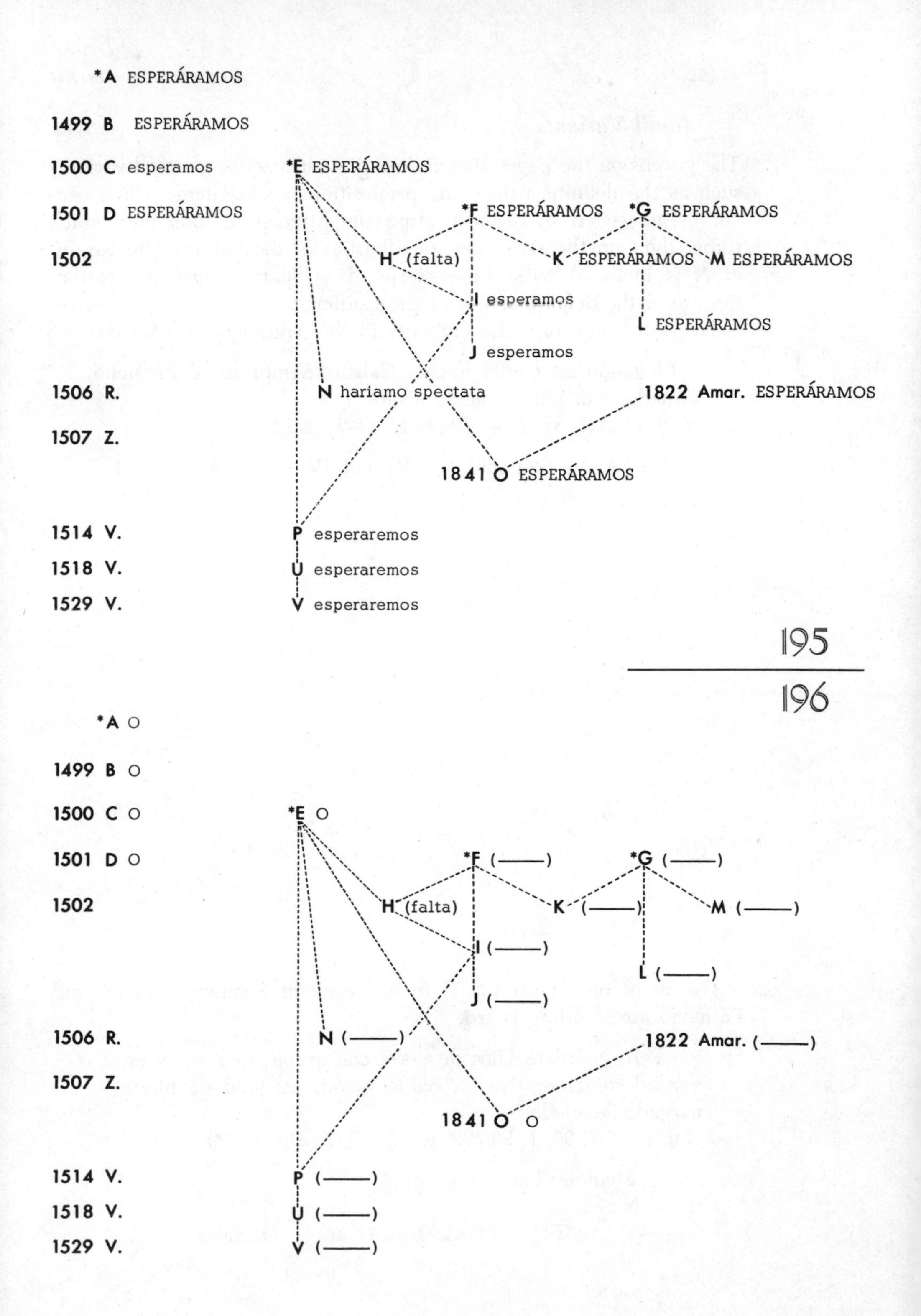
*A ESPERÁRAMOS
1499 B ESPERÁRAMOS
1500 C esperamos
*E ESPERÁRAMOS
1501 D ESPERÁRAMOS
*F ESPERÁRAMOS
*G ESPERÁRAMOS
1502
H (falta)
K ESPERÁRAMOS
M ESPERÁRAMOS
I esperamos
L ESPERÁRAMOS
J esperamos
1506 R.
N hariamo spectata
1822 Amar. ESPERÁRAMOS
1507 Z.
1841 O ESPERÁRAMOS
1514 V.
P esperaremos
1518 V.
U esperaremos
1529 V.
V esperaremos
195
196
*A O
1499 B O
1500 C O
*E O
1501 D O
*F (——)
*G (——)
1502
H (falta)
K (——)
M (——)
I (——)
L (——)
J (——)
1506 R.
N (——)
1822 Amar. (——)
1507 Z.
1841 O O
1514 V.
P (——)
1518 V.
U (——)
1529 V.
V (——)

### *Small Variants*

The graphs on the pages that follow present a series of small variants such as the definite article, the preposition A, etc.–items which cannot be neglected in reconstructing the princeps edition and which throw light on the style and peculiarities of the author. The variant of N is included with the corresponding Spanish form in cases of the use of the definite article or preposition.

The word on Graph 197 appears in the Argumento of Act XII.

> Llegando LA media noche, Calisto, Sempronio é Pármeno armados van para casa de Melibea.
> *(Cej. II, XII, 81, 1. 4 [76, 1. 4]; C–T, 203, 1. 2)*

LA *AD + Stemmas II, III, and IV + N + Amar. + O
(———) BC

The word on Graph 198 is in a speech of Sempronio as he and Pármeno are standing guard.

> . . . Pero guárdete Dios de verte con armas, que aquel es EL verdadero temor. No en balde dizen: cargado de hierro é cargado de miedo.
> *Cej. II, XII, 96, 1. 25 [90, 1. 20]; C–T, 215, 1. 14)*

EL Stemmas I and II + O
IL N
(———) *FIJ + *GKLM + Amar. (H falta)

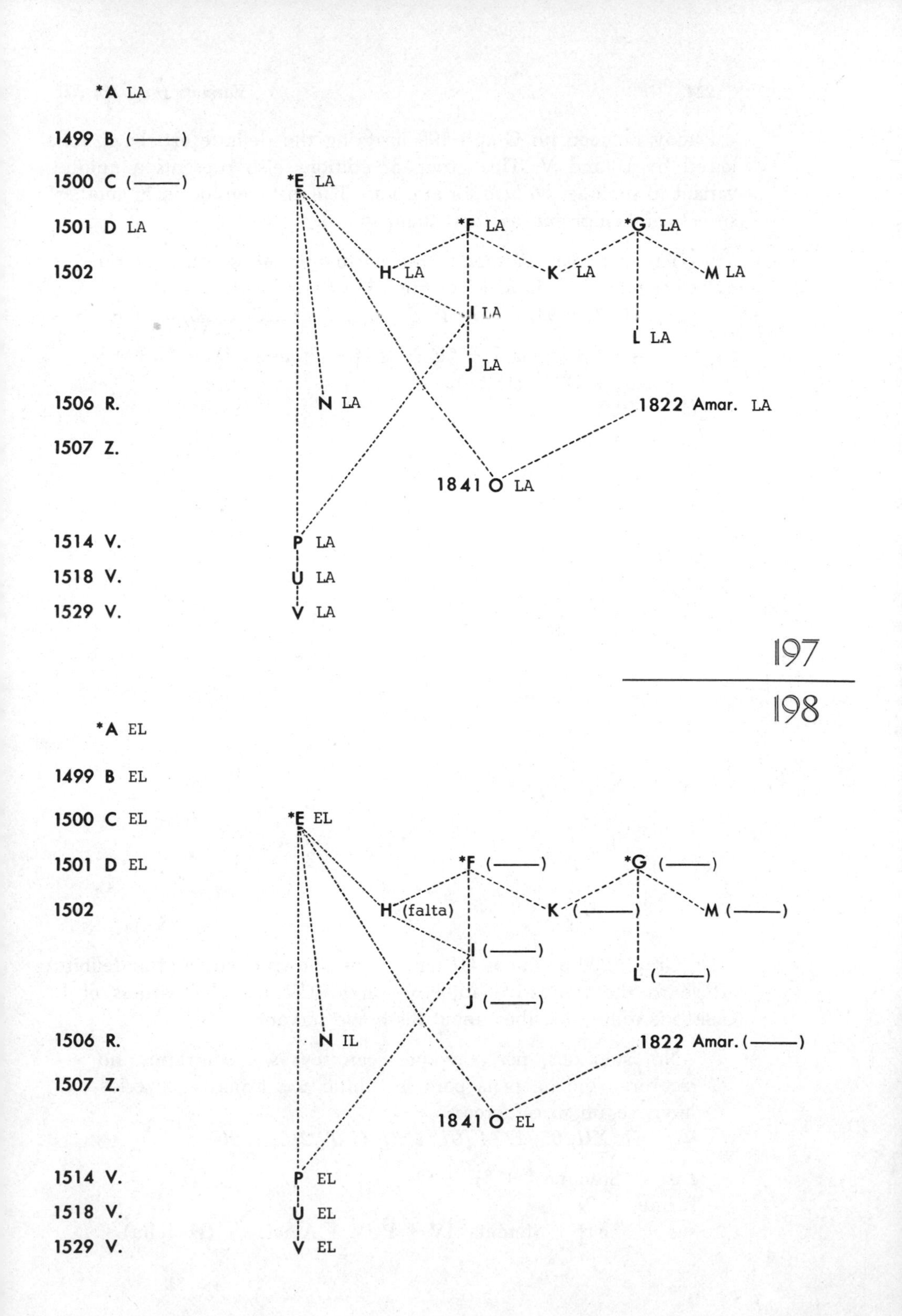
*A LA
1499 B (——)
1500 C (——)
1501 D LA
1502
1506 R.
1507 Z.
1514 V.
1518 V.
1529 V.
*E LA
*F LA
*G LA
H LA
K LA
M LA
I LA
L LA
J LA
N LA
1822 Amar. LA
1841 O LA
P LA
U LA
V LA
*A EL
1499 B EL
1500 C EL
1501 D EL
1502
1506 R.
1507 Z.
1514 V.
1518 V.
1529 V.
*E EL
*F (——)
*G (——)
H (falta)
K (——)
M (——)
I (——)
L (——)
J (——)
N IL
1822 Amar. (——)
1841 O EL
P EL
U EL
V EL

197
___
198

P may be seen on Graph 199 inserting the definite article *el*, followed by U and V. This group of editions also presents a unique variant in spelling, *bollicio* for BULLICIO. The instances occur in another speech of Sempronio as they stand guard.

> —Ya no temas, Pármeno, que harto desuiados estamos. En sintiendo———bullicio, el buen huyr nos ha de valer.
> *(Cej. II, XII, 94, 1. 18 [88, 1. 16]; C–T, 213, 1. 26)*

——— Stemma I + *E + *FIJ + Stemma IV + N + Amar. + O (H falta)
el PUV

On Graph 200 Stemmas III and IV are shown changing the definite article to the possessive adjective, and PUV use the witness of I. Calisto is telling Melibea about his brave servants.

> —Nó, sino dos; pero, avnque sean seys sus contrarios, no recebirán mucha pena para les quitar LAS armas é hazerlos huyr, según su esfuerço.
> *(Cej. II, XII, 97, 1. 14 [91, 1. 6]; C–T, 215, 1. 26)*

LAS Stemma I + *E + O
l'arme N
sus *FIJ + Stemma IV + PUV + Amar. (H falta)

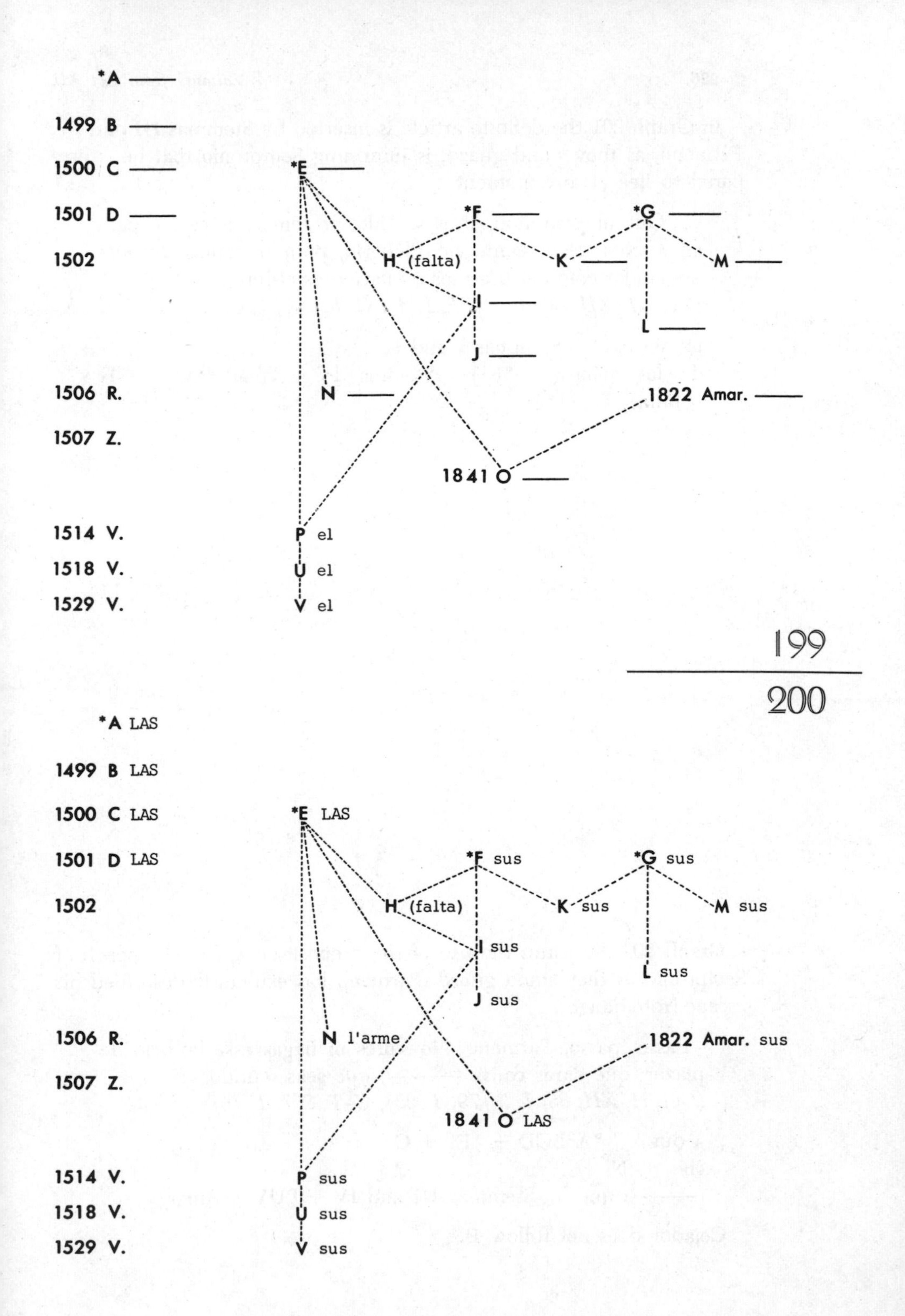
*A
1499 B
1500 C
*E
1501 D
*F
*G
1502
H (falta)
K
M
I
L
J
1506 R.
N
1822 Amar.
1507 Z.
1841 O
1514 V.
P el
1518 V.
U el
1529 V.
V el
199
200
*A LAS
1499 B LAS
1500 C LAS
*E LAS
1501 D LAS
*F sus
*G sus
1502
H (falta)
K sus
M sus
I sus
L sus
J sus
1506 R.
N l'arme
1822 Amar. sus
1507 Z.
1841 O LAS
1514 V.
P sus
1518 V.
U sus
1529 V.
V sus

In Graph 201 the definite article is inserted by Stemmas III and IV. Pármeno, as they stand guard, is informing Sempronio that he is prepared to flee at any moment.

> . . . Que nuestro amo, si es sentido, no temo que se escapará DE MANOS desta gente de Pleberio, para podernos después demandar cómo lo hezimos é incusarnos el huyr.
> *(Cej. II, XII, 86, 1. 7 [81, 1. 4]; C–T, 208, 1. 3)*

DE MANOS Stemmas I and II
de las manos *FIJ + Stemma IV + Amar. + O (H falta)
(———) N

Graph 202 illustrates the use of the preposition A, from a speech of Sempronio as they stand guard. Pármeno has exultantly described his escape from danger.

> –Passo, passo, Pármeno. No saltes ni hagas esse bollicio de plazer, que darás causa (———) *que* seas sentido.
> *(Cej. II, XII, 85, 1. 5 [79, 1. 22]; C–T, 207, 1. 12)*

A QUE *A?BCD + *E? + O
che N
(———) que Stemmas III and IV + PUV + Amar.

Cejador does not follow B.

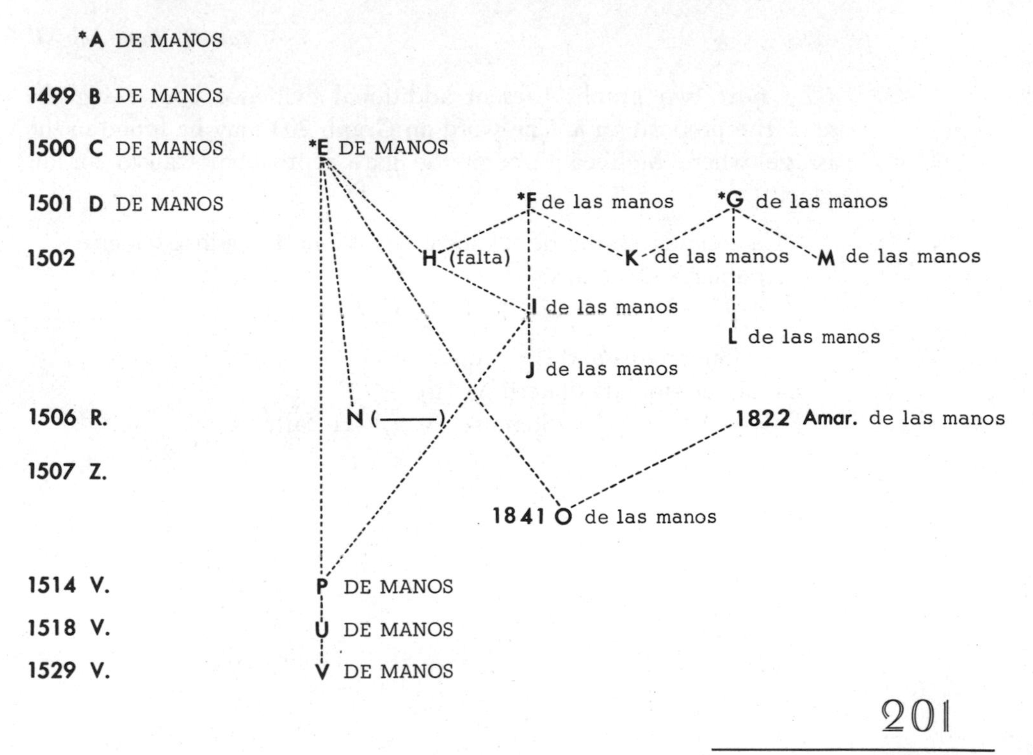

202

*A A QUE?

1499 B A QUE

1500 C A QUE

1501 D A QUE

1502

1506 R.

1507 Z.

1514 V.

1518 V.

1529 V.

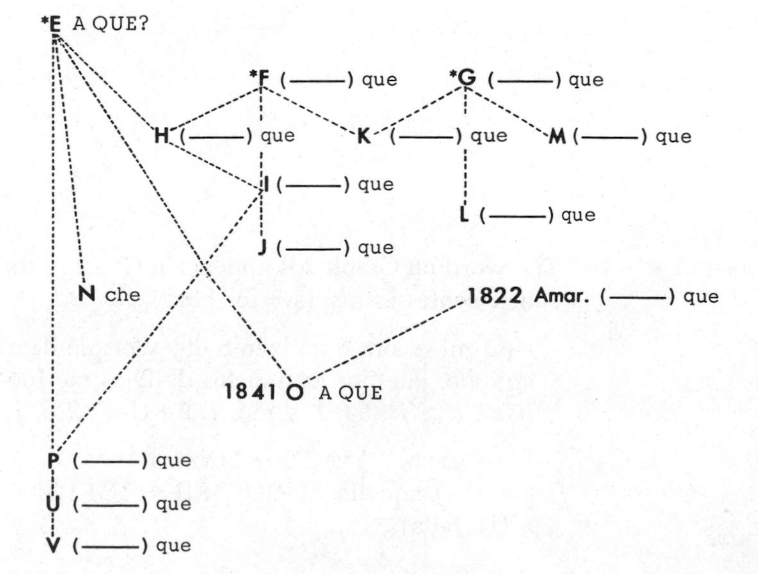

The next two graphs present additional evidence concerning the use of the preposition A. The word on Graph 203 may be found in the passage where Melibea through the gate reproaches Calisto for his audacity.

—La sobrada osadía de tus mensajes me ha forçado A hauerte de hablar, señor Calisto.
*(Cej. II, XII, 88, 1. 21 [83, 1. 4]; C–T, 209, 1. 14)*

A Stemmas I and II + Amar. + O
me hanno sforzata douerti parlare N
(———) *FIJ + Stemma IV (H falta)

The word on Graph 204 appears in Calisto's speech at the gate when Melibea confesses her love for him.

—¡O mi señora é mi bien todo! ¿Porqué llamas yerro (———) *aquello,* que por los sanctos de Dios me fué concedido?
*(Cej. II, XII, 94, 1. 4 [88, 1. 2]; C–T, 213, 1. 15)*

A AQUELLO *ACD + Stemma II
(———) aquello B + *FIJ + *GKLM + N +Amar. + O
(H falta)

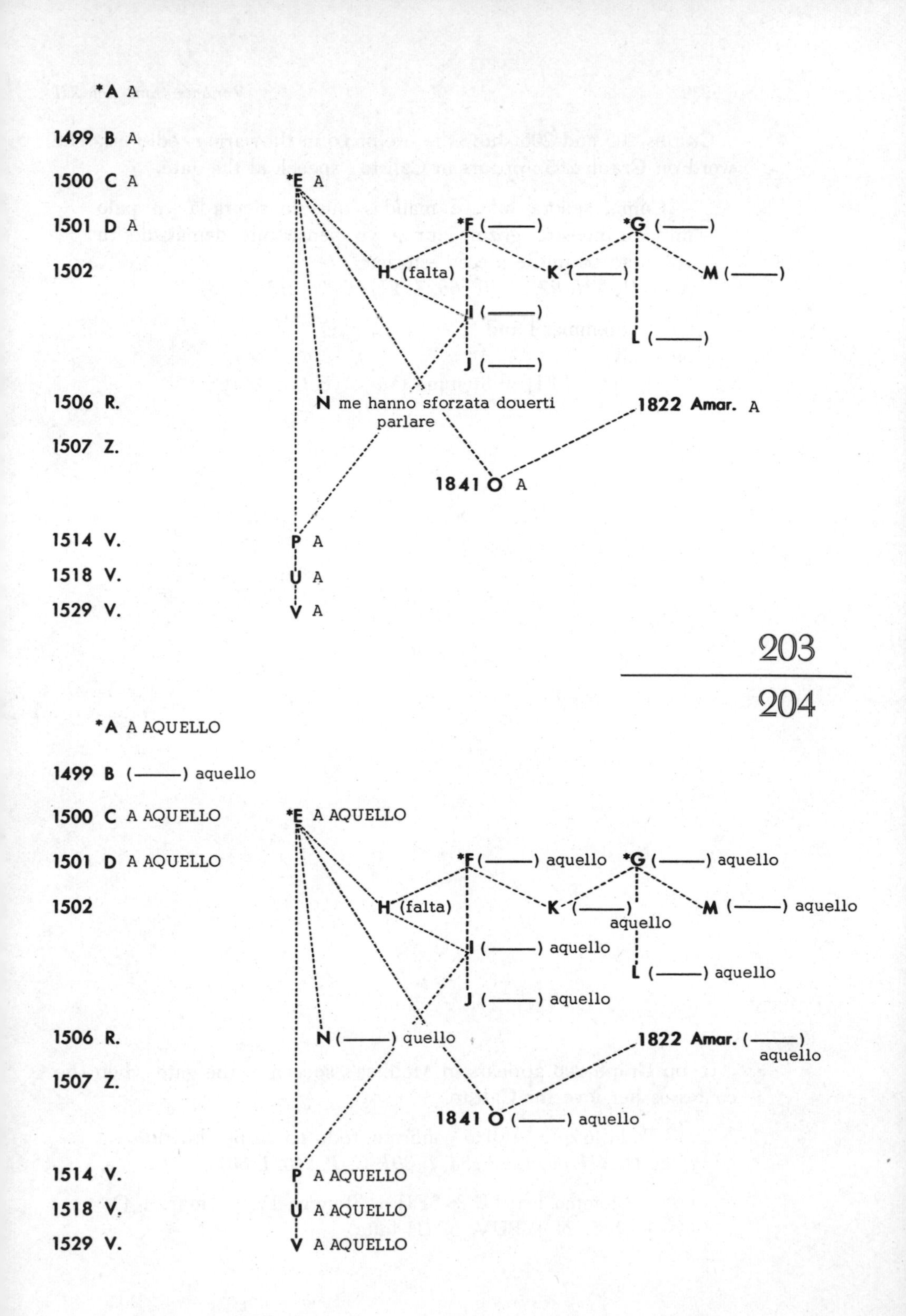
*A A
1499 B A
1500 C A
*E A
1501 D A
*F (——)
*G (——)
1502
H (falta)
K (——)
M (——)
I (——)
L (——)
J (——)
1506 R.
N me hanno sforzata douerti parlare
1822 Amar. A
1507 Z.
1841 O A
1514 V.
P A
1518 V.
U A
1529 V.
V A
203
204
*A A AQUELLO
1499 B (——) aquello
1500 C A AQUELLO
*E A AQUELLO
1501 D A AQUELLO
*F (——) aquello
*G (——) aquello
1502
H (falta)
K (——) aquello
M (——) aquello
I (——) aquello
L (——) aquello
J (——) aquello
1506 R.
N (——) quello
1822 Amar. (——) aquello
1507 Z.
1841 O (——) aquello
1514 V.
P A AQUELLO
1518 V.
U A AQUELLO
1529 V.
V A AQUELLO

Graphs 205 and 206 show the use of LO in the various editions. The word on Graph 205 appears in Calisto's speech at the gate.

> —¿Cómo, señora mía, é mandas que consienta á vn palo impedir nuestro gozo? Nunca yo pensé que demás de tu voluntad LO pudiera cosa estoruar.
> *(Cej. II, XII, 92, 1. 19 [86, 1. 21]; C–T, 212, 1. 16)*

LO Stemmas I and II + Amar. + O
ne N
(———) *FIJ + Stemma IV (H falta)

LO on Graph 206 appears in Melibea's speech at the gate when she confesses her love for Calisto.

> . . . Todo lo que te dixo confirmo, todo LO he por bueno.
> *(Cej. II, XII, 90, 1. 23 [84, 1. 30]; C–T, 210, 1. 30)*

LO Stemma I + *E + *FIJ + Stemma IV + Amar. + O
(———) N + PUV (H falta)

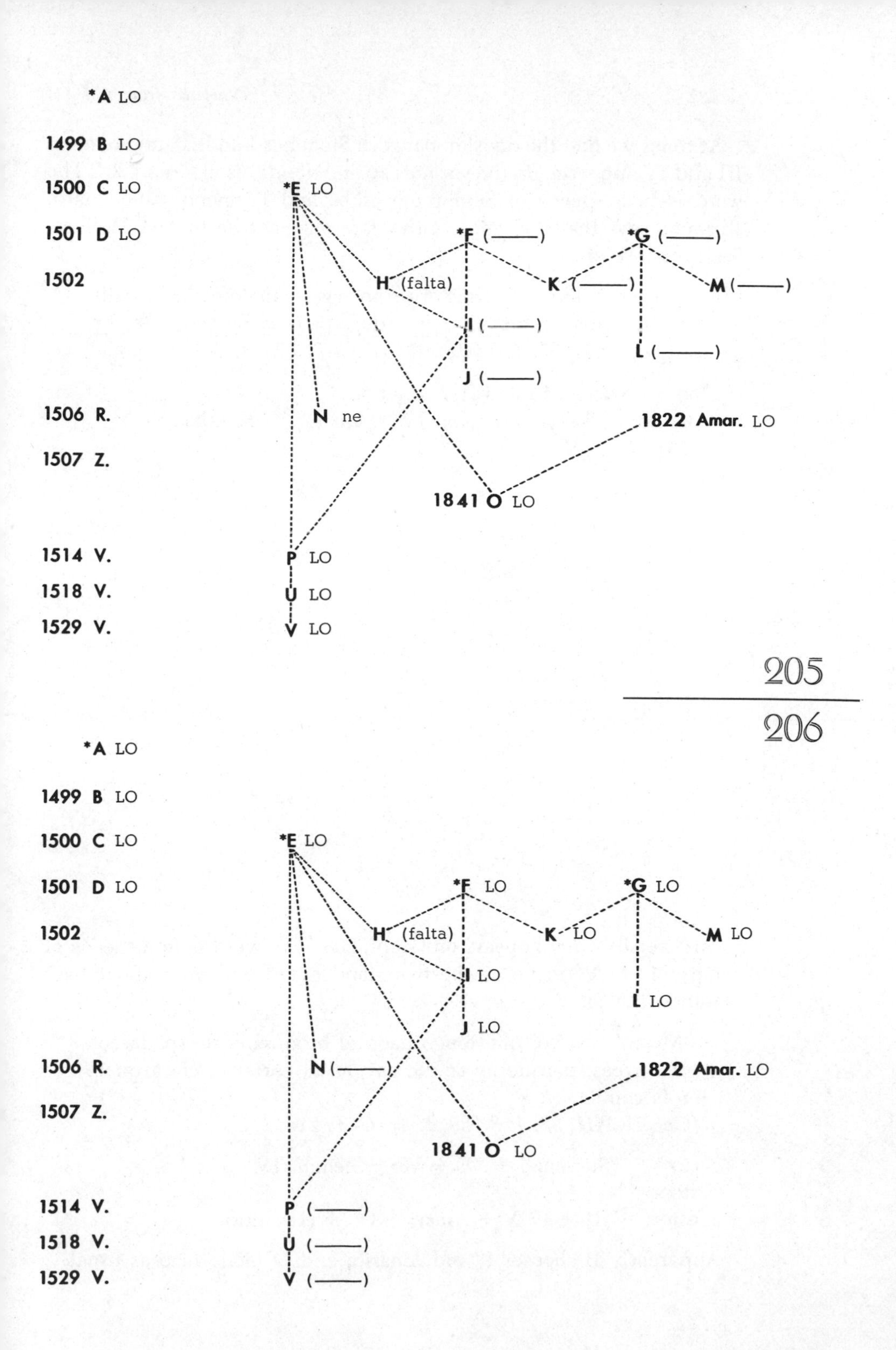

*A LO
1499 B LO
1500 C LO
*E LO
1501 D LO
*F (——)
*G (——)
1502
H (falta)
K (——)
M (——)
I (——)
L (——)
J (——)
1506 R.
N ne
1822 Amar. LO
1507 Z.
1841 O LO
1514 V.
P LO
1518 V.
U LO
1529 V.
V LO
205
206
*A LO
1499 B LO
1500 C LO
*E LO
1501 D LO
*F LO
*G LO
1502
H (falta)
K LO
M LO
I LO
L LO
J LO
1506 R.
N (——)
1822 Amar. LO
1507 Z.
1841 O LO
1514 V.
P (——)
1518 V.
U (——)
1529 V.
V (——)

At times we find the division between Stemmas I and II and Stemmas III and IV appearing in the variants DO and *donde,* as in Graph 207. The word is in a speech of Sempronio as he and Pármeno stand guard. Pármeno says that the voice at the gate may not be that of Melibea. Sempronio replies:

> —Dios nos libre de traydores, no nos ayan tomado la calle por DO tenemos de huyr; que de otra cosa no tengo temor.
> *(Cej. II, XII, 87, 1. 17 [82, 1. 4]; C–T, 208, 1. 20)*

DO  Stemmas I and II + O
donde  *FIJ + Stemma IV + Amar.  (H falta)
la qual  N

ESTÓ versus *estoy* appears on Graph 208. The word is in a speech of Sempronio to Pármeno as the two stand guard and brag about their readiness to flee.

> —Mejor ESTÓ yo, que tengo liado el broquel é el espada con las correas, porque no se me caygan al correr, é el caxquete en la capilla.
> *(Cej. II, XII, 95, 1. 8 [89, 1. 4]; C–T, 214, 1. 9)*

ESTÓ  Stemma I + *E + *F + Stemma IV
sto  N
estoy  IJ + PUV + Amar. + O  (H falta)

Apparently P chooses I, and Amarita and O modernize as usual.

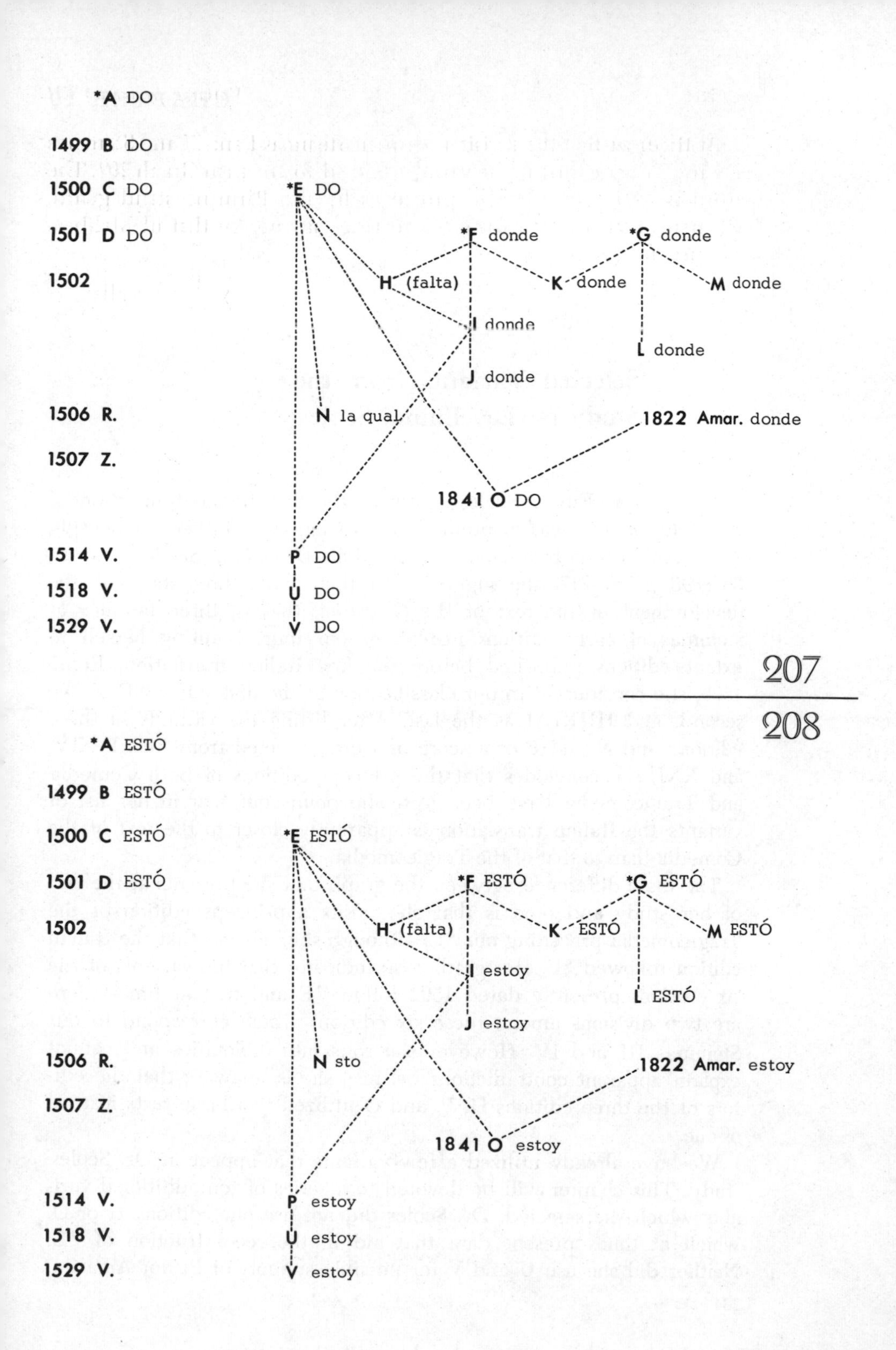

*A DO
1499 B DO
1500 C DO
*E DO
1501 D DO
*F donde
*G donde
1502
H (falta)
K donde
M donde
I donde
L donde
J donde
1506 R.
N la qual
1822 Amar. donde
1507 Z.
1841 O DO
1514 V.
P DO
1518 V.
U DO
1529 V.
V DO
207
208
*A ESTÓ
1499 B ESTÓ
1500 C ESTÓ
*E ESTÓ
1501 D ESTÓ
*F ESTÓ
*G ESTÓ
1502
H (falta)
K ESTÓ
M ESTÓ
I estoy
L ESTÓ
J estoy
1506 R.
N sto
1822 Amar. estoy
1507 Z.
1841 O estoy
1514 V.
P estoy
1518 V.
U estoy
1529 V.
V estoy

# CHAPTER 10

# Selected Variants from the Study by Dr. Emma Scoles

Dr. Emma Scoles' study of the first Italian translation of the *Celestina* (N) was mentioned in our Chapter 1. In her monograph, "Note sulla prima traduzione italiana della *Celestina*," *Studi Romanzi*, 33 (1961), 157–217, she suggests that there were three stages in the development of the text of the *Celestina;* that is, three families or stemmas of early editions instead of our four. Limiting herself to extant editions published before the first Italian translation, Rome 1506, she considers B in our classification as the first stage, CD as the second, and HIJKLM as the last. After listing the variants in these editions and N and P of a score of words selected from Acts I, XIV, and XXI, she concludes that the princeps editions of both Comedia and Tragicomedia have been lost. She points out that in her list of variants the Italian translation is apparently closer to the text of the Comedia than to that of the Tragicomedia.

The main difference between the graph that she presents at the end of her study and ours is that she posits a princeps edition of the Tragicomedia preceding our *E, although she believes that the Italian edition followed *E. Her graph also indicates that the variants of the six editions presently dated 1502 follow *E and that at times there are two divisions among these six editions which correspond to our Stemmas III and IV. However she runs into difficulties and cannot explain apparent contradictions because she is unaware that the editors of the three editions H, P, and O utilized two basic texts instead of one.

We have already utilized a few variants that appear in Dr. Scoles' study. This chapter will be devoted to a series of ten additional variants which she selected. Dr. Scoles did not use our editions H or O, which at times present data that aid in the reconstruction of *E. Neither did she use U and V for possible support of P; nor Amarita,

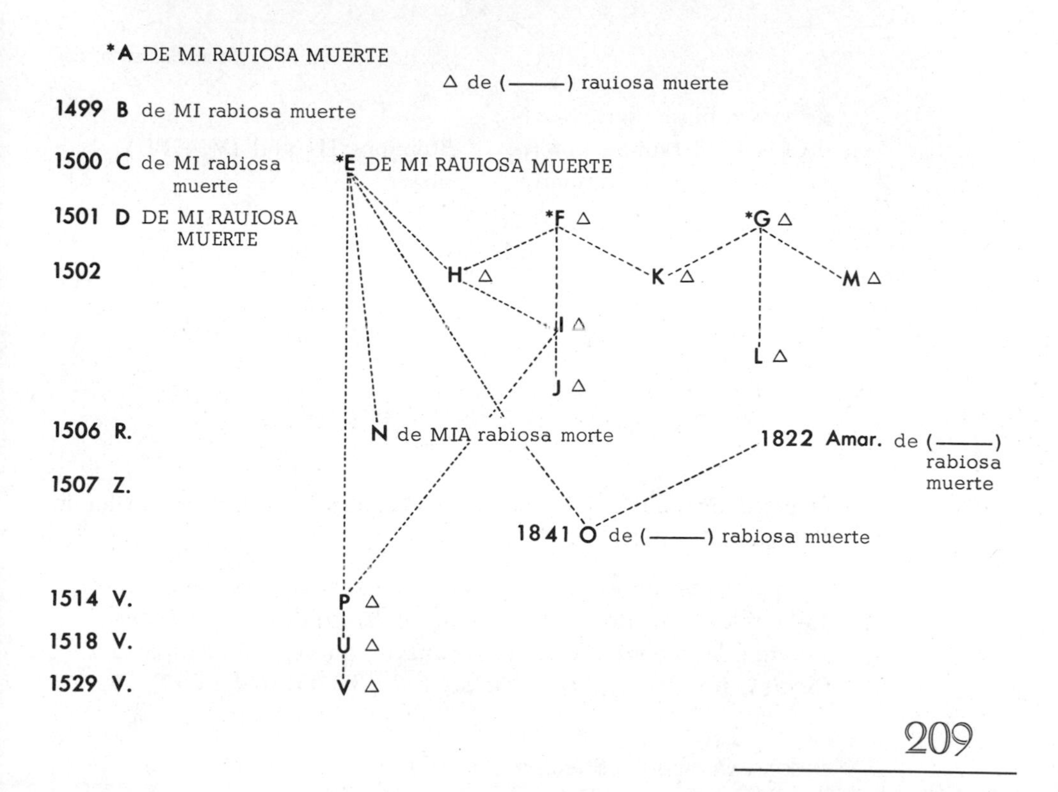


which provides help in evaluating O. The reader is already acquainted with the patterns into which the variants fall, although at times there are slight variations. In the first three instances the variant which, in our opinion, was not the original word of the princeps edition is supported by Stemmas III and IV and by PUV, Amarita, and O. On the other hand, *E is supported by Stemma I and by N in each case. In the first example, and later where several words are included as one variant and where each word of the expression may have variants, we restrict the use of capital letters to one or two words except in the first line of each summary.

The words on Graph 209 appear in a speech of Calisto threatening Sempronio in an angry voice. He has just returned home dejectedly after his first meeting with Melibea.

> —¡Vete de ay! No me fables; sinó, quiça ante del tiempo de MI rabiosa muerte, mis manos causarán tu arrebatado fin. *(Scoles, p. 198. Cej. I, I, 37, l. 3; C–T, 25, l. 8)*

| | |
|---|---|
| DE MI RAUIOSA MUERTE | *AD + *E |
| de MI rabiosa muerte | BC |

de MIA rabiosa morte N
de (———) rauiosa muerte Stemmas III and IV + PUV
de (———) rabiosa muerte Amar. + O

The word on Graph 210 appears in a speech by Calisto earlier in the dialogue just cited.

> . . . ¡Assí por infortunio arrebatado perezcas ó perpetuo intollerable tormento consigas, el qual en grado *incomparablemente* á la penosa é desastrada muerte, que espero, traspassa.
> *(Scoles, p. 197. Cej. I, I, 35, 11. 6–7 [35, 11. 3–4]; C–T, 24, 1. 20)*

INCOMPARABLE Stemma I + *E
INCOMPARABILE N
incomparablemente Stemmas III and IV + PUV + Amar. + O

On Graph 211 Pármeno is telling Calisto about his boyhood when he was in the service of Celestina.

> . . . Pero de aquel poco tiempo que la seruí, recogía la nueua memoria lo que la VEJEZ no ha podido quitar.
> *(Scoles, p. 198. Cej. I, I, 70, 1. 2; C–T, 41, 1. 18)*

VEJEZ *ABCD*E
UECCHIEZZA N
vieja Stemmas III and IV + PUV + Amar. + O

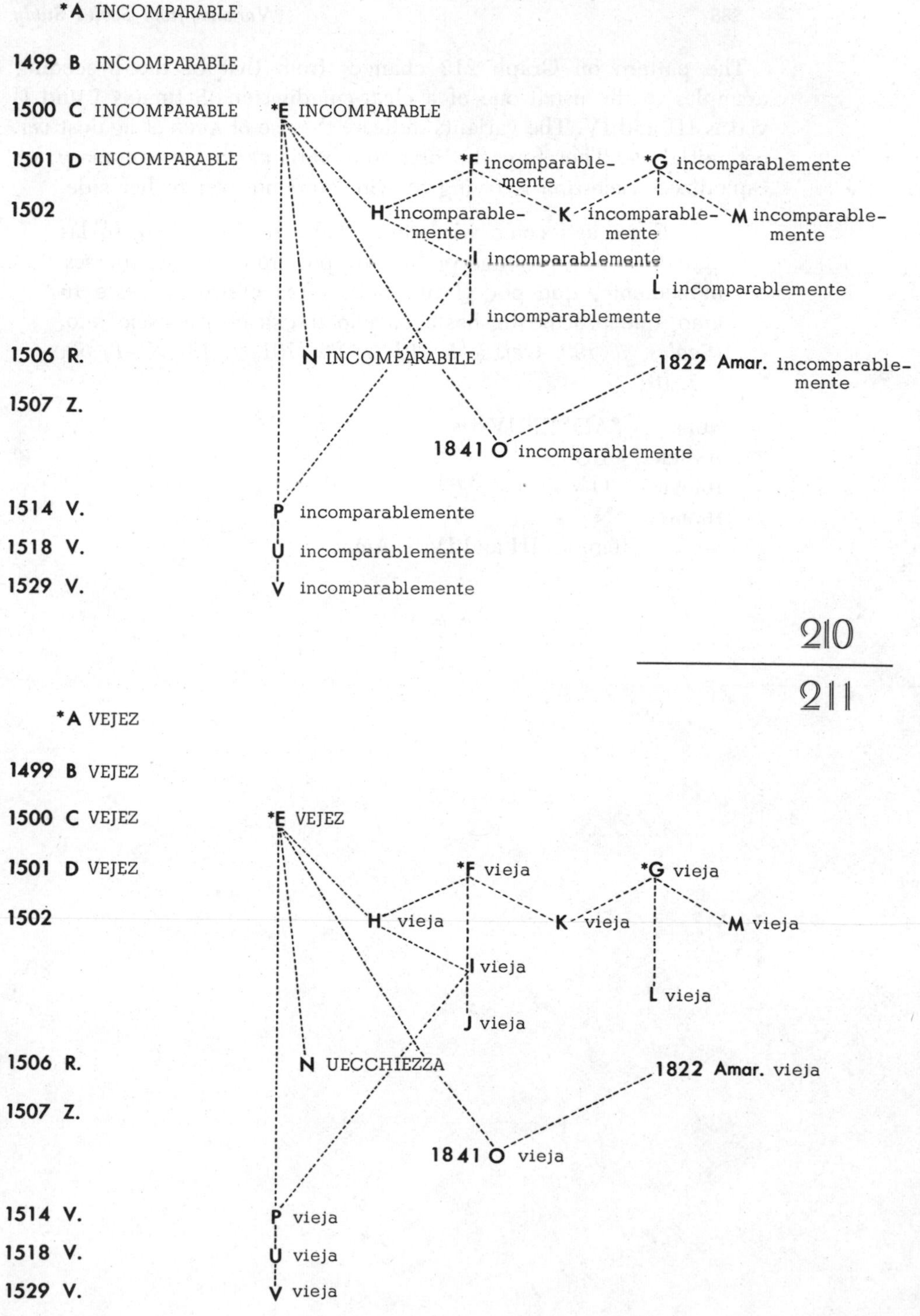
*A INCOMPARABLE
1499 B INCOMPARABLE
1500 C INCOMPARABLE
*E INCOMPARABLE
1501 D INCOMPARABLE
*F incomparable-mente
*G incomparablemente
1502
H incomparable-mente
K incomparable-mente
M incomparable-mente
I incomparablemente
L incomparablemente
J incomparablemente
1506 R.
N INCOMPARABILE
1822 Amar. incomparable-mente
1507 Z.
1841 O incomparablemente
1514 V.
P incomparablemente
1518 V.
U incomparablemente
1529 V.
V incomparablemente
210
211
*A VEJEZ
1499 B VEJEZ
1500 C VEJEZ
*E VEJEZ
1501 D VEJEZ
*F vieja
*G vieja
1502
H vieja
K vieja
M vieja
I vieja
L vieja
J vieja
1506 R.
N UECCHIEZZA
1822 Amar. vieja
1507 Z.
1841 O vieja
1514 V.
P vieja
1518 V.
U vieja
1529 V.
V vieja

The pattern on Graph 212 changes from that of the preceding examples to the usual one of a clear-cut division: Stemmas I and II versus III and IV. The variants indicate the use of AUER as against *ver*, not initial H-. Therefore the first four variants in the summary are capitalized. Celestina is trying to win Pármeno over to her side.

> . . . E yo, assí como verdadera madre tuya, te digo, só las malediciones, que tus padres te pusieron, si me fuesses inobediente, que por el presente sufras é siruas á este tu amo, que procuraste, hasta en ello HAUER otro consejo mío. *(Scoles, p. 199. Cej. I, I, 101, 1. 20 [101, 1. 19]; C–T, 53, 1. 10)*

AUER *AD*EPUV
HAUER BC
HABER O
HARAI N
ver Stemmas III and IV + Amar.

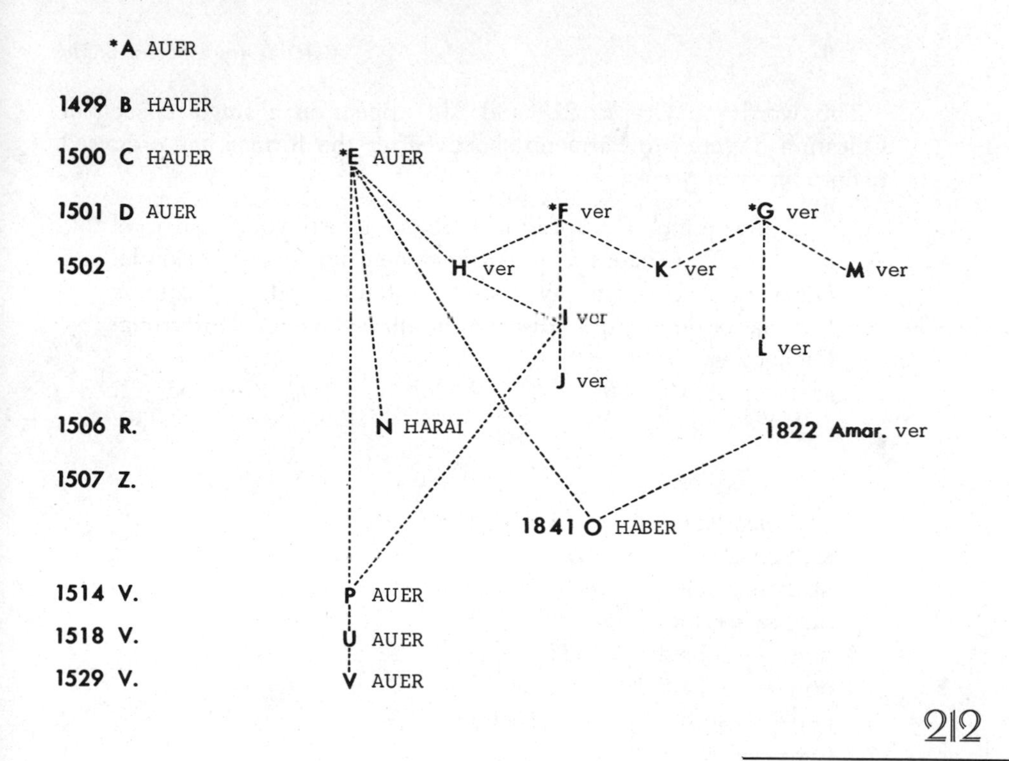
*A AUER
1499 B HAUER
1500 C HAUER
1501 D AUER
1502
1506 R.
1507 Z.
1514 V.
1518 V.
1529 V.
*E AUER
*F ver
*G ver
H ver
K ver
M ver
I ver
L ver
J ver
N HARAI
1822 Amar. ver
1841 O HABER
P AUER
U AUER
V AUER

The words on Graphs 213 and 214 appear in a single speech of Celestina directed to Pármeno shortly after the former has promised to help him win Areúsa.

> —¡O mezquino! De enfermo coraçón es NO PODER sufrir el bien. Da Dios hauas á quien no tienen quixadas. ¡O simple! Dirás que á donde ay mayor entendimiento ay MENOR fortuna é donde más discreción allí es menor la fortuna! Dichos son.
> *(Scoles, pp. 199–200. Cej. I, I, 106, 11. 9–11; C–T, 55, 11. 32–33 and 56, 1. 2)*

Graph 213

| | |
|---|---|
| NO PODER SUFFRIR | *AC*EPU |
| NO PODER sufrir | BO |
| NO PODER soffrir | D |
| NON SA PATIRE | N |
| no (———) suffrir | H |
| no (———) sufrir | Amar. |
| (———) suffrir | *FIJ + Stemma IV |
| (———) poder sufrir | V |

The next word to note in the preceding text is MENOR. The word MAYOR which precedes it has no variant except in O, where the witness is *menor*.

Graph 214

| | |
|---|---|
| MENOR | Stemmas I and II |
| MINOR | N |
| mayor | Stemmas III and IV + Amar. + O |

The MENOR used near the end of the speech "allí es MENOR la fortuna" is a nonvariant.

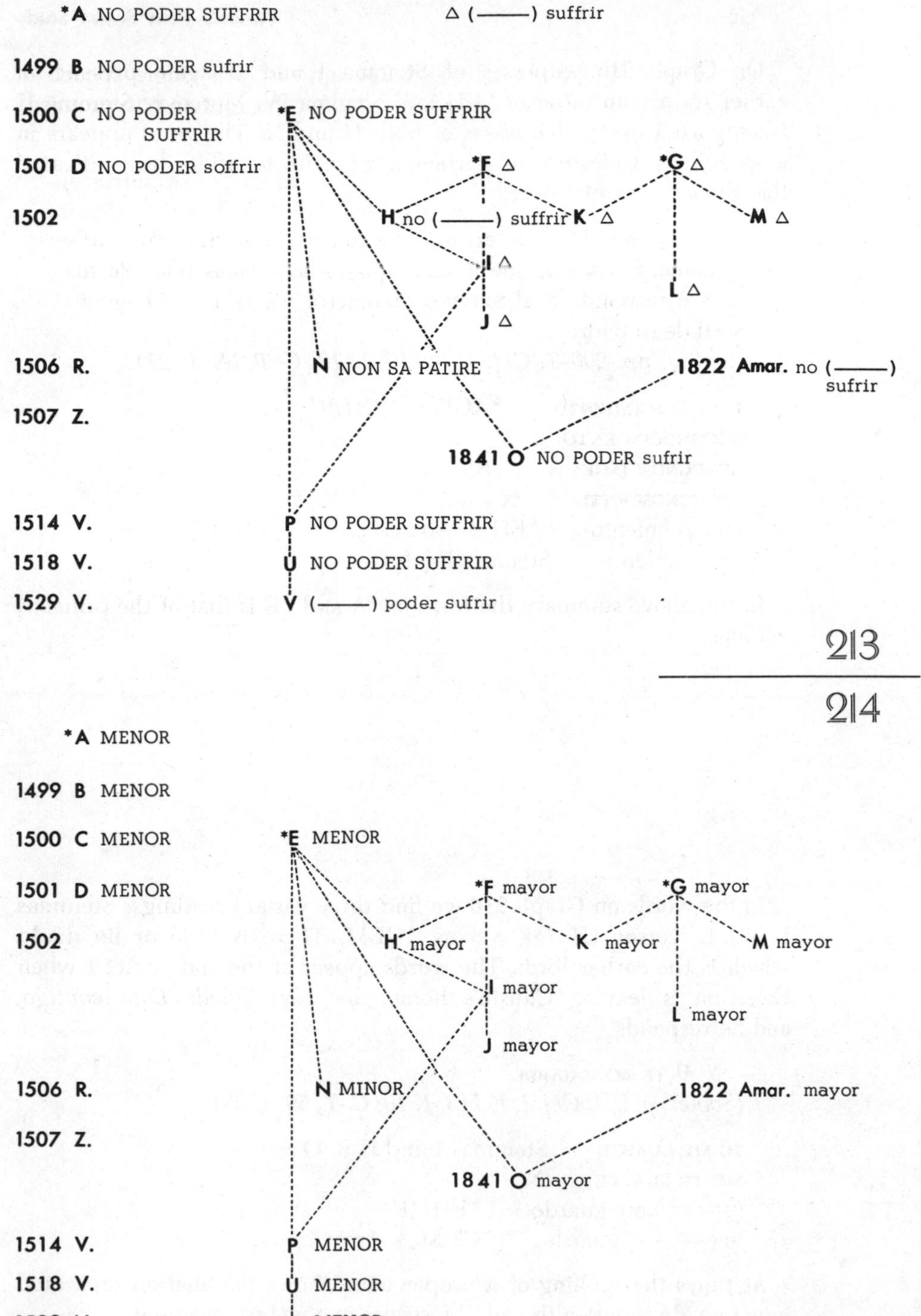
*A NO PODER SUFFRIR
△ (——) suffrir
1499 B NO PODER sufrir
1500 C NO PODER SUFFRIR
*E NO PODER SUFFRIR
1501 D NO PODER soffrir
*F △
*G △
1502
H no (——) suffrir
K △
M △
I △
L △
J △
1506 R.
N NON SA PATIRE
1822 Amar. no (——) sufrir
1507 Z.
1841 O NO PODER sufrir
1514 V.
P NO PODER SUFFRIR
1518 V.
U NO PODER SUFFRIR
1529 V.
V (——) poder sufrir
213
214
*A MENOR
1499 B MENOR
1500 C MENOR
*E MENOR
1501 D MENOR
*F mayor
*G mayor
1502
H mayor
K mayor
M mayor
I mayor
L mayor
J mayor
1506 R.
N MINOR
1822 Amar. mayor
1507 Z.
1841 O mayor
1514 V.
P MENOR
1518 V.
U MENOR
1529 V.
V MENOR

On Graph 215 witnesses of Stemma I and II again present an earlier form than those of *FIJ and Stemma IV. Moreover Stemma II is supported by the witnesses of both H and N. The word appears in a speech by Celestina to Pármeno, who, in an aside, has indicated that she has won him over.

> –De los hombres es errar é bestial es la porfía. Por ende gózome, Pármeno, que ayas limpiado las turbias telas de tus ojos é respondido al RECONOSCIMIENTO, discreción é engenio sotil de tu padre, . . .
> *(Scoles, pp. 200–1. Cej. I, I, 110, l. 18; C–T, 58, l. 21)*

RECONOSCIMIENTO *ACD + *EHPU
RECONOCIMIENTO V
RECOGNOSCIMIENTO B
RECOGNOSCENTIA N
conoscimiento *FIJ + Amar.
conocimiento Stemma IV + O

In the above summary the form in *A and *E is that of the princeps editions.

In the words on Graph 216 we find three variant readings: Stemmas I and II versus III + K versus *GLM. There is little or no doubt which is the earlier form. The words appear at the end of Act I when Celestina is leaving Calisto's home. She says *Quede Dios contigo*, and he responds:

> —Y él TE ME GUARDE.
> *(Scoles, p. 201. Cej. I, I, 112, l. 10; C–T, 59, l. 28)*

TE ME GUARDE Stemmas I and II + O
ME TE GUARDE N
(———) me guarde *FHIJK
te (———) guarde *GLM + Amar.

At times the spelling of a proper noun shows the filiation separated into two divisions–although M strays in the first example.

*A RECONOSCIMIENTO

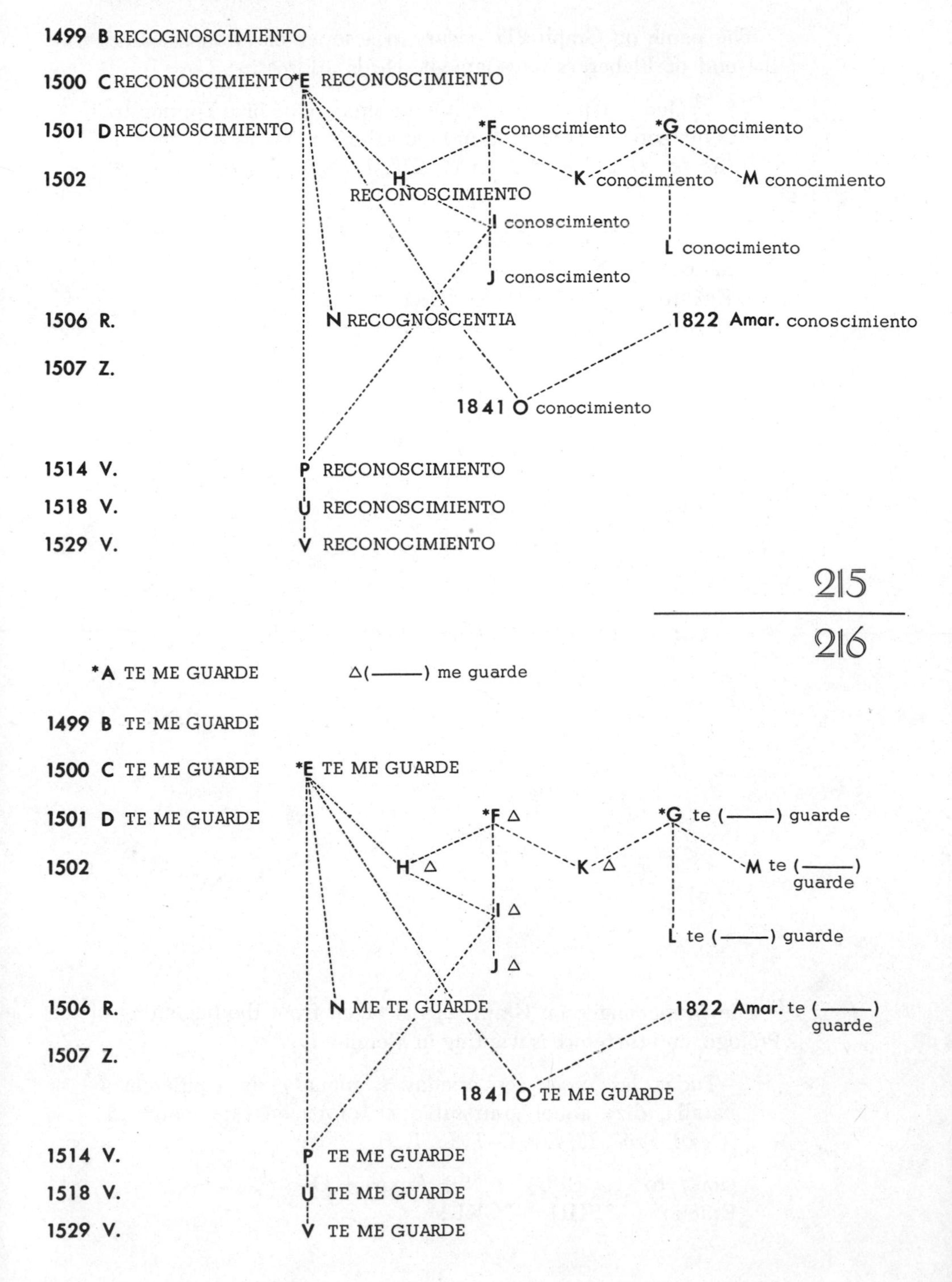
1499 B RECOGNOSCIMIENTO
1500 C RECONOSCIMIENTO
*E RECONOSCIMIENTO
1501 D RECONOSCIMIENTO
*F conoscimiento
*G conocimiento
1502
H RECONOSCIMIENTO
K conocimiento
M conocimiento
I conoscimiento
L conocimiento
J conoscimiento
1506 R.
N RECOGNOSCENTIA
1822 Amar. conoscimiento
1507 Z.
1841 O conocimiento
1514 V.
P RECONOSCIMIENTO
1518 V.
U RECONOSCIMIENTO
1529 V.
V RECONOCIMIENTO
215
216
*A TE ME GUARDE
△(——) me guarde
1499 B TE ME GUARDE
1500 C TE ME GUARDE
*E TE ME GUARDE
1501 D TE ME GUARDE
*F △
*G te (——) guarde
1502
H △
K △
M te (——) guarde
I △
L te (——) guarde
J △
1506 R.
N ME TE GUARDE
1822 Amar. te (——) guarde
1507 Z.
1841 O TE ME GUARDE
1514 V.
P TE ME GUARDE
1518 V.
U TE ME GUARDE
1529 V.
V TE ME GUARDE

The name on Graph 217 occurs in a series of classical names near the end of Pleberio's long lament. He is addressing Love.

> . . . ¿Qué hizo por tí Paris? ¿Qué Elena? ¿Qué hizo Ypermestra? ¿Qué EGISTO? Todo el mundo lo sabe.
> *(Scoles, p. 212. Cej. II, XXI, 227, l. 9 [211, l. 18]; C–T, 300, l. 19)*

| | |
|---|---|
| EGISTO | Stemmas I and II + M + O |
| AEGISTO | N |
| Egistro | Stemma III + *GKL |
| Egistor | Amar. |

The proper name on Graph 218 is taken from the beginning of the Prólogo, and therefore is wanting in Stemma I.

> —Todas las cosas ser criadas á manera de contienda ó batalla, dize aquel gran sabio ERÁCLITO en este modo: . . .
> *(Cej. I, Ról., 15, l. 2; C–T, 13, l. 2)*

| | |
|---|---|
| ERÁCLITO | *EPUV + N + Amar. + O |
| Eraclio | *FHIJ + *GKLM |

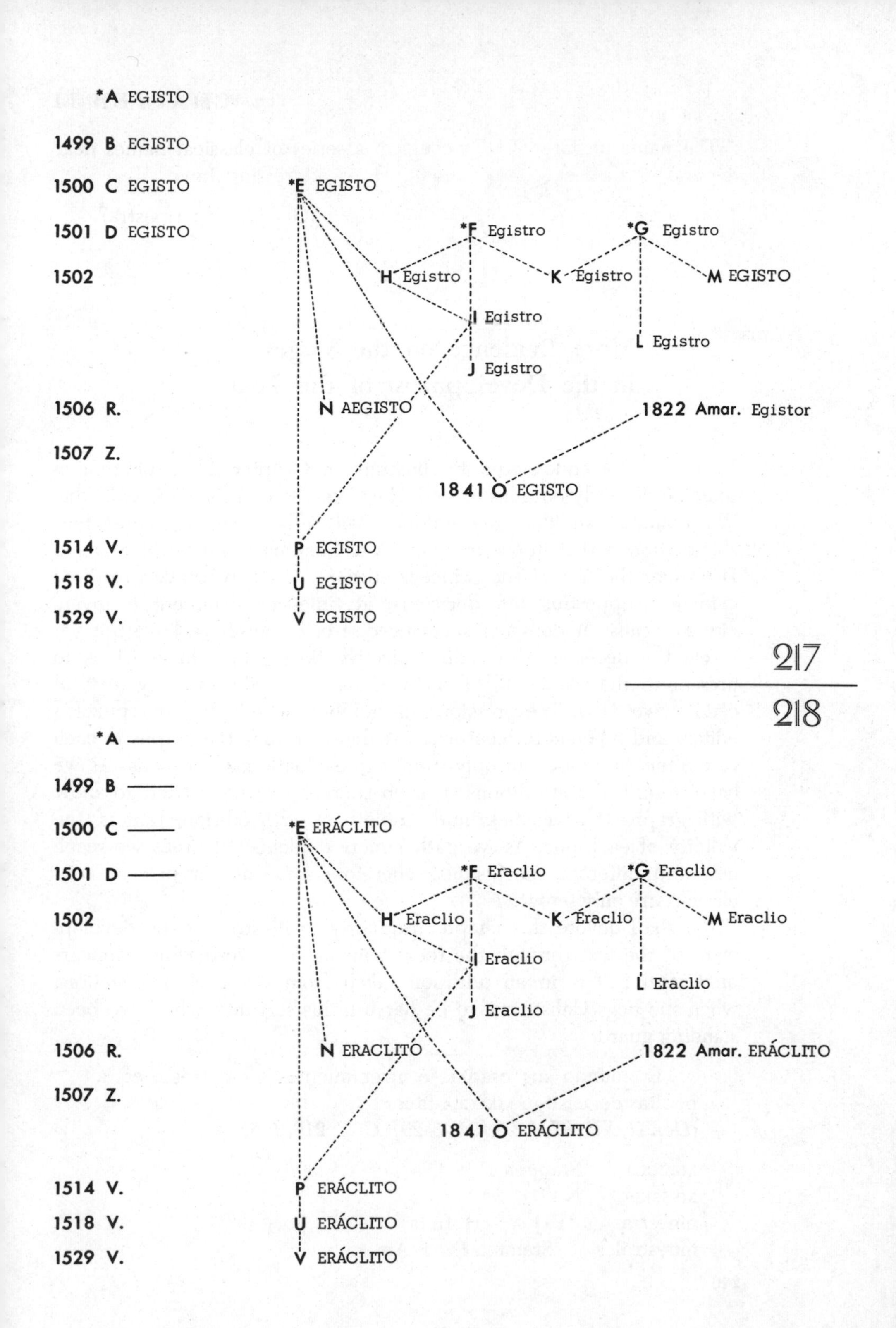
*A EGISTO
1499 B EGISTO
1500 C EGISTO
*E EGISTO
1501 D EGISTO
*F Egistro
*G Egistro
1502
H Egistro
K Egistro
M EGISTO
I Egistro
L Egistro
J Egistro
1506 R.
N AEGISTO
1822 Amar. Egistor
1507 Z.
1841 O EGISTO
1514 V.
P EGISTO
1518 V.
U EGISTO
1529 V.
V EGISTO
217
218
*A ——
1499 B ——
1500 C ——
*E ERÁCLITO
1501 D ——
*F Eraclio
*G Eraclio
1502
H Eraclio
K Eraclio
M Eraclio
I Eraclio
L Eraclio
J Eraclio
1506 R.
N ERACLITO
1822 Amar. ERÁCLITO
1507 Z.
1841 O ERÁCLITO
1514 V.
P ERÁCLITO
1518 V.
U ERÁCLITO
1529 V.
V ERÁCLITO

# CHAPTER 11

# More Evidence on the Stages in the Development of the Text

We endeavored to illustrate in Chapter 2 the filiation of some of the early editions of both the Comedia and the Tragicomedia. We pointed out that the editions fall rather regularly into four stemmata and that in our opinion *A of Stemma I and *E of Stemma II present the text of the princeps editions. Often we have furnished evidence supporting our decisions; at times no comment is given, either because it does not seem needed or because we have not yet reached a decision. Our main objective throughout this book is to present to the reader all of the variants in significant early texts of certain words and expressions, a number of which have puzzled editors and scholars for centuries. At the same time the graphs in each case offer the reader an opportunity to evaluate our decisions. As we have described the editions of each stemma, we have tried to show with graphs the weakness and strength of each edition; that is, the validity of each one. As we gather more evidence, at times we reach new and different conclusions. Therefore some of our present conclusions are only tentative.

We shall devote this chapter primarily to illustrating the development of the text through the four stemmas. The word which appears on Graph 219 is in an addition taken from a speech by Melibea when she begs Calisto not to be harsh to his servants, who have been standing guard.

> . . . É quando sus osadías é atreuimientos les corregieres, á bueltas del castigo MEZCLA fauor.
> *(Cej. II, XII, 97, 1. 28 [91, 1. 20]; C–T, 216, 1. 8)*

MEZCLA Stemma II + O
MESSEDI N
muestra *FIJ (H falta)
muéstrales Stemma IV + Amar.

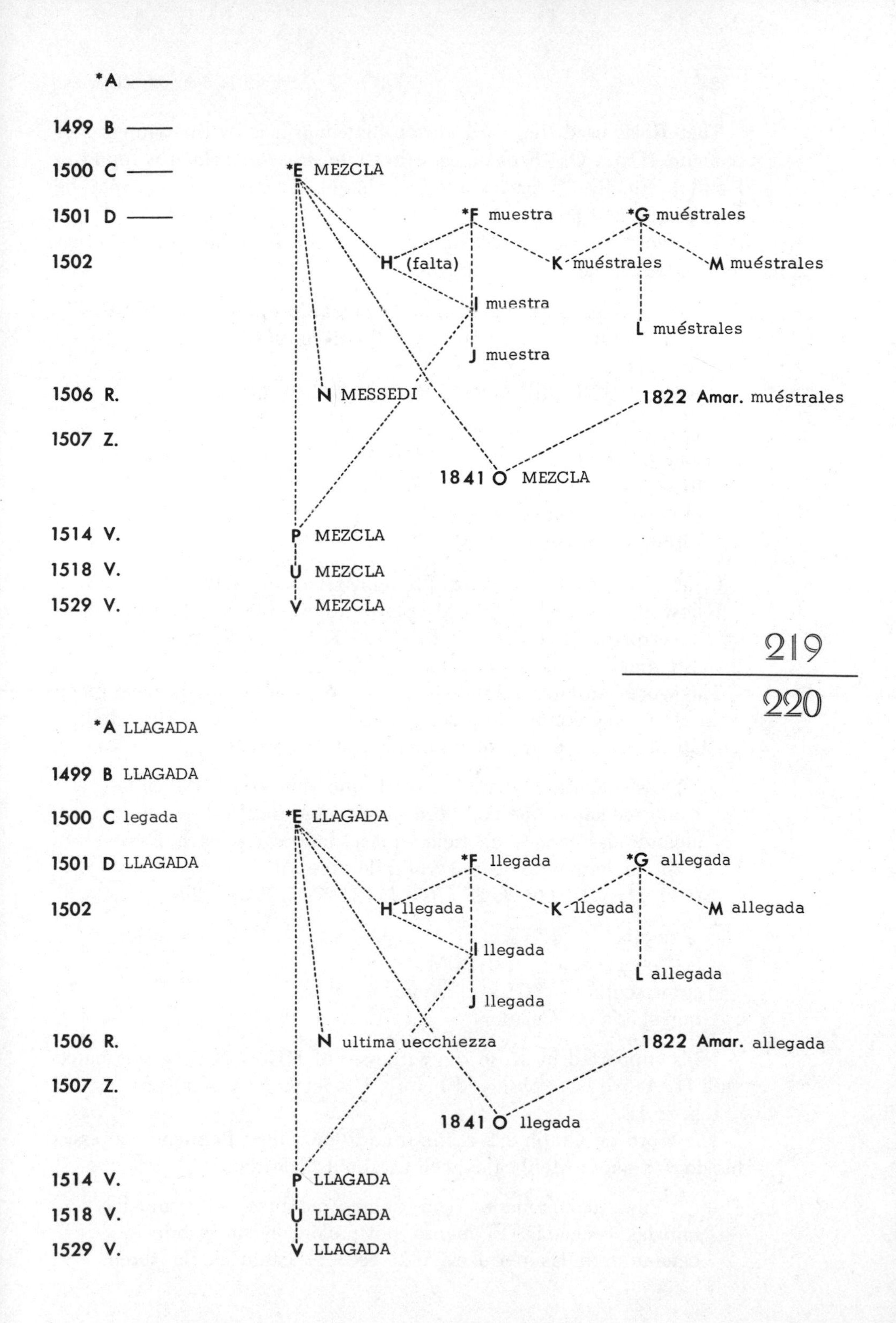

*A
1499 B
1500 C
1501 D
1502
1506 R.
1507 Z.
1514 V.
1518 V.
1529 V.
*E MEZCLA
*F muestra
*G muéstrales
H (falta)
K muéstrales
M muéstrales
I muestra
L muéstrales
J muestra
N MESSEDI
1822 Amar. muéstrales
1841 O MEZCLA
P MEZCLA
U MEZCLA
V MEZCLA
219
220
*A LLAGADA
1499 B LLAGADA
1500 C legada
1501 D LLAGADA
1502
1506 R.
1507 Z.
1514 V.
1518 V.
1529 V.
*E LLAGADA
*F llegada
*G allegada
H llegada
K llegada
M allegada
I llegada
L allegada
J llegada
N ultima uecchiezza
1822 Amar. allegada
1841 O llegada
P LLAGADA
U LLAGADA
V LLAGADA

That Rojas used the word MEZCLA is confirmed by the witnesses of Stemma II and O. *F changes MEZCLA to *muestra,* which is found in I and J. Finally *G makes another change, to *muéstrales,* as may be seen throughout Stemma IV.

The word on Graph 220 appears near the beginning of Pleberio's long lament as he is talking to Alisa.

> . . . La causa supe della; más la he sabido por estenso desta su triste siruienta. Ayúdame á llorar nuestra LLAGADA postremería.
> *(Cej. II, XXI, 216, 1. 16 [201, 1. 14]; C–T, 294, 1. 23)*

LLAGADA *ABD + *EPUV
legada C
llegada *FHIJK + O
allegada *GLM + Amar.
ultima uecchiezza N

C, as often, makes an error. Stemma III changes the meaning and is followed by K and O. *GLM creates a new spelling, an error based on the error of *FHIJKO. In this case K follows Stemma III rather than Stemma IV, that is, *F instead of *G.

The words on Graph 221, which appear in an addition, have given trouble to some editors. Cejador changes the *si* to *qué.* Sosia is telling Tristán about the deaths of Pármeno and Sempronio.

> —Ya sin sentido yuan; pero el uno con harta difficultad, como me sintió que con lloro le miraua, hincó los ojos en mí, alçando las manos al cielo, quasi dando gracias á Dios é como preguntándome *qué sentía* de su morir.
> *(Cej. II, XIII, 116, 1. 22 [108, 1. 15]; C–T, 230, 1. 14)*

SI SENTÍA *E*FK
(———) sentía HIJPUV
si me sentía *GLM + Amar. + O
qué sentía Cejador

*F is supported by K, so the witnesses of HIJ must have originated with H. As we have observed before, P selects the variant of I instead of that of *E.

The word on Graph 222 is in an addition where Pármeno expresses his doubts about Melibea as well as about Celestina.

> . . . Pues alahé, madre, con dulces palabras están muchas injurias vengadas. El manso boyzuelo con su blando CENCERRAR trae las perdizes á la red; el canto de la serena

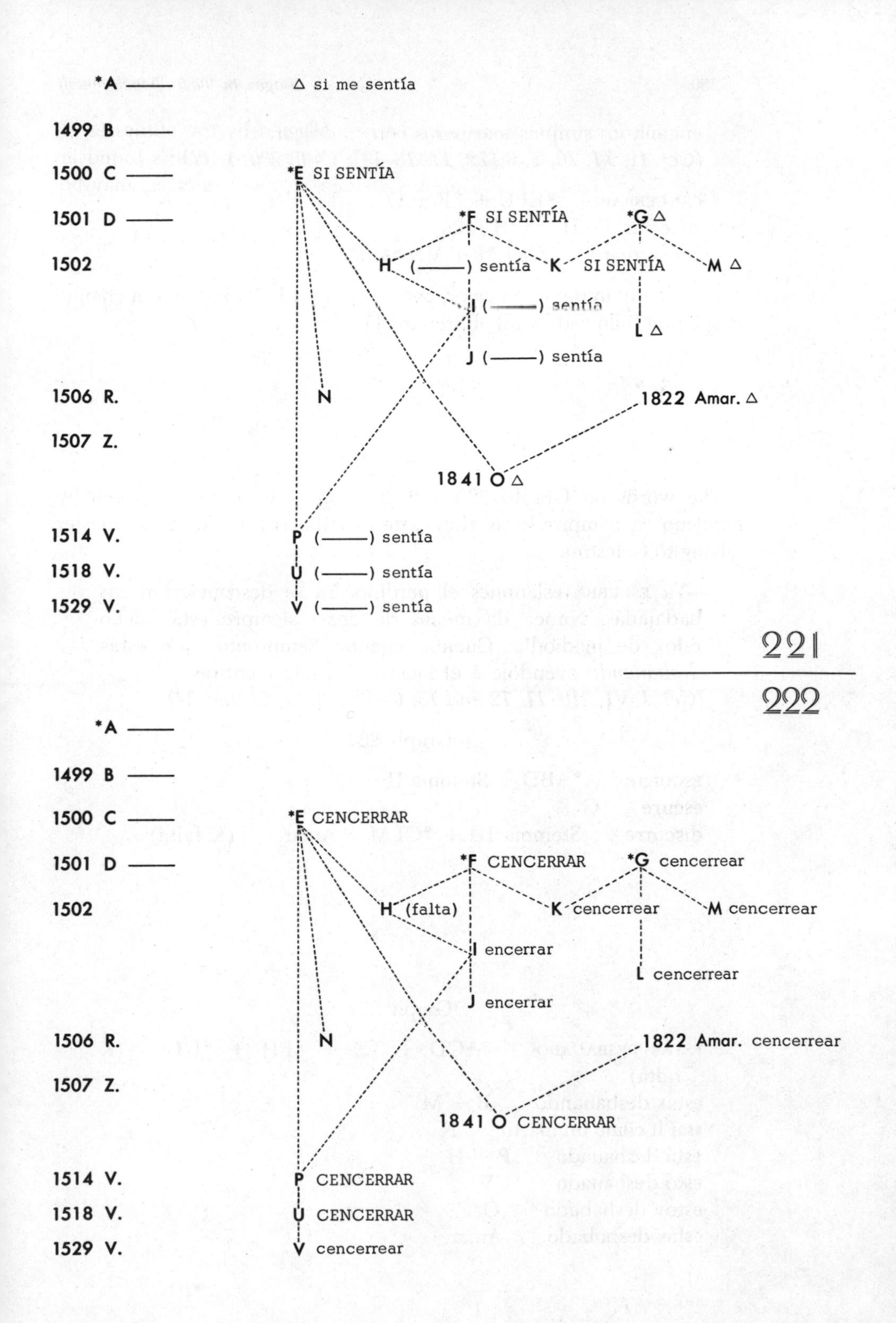
*A —— △ si me sentía
1499 B ——
1500 C —— *E SI SENTÍA
1501 D —— *F SI SENTÍA *G △
1502 H (——) sentía K SI SENTÍA M △
I (——) sentía
L △
J (——) sentía
1506 R. N
1822 Amar. △
1507 Z.
1841 O △
1514 V. P (——) sentía
1518 V. U (——) sentía
1529 V. V (——) sentía
221
222
*A ——
1499 B ——
1500 C —— *E CENCERRAR
1501 D —— *F CENCERRAR *G cencerrear
1502 H (falta) K cencerrear M cencerrear
I encerrar
L cencerrear
J encerrar
1506 R. N
1822 Amar. cencerrear
1507 Z.
1841 O CENCERRAR
1514 V. P CENCERRAR
1518 V. U CENCERRAR
1529 V. V cencerrear

engaña los simples marineros con su dulçor.
*(Cej. II, XI, 76, 1. 6 [72, 11. 18–19]; C–T, 200, 1. 17)*

CENCERRAR *EPU + *F + O
encerrar IJ (H falta)
cencerrear *GKLM + V + Amar.

I evidently initiated an error, and J followed I. *G initiated a change of spelling followed by all of Stemma IV.

The words on Graphs 223 and 224 appear in a single speech by Pármeno to Sempronio as they listen to the ravings of their master talking to Celestina.

—Ya ESCURRE eslauones el perdido. Ya se desconciertan sus badajadas. Nunca da menos de doze; siempre está hecho relox de mediodía. Cuenta, cuenta, Sempronio, que estás *desbauando* oyéndole á él locuras é á ella mentiras.
*(Cej. I, VI, 210, 11. 12 and 15; C–T, 116, 11. 21 and 24)*

Graph 223

ESCURRE *ABD + Stemma II + O
escure C
discurre Stemma III + *GLM + Amar. (K falta)

Graph 224

ESTÁS DESBAUADO *ACD + *E + *FIJ + *GL (K falta)
estás desbauando B + M
stai li como un matto N
está desbauado P + H
estó desbauado UV
estoy desbabado O
estás desbobado Amar.

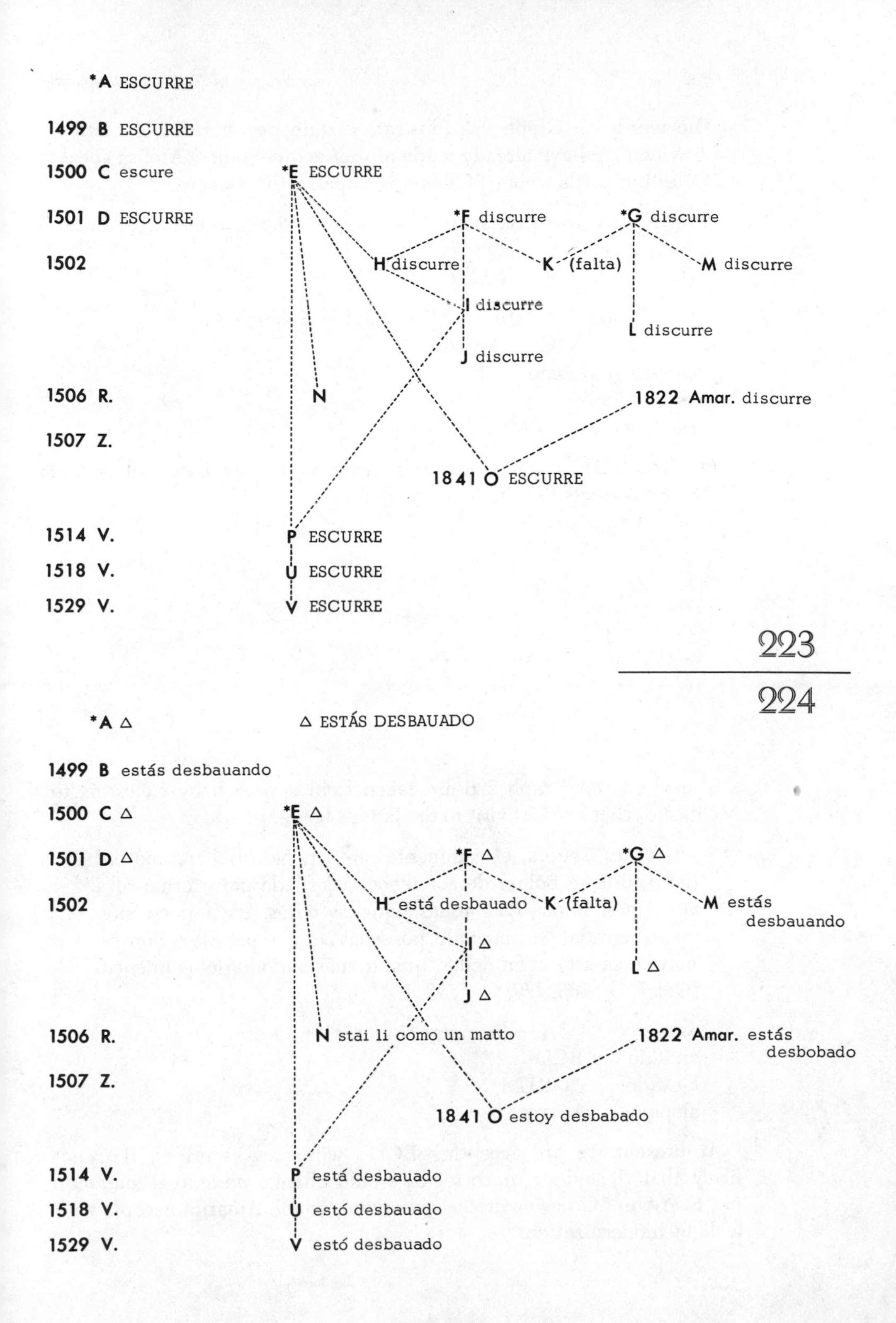
*A ESCURRE
1499 B ESCURRE
1500 C escure
*E ESCURRE
1501 D ESCURRE
*F discurre
*G discurre
1502
H discurre
K (falta)
M discurre
I discurre
L discurre
J discurre
1506 R.
N
1822 Amar. discurre
1507 Z.
1841 O ESCURRE
1514 V.
P ESCURRE
1518 V.
U ESCURRE
1529 V.
V ESCURRE
223
224
*A △
△ ESTÁS DESBAUADO
1499 B estás desbauando
1500 C △
*E △
1501 D △
*F △
*G △
1502
H está desbauado
K (falta)
M estás desbauando
I △
L △
J △
1506 R.
N stai li como un matto
1822 Amar. estás desbobado
1507 Z.
1841 O estoy desbabado
1514 V.
P está desbauado
1518 V.
U estó desbauado
1529 V.
V estó desbauado

The words on Graph 225 illustrate certain peculiarities of editions with which we have already made a brief acquaintance. Areúsa speaks to Celestina, with whom Pármeno is impatiently conversing.

> —¿Qué te dize ESSE SEÑOR á la oreja? ¿Piensa que tengo de fazer nada de lo que pides?
> *(Cej. I, VII, 258, l. 4; C–T, 146, l. 13)*

ESSE SEÑOR *ABD + *E + *FH + Stemma IV
ESE SEÑOR C + O + Amar.
questo getilhomo N
esse señora IJ
essa señora PUV

On Graph 225 P apparently selects the variant of I instead of that of *E but corrects I's mistake in gender.

The words on Graph 226 are taken from a speech by Celestina to Melibea during her first visit to the latter's home.

> —Loco es, señora, el caminante que, enojado del trabajo del día, quisiesse boluer de comienço la jornada para tornar otra vez aquel lugar. Que todas aquellas cosas, cuya possessión no es agradable, más vale poseellas, que esperallas. Porque más cerca está el fin dellas, quanto más *andado* del comienço.
> *(Cej. I, IV, 169, l. 9; C–T, 88, l. 4)*

ANDANDO *A + Stemmas II and III + O
andado BCD
alexado *GKLM
alejado Amar.

At present we are accepting BCD's witnesses as errors. It is not likely that the editor or corrector would change *andado* to *andando* in *E. Again *G has created a new word, which Amarita accepts with a slight modernization.

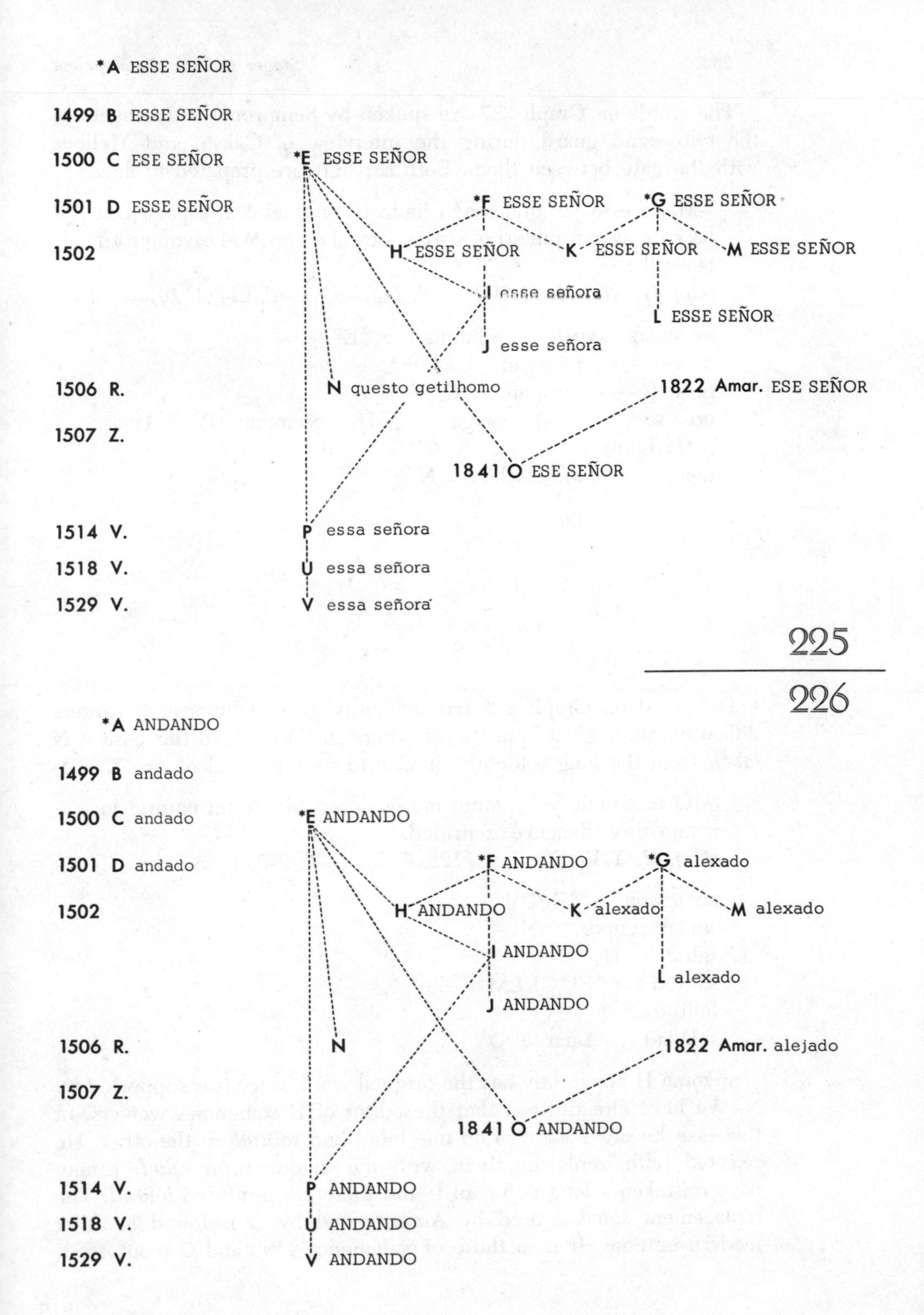
*A ESSE SEÑOR
1499 B ESSE SEÑOR
1500 C ESSE SEÑOR
*E ESSE SEÑOR
1501 D ESSE SEÑOR
*F ESSE SEÑOR
*G ESSE SEÑOR
1502
H ESSE SEÑOR
K ESSE SEÑOR
M ESSE SEÑOR
I esse señora
L ESSE SEÑOR
J esse señora
1506 R.
N questo getilhomo
1822 Amar. ESE SEÑOR
1507 Z.
1841 O ESE SEÑOR
1514 V.
P essa señora
1518 V.
U essa señora
1529 V.
V essa señora
225
226
*A ANDANDO
1499 B andado
1500 C andado
*E ANDANDO
1501 D andado
*F ANDANDO
*G alexado
1502
H ANDANDO
K alexado
M alexado
I ANDANDO
L alexado
J ANDANDO
1506 R.
N
1822 Amar. alejado
1507 Z.
1841 O ANDANDO
1514 V.
P ANDANDO
1518 V.
U ANDANDO
1529 V.
V ANDANDO

The words on Graph 227 are spoken by Sempronio to Pármeno, as the two stand guard during the interview of Calisto and Melibea with the gate between them. Both servants are prepared to flee.

—Mejor estó yo, que tengo liado el broquel é el espada con las correas, porque NO SE ME CAYGAN al correr, é el caxquete en la capilla.
*(Cej. II, XII, 95, 11. 9–10 [89, 11. 5–6]; C–T, 214, 1. 10)*

NO SE ME CAYGAN Stemma I + *E?
no se (———) caygan PUV
no se (———) caigan O
no se (———) cayga *FIJ + Stemma IV + Amar. (H falta)
non (———) me casche N

The word on Graph 228 has evidently given editors and printers difficulty, although it appears elsewhere in the text. In this case it is taken from the long soliloquy of Calisto near the end of Act XIV.

—¡O mezquino yo! quanto me es agradable de mi natural la SOLICITUD é silencio é escuridad.
*(Cej. II, XIV, 132, 1. 2 [122, 1. 9]; C–T, 240, 1. 28)*

SOLICITUD *EPUV
SOLLICITUDINE N
salud H
solitud *FI*GKLM
lolitud J
soledad Amar. + O

Stemma II apparently has the original word, since it is supported by N. We have already seen that the editor of H sometimes waivers. In this case he saw SOLICITUD on one hand and *solitud* on the other. He rejected both, replacing them with the unique form *salud.* J may have mistaken a long s- for an l- and therefore produced *lolitud.* The replacement *soledad* used by Amarita and by O is found in other modern editions. It is in those of Salamanca 1590 and Osmont 1633.

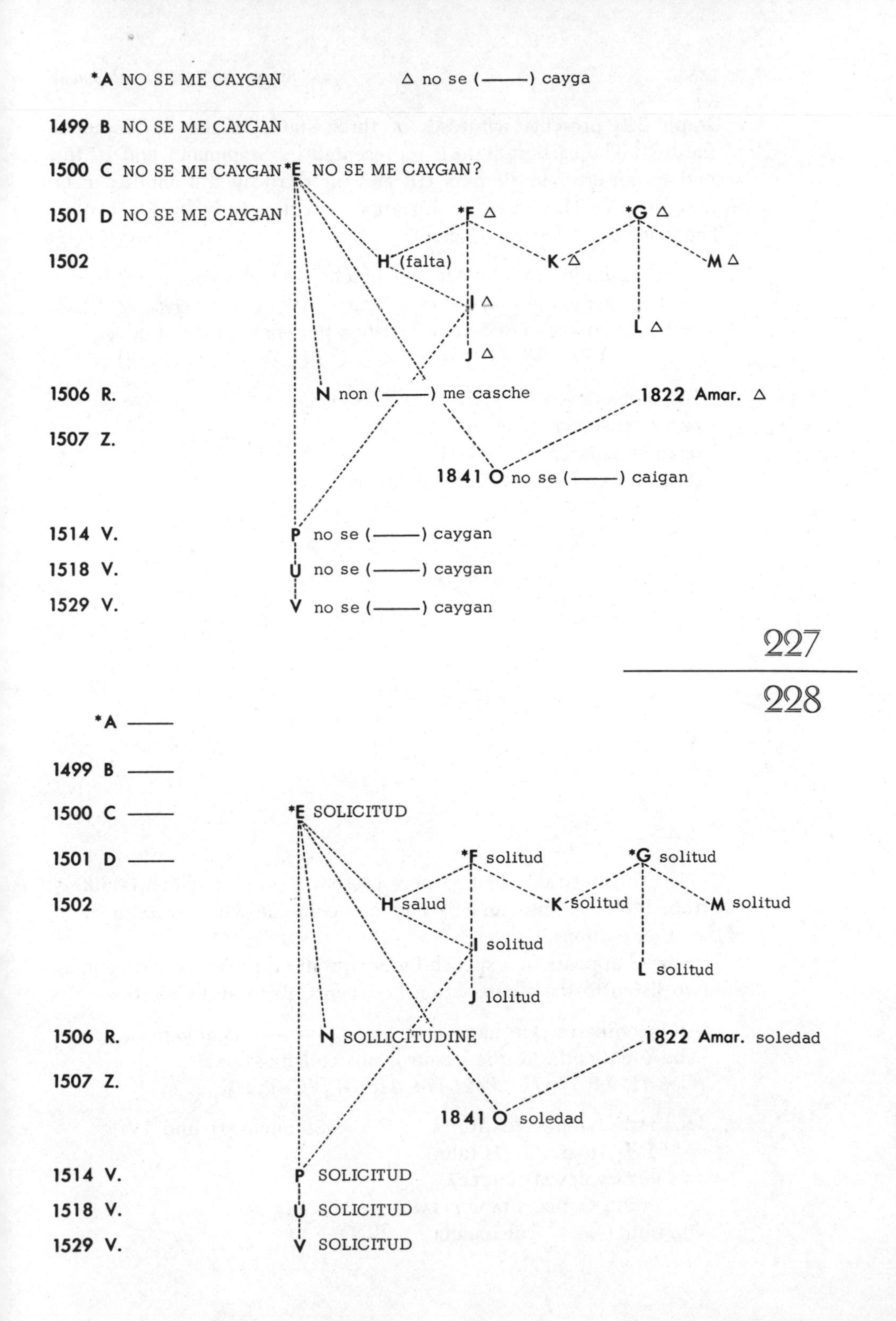
*A NO SE ME CAYGAN
△ no se (——) cayga
1499 B NO SE ME CAYGAN
1500 C NO SE ME CAYGAN
*E NO SE ME CAYGAN?
1501 D NO SE ME CAYGAN
*F △
*G △
1502
H (falta)
K △
M △
I △
L △
J △
1506 R.
N non (——) me casche
1822 Amar. △
1507 Z.
1841 O no se (——) caigan
1514 V.
P no se (——) caygan
1518 V.
U no se (——) caygan
1529 V.
V no se (——) caygan
227
228
*A ——
1499 B ——
1500 C ——
*E SOLICITUD
1501 D ——
*F solitud
*G solitud
1502
H salud
K solitud
M solitud
I solitud
L solitud
J lolitud
1506 R.
N SOLLICITUDINE
1822 Amar. soledad
1507 Z.
1841 O soledad
1514 V.
P SOLICITUD
1518 V.
U SOLICITUD
1529 V.
V SOLICITUD

Graph 229 presents witnesses of three states in the development of the text. The earliest state is represented by Stemmas I and II, the second by an error in Stemma III, and the third by still another error in Stemma IV. The variants also appear in the study by Dr. Scoles. The word is in Pleberio's lament:

> . . . ¡O mundo, mundo! Muchos mucho de tí dixeron, muchos en tus qualidades metieron la mano, á diuersas cosas por oydas TE COMPARARON; yo por triste esperiencia lo contaré, . . . *(Cej. II, XXI, 218, 11. 20–21 [203, 1. 14]; C–T, 296, 1. 10)*

TE COMPARARON *ABCD*EPUV + O
DE TE FECERO COMPARATIONE N
te acompañaron *FHIJ
de ti contaron *GKLM + Amar.

Graph 230 illustrates that O may present a variant which is different from both *E and Amarita but may coincide with errors in some of the other editions.

The word appears in a speech by Sempronio directed to Pármeno as the two listen to the conversation between Calisto and Celestina.

> —¿Qué quieres que haga *vna puta (———) alcahueta,* que sabe é entiende lo que nosotros nos callamos . . . . *(Cej. II, XI, 77, 11. 20–21 [74, 11. 6–7]; C–T, 201, 1. 18)*

VNA PUTA VIEJA ALCAHUETA *A + Stemmas II and IV + *FI + Amar. (H falta)
VNA PUTA VIEJA ALCAHUEDA J
UNA PUTTANA UECCHIA RUFFIANA N
vna puta (———) alcahueta BCD + O

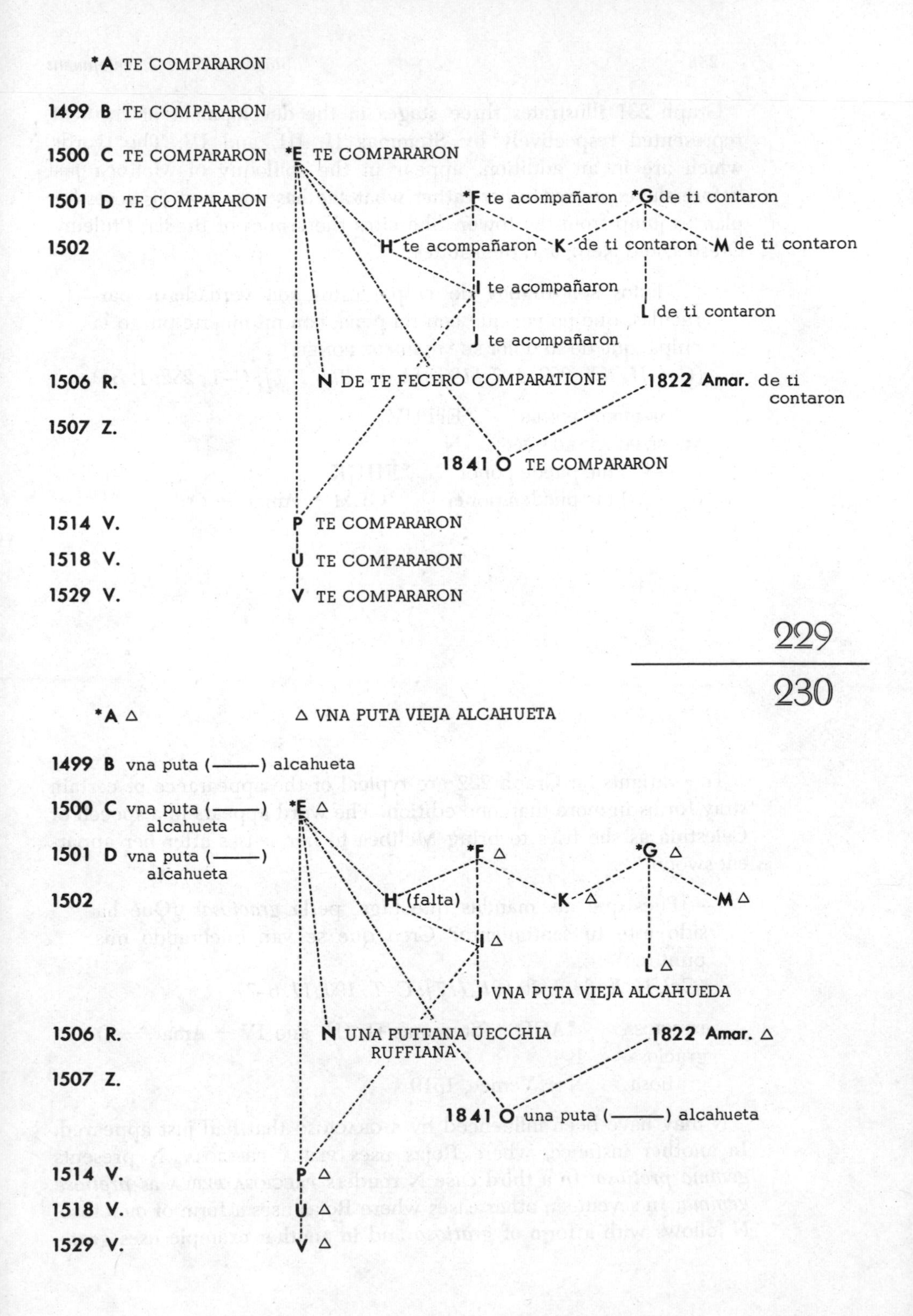

*A TE COMPARARON
1499 B TE COMPARARON
1500 C TE COMPARARON
*E TE COMPARARON
1501 D TE COMPARARON
*F te acompañaron
*G de ti contaron
1502
H te acompañaron
K de ti contaron
M de ti contaron
I te acompañaron
L de ti contaron
J te acompañaron
1506 R.
N DE TE FECERO COMPARATIONE
1822 Amar. de ti contaron
1507 Z.
1841 O TE COMPARARON
1514 V.
P TE COMPARARON
1518 V.
U TE COMPARARON
1529 V.
V TE COMPARARON
229
230
*A △
△ VNA PUTA VIEJA ALCAHUETA
1499 B vna puta (——) alcahueta
1500 C vna puta (——) alcahueta
*E △
1501 D vna puta (——) alcahueta
*F △
*G △
1502
H (falta)
K △
M △
I △
L △
J VNA PUTA VIEJA ALCAHUEDA
1506 R.
N UNA PUTTANA UECCHIA RUFFIANA
1822 Amar. △
1507 Z.
1841 O una puta (——) alcahueta
1514 V.
P △
1518 V.
U △
1529 V.
V △

Graph 231 illustrates three stages in the development of the text, represented respectively by Stemmas II, III, and IV. The words, which are in an addition, appear in the soliloquy of Melibea just before she confesses to her father what she has done and discloses her plan to jump from the tower. She cites the crimes of Bursia, Ptolemy, Orestes, and Nero, and then states:

> . . . Estos son dignos de culpa, estos son verdaderos parracidas, que no yo; que con mi pena, con mi muerte purgo la culpa, que de su dolor SE ME PUEDE PONER.
> *(Cej. II, XX, 209, l. 7 [193, ll. 12–194, l. 1]; C–T, 288, l. 31)*

SE ME PUEDE PONER *E?PUV
ME SE PO ATTRIBUIRE N
(———) me puede poner *FHIJK
(———) me pueden poner *GLM + Amar. + O

The variants on Graph 232 are typical of the appearance of certain stray forms in more than one edition. The word appears in a speech of Celestina as she tries to bring Melibea to her senses after her apparent swoon.

> —¿Pues qué me mandas que faga, perla *graciosa*? ¿Qué ha sido este tu sentimiento? Creo que se van quebrando mis puntos.
> *(Cej. II, X, 64, l. 10 [61, l. 7]; C–T, 190, ll. 6–7)*

PRECIOSA *ACD + Stemmas II, III, and IV + Amar. + O
graciosa B
gratiosa N + Venice, 1519

N may have been influenced by a GRACIOSO that had just appeared. In another instance, where Rojas uses PERLA PRECIOSA, N presents *gemma pretiosa*. In a third case N renders PRECIOSA PERLA as *pretiosa gemma*. In seventeen other cases where Rojas uses a form of GRACIOSO, N follows with a form of *gratioso* and in another example uses *grato*.

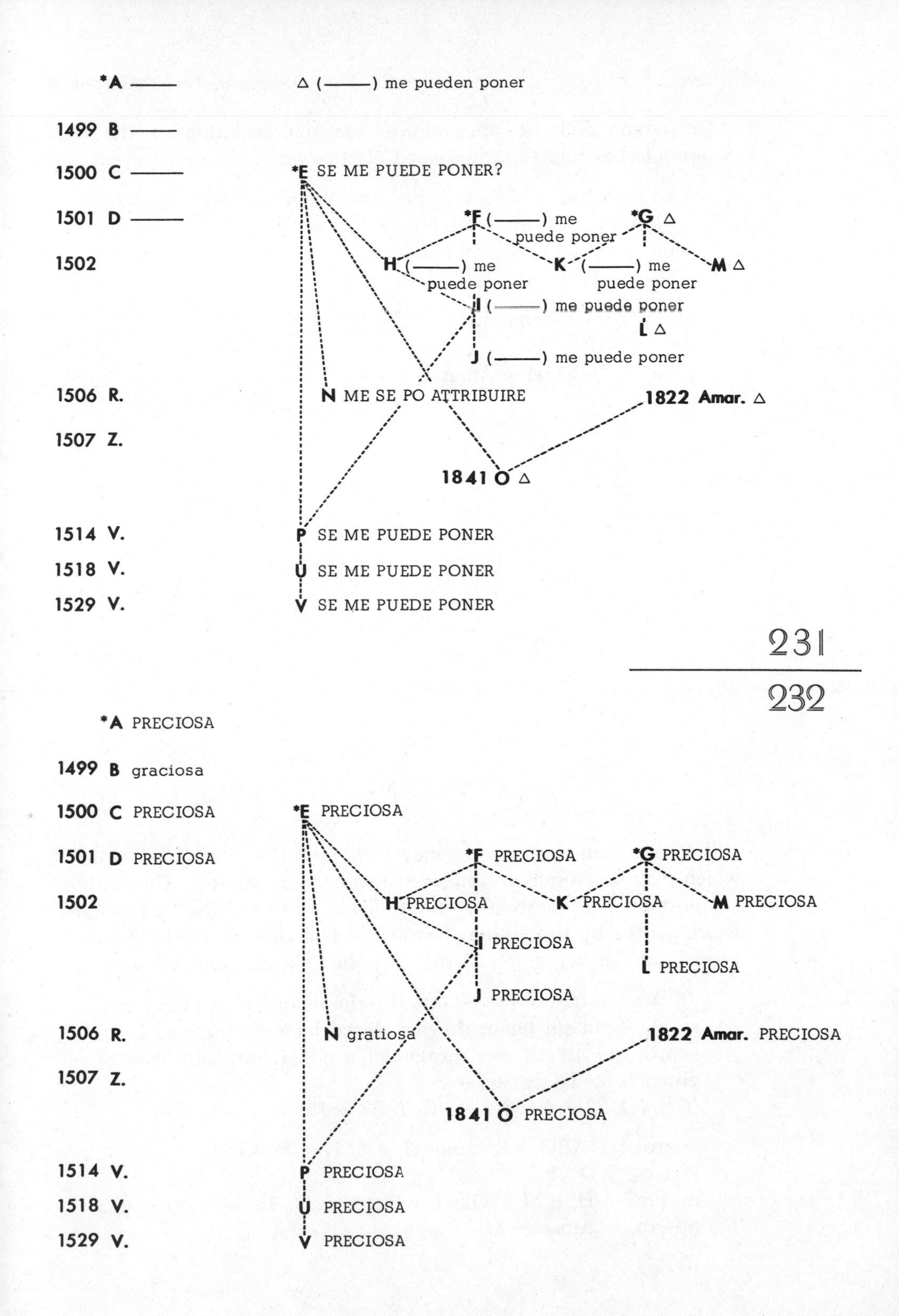

*A —— △ (——) me pueden poner
1499 B ——
1500 C ——
*E SE ME PUEDE PONER?
1501 D ——
*F (——) me puede poner
*G △
1502
H (——) me puede poner
K (——) me puede poner
M △
I (——) me puede poner
L △
J (——) me puede poner
1506 R.
N ME SE PO ATTRIBUIRE
1822 Amar. △
1507 Z.
1841 O △
1514 V.
P SE ME PUEDE PONER
1518 V.
U SE ME PUEDE PONER
1529 V.
V SE ME PUEDE PONER
231
232
*A PRECIOSA
1499 B graciosa
1500 C PRECIOSA
*E PRECIOSA
1501 D PRECIOSA
*F PRECIOSA
*G PRECIOSA
1502
H PRECIOSA
K PRECIOSA
M PRECIOSA
I PRECIOSA
L PRECIOSA
J PRECIOSA
1506 R.
N gratiosa
1822 Amar. PRECIOSA
1507 Z.
1841 O PRECIOSA
1514 V.
P PRECIOSA
1518 V.
U PRECIOSA
1529 V.
V PRECIOSA

On Graph 233 we are able to see the evolution of the text. Sempronio has told Calisto about Celestina and is leaving to visit her.

> —Yo te la traeré hasta acá. Por esso, aparéjate, seyle gracioso, seyle franco. Estudia, mientra vo yo, *de* le dezir tu pena tan bien como ella te dará el remedio.
> *(Cej. I, I, 59, l. 9; C–T, 36, l. 4)*

A *A? + Stemmas II and III + N + O
de BCD
para *GKLM + Amar.

We have seen that a word may have two, three, or more variants, which may be unique or appear in two or more editions. Under these circumstances, it is usually not difficult to reestablish the original word written by the author. Graph 234 is a case in point. The word appears at the beginning of the play, in Calisto's involved speech.

> . . . Mas ¡o triste! que en esto diferimos: que ellos puramente se glorifican sin temor de caer de tal bienauenturança, é yo, MISTO, me alegro con recelo del esquiuo tormento, que tu absencia me ha de causar.
> *(Cej. I, I, 33, l. 6 [33, l. 4]; C–T, 23, l. 15)*

MISTO *ABC + Stemma II + *FIJ + *GKL + N
MIXTO D
mismo H + M + Officina Plantiniana, 1595; Milan, 1622
mísero Amar. + O

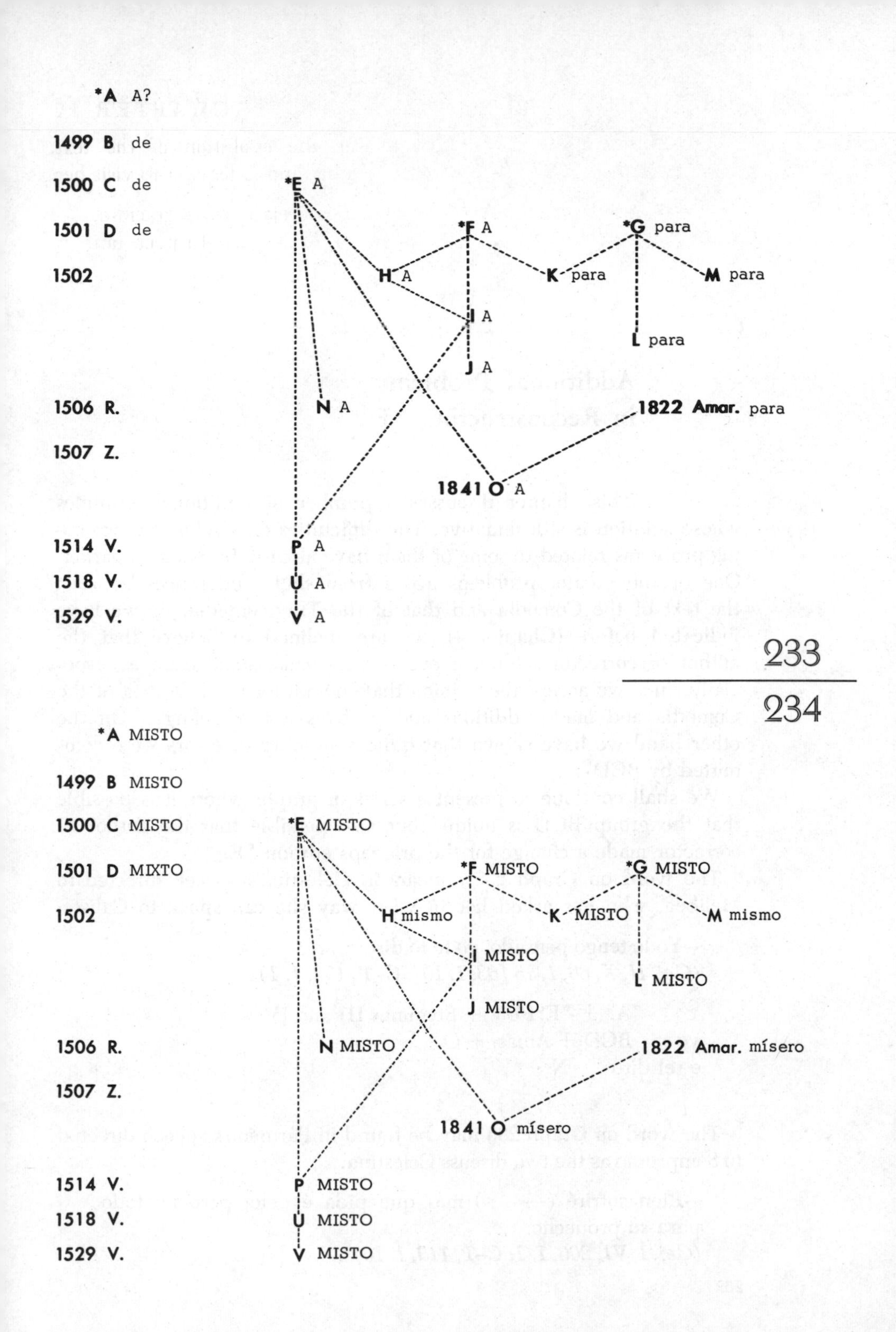
*A A?
1499 B de
1500 C de
1501 D de
1502
1506 R.
1507 Z.
1514 V.
1518 V.
1529 V.
*E A
*F A
*G para
H A
K para
M para
I A
L para
J A
N A
1822 Amar. para
1841 O A
P A
U A
V A
233
234
*A MISTO
1499 B MISTO
1500 C MISTO
1501 D MIXTO
1502
1506 R.
1507 Z.
1514 V.
1518 V.
1529 V.
*E MISTO
*F MISTO
*G MISTO
H mismo
K MISTO
M mismo
I MISTO
L MISTO
J MISTO
N MISTO
1822 Amar. mísero
1841 O mísero
P MISTO
U MISTO
V MISTO

# CHAPTER 12

# Additional Problems in Reconstructing *E

This chapter discusses a number of additional examples whose solution is still tentative. The difficulties encountered in resolving problems related to some of them have already been stated earlier. One of the greater problems arises from slight differences between the text of the Comedia and that of the Tragicomedia. As we have indicated before (Chapter 4), we are inclined to believe that the author or corrector seldom if ever would make small changes, especially since we accept the opinion that the author used the text of the Comedia and made additions and perhaps a few changes. On the other hand we have shown that quite a number of errors were committed by BCD.

We shall continue to present a series of graphs where it is possible that the group BCD is unique but also possible that the author or corrector made a change for the princeps edition *E.

The word on Graph 235 appears in Celestina's speech directed to Melibea, who has asked her in what way she can speak to Calisto.

—Yo lo tengo pensado, *yo* te lo diré: . . .
*(Cej. II, X, 66, l. 15 [63, l. 10]; C–T, 192, l. 1)*

Y *A? + *E?PUV + Stemmas III and IV
yo BCD + Amar. + O
e tel diro N

The word on Graph 236 may be found in Pármeno's speech directed to Sempronio as the two discuss Celestina.

—Bien sofriré (———) más que pida é pele; pero no todo para su prouecho.
*(Cej. I, VI, 206, l. 1; C–T, 113, l. 16)*

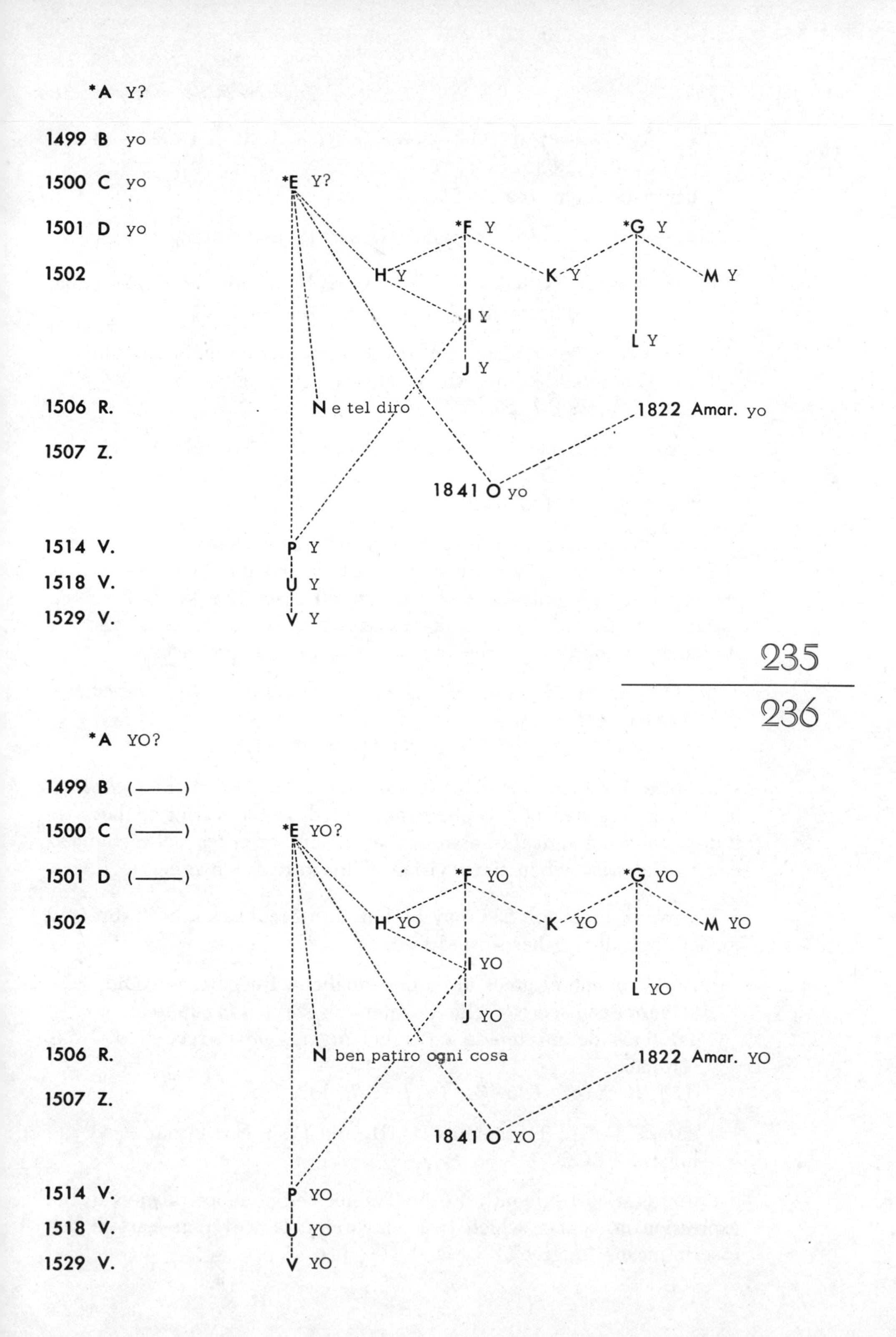
*A Y?
1499 B yo
1500 C yo
*E Y?
1501 D yo
*F Y
*G Y
1502
H Y
K Y
M Y
I Y
L Y
J Y
1506 R.
N e tel diro
1822 Amar. yo
1507 Z.
1841 O yo
1514 V.
P Y
1518 V.
U Y
1529 V.
V Y
235
236
*A YO?
1499 B (——)
1500 C (——)
*E YO?
1501 D (——)
*F YO
*G YO
1502
H YO
K YO
M YO
I YO
L YO
J YO
1506 R.
N ben patiro ogni cosa
1822 Amar. YO
1507 Z.
1841 O YO
1514 V.
P YO
1518 V.
U YO
1529 V.
V YO

YO *A? + *E?PUV + Stemmas III and IV + Amar. + O
(———) BCD
ben patiro ogni cosa N

The *más* is deleted in Stemmas III and IV and Amar.

The words on Graph 237 are in a speech by Sempronio to Celestina, who has returned from her first visit to Melibea.

> —Lo que vengo diziendo, *madre mía,* es que no me marauillo que seas mudable, que sigues el camino de las muchas.
> *(Cej. I, V, 198, 1. 20; C–T, 107, 1. 9)*

MADRE CELESTINA *A? + Stemmas II, III, and IV + N + Amar. + O
madre mía BCD

Aside from this case, our data indicate that Celestina is addressed as MADRE on some fifty occasions, as MADRE MÍA on about ten, and as MADRE CELESTINA only once. In almost all cases the words are nonvariant. The single instance of MADRE CELESTINA appears in another speech by Sempronio at the beginning of the banquet scene.

> —Después reñiremos; comamos agora. Assiéntate, MADRE CELESTINA, tú primero.
> *(Cej. II, IX, 29, 1. 5 [27, 1. 22]; C–T, 166, 1. 14)*

In spite of the frequency of *madre mía* in the text of the *Celestina,* in this case we are not accepting these words as the text of *A because it does not seem logical to assume that the author or corrector changed *mía* to *Celestina* when the revision of the text was made.

The word on Graph 238 may be found in Melibea's speech directed to Celestina during her second visit.

> . . . Catiuóme el amor de aquel cauallero. Ruégote, por Dios, se cubra con secreto sello, porque yo goze de tan suaue amor. Tú serás de mí tenida en aquel *lugar,* que merece tu fiel seruicio.
> *(Cej. II, X, 67, 1. 5 [64, 1. 1]; C–T, 192, 1. 17)*

GRADO *A? + Stemmas II, III, and IV + N + Amar. + O
lugar BCD

GRADO is used frequently in the Tragicomedia, almost always in the expression DE GRADO, which is a nonvariant. However at least in one case it means "degree":

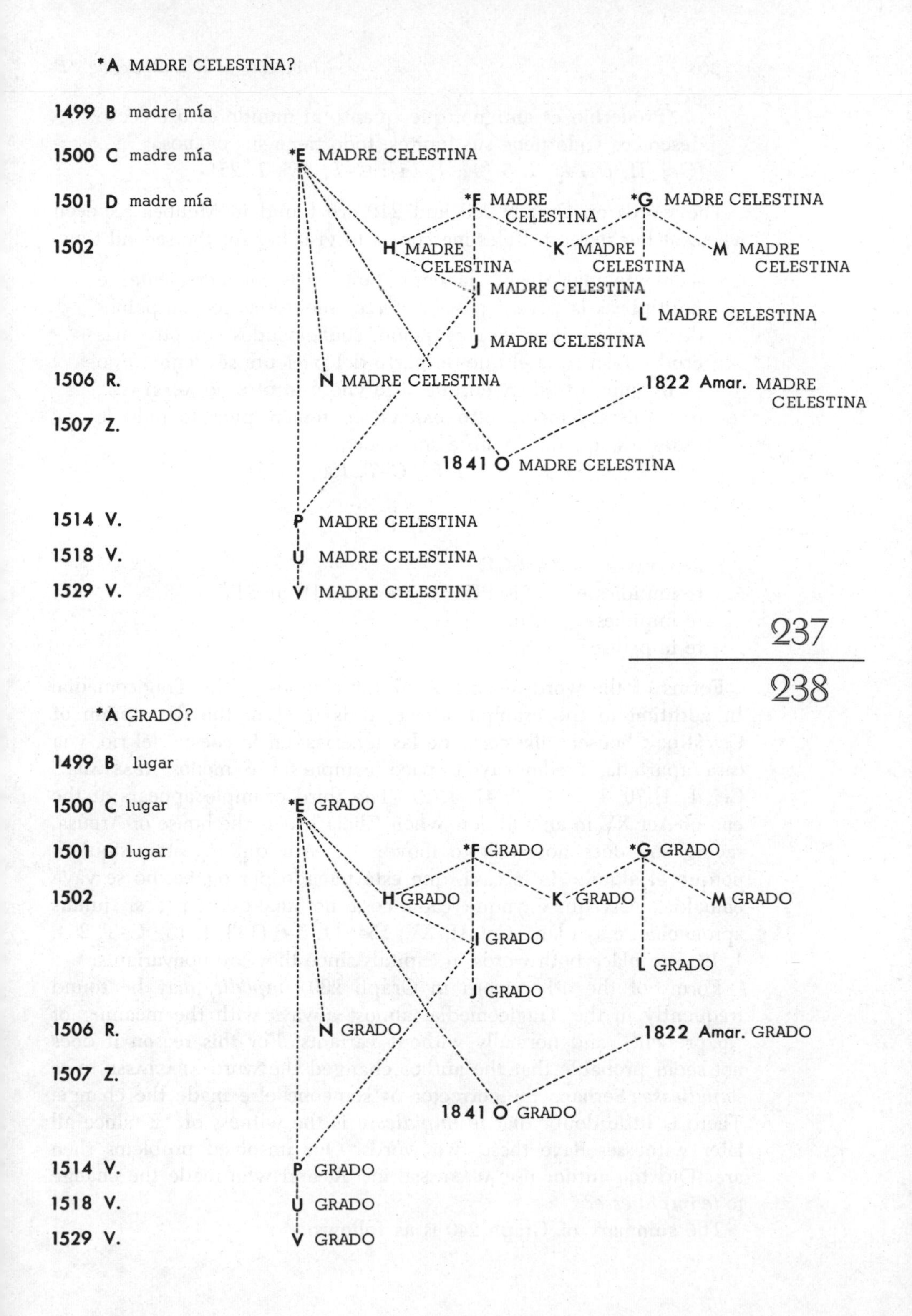
*A MADRE CELESTINA?
1499 B madre mía
1500 C madre mía
*E MADRE CELESTINA
1501 D madre mía
*F MADRE CELESTINA
*G MADRE CELESTINA
1502
H MADRE CELESTINA
K MADRE CELESTINA
M MADRE CELESTINA
I MADRE CELESTINA
L MADRE CELESTINA
J MADRE CELESTINA
1506 R.
N MADRE CELESTINA
1822 Amar. MADRE CELESTINA
1507 Z.
1841 O MADRE CELESTINA
1514 V.
P MADRE CELESTINA
1518 V.
U MADRE CELESTINA
1529 V.
V MADRE CELESTINA
237
238
*A GRADO?
1499 B lugar
1500 C lugar
*E GRADO
1501 D lugar
*F GRADO
*G GRADO
1502
H GRADO
K GRADO
M GRADO
I GRADO
L GRADO
J GRADO
1506 R.
N GRADO
1822 Amar. GRADO
1507 Z.
1841 O GRADO
1514 V.
P GRADO
1518 V.
U GRADO
1529 V.
V GRADO

. . . Prouerbio es antiguo, que quanto al mundo es o crece o descrece. Todo tiene sus límites, todo tiene sus GRADOS.
*(Cej. II, IX, 46, 1. 5 [44, 1. 14]; C–T, 175, 1. 25)*

The words on Graphs 239 and 240 are found in Melibea's speech when, at her request, Celestina comes to visit her for the second time.

—Quanto más dilatas la cura, tanto más me acrecientas é multiplicas la pena é passión. O tus melezinas son de poluos de infamia é licor de corrupción, conficionados con otro más crudo dolor, que el que de parte del paciente se siente, ó no es ninguno tu saber. Porque si lo vno ó lo otro no ABASTASSE, qualquiera remedio otro DARÍAS sin temor, pues te pido le muestres, quedando libre mi honrra.
*(Cej. II, X, 59, 1. 7 [56, 1. 6]; C–T, 186, 1. 15)*

Graph 239

| | |
|---|---|
| ABASTASSE | *A?BCD |
| te impidiesse | *E?PUV + Stemmas III and IV |
| te impidiese | Amar. + O |
| te impedisce | N |

Forms of the word ABASTA occur three times in the Tragicomedia. In addition to the example above, it is used in the description of Celestina's house: "allá cerca de las tenerías, en la cuesta del río, vna casa apartada, medio cayda, poco compuesta é menos ABASTADA." Cej. I, I, 70, 1. 6; C–T, 41, 1. 21. The third example appears at the end of Act XV in an addition, when Elicia leaves the house of Areúsa, saying she does not wish to move: ". . . Allí quiero estar, siquiera porque el alquile de la casa, que está pagado por ogaño, no se vaya embalde. Assí que, avnque cada cosa no ABASTASSE por sí, juntas aprouechan é ayudan." Cej. II, XV, 154, 11. 5–6 (143, 1. 13); C–T, 254, 1. 12. We place both words in capitals since they are nonvariants.

Forms of the other word in Graph 239, *impedir,* may be found frequently in the Tragicomedia, almost always with the meaning of "to prevent," and normally without variants. For this reason it does not seem probable that the author changed the word ABASTASSE to *te impidiesse.* Perhaps the corrector or someone else made the change. There is little doubt that *te impidiesse* is the witness of *E, since all later witnesses have these two words. Our unsolved problems then are: Did the author use ABASTASSE in *A, and who made the change to *te impidiesse?*

The summary of Graph 240 is as follows:

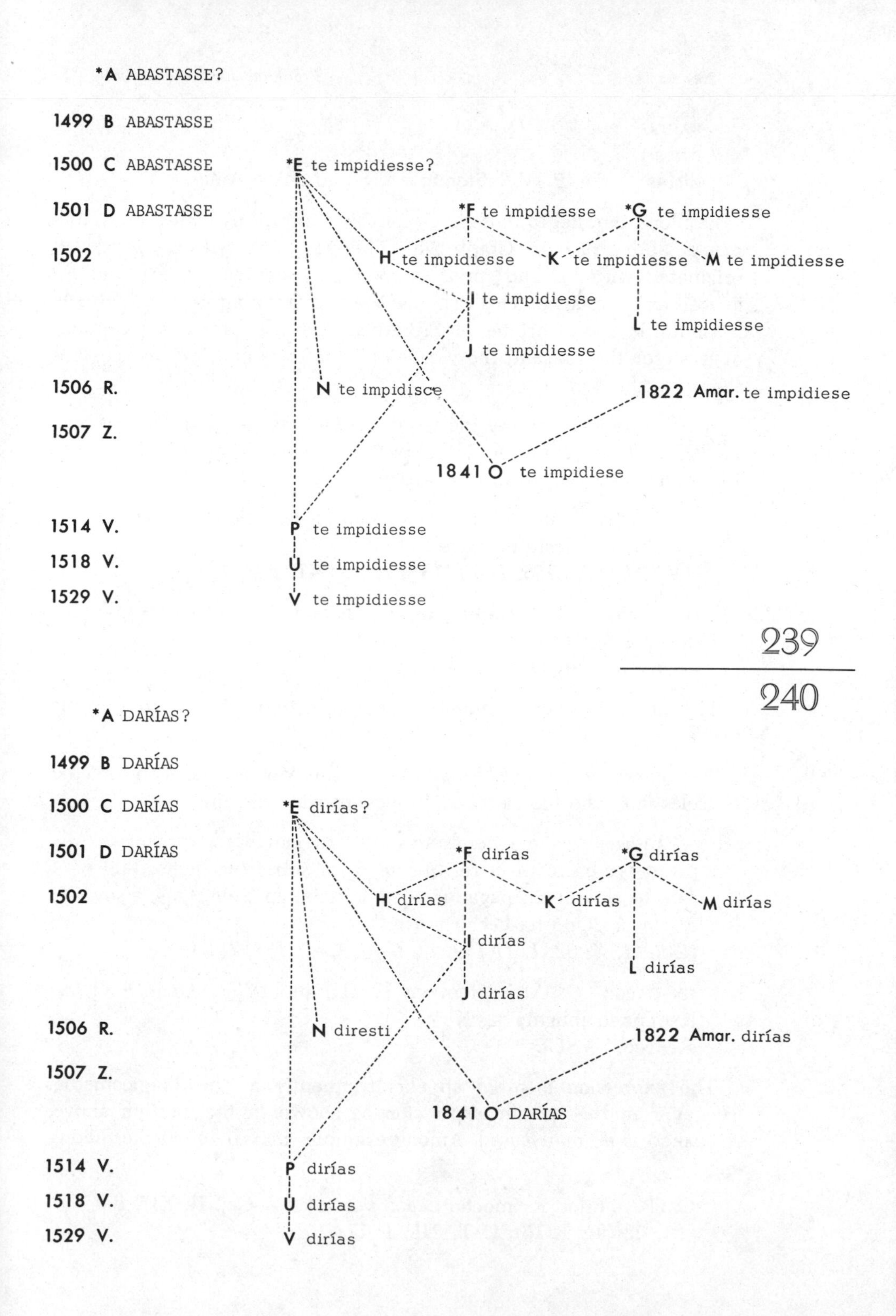
*A ABASTASSE?
1499 B ABASTASSE
1500 C ABASTASSE
*E te impidiesse?
1501 D ABASTASSE
*F te impidiesse
*G te impidiesse
1502
H te impidiesse
K te impidiesse
M te impidiesse
I te impidiesse
L te impidiesse
J te impidiesse
1506 R.
N te impidisce
1822 Amar. te impidiese
1507 Z.
1841 O te impidiese
1514 V.
P te impidiesse
1518 V.
U te impidiesse
1529 V.
V te impidiesse
239
240
*A DARÍAS?
1499 B DARÍAS
1500 C DARÍAS
*E dirías?
1501 D DARÍAS
*F dirías
*G dirías
1502
H dirías
K dirías
M dirías
I dirías
L dirías
J dirías
1506 R.
N diresti
1822 Amar. dirías
1507 Z.
1841 O DARÍAS
1514 V.
P dirías
1518 V.
U dirías
1529 V.
V dirías

DARÍAS *A?BCD + O
diresti N
dirías *E?PUV + Stemmas III and IV + Amar.

Problems parallel to those in Graph 239 confront us with the variants DARÍAS and *dirías* on Graph 240. The new form *dirías* apparently originated with *E and spread throughout Stemmas II, III, and IV as well as to Amarita. This case may be one of a simple error, perhaps attributable to the printer of *E. At any rate we are not accepting, at least for the present, the words *te impidiesse* or *dirías* as those of the author himself.

We at present attribute the words on Graphs 241 and 242 to errors of BCD. Those on Graph 241 appear in Melibea's speech as she and Lucrecia await Calisto in the garden.

> . . . Mas *escucha,* que passos suenan en la calle é avn parece que hablan destotra parte del huerto.
> *(Cej. II, XIV, 125, 1. 3 [115, 1. 22]; C–T, 236, 1. 21)*

OYE, OYE *A? + Stemmas II, III, and IV + Amar. + O
ODI, ODI N
escucha BCD

The author rather frequently uses repetitions similar to the one above.

The words on Graph 242 may be found in Melibea's speech directed to Celestina, who has been analyzing her state of mind.

> –Tantas vezes me nombrarás esse tu cauallero, que ni mi promessa baste ni la fe, que te dí, á sofrir tus dichos. ¿De qué ha de quedar pagado? ¿Qué le deuo yo á él? ¿Qué le soy *a cargo*? ¿Qué ha hecho por mí?
> *(Cej. II, X, 62, 1. 11 [59, 11. 6–7]; C–T, 188, 1. 24)*

EN CARGO *A? + Stemmas II, III, and IV + Amar. + O
li sonno io obligata N
a cargo BCD

The expression *a cargo* appears frequently in the Tragicomedia. However in the specific expression as shown in the citation above, EN CARGO is normally used. Among examples may be cited the following:

CAL. . . . Fijos, EN mucho CARGO vos soy.——Cej. II, XII, 100, 1. 22 (94, 1. 16); C–T, 218, 1. 17

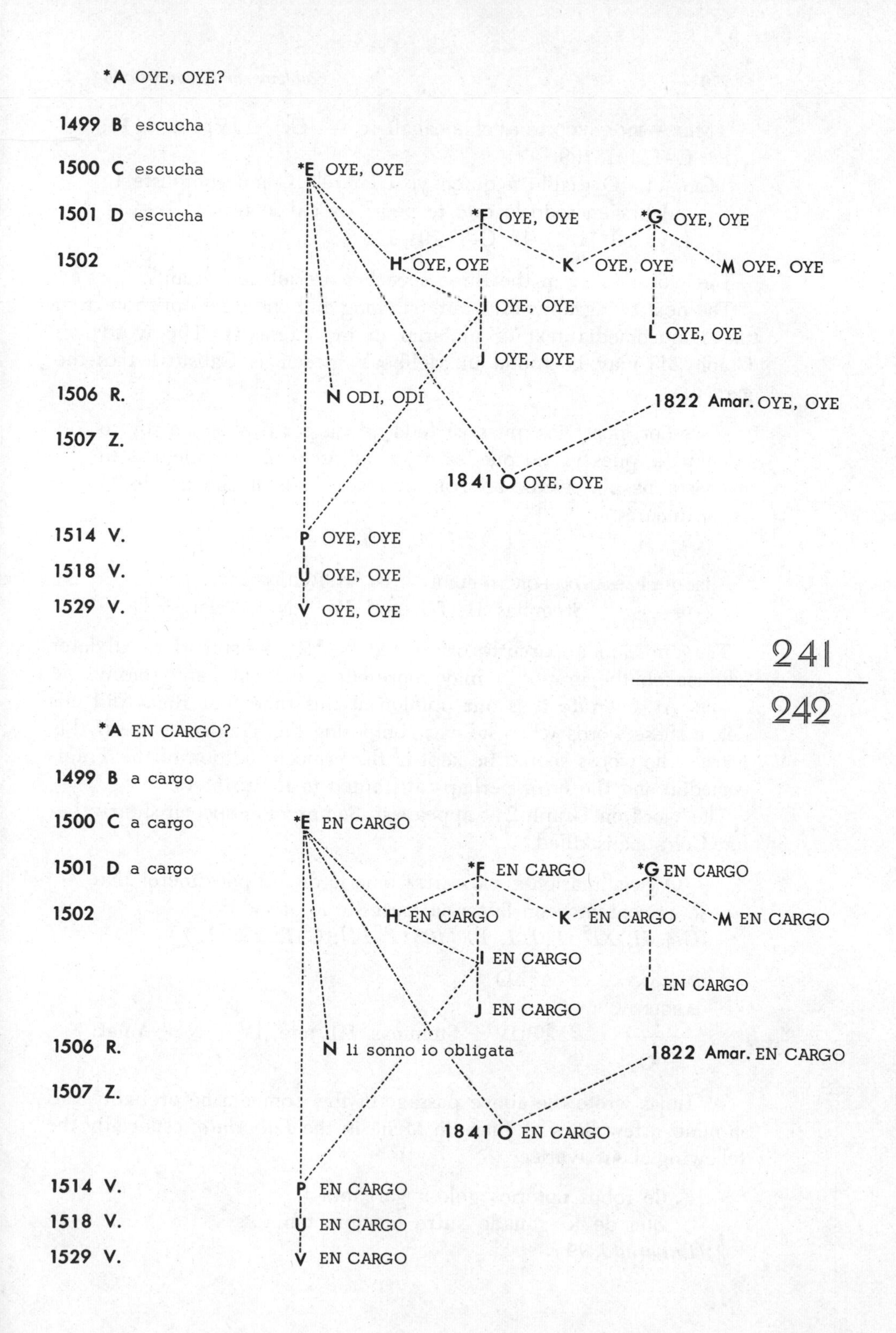
*A OYE, OYE?
1499 B escucha
1500 C escucha
1501 D escucha
1502
1506 R.
1507 Z.
1514 V.
1518 V.
1529 V.
*E OYE, OYE
*F OYE, OYE
*G OYE, OYE
H OYE, OYE
K OYE, OYE
M OYE, OYE
I OYE, OYE
L OYE, OYE
J OYE, OYE
N ODI, ODI
1822 Amar. OYE, OYE
1841 O OYE, OYE
P OYE, OYE
U OYE, OYE
V OYE, OYE
241
242
*A EN CARGO?
1499 B a cargo
1500 C a cargo
1501 D a cargo
1502
1506 R.
1507 Z.
1514 V.
1518 V.
1529 V.
*E EN CARGO
*F EN CARGO
*G EN CARGO
H EN CARGO
K EN CARGO
M EN CARGO
I EN CARGO
L EN CARGO
J EN CARGO
N li sonno io obligata
1822 Amar. EN CARGO
1841 O EN CARGO
P EN CARGO
U EN CARGO
V EN CARGO

MEL.—EN CARGO te es esse cauallero.——Cej. I, IV, 192, 1. 14; C–T, 101, 1. 9

CEL. . . . ¡O diablo á quien yo conjuré! ¿Cómo compliste tu palabra en todo lo que te pedí? EN CARGO te soy.——Cej. I, V, 193, 11. 17–18; C–T, 104, 1. 6

The words cited in the three speeches are all nonvariants.

The next two graphs illustrate one long and one brief omission from the Tragicomedia text of material in the Comedia. The words on Graph 243 may be found in Melibea's speech as Calisto leaves the garden.

–Señor, por Dios, pues ya todo queda por tí, pues ya soy tu dueña, pues ya no puedes negar mi amor, no me niegues tu vista DE DÍA, PASSANDO POR MI PUERTA; de noche donde tú ordenares.
*(Cej. II, XIV, 129, 1. 13 [120, 1. 4]; C–T, 239, 1. 22)*

DE DÍA PASSANDO POR MI PUERTA *A?BCD
(———) Stemmas II, III, and IV + N + Amar. + O

The omission apparently originated in *E and spread to all later editions on the graph. It may represent a case of haplography: DE . . . DE. At any rate it is our opinion at this time that Rojas did not delete these words when he was composing the Tragicomedia. If this is true, the words should be kept in the princeps edition of the Tragicomedia, and the error perhaps attributed to the printer.

The word on Graph 244 appears in Sempronio's speech shortly before Celestina is killed.

–¡O vieja auarienta, GARGANTA muerta de sed por dinero! ¿No serás contenta con la tercia parte de lo ganado?
*(Cej. II, XII, 110, 1. 10 [103, 1. 14]; C–T, 225, 1. 7)*

GARGANTA *A?BD
GARGENTA C
(———) *E?PUV + Stemmas III and IV + N + Amar. + O

As Rojas wrote the above passage of the Comedia he probably had in mind a few lines of Juan de Mena in the *Laberinto*, especially the following about avarice:

. . . de robos notorios golosa garganta
que de lo ganado sufre mengua tanta . . . .
*(Laberinto, 99 f.)*

*A DE DÍA, PASSANDO POR MI PUERTA?

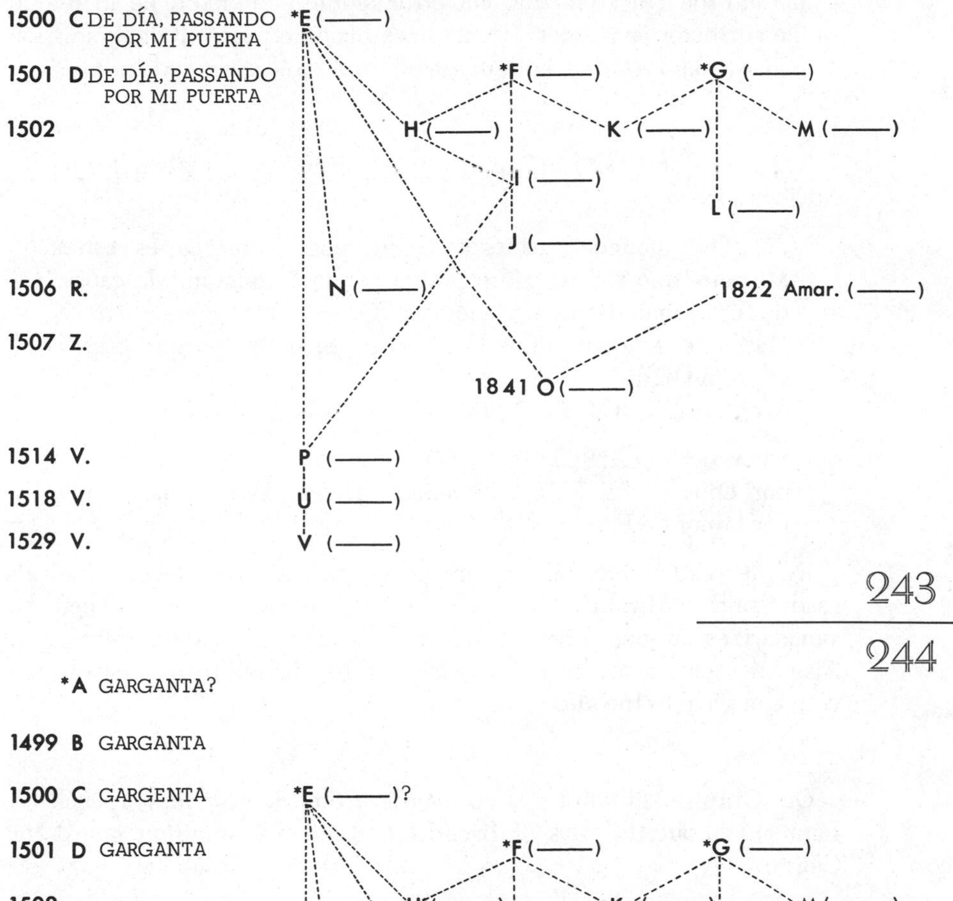


243
———
244

*A GARGANTA?

1499 B GARGANTA

1500 C GARGENTA

1501 D GARGANTA

1502

1506 R.

1507 Z.

1514 V.

1518 V.

1529 V.

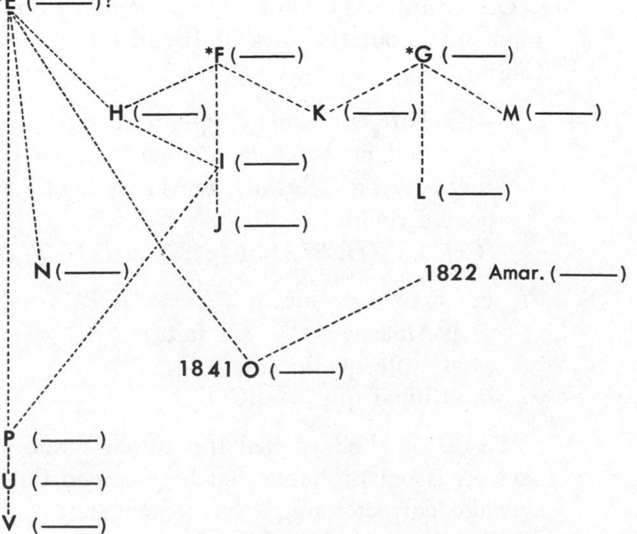

It does not seem probable that he deleted GARGANTA when he composed the Tragicomedia. The error should more likely be attributed to the corrector or printer. It may have been an unintentional omission caused by the fact that both *avarienta* and GARGANTA end in -nta.

The words on Graph 245 appear in Pleberio's speech when he reaches Melibea's room.

> . . . ¿Qué nouedad es ésta? ¿Qué poco esfuerço es este? Mírame, que soy tu padre. Fabla comigo, cuéntame la causa de tu arrebatada pena. ¿Qué has? ¿Qué sientes? ¿Qué quieres? Háblame, MÍRAME, dime la razón de tu dolor, porque presto sea remediado.
> *(Cej. II, XX, 204, 1. 11 [189, 1. 11]; C–T, 286, 1. 14)*

MÍRAME *A?BCD
por Dios *E?PUV + Stemmas III and IV + Amar. + O
per lamor de Dio N

As the reader may observe in the citation above, Pleberio had already said: "Mírame, . . . Fabla comigo, cuéntame . . . ." Then he summarizes in one brief sentence: "Hablame, MÍRAME, dime . . . ." Again it seems more logical to attribute the change to *por Dios* to the corrector than to the author.

On Graph 246 appear two words from Sempronio's speech to Pármeno about the joys of friendship. Both are standing guard for Calisto.

> —¡O Pármeno amigo! ¡Quán alegre é prouechosa es la conformidad en los compañeros! Avnque por otra cosa no nos fuera buena Celestina, era harta *la vtilidad que* por su causa nos ha venido.
> *(Cej. II, XII, 87, 1. 4 [81, 1. 10]; C–T, 208, 11. 8–9)*

VTILIDAD LA QUE *A? + *E?PUV + *FIJ + Stemma IV + Amar. + O (H falta)
assai utile quello che N
la vtilidad que BCD

We do not believe that the author wrote *la vtilidad que* in *A because it is not probable that he changed the word order in *E. However the corrector might have done so.

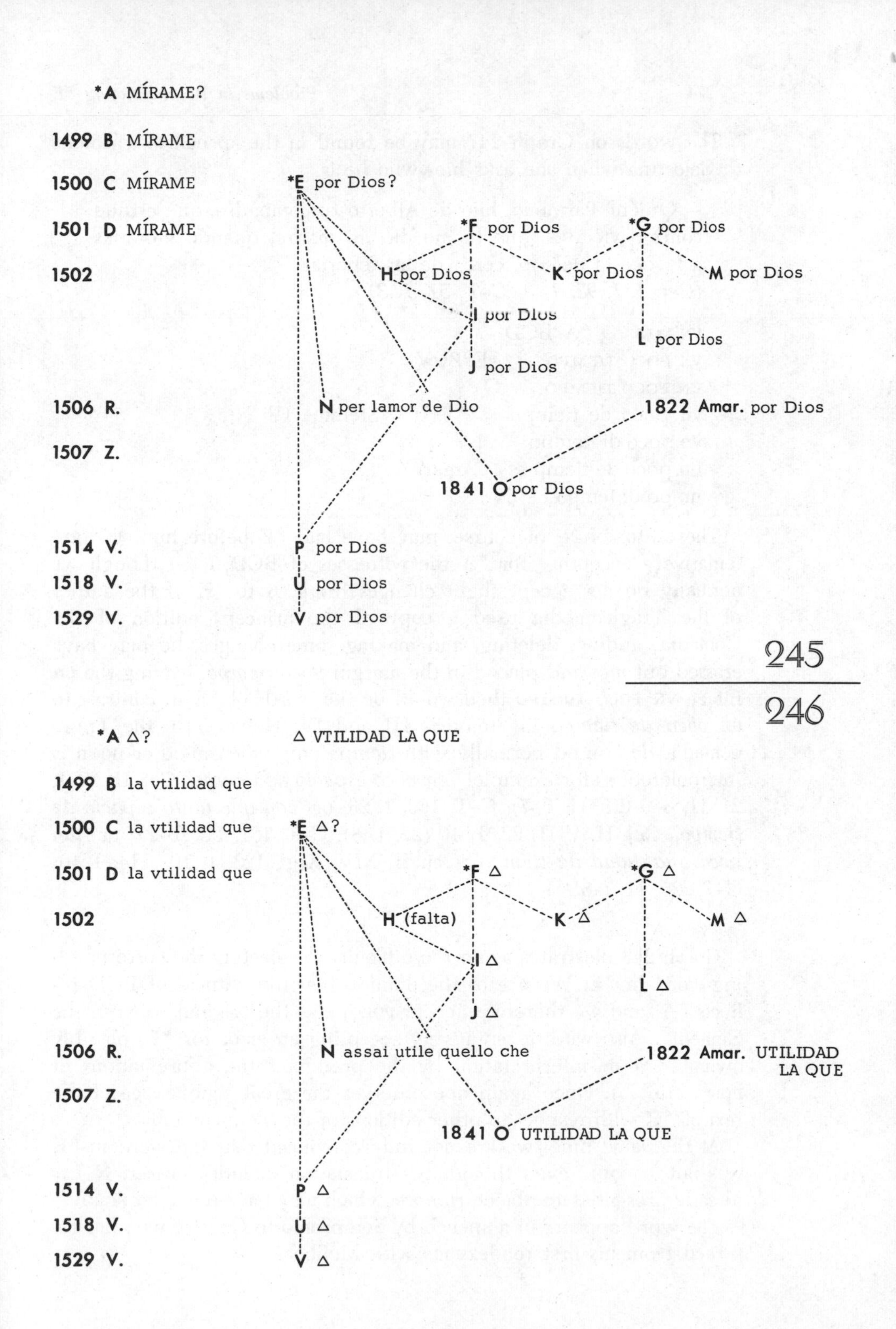
*A MÍRAME?
1499 B MÍRAME
1500 C MÍRAME
*E por Dios?
1501 D MÍRAME
*F por Dios
*G por Dios
1502
H por Dios
K por Dios
M por Dios
I por Dios
L por Dios
J por Dios
1506 R.
N per lamor de Dio
1822 Amar. por Dios
1507 Z.
1841 O por Dios
1514 V.
P por Dios
1518 V.
U por Dios
1529 V.
V por Dios
245
246
*A △?
△ VTILIDAD LA QUE
1499 B la vtilidad que
1500 C la vtilidad que
*E △?
1501 D la vtilidad que
*F △
*G △
1502
H (falta)
K △
M △
I △
L △
J △
1506 R.
N assai utile quello che
1822 Amar. UTILIDAD LA QUE
1507 Z.
1841 O UTILIDAD LA QUE
1514 V.
P △
1518 V.
U △
1529 V.
V △

The words on Graph 247 may be found in the speech of Pármeno to Celestina when she asks him who he is.

> —¿Quién? Pármeno, hijo de Alberto tu compadre, que estuue contigo VN MES, que te me dió mi madre, quando morauas á la cuesta del río, cerca de las tenerías.
> *(Cej. I, I, 98, l. 9; C–T, 51, l. 3)*

VN MES *A?BCD
VN POCO TIEMPO *E?PUV
UN POCO TIEMPO O
vn poco de tiempo *FHI + Stemma IV
vn poco di tiempo J
un poco de tiempo Amar.
un po di tempo N

The editor of N, of course, may have had *E before him. We are tentatively accepting for *A the witnesses of BCD, even though we normally do not accept slight changes from *A to *E. If the author of the Tragicomedia used a copy of the princeps edition of the Comedia, adding, deleting, and making some changes, he may have crossed out *mes* and placed in the margin *poco tiempo,* leaving the *vn* intact. VN POCO TIEMPO then would be the words of *E in contrast to *vn poco de tiempo* in Stemmas III and IV. However in the Tragicomedia *de* is used normally with *tiempo* only when another noun is interpolated, as for example: "*en poco espacio de tiempo*" Cej. II, VIII, 21, ll. 8–9 (21, ll. 6–7); C–T, 160, l. 26; or "*con que tanto espacio de tiempo*" Cej. II, VIII, 22, l. 10 (22, l. 8); C–T, 161, ll. 20–21; or "*tan poca quantidad de tiempo*" Cej. II, XIV, Arg., 123, l. 10 (114, l. 9); C–T, 235, ll. 7–8.

Graph 248 illustrates again the difficulty in selecting the corresponding word in *E. We are of the opinion that the witness of BCD reflects *A, and we therefore accept PORQUÉ as the original word in the Comedia. Also we are tentatively accepting an error for *E, possibly owing to a misinterpretation by the printer of the abbreviations of PORQUÉ in *A. Once again one observes the great significance of the text of *E with respect to other editions of the Tragicomedia.

At the same time, we are not fully convinced that the word in *E was not PORQUÉ; even though N's translation includes posser. N has already presented an object, *rumore,* which may have reflected PORQUÉ.

The word appears in a speech by Sempronio to Calisto, who has returned from his first rendezvous with Melibea.

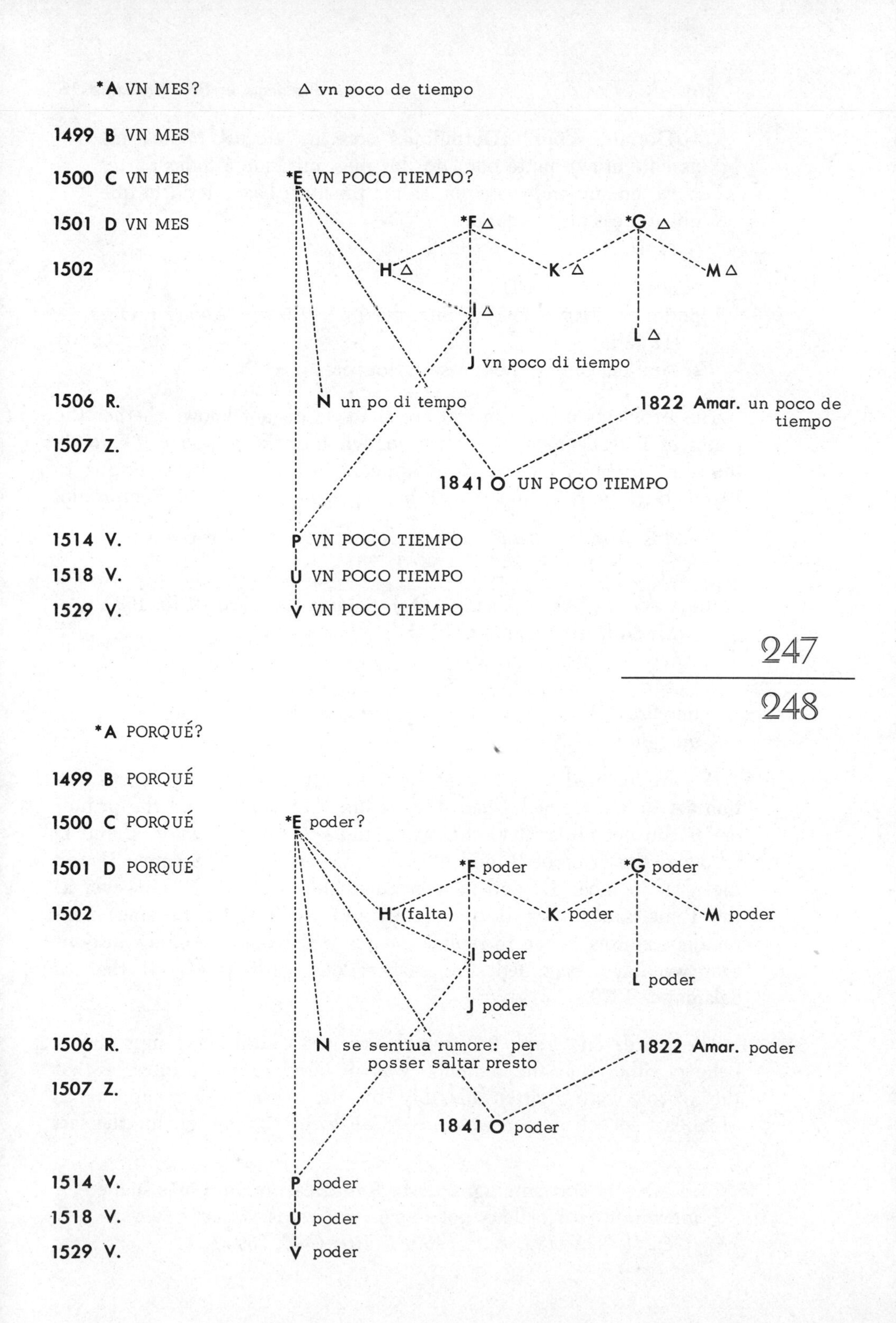
*A VN MES?
△ vn poco de tiempo
1499 B VN MES
1500 C VN MES
*E VN POCO TIEMPO?
1501 D VN MES
*F △
*G △
1502
H △
K △
M △
I △
L △
J vn poco di tiempo
1506 R.
N un po di tempo
1822 Amar. un poco de tiempo
1507 Z.
1841 O UN POCO TIEMPO
1514 V.
P VN POCO TIEMPO
1518 V.
U VN POCO TIEMPO
1529 V.
V VN POCO TIEMPO
247
248
*A PORQUÉ?
1499 B PORQUÉ
1500 C PORQUÉ
*E poder?
1501 D PORQUÉ
*F poder
*G poder
1502
H (falta)
K poder
M poder
I poder
L poder
J poder
1506 R.
N se sentiua rumore: per posser saltar presto
1822 Amar. poder
1507 Z.
1841 O poder
1514 V.
P poder
1518 V.
U poder
1529 V.
V poder

—¿Dormir, señor? ¡Dormilones son los moços! Nunca me assenté ni avn junté por Dios los piés, mirando á todas partes para, en sintiendo PORQUÉ, saltar presto é hazer todo lo que mis fuerças me ayudaran.
*(Cej. II, XII, 100, 1. 8 [94, 1. 2]; C–T, 218, 1. 4)*

PORQUÉ *A?BCD
poder *E? + *FIJ + Stemma IV + PUV + Amar. + O (H falta)
se sentiua rumore: per posser saltar presto N

The problems on Graph 249 are that we do not know whether the editor of B read *mayor* for MARÓN or whether the printer of *E made the same error as B. The word appears in a speech by Celestina to Pármeno as she tries to persuade him to make friends with Sempronio.

—Mas dí, como *mayor,* que la fortuna ayuda á los osados.
*(Cej. I, I, 104, 1. 8; C–T, 54, 1. 25)*

MARÓN *A? + Amar. + O + Salamanca, 1570, 1575, 1590; Madrid, 1619; Osmont, 1633
MARÓ Tarragona, 1595
Varón Sevilla, 1596
mayor BCD + *E?PUV + Stemmas III and IV
maggiore N

We are inclined to believe at the present time that the princeps edition *A of the Comedia had MARÓN but that both B and the printer of *E did not understand this word and substituted *mayor.* C and D followed the error of B, and all the other editions of Stemma II and those of Stemmas III and IV continued the error of *E. However as the Renaissance took deeper roots and the classics became more familiar, editors began to replace *mayor* with MARÓN. Among editions that we have examined, the earliest one with MARÓN is that of Salamanca 1570.

The words on Graph 250, which are in an addition, tempt one to believe either that the sentence was dictated to the printer or that the words were written illegibly by the author. They appear in Melibea's speech as she welcomes Calisto to the garden for the last time.

. . . Oye la corriente agua desta fontezica, ¡quánto más suaue murmurio *su río* lleua por entre las frescas yeruas!
*(Cej. II, XIX, 194, 1. 16 [180, 1. 10]; C–T, 280, 1. 1)*

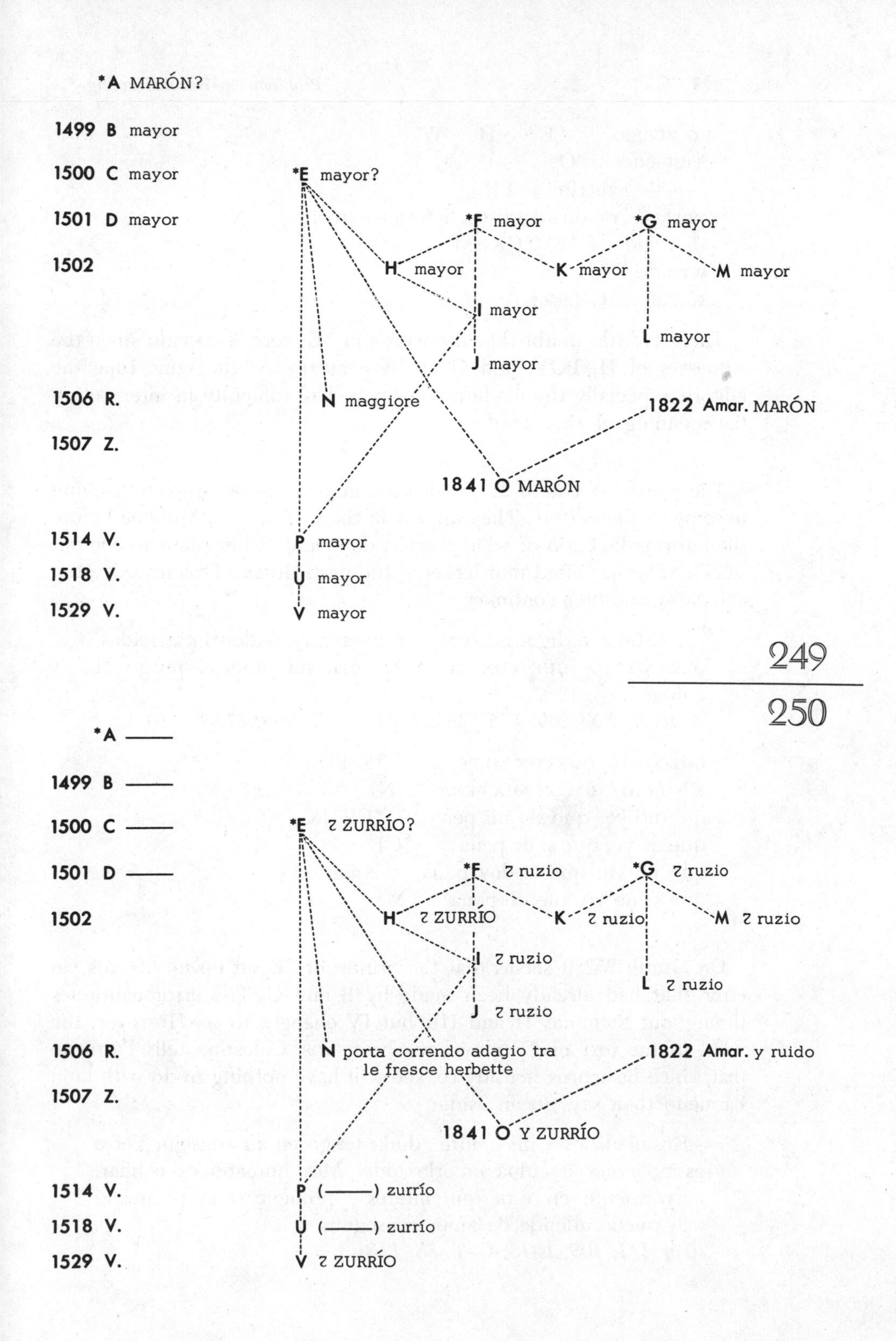

*A MARÓN?
1499 B mayor
1500 C mayor
*E mayor?
1501 D mayor
*F mayor
*G mayor
1502
H mayor
K mayor
M mayor
I mayor
L mayor
J mayor
1506 R.
N maggiore
1822 Amar. MARÓN
1507 Z.
1841 O MARÓN
1514 V.
P mayor
1518 V.
U mayor
1529 V.
V mayor
249
250
*A ——
1499 B ——
1500 C ——
*E ⁊ ZURRÍO?
1501 D ——
*F ⁊ ruzio
*G ⁊ ruzio
1502
H ⁊ ZURRÍO
K ⁊ ruzio
M ⁊ ruzio
I ⁊ ruzio
L ⁊ ruzio
J ⁊ ruzio
1506 R.
N porta correndo adagio tra le fresce herbette
1822 Amar. y ruido
1507 Z.
1841 O Y ZURRÍO
1514 V.
P (——) zurrío
1518 V.
U (——) zurrío
1529 V.
V ⁊ ZURRÍO

Ƨ ZURRÍO *E? + H + V
Y ZURRÍO O
(———) zurrío PU
porta correndo adagio tra le fresce herbette N
Ƨ ruzio *FIJ*GKLM
y ruido Amar.
su río Cejador

There is little doubt that the words in *E were Ƨ ZURRÍO since the witnesses of H, PUV, and O all have *zurrío*. At the same time the editors, especially the modern ones, have had difficulty in interpreting the meaning of this word.

The words on Graph 251, which are in an addition, were perplexing to some of the editors. They appear in the soliloquy of Melibea before she informs Pleberio of what she has done and of her plans to commit suicide. She has cited murderers of the past, Bursia, Ptolemy, Orestes, and Nero, and then continues:

> . . . Estos son dignos de culpa, estos son verdaderos parricidas, QUE NO YO; QUE CON MI PENA, con mi muerte, purgo la culpa, . . .
> *(Cej. II, XX, 209, 1. 5 [193, 1. 11]; C–T, 288, 11. 29–30)*

QUE NO YO; QUE CON MI PENA *E?PUV
& NON IO CHE CON MIA PENA N
que no yo; que do mi pena *FHIJK
que no yo; que si do pena *GL
que no yo; que si doy pena Amar. + O
que si no yo que do pena M

On Graph 252 it seems that the printer of *E set up *no* for NOS, an error that had already been made by B and C. The error continues throughout Stemmas II and III; but IV changes to *se*. However, the word in the text of *E may have been NOS. Celestina tells Pármeno that, since he scorns her advice, she will have nothing to do with him. Pármeno then says in an aside:

> –Ensañada está mi madre: duda tengo en su consejo. Yerro es no creer é culpa creerlo todo. Más humano es confiar, mayormente en ésta que interesse promete, ado prouecho NOS puede allende de amor conseguir.
> *(Cej. I, I, 109, 1. 15; C–T, 58, 1. 3)*

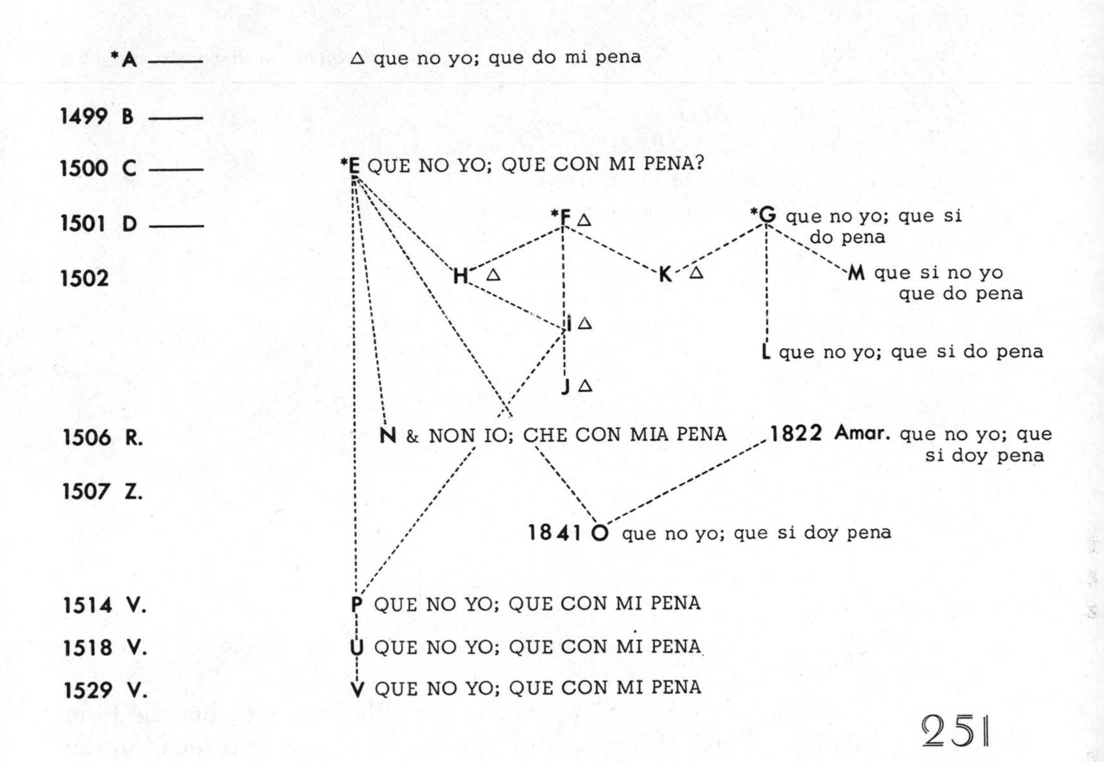

*A —— △ que no yo; que do mi pena
1499 B ——
1500 C —— *E QUE NO YO; QUE CON MI PENA?
1501 D —— *F △ *G que no yo; que si do pena
1502 H △ K △ M que si no yo que do pena
I △
L que no yo; que si do pena
J △
1506 R. N & NON IO; CHE CON MIA PENA
1822 Amar. que no yo; que si doy pena
1507 Z.
1841 O que no yo; que si doy pena
1514 V. P QUE NO YO; QUE CON MI PENA
1518 V. U QUE NO YO; QUE CON MI PENA
1529 V. V QUE NO YO; QUE CON MI PENA


251
252

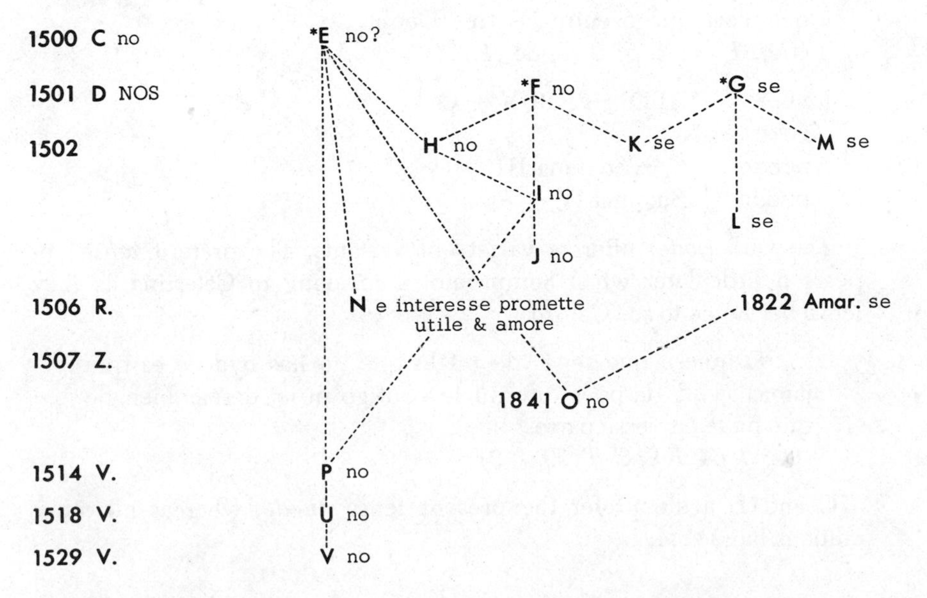

*A NOS?
1499 B no
1500 C no *E no?
1501 D NOS *F no *G se
1502 H no K se M se
I no
L se
J no
1506 R. N e interesse promette utile & amore
1822 Amar. se
1507 Z.
1841 O no
1514 V. P no
1518 V. U no
1529 V. V no

NOS *A?D
no BC + *E?PUV + Stemma III + O
se Stemma IV + Amar.
i interesse promette utile & amore N

The word on Graph 253 presents two other variants, but the form given for *A and *E appears to be the correct one. It is found in the passage where Calisto is describing the perfection of Melibea to Sempronio.

> . . . Aquella proporción, que veer yo no PUDE, no sin duda por el bulto de fuera juzgo incomparablemente ser mejor, que la que Paris juzgó entre las tres Deesas.
> *(Cej. I, 56, l. 5; C–T, 34, l. 15)*

PUDE *ABD + *EPUV + O
POTE N
puede C + Stemma III
puedo Stemma IV + Amar.

The verb *poder* offers a variety of variants. The preterit tense appears a little later when Sempronio is speaking to Celestina as they leave her home to see Calisto.

> . . . E quiero que sepas de mí lo que no has oydo é es que jamás PUDE, después que mi fe contigo puse, desear bien de que no te cupiesse parte.
> *(Cej. I, 64, l. 9; C–T, 39, l. 2)*

C and L again prefer the present tense *puede,* whereas all other editions have PUDE.

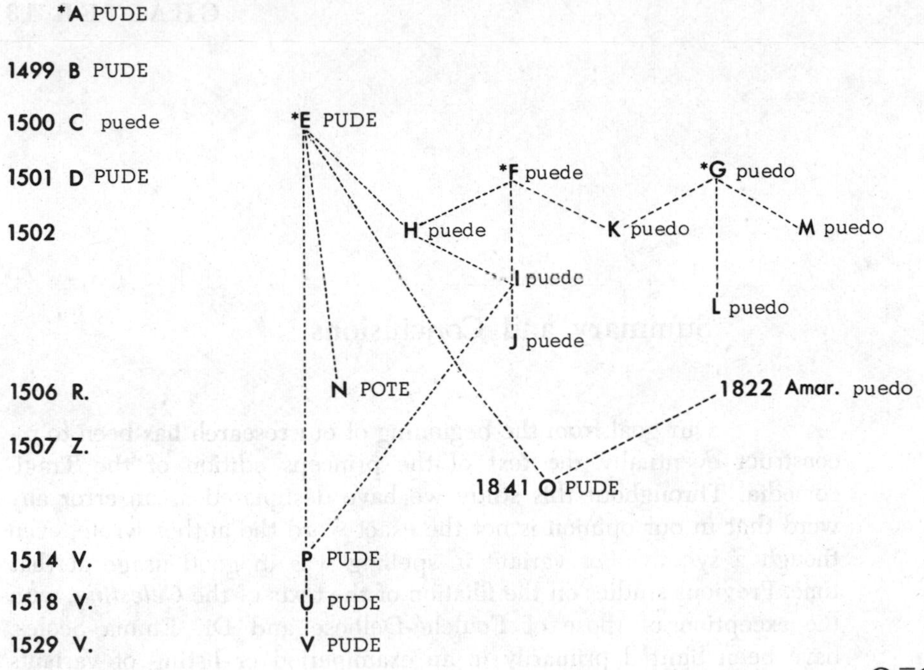
*A PUDE
1499 B PUDE
1500 C puede
1501 D PUDE
1502
1506 R.
1507 Z.
1514 V.
1518 V.
1529 V.
*E PUDE
*F puede
*G puedo
H puede
K puedo
M puedo
I pucdc
L puedo
J puede
N POTE
1822 Amar. puedo
1841 O PUDE
P PUDE
U PUDE
V PUDE

# CHAPTER 13

# Summary and Conclusions

Our goal from the beginning of our research has been to reconstruct eventually the text of the princeps edition of the Tragicomedia. Throughout this study we have designated as an error any word that in our opinion is not the exact word the author wrote, even though a synonym or variant in spelling was in good usage at that time. Previous studies on the filiation of the texts of the *Celestina,* with the exception of those of Foulché-Delbosc and Dr. Emma Scoles, have been limited primarily to an examination or listing of variants of very few editions, usually two or three. Foulché-Delbosc believed that I (E in his classification) was the princeps edition. The data presented in this study demonstrate that this premise is not valid.

We began our study by collating all extant Spanish editions issued before 1530 and two Italian translations, Rome 1506 and Milan 1514. Other editions and translations were utilized but only for reference. Scholars in the past had indicated that certain editions are quite close to one another, for example, that J often follows I, and that many times the pair is unique. Krapf in his Vigo 1900 edition based on P points out that often the variant of P coincides with that of N, or of O (based on Zaragoza 1507), or both. His primary premise that P used as a basic text the lost princeps edition of the Tragicomedia, *E, is in our opinion correct. The weakness of his edition stems from the fact that he had too great confidence in the text of P, altering it only in case of obvious error, and that he was unaware that from time to time the editor of P also utilized another edition, I.

Even before the collation was finished, it was evident that certain editions, for example, L and M, were similar and belonged to the same family. At times K coincided in its variants exclusively with L and M; at times it did not. Moreover, from omissions, additions, and other variants unique to each of the three editions, it became evident that no one of these three was based directly on another but that all three stemmed from a lost prototype. This situation seemed to exist with respect to all other editions in the collation except I and J. At this stage of our investigations we tried to solve the problems facing us by positing from one to as many as ten lost editions before 1502. Since some editions followed others rather closely we considered that an editor utilized one basic text for his edition.

It was also clear as the collation advanced that most of the variants fall into four principal stemmas. However scores of exceptions still existed; and it was only when we tested the premise that an editor may have used two basic texts instead of one that many of the problems dissipated. Three editors—H, P, and O— who used two basic texts offer significant aid in reconstructing the lost princeps edition of the Tragicomedia. In each case the editor used a second text belonging to a different stemma, an interrelationship which has been a source of much confusion in the past. P of Stemma II normally follows *E but at times follows I of Stemma III. The editor of H in Stemma III normally follows the prototype *F but at times he uses *E. O, the modern edition of Gorchs, follows either Amarita or the Zaragoza 1507 edition, which in turn reflects *E. K of Stemma IV normally follows the prototype *G but at times turns to *F of Stemma III.

Two major problems still remained unsolved. In Act IV a passage of five lines beginning *El pelicano,* and which we call the Pelican Episode, was incorrectly transposed to the end of Celestina's next speech. This error apparently first appeared in the princeps edition *E and continued throughout all the editions of Stemmas II and III as well as in many translations. We began to test a logical hypothesis which we soon accepted and which has helped us to reach decisions in many doubtful cases. Rojas worked on a printed copy of the Comedia as he composed the Tragicomedia. If he made his small changes in the text or margins of the printed book and his longer additions on sheets of paper, we could expect the witnesses of *E to be like those of *A except for author's and editor's changes and possible typographical errors. In the case of the Pelican Episode, the author wrote the addition on the margin, or perhaps on sheet of paper, indicating that the passage should be inserted in Celestina's speech. The printer inserted it but in Celestina's next speech, which comes three lines later.

The next major problem concerned the many variations in spelling of the same word in all early editions of the *Celestina.* Searching for a clue to help solve the problem, as we made the collation we also compiled a complete word list of the *Celestina* and a list of nonvariant words appearing in both the Comedia and the Tragicomedia. The nonvariant word list, which contains some 85 percent of all the words in the *Celestina,* demonstrates that Rojas was much more consistent both in his selection of words and in his spelling than has been believed in the past. For example, although initial H- and f- were both good usage in the late fifteenth century he consistently used H-.

In this study we have endeavored to establish the interrelationship of sixteen early Spanish editions, including four which have been lost. In addition to these, the first Italian translation, Rome 1506, and two modern Spanish editions, Amarita and Gorchs, are included on the graph, in order to help the reader understand the development of the text and, specifically, to aid in the reconstruction of the princeps edition *E. Among early Spanish editions not included are Seville 1523, which follows Stemma III closely; and Seville 1525, Toledo 1526, and Seville 1528, all of which follow Stemma IV. None of these four editions would help the reader understand the development of the text.

The sixteen editions fall naturally into four stemmas. Unfortunately the prototype of each stemma has been lost. However, in each case the prototype of each can usually be established by examining the three witnesses in that stemma. At times, especially in the cases of H and K, there are lacunae; and on other occasions the witnesses may present two or even three variants. On the other hand, frequently one stemma supports another, as in the cases of Stemma I and II or III and IV. The position of any edition of the graph cannot be changed; no extant edition on the graph can replace any of the lost editions.

*A, which represents the princeps edition of the Comedia, and the three other editions of Stemma I—B, C, and D—reflect the earliest stage of the development of the text. The second stage, Stemma II, is represented by *E, the princeps edition of the Tragicomedia, which is usually confirmed by PUV, and frequently supported by N or O and sometimes by H of Stemma III, or a combination of two or all three of these editions.

The four editions of Stemma III, *FHIJ, represent the third stage in the development of the text. The editor of *F, the prototype, did not follow the text of *E faithfully but often replaced the original with new words or expressions of his own. The three other editions of the stemma are less stable than those in Stemmas II and IV; but they usually reflect *F, whether it is an error or not.

The fourth and last stage on our graph is represented by Stemma IV, *GKLM. *G, the prototype, normally used *F as a basic text but at times created a new form which may be reflected in one, two, or all the witnesses of Stemma IV. We then have a variant or error unique to Stemma IV. Most of the later editions up to the present time follow Stemma IV rather closely, although in a considerable number of cases the text does not reflect faithfully the princeps edition of the Tragicomedia.

The early Spanish editions on the graph present some ten thousand variants, if the symbols for ET are included. However 40 percent of these are unique errors, where a variant is found in only one edition. The edition with the largest number of unique errors is J, followed in decreasing order by C, H, D, B, M, L, I, and K. In this treatise the few graphs that illustrate errors unique to one edition are included primarily to help the reader catch a glimpse of the traits of a given editor.

There are also many examples in the *Celestina* in which a single pair of editions, such as BC, IJ, etc., presents a unique variant. At other times a single variant may appear in one group of three editions, especially BCD, HIJ, or PUV. It is usually not difficult to reestablish the text of the princeps edition of the Tragicomedia when there is a unique variant in only one edition on the graph or even in a group of two or three editions. Nevertheless, there are many cases in this study which present problems still with no definitive solution. Chapter 12 has been devoted to various problems that may be found scattered throughout this study. Among the difficult problems is the source of an error in Stemma III. If H had no lacunae, in many cases light would be shed not only on this problem but also on the reconstruction of *E. We have presented a few cases where the printer of the princeps edition *E undoubtedly was the source of an error and others where he probably was. Other cases, in which the printer of either *A or *E may have made an error which contaminated all later editions, must still be studied. As data accumulate we are able to reexamine these problems and at times to reach a more definitive conclusion.

It would be possible to present a thousand graphs illustrating patterns of filiation with from one to three, four, or more examples without helping the reader to catch more than a vague glimpse of the interrelationships among editions, of the stemmas, of the early stages of the developments of the text and of certain characteristics of early editions. We have tried to simplify as much as possible the presentation of new premises and of more than five thousand citations and references. In order to aid the reader to keep in mind the new premises as well as the new filiation of texts and the significance of each, we have deemed it advisable at appropriate times to repeat opinions which have already been stated.

Finally, as we suggested earlier, the witnesses of these early editions fall so naturally most of the time into the four stemmas, even in the slightest details, that we cannot foresee that the discovery of new editions or the positing of other lost editions, even a princeps edition of the Tragicomedia earlier than *E, would alter the filiation of early editions as presented on the graphs.

If future studies should find valid reasons for changing the date or place of publication of any of the 1502 editions, or others, the four stemmas would still remain intact or be changed very little.

# *Index*

Boldfaced type refers to graph numbers; lightfaced type refers to page numbers. The abbreviation c. stands for citation and r. for reference, especially to information based on our data. When appropriate, all forms of a verb are included under the infinitive.